THE MAKING OF LAW

THE MAKING OF LAW

THE SUPREME COURT AND LABOR LEGISLATION IN MEXICO, 1875–1931

William J. Suarez-Potts

STANFORD UNIVERSITY PRESS
Stanford, California

Stanford University Press
Stanford, California

This book has been published with the assistance of Kenyon College.

Library of Congress Cataloging-in-Publication Data
Suarez-Potts, William J., author.
The making of law : the Supreme Court and labor legislation in Mexico, 1875–1931 / William J. Suarez-Potts.
pages cm
Includes bibliographical references and index.
ISBN 978-0-8047-7551-9 (cloth : alk. paper)
1. Labor laws and legislation—Mexico—History. 2. Mexico. Suprema Corte de Justicia—History. I. Title.
KGF1777.S83 2012
344.7201—dc23

2012009456

Typeset by Westchester Book Services in 10/15 Sabon

To Mimi and Moramay

Contents

Acknowledgments

I COULD NOT HAVE WRITTEN THIS BOOK without the support of many individuals and institutions. Kenyon College has assisted me in the realization of this project since 2006. The Center for U.S.–Mexican Studies at the University of California, San Diego, and its staff provided a hospitable environment that facilitated writing the dissertation on which this book is based. Eric Van Young was particularly supportive of a legal history covering modern Mexico. Javier Garciadiego graciously authorized my affiliation with the Colegio de México while I was still a graduate student residing in Mexico City. Mellon Foundation fellowships helped fund early research from which this book evolved. Norris Pope of Stanford University Press as editor and Michael Haggett as production editor have greatly facilitated this publication.

The staff at the Archivo Histórico de Vicente Lombardo Toledano, located at the Universidad Obrera de México, in Mexico City, warmly nurtured my research there. The staff at Harvard Law School's international legal studies library patiently found and retrieved old Mexican legal tomes on countless occasions. The Hemeroteca Nacional at the UNAM in Mexico City welcomed me to their alcove. Kenyon College librarians have tirelessly sorted interlibrary loan books related to this study.

Parts of Chapter 6 of this book appeared as "The Mexican Supreme Court and the *Juntas de Conciliación y Arbitraje*, 1917–1924: The Judicialisation of Labour Relations after the Revolution," in the *Journal of Latin American Studies*, vol. 41, no. 4 (2009): 723–55. And an earlier version of a section of Chapter 7 was published as "The Railroad Strike of 1927: Labor and Law After the Mexican Revolution," in *Labor History*, vol. 52, no. 4 (2011): 723–55.

While the legal historiography of Mexico since independence is scant, there is much scholarship on the nation's labor movements, and this book has benefited from it. Studies by Kevin Middlebrook, Graciela

Bensusán, Rodney Anderson, and the multiple volumes of *La clase obrera en la historа de México*, coordinated by Pablo González Casanova, to name but a few, have invaluably informed my narrative. It is also appropriate to acknowledge the legal scholarship of Mario de la Cueva and Vicente Lombardo Toledano, and that of Christopher Tomlins, Morton Horwitz, Duncan Kennedy and Karl Klare. This legal and historical scholarship have influenced my interpretation of Mexican legal and labor history. Any misreading is of course my doing.

A few of the colleagues who have shared their perspectives about Mexican legal studies and labor history, or in some manner furthered this project since its inception, include Oliver Dinius, Aurora Gómez-Galvarriato Freer, Daniel Gutiérrez, Aaron Navarro, Halbert Jones, Line Schjolden, Juan Manuel Palacio, Miles Rodríguez, José Miguel Torres, Amilcar Challú, Alejandra Núñez-Luna, T. M. James, Pablo Mijangos y González, Emilio Kourí, and, especially, Moramay López-Alonso. Edward Beatty constructively suggested changes to a draft of this book. Louis Suárez-Potts and Mimi Potts gave of themselves so that I could complete this book.

Among the mentors who guided this project initially, the professors on my dissertation committee at Harvard University stand out. John Coatsworth's incisive awareness of the importance of legal history for a more complete understanding of Mexico since independence provided the first and essential orientation needed to begin contemplating this study. Had he not insisted that law might have mattered during the national period in Mexico, it is doubtful that I would have pursued such a project. (My skepticism then about the value of the legal historical study of modern Mexico was similar to that of other scholars of Latin America.) Charles Donahue Jr. taught me legal history as no other legal historian could have, generously sharing his approaches to the subject. More recently, he has encouraged me to persist with the study of a region whose legal history merits attention. John Womack Jr. first unobtrusively guided me throughout the duration of graduate study and the writing of a dissertation. Since then, he has provided further moral support. The value of his counsel has been incommensurable. The shortcomings of this book, however, are solely the result of my work.

THE MAKING OF LAW

Introduction

THIS BOOK IS A HISTORY of the development of labor law in Mexico from 1875 to 1931. Contemporaries from the late nineteenth century through the 1930s considered labor law progressive, reformist, or a threat to private property and capitalism. Arguably, labor law sometimes manifested these characteristics. It did, from almost any viewpoint, matter in the constitution of the state after 1917, as well as for workers and businesses negotiating conditions of employment and production both before and after the 1910 revolution. That labor law was important politically, socially, and economically in Mexico, however, may seem peculiar for two reasons. Since the country was predominantly agricultural throughout the period in which labor law largely evolved—1875 to 1931—it is counterintuitive that a field of law normally associated with industrial relations should have been so significant for the nation's polity and economy. Moreover, in view of the reality that "the rule of law," or *estado de derecho*, did not typify the nation's social and political systems in this period, it appears contradictory that legal institutions and discourses became central elements of industrial relations. Yet as peasants' lands were divided and then concentrated in large landholdings in the second half of the nineteenth century, more agricultural production was organized with wage labor.[1] By the turn of the century, Mexico had a substantial agricultural proletariat; and a large fraction of the peasantry performed wage labor at least part of the year.[2] And the country began to industrialize in the 1880s and 1890s, which led to the constitution of a working class. Although this working class remained a minority of the total population productively engaged, it was situated in the more dynamic sectors of the economy and, accordingly, could affect the nation's development.[3] Furthermore, liberal ideologies dominant after 1867 among political elites and other social actors were grounded in constitutional and legal vocabularies. Political and social leaders, even revolutionaries in some instances, frequently expressed their positions in legal terms. Even if the rule of law remained an unrealized ideal, law was normally referenced in the political and social worlds ruled by men.[4]

Nineteenth-century liberal legal principles and institutions, however, were inadequate to accommodate fully workers' interests by the first years of the twentieth century. A new legal field was necessary if legal discourse was to be relevant in the modern world. The "social (or labor) question," as it came to be called, demanded an answer. That phrase had been used since at least the mid-1800s, and it circulated throughout the Atlantic world by the end of the nineteenth century, including Latin America.[5] By then, it normally referred to the problematic social consequences of industrialization. These encompassed the general indigence of workers, urban conditions of unhygienic overcrowding, crime—and industrial conflict, especially militant labor movements and strikes. In Mexico, intellectuals, including lawyers, perceived especially threatening to the economic and political order the strikes of 1906–8. And as legalistic liberalism proved incapable of addressing convincingly such conflict, an alternative response to the labor question short of revolution developed from principles of social legislation current among legal reformers in France in the early twentieth century. Among the social reform projects inspired by French legal thought that attracted interest in Mexico was labor legislation.[6]

Labor law like workers' movements in this country became interrelated with the events, political contests, and social struggles of 1910–20 and thereafter: the Mexican Revolution. Labor reform certainly was one item of the social agendas or pronouncements of the revolutionary factions who fought one another; still, the relationship among workers, other classes, revolutionary leaders, and social reform was complex. The insurrection and civil wars of 1910–17, insofar as they were not primarily political contests, largely had an agrarian social basis.[7] The role of industrial labor in the armed conflict was less extensive, in comparison. *Campesinos* and other rural people more than urban workers joined the armies to fight against the ancien régime.[8] The 1917 constitution nevertheless dedicated an entire chapter, Article 123, to stating the rights of workers, while in the ensuing years state governments passed labor statutes; and the federal government enacted comprehensive labor legislation in 1931. At the same time, federal and several state government leaders formed alliances with labor organizations, preeminently the CROM (Confederación Regional Obrera Mexicana or Mexican Regional Labor Confederation). The constitution of 1917, of course, also contained a provision authorizing land reform and the nationalization of property, Article 27; agrarian property relations remained the nation's great problem through the period of this study.[9] But as scholars have noted repeatedly, labor law, along with workers' movements, came to play a central role in the organization of the new state and its corresponding revolutionary ideology.[10] This book suggests further that given the importance of labor law for the new state and workers' organizations, the federal judiciary's adjudication of labor disputes and interpretation of new legal principles were also significant in the evolution of the nation's political and social contours after 1917.

As the following chapters show, social and political actors paid attention to the rulings of Supreme Court justices in labor cases. Judge-made law sometimes could preoccupy contemporaries, notwithstanding the nation's civil law tradition, weak judiciary, authoritarian government, and pervasive corruption. Indeed, probably because of such presumptions or observations (not restricted to Mexico), the legal history of modern Latin America as a discipline has less scholarly production to its name than many other historical specialties.[11] But for Mexicans, that the judiciary was relatively weak, dependent on the executive power, or corrupt did not detract from the point that it mattered politically or in industrial relations. In his revealing parting message, on the cusp of a new generation of Supreme Court justices taking office in December 1928, the president of the Court, Jesús Guzmán Vaca, acknowledged many of the faults of the federal judiciary as well as the difficult circumstances confronting the justices.[12] The federal courts had faced armed revolt and powerful and defiant local bosses who disregarded judicial orders and legal norms. No other era had witnessed such corruption of judges as "these dangerous and ill-fated days." Yet Guzmán Vaca insisted that the Court for the most part had operated ably, dealing with backlogs of cases, applying the law assiduously. The editors of *El Universal*, a major Mexico City daily, queried the high court's efforts to ameliorate corruption or hold government officials accountable for their failure to implement or obey judgments; but its editorial criticizing the departing justice's message recognized that most of the high court judges were not venal and that the social and political situation of the country had been abnormal.[13]

Consistent with these statements, while presenting a personal glimpse of Mexico's judicial system, is Ernest Gruening's *Mexico and Its Heritage*. Around 1927, this American writer and later senator interviewed numerous lawyers of the Mexico City bar about their perceptions of judicial corruption and judges' weaknesses or vulnerability to political pressures, especially from the presidency. His conclusion, derived from the interviews, was that corruption existed in the federal judiciary, was overstated, and was most extensive in cases involving petroleum companies. A couple of the justices whose terms ended in 1928 had been open to subornation, but the rest were honest. Historians have noted the notorious external pressure exerted on the federal judiciary in oil cases, some of which implicated the nation's security.[14] In most labor cases, however, it is apparent that the justices reacted to changing circumstances, ideologies, and constant litigation more than to direct pressure from the president.[15]

MEXICO'S LEGAL SYSTEM

Mexico's legal system partly resembles both continental Europe's civil law tradition and aspects of American constitutionalism. As in other Latin American countries with an Iberian legacy, Roman legal concepts, codified in the early nineteenth century by France and subsequently by Spain and other continental European states, influenced Mexican legal education and practice. In Europe, Roman-based law consisted mostly of judicial procedure and a set of categories of rules addressing relations between individuals—that is, private law, including contract and property law.[16] In the civil law tradition, clear distinctions have been drawn between private and public law and among the three branches of government (the separation of powers). Legal scholars theorized that the main source of written law should be the legislature. Judicial opinions have been accorded less weight as legal statements, frequently resulting in the absence of a rule of *stare decisis* or controlling precedent. Thus, following the paradigm of the French civil code of 1804, legal experts drafted under legislative auspices detailed, statutory codes; in Mexico, the government codified the principal areas of private law with the promulgation of the civil code in 1870 for the federal district.[17]

Mexico's legal system also shares aspects of its American counterpart. The U.S. constitution impressed the drafters of the 1857 constitution, on which the 1917 constitution was modeled. Both the 1857 and 1917 texts outlined a federal system of government. Each state has a governor, legislature, and courts. The federal government similarly has three branches or powers: the presidency, a bicameral congress, and judiciary. The latter has consisted of federal district courts located throughout the republic, sometimes an intermediate level of appellate courts, and a supreme court that, among other tasks, regularly reviews appeals directly from district courts.[18]

If litigation has not been as pervasive in Mexican society as in the United States, courts still have been involved substantially since the colonial era in the resolution of individual and group conflict. And since the restoration of the liberal republic in 1867, the most important institution for challenging state action or seeking relief from its effects has been the *juicio de amparo*. In connection with the development of labor law, this has been a lawsuit initiated in federal court by an individual who seeks the judiciary's protection against an action of a public authority, including its application of a law, which violates the constitutional rights of the individual.[19] The remedy of the *amparo* (literally, support or protection) is essentially injunctive: the federal judge orders the public authority to carry out an action or refrain from doing so, on the grounds that otherwise the authority would infringe the petitioner's rights. Encompassed within such injunctive relief can be a federal judge's declaration that since a state court's decision, or that of an administrative agency, infringes the petitioning individual's rights, it is legally unenforceable.[20]

The distinctive characteristic of the *amparo* has been its "Otero formula." In the period of this study, the federal judiciary's order could protect only the individual petitioner granted the amparo. That is, the judicial ruling did not have general applicability, even if the court found a law, widespread policy, or governmental practice unconstitutional. The judiciary could not derogate a law in general or enjoin an entire policy or practice of another branch of government except to the extent necessary to obtain relief for the individual in the particular case before it.[21] In actuality, after 1917, the Supreme Court's amparos declaring that a law or practice contravened an individual's rights, especially if more than one individual filed an action at the same time, had the practical effect of undermining the law in question.[22]

In the types of amparo cases examined in this book, the litigant filed a complaint in a federal district court, normally located in the state where the public authority's challenged action had occurred, while the Supreme Court, located in Mexico City, ruled as the final court of appeal.[23] These amparo actions normally had two basic, remedial stages: the judge's suspension order and the amparo judgment.[24] The individual petitioning for an amparo could request of the federal judge an order suspending execution of the offending state action at the time the complaint was filed. The judge might enter a provisional suspension order on the basis of whether the petitioner risked irreparable harm, balanced against the public interest, pending further review of the substantive merits of the amparo petition. Litigants could appeal the suspension order, as they could an amparo order of the federal judge. In the cases relevant to this study, during the Porfirian era (1876–1911), the Supreme Court issued the final decision. Since 1917, the policy of the Court's final review of amparo (and suspension) proceedings continued, although the volume of amparo cases pending before it increased through the 1920s.[25]

Under the post-1917 governments, as well as intermittently before then, the federal judiciary adhered to a narrow policy of *stare decisis*. In general, five consistent, consecutive rulings by the Supreme Court on a legal point (*tesis*) established a controlling precedent, *jurisprudencia*, on lower federal courts and on its own subsequent decision making, which only it could overrule if it did so explicitly.[26] A *tesis* typically is stated in a few sentences, phrased abstractly, and collected in the Supreme Court's reporter and other publications.[27] *Jurisprudencia*, the Court's interpretation of constitutional provisions, statutes, or other legal sources, in connection with cases before it, and as articulated in *tesis*, is a form of judge-made law, or case law. Even in instances where the opinion of a Supreme Court ruling is not binding in subsequent cases (because it does not comprise one of five consistent rulings), it may have some persuasive effect. More broadly if inexactly, written and published opinions of the high court might be deemed a part of judicial doctrine on a legal issue, hence *jurisprudencia,* too, although such opinions technically would not be applicable as law in the same sense as a controlling decision.

The Porfirian Supreme Court ceased its operation in August 1914, following the defeat of Victoriano Huerta in the revolutionary civil war.[28] The victorious Constitutionalists reestablished the Court under the 1917 constitution. The Court with different justices began to operate again in June 1917. The constitution of 1917 conserved the amparo action, outlined in Articles 103 and 107, and directed that the Court would decide amparo appeals as one body: all eleven justices voting jointly, if present, in public conferences.[29]

The drafters of the 1917 constitution sought to ensure greater independence for the federal judiciary than it had under the authoritarian rule of Porfirio Díaz by gradually introducing between 1917 and 1923 lifetime tenure for justices and by placing the nomination of justices and judges outside of the control of the federal executive.[30] In 1928, amendments to the constitution modified the structure of the Supreme Court, increasing the number of justices from eleven to sixteen and dividing the tribunal into three chambers or *salas*, each of which would decide amparo appeals separately and specialize in specific legal areas. The second, administrative, chamber was to review most amparos involving labor matters, as they normally resulted from the determinations of administrative agencies. The amendments also changed the procedure for selecting justices. Henceforward the president nominated them, with the Senate ratifying the choices.[31]

LAW, POLITICS, AND IDEOLOGY

Liberal belief has distinguished law from politics at least since the nineteenth century.[32] To a degree, the constitutional separation of powers and the distinction between public and private law have the function of delegating political decision making to the sovereign (in modern republics normally the legislature) and application of the laws to the judge. Jurisprudential theories have defined law variously and in turn have envisioned the social function of law and adjudication differently.[33] Advocates of social legislation in the early twentieth century engaged in a critique of what law was, who made it, and what its purposes were. In Mexico, justices opined about these issues, too, as concepts of law changed with the advent of labor legislation. At the same time, the belief persisted that judicial decision making differed substantially—and should—from politicking or legislating. In the editorials of major newspapers, politics had a pejorative connotation, and editors leaned toward tagging politics and politicians with corruption. Ideally, the judge or justice should be independent of such politics, knowledgeable in the science of law, and honorable. Such overarching values transcended the legal community, implicating political discourse—even revolution.

The formal separation of powers within the state that the drafters of the 1917 constitution designed did not result, as contemporaries and scholars since then have observed, in complete judicial independence. In the mid-1920s, Vicente Lombardo Toledano, an early scholar of labor law as well as then a CROM leader and lawyer, remarked that Mexico's federal government centered on executive power: it was a presidential system.[34] Scholars have used the word *presidencialismo* to describe an all-powerful presidential system, which, however, was not consolidated until the mid-1930s.[35] Given such appraisals, one can readily conclude that the judiciary was a dependent adjunct of the executive branch and law epiphenomenal of other political processes. But it is also evident that the state's chief executives from 1917 to 1935 presided over inherently weak administrations. Nor was the national legislature a strong, unified, lawmaking body during most of the 1920s; throughout much of the decade, successive presidents failed to control it.[36] The federal government barely maintained its authority over the nation between 1917 and the early 1930s. Each president during his administration confronted rural violence, army revolts, challenges from the Catholic Church and U.S. interests, or persistent regional opposition—as well as perennial labor conflict.

In such a political and social context, the federal judiciary is more accurately perceived as one among several weak but not insignificant governmental actors. Contemporaries certainly realized this; more recently scholars have argued that the Supreme Court, which the federal executive efficiently subordinated with the 1934 constitutional reforms adopted by Lázaro Cárdenas, maintained a degree of autonomy in the 1920s, partly due not only to the weaknesses of the presidencies but also to the selection process of justices. A review of their nominations in 1917, 1919, and 1923 suggests that it was a political process, but not one completely determined by the president.[37]

The very nature of the amparo action, structured pursuant to the Otero formula so as not to implicate political issues, has an inherent political element. Until Díaz's first presidency, the Supreme Court had frequently played an independent and substantial role in the nation's politics.[38] Many of the justices sided with the president of the Court in his defiance of President Sebastián Lerdo de Tejada's attempt to orchestrate his reelection in the three-way struggle that resulted in Díaz's military overthrow of Tejada in late 1876. One early Díaz ally, the renowned justice Ignacio Vallarta, advocated for a more politically restrained judiciary while promoting judicial review and the value of jurisprudencia in amparo cases. By the early 1880s, Díaz regarded Vallarta a rival. Vallarta resigned, and soon the Court posed less of a challenge to Díaz.[39] The amparo action, however, continued to allow the Court to voice an independent position; but this occurred partly because the impact of its judgments was legally constrained—which was an initial political choice and premise about the amparo institution.[40]

Political factors external to the deliberative process of judicial decision making certainly have continued to influence it. But legal positions and judicial language are political acts, too, insofar as they are actions by state officers that imply a relationship between the state and individuals or relations between individuals and groups that the state attempts to govern. And as the judiciary operated in a context of social and political conflict, it could not have been immune to it. The recurring aspiration to segregate law from politics was perhaps utopian and was, in any event, unachievable in practice. In particular, the discourses around labor law tended toward acknowledging by the mid-1920s that the new legal field and its application were connected with the public interest. Justices couched their opinions implicitly or explicitly in language referring to the consequences of their decisions and extant social realities: judgments were policy oriented, not simple applications of legal text. Employers avoided pro-labor determinations of administrative agencies by asserting their constitutional rights in federal courts when they petitioned for amparo orders, thereby raising fundamental questions implying state conduct and federal-state relations as well as industrial relations. The legislating of labor rights, meanwhile, made explicit references to the constitutional rights of labor and capital, as the labor movement invoked the evolving rhetoric of the triumph of the revolution, embodied in Article 123.[41] As the politicization of law was more explicitly pronounced, the politics of industrial relations came to be expressed in legal terms.[42]

METHODOLOGY

The Supreme Court began to publish regularly its legal opinions in 1871, in the *Semanario Judicial de la Federación*. There are a few lacunae, from 1875 to 1880 and from 1914 to 1917; still, the continuity of published decisions is impressive. In both a narrow and expansive sense, the Court's published opinions form a body of judge-made law and include doctrines of labor law, a point noted by Mexican legal scholars like Lombardo Toledano.[43] As John Dawson argued in his study of the evolution of judge-made law throughout Western Europe since the Middle Ages, even in the absence of a rule of controlling precedent, decisions and their corresponding rationales tend to become normative in the resolution of subsequent disputes brought before judges when they are organized and made accessible to litigants and their lawyers.[44] This book relies on Dawson's observation to demonstrate how adjudication has been an integral part of the making of law in Mexico during a period when the Supreme Court was able to play an important role (and more than at some other times in the nation's history). More generally, the arguments in this book are influenced by legal realist conclusions (derived from study of the common law system dominant in the United States) that the law is the consequence of what judges and other government officials do.[45] In Mexico, within the civil law tradition where judges' actions have been limited, such a definition of law should be qualified. It is noteworthy, nonetheless, that by 1930 Lombardo Toledano, for one, apparently independently of American legal realist thought, approached holding a similar viewpoint that law, in part, was the result of the decisions and actions of officials, including judges. By then, another major legal and public intellectual, Narciso Bassols, had also concluded that the Supreme Court's *jurisprudencia* on labor issues was crucially important for labor law, perhaps more so than in any other legal area at the time.[46]

The published opinions of the *Semanario Judicial* over the period of this study vary in length and detail. They are collected in five series (*épocas*) of volumes, the fifth covering the post-revolutionary years after 1917. Under the Porfirian regime, the Supreme Court published relatively few cases about servitude and the constitutional right to work or pursue an occupation, which was the extent of its explicit adjudication of labor matters. By the late 1920s, labor cases were numerous and encompassed a wide scope of employment-related issues. Many volumes of the *Semanario Judicial* have several indices, including typically a subject index and one for cited constitutional provisions. From them it was possible to identify cases that dealt with labor. The *Semanario Judicial* also collects *tesis* in some volumes and appendices, as have independent treatises edited by legal scholars. After identifying labor cases by perusing indices of the *Semanario*, I compared findings with the tesis grouped in the *Semanario* and in other treatises. In view of the evident changes in publication over decades, it is doubtful that this method yielded every relevant labor case, but the approach did produce a fairly reasonable and accurate sense of the case law as it evolved over time.[47] Since this study is concerned with detailing the development of the doctrinal content of labor law, the legal, political, and social reasons for this evolution, and some of the political and legal implications of it, quantification of the cases was not necessary. Quantification, of course, would be important for several arguments about the actual effects of Supreme Court opinions on both the parties to a case and for the populations that were surely interested in the issues the Court reviewed.[48] But by identifying the trajectory of judicial decisions and legislative enactments, and their content, with reference to their discussion in contemporaneous periodicals and other records, it at least should be clear that labor law and its adjudication were at times important elements in the political discourses of the period 1875–1931 and significant for postrevolutionary industrial relations.[49]

A schematic outline that is helpful for the analysis of institutions classifies related phenomena as to whether they are the specification or articulation of a norm, the application or execution of it, or the response by interested actors to the application or administration of the specified norm.[50] This study is concerned with the articulation and application of legal norms through specifically recognized governmental branches, legislatures and federal courts, which in the Western legal and liberal tradition ideally enact and apply law.[51] It argues that in the application of the law, further law is frequently made: specification and application are often closely related even when they are ideally distinguished (in view of the perception of a separation of powers).[52] Indeed, it is suggested that the conduct of social actors—for example, their turning to the courts for adjudication—further shapes the law in that it provides courts the basis for their decisions and their rationales: thus, if businesses had not sought injunctive orders against administrative organs regularly after 1917, the federal judiciary would not have developed a body of law about their nature.

Mexican legal scholars and government officials, educated primarily in the civil law tradition, came to envision that systematic codification of labor law would eventually follow the drafting of the 1917 constitution. Fourteen years transpired before the promulgation of comprehensive national legislation. Because this was both manifestly a political and a legal process, this book discusses the text and earlier draft bills and narrates the events that led to passage of the federal labor law. It relies on the reported legislative history, as well as on extensive correspondence of the American embassy, which was keenly interested in the matter. The result is a piecing together of the formulation of the legislation by close readings of legal text and U.S. State Department records. Private archives were also examined, as were published memoirs. To the extent that such an approach was possible in the case of the drafting of Article 123 and its antecedents, this was also done. Lastly, law and policy journal articles published between the 1880s and 1934 were reviewed, as these often influenced or foreshadowed the contours that legislation and judicial decisions assumed.

Translating terms embedded in Mexico's legal system and culture has been problematic.[53] Many legal concepts have been part of a distinct institutional and discursive history that might be analogous to that of the United States, or share much in common with it; nonetheless, the vocabulary is also historically specific and sometimes not directly equatable. To the extent that there is an English equivalent to the Spanish term, this has been used; one example is the word *jurisprudencia*, or case law, or judge-made law; but the word also can be mistakenly translated as jurisprudence. Where the term has comparable English elements but is unique to Mexico or Latin America, the Spanish sometimes has been kept and initially italicized: the outstanding instance is that of the *juicio de amparo*, which if translated as a writ, as has been done, could be misleading, in that the connotation for English readers would be the common-law writ system.[54]

HISTORICAL BACKGROUND AND SUMMARY OF CHAPTERS

Chapter 1 presents an overview of liberal principles that informed workers' rights in the nineteenth century. These were not negligible: the right to work or freedom of labor, the right to organize and strike. In 1875 liberal intellectuals construed the 1857 constitution to guarantee these rights. They also utilized political economic ideas in their recommendations for better and less exploitive relations between capital and labor. Generally underlying such principles was the liberal belief that the state should let economic actors, including employers and employees, enter into contracts voluntarily. To a marked extent, the nation's Supreme Court during the Porfirian era concurred with these liberal tenets. Chapter 2 observes how the high court between 1875 and 1910 repeatedly upheld the right of free labor of mostly poor agricultural laborers petitioning the federal judiciary for relief against their employers and local authorities. While the same justices apparently avoided involvement in industrial disputes, it is still noteworthy that the Supreme Court applied the 1857 constitution on behalf of those laborers who were able to reach a federal court.

Chapter 3 describes the labor policies of Díaz's regime in the first decade of the twentieth century. Porfirio Díaz was a dictator, but his dictatorship maintained constitutional and legal forms of rule. Díaz, moreover, came to power in 1876 as a liberal as well as a military leader, subscribing to the political ideology consolidated after 1867 first under Benito Juárez and then Lerdo de Tejada. Díaz's very legitimacy as president relied on the maintenance of liberal, legal, and constitutional forms of governance. And like Lerdo de Tejada before him, Díaz cultivated popular, urban groups, including artisanal and labor associations, for their support. But as the country industrialized, strike activity increased and risked affecting economic progress. Facing substantial labor unrest, government officials, including Díaz, personally responded in an ad hoc manner, to some extent continuing the strategy of encouraging and then coopting some labor organization, a strategy that had proven relatively successful in earlier decades, but which failed in 1906–7. By then, it is evident that Díaz's closest circle of advisers, the *científicos*, was considering labor legislation, mostly repressive. In contrast, by the first decade of the twentieth century, major law and policy journals had published articles or excerpts of books by European legal scholars that sympathetically portrayed the new social legislation. This is the subject of Chapter 4, which reviews such articles published in Mexico, thereby pointing to how European legal concepts were disseminated under the Porfirian regime and comprised one of the early sources of labor law.

Díaz failed to implement any substantial social reforms in the last years of his administration or hold fair elections when Francisco Madero contested his reelection in 1910. After the suppression of his electoral campaign, Madero called for an insurrection to begin on November 20, in the Plan of San Luis Potosí. The Plan denounced the regime for, among other things, violating the constitution, subordinating the judicial and legislative branches to executive power, and maintaining a judicial system that legalized the depredations of powerful interest groups.[55] It was a critique echoing Luis Cabrera's, which had reviled the *científico* lawyers and the Porfirian courts for cronyism and corruption.[56] The Plan did not speak directly to the social question, but Madero had promised to recognize labor's constitutional rights. If his earlier campaign rhetoric did not transcend the parameters of the 1857 constitution, Madero's defiance of Díaz resonated with labor, in contrast to the mixed overtures of Porfirian politicians to workers, which were belied by their moderation or by recent memories of repression of strike movements.

Madero's presidency (1911–13) represented a shift in the state's approach to industrial relations, and one to which labor had contributed. Workers, observing the oscillation in official positions, beginning with Díaz's resignation, launched unionizing movements—and strikes.[57] Madero generally tolerated the surge in labor mobilization, although government officers repressed some strikes.[58] Notably, Madero's administration coordinated negotiations in the textile industry between labor and capital, with a newly created labor department playing an active role, in order to end disruptions in this economic sector by reaching an industry-wide collective agreement. The textile conventions that resulted from the negotiations ultimately failed on both counts. But they marked the beginning of a formal institutionalization of industrial relations with the state's routine participation. Similarly, draft legislation sponsored by liberal members of the Twenty-Sixth Congress, the *renovadores* or renovators, was an early sign of positive labor law in the country, even if it was not passed.[59]

Victoriano Huerta overthrew Madero in February 1913. In March, Venustiano Carranza, governor of the northern state of Coahuila, initiated the Constitutionalist revolution against Huerta's usurpation of legitimate authority. Carranza would lead the Constitutionalist revolution as *primer jefe*, or first chief, pursuant to the Plan of Guadalupe, proclaimed on March 26. It accused Huerta of treason and the Congress and Supreme Court with violation of the nation's laws and constitutional precepts for its support of Huerta.[60] But the plan omitted any allusion to social rights. Although Carranza eschewed a social orientation for the struggle against Huerta, many leaders of the armed bands that coalesced in northern Mexico and loosely formed the Constitutionalist armies differed from him in this respect.[61] Meanwhile, Zapatistas—peasants in southern Mexico—sustained their social struggle for land; and workers in Mexico City and elsewhere continued to defend, if not advance, their interests. Huerta recognized the advantages of state mediation of industrial conflict and moderate social reform; now under his rule, the labor department continued to operate. Only belatedly, Huerta repressed the anarchist-leaning Casa del Obrero Mundial (COM, the House of the World Worker) that had formed in 1912 in Mexico City.[62]

Carranza remained ambivalent toward independent workers' movements, even as many of his generals sought alliances with labor leaders. After Huerta's defeat, when civil war ensued between the major revolutionary armies (Conventionists against Constitutionalists or rather Villistas and Zapatistas against Carrancistas), Carranza and his closest advisers did redefine the Constitutionalist revolution as one for social transformation. In December 1914, the first chief amended the Plan of Guadalupe to allow for labor reform. Constitutionalist generals decreed reforms to end servitude and other forms of excessive exploitation in territories they controlled. In February, the Constitutionalists entered into an agreement with the COM, with the encouragement of Carranza's leading general, Álvaro Obregón, and some of his sympathizers. This agreement enabled the COM to undertake propaganda campaigns under the aegis of Constitutionalist military commanders and to organize workers, albeit sometimes in competition with the labor department, particularly in the state of Veracruz. In return, the Constitutionalists gained some labor support, skilled munitions workers, and more soldiers for their struggle against the Villistas and Zapatistas.[63] Following major victories against Pancho Villa, however, Carranza demobilized the COM and hardened his position against organized labor. It was a stance not fully shared by many Constitutionalists, including powerful military commanders.

When Carranza convened a constitutional congress in late 1916, ostensibly to reestablish legal and constitutional rule reflective of the changes that had occurred in the preceding years of revolutionary civil war, the Constitutionalists were divided amongst themselves as to the extent that social reforms should be incorporated into the new constitution. Ultimately, of course, the revised charter did include provisions for land—and labor—reform. More important for the first chief, the 1917 constitution also legitimized his subsequent presidency and augmented the strength of the executive.

On May 1, Carranza became Mexico's constitutional president. He nearly completed his term, which would have run to November 30, 1920. Carranza ostensibly tried to govern as a civilian, but most of the governors and regional powers in the country were military leaders, a few of them allied with mobilized popular groups to varying degrees, such as in Veracruz, or committed to social reform, such as in Yucatán. Carranza's hold on power was actually tenuous, and it deteriorated over the next few years. His attempt to co-opt labor through the indirect sponsorship of the founding convention of the CROM in March 1918 failed. The CROM was disposed to collaborate with politicians but not with Carranza. The president was able to designate a pliable civilian successor, but this too backfired: Carranza could not check Obregón's plan to run for the presidency; his awkward attempts to thwart Obregón led to a political-military revolt, seconded by a broad range of popular groups. Carranza's government collapsed in the spring of 1920. The president evacuated Mexico City, with much of the apparatus of civilian government, including Supreme Court justices. Anti-Carrancistas foiled his attempt to retreat to Veracruz and killed him.[64]

Obregón succeeded to the presidency after the interim government of Adolfo de la Huerta promptly held elections. Obregón would complete his presidential term, but he, too, faced a major military revolt in late 1923, as well as constant regional challenges to federal and presidential power. Obregón, unlike Carranza, countered the revolt and political rivalries from state governors in part by successfully collaborating with labor and agrarian groups. His relationship with the CROM in particular was significant. The CROM and Obregón, while a presidential candidate, had entered into a secret pact in 1919, which would have consolidated a close relationship between the CROM and the president, in return for the federation's assistance.[65] To a modest degree, Obregón tried to honor the stipulations of the pact; the CROM, too, crucially aided his presidency during the 1923–24 military rebellion.

Chapter 5 reviews these events of the revolution and postrevolutionary years (through 1924) in relation to the development of labor law, including the establishment of the federal labor department in 1911, and the formulation of Article 123. Labor's social and political importance grew in this period. By 1924, labor federations or unions were crucial partners of governors or other regional political bosses in a number of states, and the CROM had become a pivotal constituent of the executive power. Significantly, Obregón, who had to compromise substantially with American interests and regional strongmen when he assumed the presidency, was pushing for comprehensive federal labor legislation by 1924.[66] The president had realized that the federal government needed to regulate labor relations, in view of the alternative: states doing so in a way that antagonized industrial interests, undermined the national economy, and jeopardized the very viability of a central state.

The nation's reestablished Supreme Court quickly began in 1917–18 to adjudicate labor disputes that were related to major political and social conflicts then unfolding in several states. This is historically significant: during the Porfirian era the Court's judgments in labor matters had limited applicability and, as noted, were unrelated to major industrial conflicts. The Court now became involved in the organization of industrial relations. At a time when the presidency was not legally or constitutionally enabled (and at times politically unable) to address routine and recurring industrial conflict in different states, the Court's amparo orders functioned to counter state governments' policies or laws.

Among the more important institutions for the development of industrial relations and labor law in Mexico were the boards of conciliation and arbitration.[67] These administrative organs constituted a mechanism for the states to regulate labor relations and, in doing so, were also a novel innovation in the development of the postrevolutionary state. Composed of business, labor, and government representatives, they tended to rule against employers, cementing labor-governmental blocs at the local or state level and providing additional leverage to unions against employers. Supreme Court decisions in amparo cases frequently interpreted the enforceability of the awards of labor boards; the decisional law that evolved was thus consequential both for the development of labor law and the formation of an industrial relations system. Additionally, the Court dealt with constitutional questions related to the legality of the federal executive's promulgation of decrees that attempted to establish the latter's jurisdiction in labor matters. Again, the stakes were high.

Chapters 6 and 7 analyze, as a legal, historical process, the Court's case law fashioned in response to labor disputes arising between the effective date of the 1917 constitution and passage of the federal labor law in 1931. The analyses are fairly detailed for three reasons. First, outlining the sequential order of the judge-made law suggests how the Court's decision-making process constrained its discretion to adjudicate labor cases and contributed to the structure of its legal doctrine. Second, explaining the opinions that justified the Court's decisions illustrates how underlying labor conflicts about which the Court deliberated were conceptualized in legal terms. Third, the combination of analysis and narration demonstrates how the Court helped shape labor law in the social and political context of the 1920s. This focus on legal decision making, however, is not meant to deny that political factors contributed to the outcomes of judicial decisions and in some instances were presumably decisive. The argument, rather, is that the Court's case-by-case decision making, which required a rationale in each case, should not be imputed solely to external, political determinants.

Not only Obregón (1920–24), but also Plutarco Elías Calles (1924–28), as president, tried to pass labor legislation, with the expectation that it would institutionalize the federal government's role in industrial relations, thereby stabilizing them. Neither succeeded. It was Calles's near puppet (and politically feeble) president who finally promulgated a comprehensive labor statute. Despite the CROM's desire for national labor legislation, along with that of two presidents, passage of it was actually not feasible before 1931. The political context was extremely difficult for national legislation that required endorsement by adversarial parties. Chapter 8 recounts the attempts to enact federal labor legislation, which culminated in August 1931 with the promulgation of the federal labor law (Ley Federal del Trabajo).[68]

The CROM had already formed a strong relationship with Calles before he became president in 1924. He appointed the CROM leader

Luis N. Morones as minister of the Secretariat of Industry, Commerce, and Labor (Secretaría de Industria, Comercio y Trabajo, or SICT). Morones became the most powerful minister in the president's cabinet. Even while the CROM continued to utilize racketeering tactics against its adversaries, Morones and Calles also adopted a more conciliatory approach to employers, emphasizing cooperation between the factors of production over class war. Morones, both as government minister and the head of the CROM, discouraged strikes. The SICT endeavored to arbitrate strike activity, declaring some concerted actions illegal and a few legal (and hence meriting state support). Meanwhile, Morones attempted to extend CROM influence among unions and workers and to marginalize independent labor organizations, some of which were more militant than the CROM. The General Confederation of Workers (Confederación General de Trabajadores or CGT), nominally anarchist, was anti-statist and anti-CROM. It also was influential in textile factories in parts of the country. The railroad unions especially were independent of Calles, strategically important for the national economy, and also anti-CROM.

Between 1925 and 1928, Morones promoted union campaigns and government policies to replace these and other unions with CROM organizations that would collaborate more harmoniously with employers and government and contribute to the nation's economic growth. Until the economic crises of the late 1920s, such policies and CROM campaigns were relatively successful. In the first year of Calles's administration, amidst a depressed textile industry torn by labor conflict, Morones sponsored a convention that brought together hundreds of employer and (mostly CROM) union delegates for a series of meetings to negotiate an industry-wide collective contract. Between 1925 and 1927, labor and capital representatives met, reaching a comprehensive agreement, which aimed to rationalize wages across the industry; it also conceded to unions control over hiring. A system of mixed factory commissions, then district and regional committees, would resolve labor disputes, with the SICT as final arbiter (or, once created, the federal labor boards of conciliation and arbitration). This was an impressive system of industrial relations, surpassing Madero's earlier efforts to establish an industry-wide convention and, indeed, Díaz's notorious arbitral award of January 1907. In contrast to earlier agreements, the 1925–27 convention had included the full participation of unions.[69] Interestingly, the Supreme Court was ambivalent about the legal implications of the federal government's effort to regulate a national industry; in several decisions it enjoined aspects of it, as noted in Chapter 7.

In the transport sector, Morones and Calles tried to eliminate the independence of rail unions and downsize the labor force of the largest rail company, in which the government had a majority interest and whose ballooning debt was held by foreign creditors. The consequences of Morones's strategy were more disruptive than in the textile manufacturing: a widespread strike occurred in early 1927, which led to Morones declaring it illegal, the Supreme Court finding Morones's declaration unconstitutional, and Calles decreeing the creation of the federal labor boards to resolve such strikes. Again, as detailed in Chapter 7, the Supreme Court's decisions influenced the development of labor law, pinpointing some of the issues that Calles as president had to address to ground federal, executive authority more firmly on a legal base.

This legal imperative was not trivial. Calles exercised substantial power informally; the reliance on the CROM during elections in any number of instances attested to this.[70] At the same time, the legitimacy of Calles's rule was disputed: major military revolts occurred in 1927 and 1929; American oil interests had challenged his and Morones's attempts to regulate them more closely; and, in 1927, Calles confronted a large-scale rural insurrection of Catholic militants opposed to the anti-clerical policies of the federal government—and of Morones. Meanwhile, Obregón's campaign for the presidency (which necessitated a constitutional amendment) accelerated; arguably, by 1927, the general and ex-president also wielded extensive political influence.[71] This presaged the decline of the CROM. Obregón had strengthened his ties with the CROM's popular and political enemies since 1924 and indicated he would not compromise with the labor federation. Calles's stance toward the duel between Obregón and Morones has been difficult to decipher.[72] In May 1928, Obregón, who did not hold a state office, persuaded the national Congress to amend the constitution on two points. The first derogated the independent status of the federal district's government (the

CROM had controlled it). The second, as mentioned, restructured the Supreme Court; and the incoming president, presumably Obregón, would nominate new justices to begin serving their terms on December 20, 1928. Clearly, Obregón wanted a Supreme Court he could control more completely. The constitutional reform suggests that whatever the prior susceptibility of the Court to executive pressure was, it had not been sufficient to satisfy Obregón; at the time, he justified the need for reform by asserting that the Court had enjoined agrarian reform decisions—prejudicing his new agrarian allies. The reform prompted accusations of imminent executive subordination of the judiciary.[73]

The assassination of Obregón immediately after he won the presidential elections in July 1928, meant, among other things, that the interim president, Emilio Portes Gil, who was educated in law, nominated the new justices. The political implications of Obregón's death, however, remained inimical for the CROM. Portes Gil, inaugurated at the end of 1928, was not only an Obregonista but also an enemy of the CROM; as governor of Tamaulipas, he had sponsored rival organizations and had passed comprehensive labor legislation.[74] Even before Portes Gil's inauguration, Obregón's followers accused Morones of masterminding the assassination. He resigned from the SICT and other CROM leaders in the government soon followed. To appease further the Obregonistas, Calles sacrificed his ties with the CROM, tilted his government to include more of Obregón's partisans, and, in September 1928, announced he would not seek the presidency again. In his address to the national Congress, the president said that Mexico would move from "a country ruled by one man" to a "nation of institutions and laws." Henceforth, a government of institutions would replace rule by caudillos (that is, military leaders, like Obregón, for one).[75] In early 1929, Calles founded a party, the PNR (National Revolutionary Party), to preside over national and state elections and channel military commanders' rivalries.

This political and legal context framed the legislative efforts described in Chapter 8. Through the late 1920s, presidential control of the legislature remained problematic;[76] and Obregón practically countered Calles's executive power by April 1926.[77] Different actors in the 1920s favored federal legislation to varying degrees. Industrialists wished to avoid the reach of popular, quasi-radical state governments that sometimes had supported unions over them in industrial conflicts; but they also feared federalization insofar as it might incorporate provisions or arrangements that would strengthen a militant labor movement. Organized labor (the CROM, but also the railroad workers' confederation and other groups) generally desired federal legislation, but by 1931 union leaders were anxious that a federal statute would undermine what they had achieved until then. Notions of social legislation and liberal doctrine informed the political process of passing the legislation, as did the labor conflicts of the 1920s and their judicial manifestation. The conclusion reiterates these points, as the main themes of this study are reviewed: how liberal and then social legal norms and doctrines contributed to the shaping of an industrial relations system with an essential legal component by 1931; and how judge-made law developed and variously influenced labor legislation and industrial relations under Porfirian and postrevolutionary regimes.

CHAPTER I

The Rights of Free Labor, 1875–1910

INTRODUCTION

The constitution of 1857, with the civil and penal codes, largely comprised the law affecting labor relations in Mexico in the Porfirian era. Although in the early 1900s a few state governments began to introduce piecemeal social legislation while the federal government considered doing so, the constitution remained the main positive law for workers. The federal judiciary throughout the thirty-five years of *Porfirismo* recognized the freedom of labor guaranteed by the constitution, while the federal executive grudgingly acknowledged the right of workers to organize and strike implied in the 1857 document, even if in actuality government officials frequently sought to contain independent labor movements and sometimes repressed strikes when they jeopardized production. Further, liberal intellectuals and the artisan or working-class press couched language supportive of workers' interests with references to the constitution.

During Díaz's presidential terms (1877–80, 1884–1911) and Manuel González's (1880–84), the federal government promulgated a number of codes or statutes to facilitate investment in mining, commerce, and industry. Mexican government officials endeavored to use law to promote economic growth and the modernization of the country. The government reformed property rights so as to rationalize them and codified a number of areas of law to lower transaction costs for businesses disposed to invest and operate in Mexico—to overcome the perceived "obstacles to growth" that were the legacy of the *ancien*, colonial regime.[1] A new mining code was adopted in 1884 and a commercial code in 1884, to name a couple of major projects (both codes were later amended).[2] The federal government, however, did not deem it necessary in the late nineteenth century to pass legislation to regulate industrial relations. Initially, labor's challenge to industry and the government was largely dismissed, in ideological terms, by reference to laissez-faire principles. In one widely quoted instance, in 1892, Matías Romero (then minister of foreign relations and promoter of foreign investment in Mexico) replied to organized workers pleading for government intervention and aid in a dispute with their employers as follows:

> The government has the law as its norm and justice as its aspiration. Given the institutions that govern us, it is unfeasible to restrict freedom of hiring or to intervene directly in the improvement of basic working conditions. No legal text authorizes . . . the government to decree salaries, prices, or hours of work; our institutions based on the high principles of human liberty and respect for property prohibit the government from all direct interference in labor-management relations. . . . You invoke . . . your right to work [freely]. . . . Labor is subject by ineluctable natural phenomena to the law of supply and demand.[3]

Workers did indeed invoke the right to work and the constitutional right of free labor. This chapter, therefore, first discusses the constitution and some of the debates about free labor of the delegates who drafted the constitution, before turning to an examination of relevant provisions of the civil and penal codes. The chapter concludes with a discussion of a symposium held in 1875 on the right to strike, during which speakers construed the constitution with the penal code to affirm the right of workers to strike peacefully. As the speakers insisted, both the constitution and codes could provide a basis on which to maintain the rights of free labor; the liberal ideology that prevailed among Mexicans under the Porfirian regime encompassed a vision of the free laborer, however compromised in practice workers' rights were by economic trends or business interests.

THE CONSTITUTION OF 1857 AND THE RIGHTS OF LABOR

The liberal constitution of February 5, 1857, emphasized individuals' rights—in connection with social institutions. The first article made the fundamental basis and object of social institutions the rights of man.[4] Many of the other provisions in the first section concerned labor and the freedom of the worker and guaranteed his or her civil and political rights in universally applicable language. Article 2, banning slavery, the absolute, legal form of forced labor, declared that everybody in the republic was born free. Article 3 guaranteed the freedom of instruction. The fourth and fifth articles particularly focused on the freedom of labor (*libertad de trabajo*). Article 4 stated: "Every man is free to embrace the profession, industry or work that suits him, provided it is useful and honest; and to enjoy its fruits. Neither one nor the other can be impeded, except by judicial sentence when the individual has interfered with the rights of a third person, or by governmental resolution, dictated within the terms of the law, when society is offended."

Article 5, in its first sentence, contained the strongest statement of labor's rights: "No one can be obliged to furnish his work, without just compensation and his full consent." It was a radical assertion of the right of all workers to be free from any form of coercion. Indeed, the stipulation of just compensation went further than simply requiring that labor be voluntary. It raised the question of what could be fair compensation. In the mid-1870s, one jurist, José María Lozano, tried to grapple with the question; he answered it by applying rudimentary market notions.[5] In any event, in the context of labor relations, the core of Article 5 was its proscription against involuntary labor. Combined with Article 17, which prohibited the imprisonment of anybody for a civil debt, the constitution precluded the use of incarceration to coerce anybody to work to repay a debt, including advanced wages. Together or separately, these two articles rendered any form of servitude, including debt peonage, unequivocally unconstitutional.

Other constitutional provisions affirmed civil and political rights for workers. Article 7 established freedom of the press. Article 9 ensured the right to associate and meet peacefully. Arguably, it could guarantee the right of labor associations to form and assemble. Article 11 guaranteed freedom of movement throughout the republic, as well as entering and leaving it. Binding workers to specific estates, or employees to their employers, was therefore unconstitutional. Articles 12 and 13 established the principle of equality before the law, the thirteenth by proscribing special courts and privileges or immunities for any social group, apart from military tribunals. Article 14 prohibited state authorities, including judges, from violating standards of due process or applying laws retroactively. Article 16 guaranteed the individual's right against unauthorized governmental action against his or her person, family, domicile, papers or possessions. Article 21 charged the judiciary exclusively with the application of penal sanctions. Administrative or political authorities could impose a correctional fine only to a maximum of 500 pesos or one month's sentence of detention. Articles 18, 19, 20, and 22 further guaranteed due process procedures in criminal matters. The federal judiciary and litigants cited these articles in cases against local authorities using the criminal process or detaining workers to press them to work for an employer. The delimitation of jurisdiction over criminal matters to specific state authorities, moreover, aimed to prevent private entities—*hacendados* (large landholders) and their overseers, for example—from operating private jails and applying corporal punishment to their workers, in a quasi-feudal manner.[6]

Article 28 prohibited monopolies. Article 32 in part mandated the enactment of laws to improve the condition of working Mexicans. Article 34 granted citizenship to those with Mexican nationality who, as well as being of age, had an honest mode of living. Citizenship thereby was not predicated on property or any other privileged status but was related to productive activity. All Mexican workers could enjoy it and its benefits provided they had an honest occupation. This latter condition was not an incidental or rhetorical requirement. Many state laws earlier in the century had aimed to suppress vagrancy by obliging individuals to work for various employers, and vagrancy was understood as being the antithesis of having an honest mode of living.[7] In the precursor to the constitution, the provisional, organic statute of 1856, a vagabond could lose citizenship rights.[8] The constitution thus posited the individual as a free person with the right to work or engage in productive activity, against corporate privilege and political despotism. It was not a workers' charter, but its liberalism encompassed laborers and affirmed their equality with all other individuals in the nation's society and polity. The constitution affirmed an ideology to which workers recurred.

The signing of the 1857 constitution followed after prolonged debates in a convention that met for nearly a year, in the context of a looming civil war and finally foreign intervention.[9] Liberals, divided between moderates and radicals (*puros*), drafted the document. Many of the debates concerned the relationship between the Catholic Church and the state, federalism, relations among the branches of government, and the institution of property. There were also broad and pointed discussions about the status of the nation's rural workers—its large, dependent, agricultural population and that population's relationship with large estates (*haciendas* or *fincas*). The record of the debates reveals the perception of radical delegates of an underlying social problem in the country and their attempts to remedy it within a framework of liberalism. For them, the monopoly privileges enjoyed by the Catholic Church and hacendados not only retarded economic and social progress but also oppressed and pauperized much of the country's population by sustaining servitude.

The debate over the first section of Article 5 reflected the tension between the right to be free from any form of coercion and the obligation to perform an agreed upon service pursuant to a civil contract, which at least nominally structured rural labor relations; the debate thereby also reflected the underlying social reality of systems of servitude that still existed in parts of the country. One delegate, Juan Morales Ayala, insisted that Article 5 would authorize men to abandon their employment, violate their contracts, or refuse to complete the work to which they had agreed, since the remedy of monetary damages for breach of contract was illusory in the instance of indigent workers or artisans. In rebuttal, Ignacio Ramírez alluded to the peonage existent in the country: "money is advanced to day laborers [*jornaleros*], not to favor them, rather to enslave them. . . . One speaks of contracts between proprietors and day laborers, and such contracts are nothing more than a means to support slavery . . . the debtor is sold to a creditor, something that happens in haciendas far from the capital and also in those which are very close." Ramírez, one of the more renowned liberal intellectuals of the nineteenth century, as well as later a supreme court justice, added: "If liberty is not to be an abstraction, if it is not to be a metaphysical entity, it is necessary that the fundamental code protect all the rights of the citizen, and that instead of one master, thousands of masters are not created who would traffic with the life and labor of the proletariat." The convention loudly applauded

Ramírez. Guillermo Prieto, another major liberal intellectual, sought to avoid confusing the question of labor with civil law (i.e., the law of contracts or obligations), denounced the tyrannical hacendado, and insisted that the constitution should establish the rights of man, thereby distancing himself from Morales Ayala.[10] Delegates divided closely over the categorical language of the first sentence of Article 5: the final vote to adopt it was 43 to 37. In contrast, the second sentence of the article, which dealt in particular with restrictions imposed in monasteries, monastic vows, and with an apprentice's subordination to his master, passed with a larger majority: 69 to 22.[11]

As divisive as were the arguments regarding the prohibition of involuntary labor, the convention deliberated more over the original language of Article 4, which would have legally inhibited any curtailment of the free exercise labor by property holders. This would have impinged on the practices of hacendados. The convention eventually deleted the far-reaching language from the original article, initially introduced as Article 17.[12] Before it did so Ignacio Vallarta, who would become an influential jurist and early ideologue of the *Porfirisimo*, articulated both the limits of law as a form of social legislation and the laborer's condition. He also said that the right to free labor (*el derecho al trabajo libre*) was a necessary requirement of man, "because it is an indispensable condition for the development of his person." And Vallarta acknowledged the exploitation of the master—whether factory or estate owner—of the laborer: "The master, the proprietor, the owner of primary resources, of the factory or of the estate where the worker exercises his industry, commit, there is no doubt, an abuse in obliging him to lend his services in a mode that curtails his liberty."[13] According to Vallarta, the constitution should guarantee the general right of free labor but not specific protections for workers. He acknowledged the promise of socialism, although he still grounded his analysis of appropriate constitutional language partly on a formally legalistic view and partly on the premise that the state should not interfere in market relations. It was quintessential liberalism, hesitant in the face of Ramírez's preoccupation with the social question.[14] Yet Vallarta insisted that law need not be meaningless: "The law can indeed improve the fortune of the poor classes; and to this it should tend with all its force, removing impediments and obstacles, punishing abuses respecting free property as much as free labor, because in the ultimate analysis, labor is the only property of the poor, who do not have estates, factories or any other class of assets."[15] This was a conclusion that liberal jurists and legally educated intellectuals, like Matías Romero, could uphold, at least nominally, under the Porfirian regime that ostensibly was a liberal state.

THE CIVIL AND PENAL CODES

Insofar as Mexico's civil codes addressed labor relations, they conceived of the employment relationship as a contract made between individuals.[16] As the principal statutory framework supposedly organizing social relations in civil society, this in itself was significant, and typical of nineteenth-century codes modeled on France's.[17] Under the civil code, the essential element of a contract was that the parties agreed to it voluntarily; an employment contract was the expression of the wills of the individuals who committed themselves to the terms and conditions of the agreement in connection with the provision of services by one individual to another. The introductory exposition of the federal district's code recognized that human beings were contracting for services, not merely arranging for the letting of things, as the French code (and Roman law) normally conceived of the provision of labor. Thus, "nobody can lend a service . . . without employing his or her free will and exercising one of the faculties peculiar to man." The exposition added that perpetual contracts were void, in accord with the constitution.[18] Also consistent with the constitutional right of free labor was the code's limitation of the remedy for the abandonment of employment (and breach of contract) exclusively to monetary damages. The employee might forfeit any wages not paid—but an employer could not force him or her to work, and complete the contractual obligation, even if it had been entered into voluntarily.[19]

The code defined the various employment relationships between individuals.[20] It contemplated four types of employment, those of domestic servants, day laborers (*jornaleros*), contractors, and apprentices. The legal drafters did not conceive of an abstract form of work or employment, such as the wage laborer per se. The codes were written before industrialization had progressed very far in Mexico. The civil code did require employees, such as servants and day laborers, to obey completely the employer unless the request contravened the law or contract; to discharge their service loyally and with all the diligence commensurate with their abilities; and to care for things received while in service, avoiding damage to them.[21] The worker was responsible for the value of all entrusted instruments and objects, except when faultless for any damage or loss.[22]

The civil code, while centered on relations among individuals, also governed their freely constituted associations, including those of workers and artisans who organized groups and meetings for mutual support and aid.[23] Article 47 subjected all private interest associations, as any labor association would have been deemed, to the rules of the *contrato de sociedad.* The conditions for this contract of an association did not specifically require its registration with any authority but did refer to a need for a public writing, possibly a charter of its constitution and bylaws reached in a public meeting.[24] The code set out the definitions of moral and legal entities or persons, that is, of collective associations:

> Art. 43. Moral persons are associations or corporations, temporary or perpetual, founded with a joint public and private end or reason, which in their civil relations represent a legal entity.
>
> Art. 44. No association or corporation is a legal entity unless it is legally authorized.
>
> Art. 45. Associations or corporations that are legal entities can exercise all civil rights relative to the legitimate interests of their institution.[25]

The code did not outline how a legal entity was authorized or whether a public authority had to license an organization for it to be "legally authorized."

The Penal Code of 1871 addressed the strike. Article 925 imposed a fine ranging from 25 to 500 pesos or incarceration lasting between eight days and three months, or both on "those who cause a disturbance or riot, or employ any other kind of physical or moral violence, with the purpose of causing the raising or lowering of salaries or wages of workers, or impeding the free exercise of industry or work."[26] The sanction against a riot or (physical) violence was clear; in contrast, the notion of moral violence was ambiguous. Article 925 did not define the term, although moral violence was understood as intimidation or a threat of future and imminent harm, capable of sufficiently debilitating the individual's will.[27] Thus, the same code in the chapter on robbery described moral violence present when the robber threatened a person with grave harm, actual or immediate, which was capable of intimidating him or her.[28]

If one reads Article 925 in the context of its surrounding provisions in the same section of the code, it seems clearer that the penalties against certain strike activity aimed to punish rioting and tumultuous mass behavior capable of intimidating the employer or nonstriking workers. Article 922 penalized a public reunion of three or more people, which even if formed with a licit purpose degenerated into a tumult disturbing the repose of others with yelling, fighting, or disorderly behavior; Article 928 penalized those who caused a riot, tumult, or fight, with the objective of provoking the pillage of a fair or market so that, intimidated, the vendors sold their merchandise at a lower price. Article 926 targeted a verbal act—defamation—uttered in order to affect the price of merchandise or credit documents, but it did so without using the phrase "moral violence," which suggests that the drafters of the code distinguished such injurious, nonviolent verbal behavior from intimidation akin to moral violence.[29] In general, these articles concerned the maintenance of public order and prevention of harm to economic interests: aside from Article 926 they covered physical acts. The entire section (Title Eight) in which the drafters placed Article 925 was entitled "delicts against the public order." If the strike were undertaken to pressure an economic interest forcefully or threateningly, the state could punish strikers. The strike understood as the peaceful withdrawal of labor was another matter.

THE RIGHT TO STRIKE

The hatters' strike in the spring of 1875 in Mexico City was practically a paradigm of the kind of concerted action that liberals then could tolerate or support under the constitution and codes.[30] The strike was peaceful; hatters simply desisted from working. Their action did not violate Article

925 of the penal code. The then radical newspaper *El Socialista* stressed the lawfulness of the strike.[31] Guillermo Prieto advised and represented strikers in negotiations with employers; Francisco T. Gordillo, whom one periodical wrote was a learned and eloquent attorney, also served as their counsel.[32]

Striking hatters founded a society on May 3, 1875, that set a wage rate (*tarifa*) to which employers had to accede for hatters to return to work. [33] An extensive set of bylaws or statutes was drafted for the association, the Sociedad Reformadora del Ramo de Sombrerería.[34] In most respects its bylaws typified those of artisans' mutual aid societies.[35] Distinctively, one of the objectives of the bylaws was to protect the interests of the striking workers; and they contemplated the need to discipline members.[36]

Press sympathetic to the strike emphasized the value of cooperation among workers and producers. *La Firmeza* urged compromise because labor and capital needed each other: rights and obligations were identical, and consequently both should compromise to reach a satisfactory arrangement.[37] *El Socialista*, in an essay entitled "La Asociación," enumerated the practical benefits of association. After the strike ended, consistent with an ethic of cooperativism, the governing board of the society projected a conciliatory stance to employers and government. It explicitly thanked the nation's president and the government of the federal district, which "had facilitated the peaceful transaction of our and the proprietor's interests."[38] The sources do not indicate whether the society submitted its statutes to any government office for approval or review.

Following the hatters' strike, and in response to it, the prestigious Colegio de Abogados in Mexico City sponsored a symposium on the right to strike in August 1875.[39] Speakers included the eminent lawyer Rafael Martínez de la Torre,[40] and the rising attorney Emilio Velasco. Prieto also spoke; he called the symposium "transcendental." Plainly, it represented an important event: the nation's president Lerdo de Tejada attended, in addition to a couple of hundred other people.[41] It is significant, then, how the mentioned speakers concluded that workers had the legal right to strike. They based their analyses on the constitutional rights of free labor and association, also finding substantial support in political economic theory. Their discourse, particularly Martínez and Prieto's addresses, illustrates how liberalism and legal thought by 1875 had established an essential element of labor law.

Martínez de la Torre and Prieto theorized that workers had a property right in their labor, and that this right to furnish labor freely implied the right to withhold it, in a concerted manner, under Article 9 of the constitution. If peaceful, the strike was lawful. Each acknowledged that the civil code's Articles 43–45 applied to labor groups just as to other civil associations. Prieto qualified the reach of the civil code insofar as these articles might be construed to require state approval for the formation or existence of an association (its legal authorization), which association Article 9 guaranteed as a right. Both concurred that pacts for strikes could be lawful but believed that organizations could not apply penal sanctions to their members. Prieto allowed that organizations could fine members.[42]

The two thus shared a liberal ideology that centered partly on individual rights as articulated in the 1857 constitution and which conceived of individuals freely forming associations and acting through them. They also believed that the state should refrain from involvement in labor relations. Political economic principles largely supported their argument for state abstention. Prieto especially championed the relevance of political economic theory for his analysis of the conflict between labor and capital, while Martínez cited political economic notions to supplement legal arguments that included references to Roman law as well as foreign examples.

Martínez viewed the scope of the constitution more circumspectly than did Prieto. Article 9 barely adumbrated the nature of the association; and a fundamental condition of the right to associate had to be the conservation of individuals' liberty, free from any form of coercion or intimidation, including from other association members. For the lawyer, there were two sources for regulation of the association: positive law, in the form of statutory and constitutional conditions, and the contractual agreement of the association, originating from the exercise of the will of its members, in their full, individual autonomy. Ideally, law set the parameters of form while the association itself had wide discretion in fashioning its own internal rules.[43]

Martínez defined the strike as the abstention of labor "with the end of obtaining better compensation," which followed from the concept of free labor, as did property.[44] Turning to political economic doctrine, which he asserted represented a broader discipline than positive law, Martínez posited that the interests of capital and labor could be harmonized, as mutually dependent competitors. He redefined the strike as the suspension of these reciprocal relations, analogous to the capitalist's closing of his operations. Both capitalist and worker exercise a property right. The liberalism of the lawyer is evident again: the struggle between labor and capital would be pointless if not for the existence of privileged associations and monopolies; the full exercise of liberty was the antidote. As for Article 925, the lawyer construed it narrowly, citing jurists and political economists for the principle that law should proscribe rather than prescribe conduct. Even when the strike was economically harmful, it still was not necessarily unlawful: "The *estado de derecho*, as necessary for the good, should be maintained in society against every contrary pretension; legal obligations are coercive, and unjust acts should be punished by tribunals. Actions purely immoral or uneconomic, so long as they are not contrary to law, are not subject to any jurisdiction."[45] The strike, therefore, was not punishable, as long as it remained nonviolent. The liberal lawyer, however, understood violence to encompass intimidation, bending the exercise of the free will guaranteed in constitutional articles.

Prieto's disputation emphasized the importance of Article 9.[46] It recognized preexisting, post-independent, republican conditions, ratifying them.[47] If there were a conflict between it and the civil code, the constitution had to prevail. State authorization of the labor association was definitely not necessary. The association, pursuant to the civil code, however, could rely on the law for contractual enforcement. Prieto approached the potential conflict between Article 925 and the right to associate similarly. He construed the penal code to apply only to violent and coercive conduct, and in the case of inconsistent interpretations, the code had to be amended.[48]

Citing numerous political economists and especially Frédéric Bastiat, Prieto suggested that the relationship between labor and capital had been structured oppressively and wastefully. If the two factors were reorganized to conform to their legitimate conditions, the solution to the social problem would be easy. The liberal animus against governmental privilege and monopoly is also evident in Prieto's discourse, as is his criticism of socialism. Rather than proposing the abolition of capital, Prieto argued that the mutual dependency of the two factors should be recognized. The distribution of wealth was an economic question of supply and demand. Significantly, Prieto referenced the ideal of an equilibrium between the forces of capital and labor. Along with this economic argument, Prieto elaborated Martínez's argument that the right to strike was equivalent to the right to withdraw one's property. Although Prieto qualified the argument with the statement that any violent appreciation in the value of commodities was truly an outrage against property, he emphatically stated that the strike was an exercise of a property right protected by the right of association to avoid the tyranny of capital.[49]

Echoing Martínez's liberal interpretation of history, Prieto contrasted the present, liberal era from the past: labor historically had been coerced, the state regulating its compensation. Prieto lauded recent positions taken by Mexico's Supreme Court and presidency. The former had ruled against governmental regulation of the wages while the latter abstained from interfering in labor relations, allowing businesses and workers to exercise their respective rights. Bastiat provided authority for the argument that the state should not interfere in labor relations, on the assumption that when it did it repressed labor.[50] Ideally, as labor and capital freely made contracts, the resolution of labor's problems would be found in cooperativism, namely, the association. Concluding, Prieto proclaimed the beginnings of an approach to social problems based on political economy, as pioneered by his address.[51] His subsequent review of Emilio Velasco's address to the college of lawyers, approving the young lawyer's application of political economy, emphasized the value of the new, scientific approach.[52]

CONCLUSION

The constitution of 1857 established the principle of free labor. It was a central element of the document, and closely related to the concept of the free individual and citizen. Many liberal intellectuals circa 1875, including jurists, embraced this point. For example, the jurist José María Lozano, in his 1876 treatise, in connection with Article 4, wrote:

> Labor is the principal element that man has at his disposition to meet the ultimate objectives of his conservation, development and perfection . . . it provides him with his necessities and it puts him in position to discharge the principal duties that he has to society; it is one of his first rights, because it corresponds to one of his first duties; it matters as [do] all the rights of man, as an indispensable condition of his nature; consequently, the law that impedes work, that restrains it, that imposes on it irrational conditions, violates the rights of humanity.[53]

As to Article 5's prohibition of forced labor, Lozano said that the freedom of labor constituted one of the most natural forms of human liberty.[54] Complementing this viewpoint was the theory that workers had a property interest in their labor, so they could dispose of it as they wished. One could infer this property right from the civil code, which articulated the employment relationship as a contract to lease, with the worker letting his labor to the employer. Ignacio Ramírez and Vallarta repeatedly noted the significance of the condition of the indigent worker, whether agricultural or urban, whose only property was his or her labor—and the laborer's rights guaranteed by the constitution. Prieto and Martínez said that the worker has a property right in his labor, analogous to the owner's property right in his business.

The immediate precursor of the 1857 constitution, the organic, provisional statute decreed in 1856, further illustrates the relationship between the rights of the citizen and the worker as conceived by liberals by the mid-nineteenth century.[55] The main individual rights that the organic statute set forth concerned labor: after a general proclamation, the prohibition of slavery followed. Article 33 regulated apprenticeships of minors in order to prevent their exploitation due to their limited capacity (or legal incapacity) to contract for themselves. Article 32 proscribed coercive labor; but in contrast to its counterpart in the 1857 constitution, this provision allowed for obliging workers to complete their contracts.[56] Lastly, the organic statute equated the exercise of one's labor with property: "Every inhabitant of the Republic is free to employ his or her labor or capital in the trade, business or honest occupation that he or she wishes."

And even more definitively: "[p]roperty is inviolable, whether it consist of goods, rights or in the exercise of any occupation or industry."[57] In brief, the free citizen and the free laborer were interrelated, as were property and labor.

Article 32 of the organic statute reflected the tension that Morales Ayala later discussed: between the requirement to fulfill a contract and the freedom to terminate it at will. It was a problem inherent within the employment contract across the Atlantic world, as one legal historian has argued.[58] Thus, in England until 1875, under the Master and Servant Acts, workers faced penal sanctions if they abandoned their employment; in the United States, of course, slavery existed until the mid-1860s. France did not allow the coercion of labor after the Revolution of 1789; but French law did require, at least nominally, that workers furnish prospective employers with a notebook (*livret*) indicating their satisfaction of any debts incurred with their previous employer.[59] In this Atlantic world, it is noteworthy that the Mexican civil code for the federal district permitted employers to sue their ex-employees only for monetary damages when they quit in breach of their contract. Legally and in ideal terms, the constitutional right of free of labor prevailed.

Free labor as a legal concept transcended the relationship between individual workers and employers. As the symposium held in the aftermath of the hatters' strike demonstrates, the right to organize and strike could be inferred from the right of free labor combined with the right to associate.[60] In the decades after 1857, by 1875, and certainly through 1910, most artisanal and worker movements grounded their demands and aspirations largely in the guarantees of the 1857 constitution, even if they sometimes considered other currents of political and social thought, including anarchist or socialist ones.[61] In view of what the constitution promised, and its focus on the rights of man that specifically included the rights of labor, it was not an unreasonable stance for labor to adopt, whether it did so for practical, instrumental reasons or for more symbolic and ideological ones.[62]

Lozano as a jurist exemplified the social liberalism of the mid-1870s with his discussion of the rights of association and, obliquely, the hatters' strike, referencing constitutional Articles 9 and 28.[63] Lozano even stated what would become a union slogan, that unity creates strength (*la unión hace la fuerza*).[64] Interestingly, he argued that Article 28, which prohibited monopolies, and as such was an important liberal statement against privilege, applied only to state-enforced monopolies—hence could not apply to the union, which tried to control the supply of labor. He also argued, however, that neither the union agreement to sanction a member who disregarded a stipulated wage rate (such as the hatters'), nor an employer's agreement that tried to maintain a specific wage rate was fully enforceable: the union could not enforce a fine against the dissident worker, and the employer could not force the worker to work at the rate on which he insisted.[65] This was a liberal law of labor, based on constitutional Articles 4 and 5.

It was a labor law in which the state was absent. This was not an incidental omission from the liberal vision of labor relations. Nor was it altogether inconsistent with Matías Romero's response to workers. In September 1875, for example, J. P. Gallardo y Rionda in *El Socialista*, connecting the disputations recently held in the Colegio de Abogados with the hatters' strike, advised that the state not become involved in labor relations. For him, state intervention implied repression of the strike.[66] This was one approach to the question of the appropriate role of the state in industrial relations, and it echoed Prieto's position in the symposium. In determining the limits of the lawful strike, both Martínez and Prieto had largely relegated state activity to a police one: enforcing the law when somebody violated it, especially when violence occurred.

The right to strike in political economic terms had already been discussed in 1872 by José María Vigil in "La Cuestión de Huelgas." Using an analytic framework similar to Prieto's, Vigil posited the mutual dependence of the factors of production, capital and labor.[67] Vigil recognized a traditional antagonism between the two factors, which occasionally led to violent crises, the most common of which was the strike. The solution for Vigil was liberty: to allow the two factors to deal between themselves freely. Vigil recommended that the state refrain from attempting to regulate the complex question of industrial relations; the legislator's intervention would cause only an unjustifiable inclination to one side or another of the balance between the entrepreneur and worker. The legislator's action altered the natural relationship between supply and demand. In contrast, if the laboring classes were permitted to organize, they would act prudently and cautiously, ultimately favoring mediation and arbitration over the strike.[68]

All of the liberals discussed here recognized the constitutional right to organize and found that the worker had the right to withdraw his labor from employment, construed as the exercise of a property interest, derived from the right of free labor and, once promulgated, implicitly, the civil code.[69] The emphasis on the value of the voluntary will of the individual, which should not be coerced, placed the fundamental limitation not just on the right to strike but also on the labor organization, as Martínez de la Torre had contended. The basic pending question, however, was another one, already anticipated in the constitutional debates over the early draft version of Article 4. It concerned the appropriateness of social legislation to regulate industrial relations. Martínez made merely one brief allusion to the possibility of social legislation. In practical terms, this possibility raised the question of the role of the state. The law of labor should consist of the normative relations of individuals entering into voluntary contracts in which labor was exchanged for just compensation—and regarding which the state would be nearly absent, committed to enforcing said contracts, but not, significantly, to the extent of requiring or ordering their completion if this meant the coercion of labor. All Mexican workers were free citizens of the republic, who could not be forced to work, indeed, could withdraw their labor and form associations to pursue their lawful interests.

CHAPTER 2

Free Labor and the Federal Judiciary, 1875–1910

INTRODUCTION

Forced labor existed in different regions of Mexico under the Porfirian regime, especially in agriculture—and Porfirian Mexico was mostly agricultural. Employers maintained coercive labor practices in the southeastern region of the country, including Tabasco, Campeche, Yucatán, and parts of Oaxaca and Veracruz, as well as in the central states of Puebla and Tlaxcala. But the nature of servitude varied across the country. One historian, Alan Knight, proposed a typological classification of peonage in Mexico, extending from a traditional, quasi-paternalistic institution to practices in southeast Mexico that were modified during the commercialization of agriculture toward the end of the nineteenth century and became markedly more coercive.[1] Another historian, Friedrich Katz, pointed out that the precise extent of forced labor in Porfirian Mexico has been difficult to ascertain not only because actual employment practices differed and changed, as rural economies developed and population grew, but also because of the lack of primary sources illuminating agricultural labor relations and, specifically, the viewpoints of laborers.[2]

Employment arrangements were nuanced: even where peonage prevailed, labor systems on estates encompassed various forms. Large estates contracted both temporary laborers and residential workers, and whether either type of worker was free or not depended on particular circumstances. Employers or contractors frequently advanced wages or furnished maize and necessary articles on credit, but indebtedness did not necessarily equate with peonage. Wages advanced to recruit workers sometimes signaled the difficult position of employers who needed labor where workers were not readily available; advances even represented a relative advantage or benefit for workers in an imperfect market.[3] Employers, of course, who advanced wages hardly could be indifferent to anybody who later absconded without repayment. At the same time, the federal government forcefully relocated Mayans and Yaquis to work on Yucatán's plantations, while convicts and individuals deemed vagrants were also sent by government officers or contractors to work in the southeastern plantation regions.[4]

Whether legal or not, a coercive labor system required enforcement. In regions where employers relied on forced labor, public authorities might enforce labor obligations, returning fugitive workers to their haciendas or fincas. Or large landholders might use private agents to capture and return fugitives with the tolerance of public authorities. Historians have observed and theorized that servitude existed in isolated areas where demand for labor was greater than its availability, escape by estate workers was impractical, and employers' local influence was significant.[5] Apart from the federal army, which deported the defeated Yaquis and Mayans to plantations, most of the political authorities cooperating with hacendados were locally based, such as the political prefect or chief (*jefe político*), judges or justices of the peace, and mayors.[6]

State governments in the north, south, and center legislated in the nineteenth century to regulate peonage.[7] Many state laws deemed it a form of fraud (*estafa*) when a worker quit his job while in debt to his employer. During the 1880s and 1890s, the issue of debt peonage recurred in national debates. Several northern state governments, notwithstanding their labor fraud statutes, endeavored to limit the amount of a laborer's debt that could be recognized legally, with the aim of facilitating the repayment of the debt and emancipating the worker from his or her employer. Katz argues that such reforms in northern Mexico were a compromise among the national government, northern industrialists, and mine owners, who needed more workers, and the hacendados, who wanted some compensation for the loss of the their investments in labor.[8] There was an ideological facet to the debate, too. When the governor of Tamaulipas in 1894 proposed amending Article 5 of the constitution so as to allow forced labor, state legislatures in their statements to the federal Congress opposed the proposal, invoking principles of liberalism, patriotism, and the right of free labor against the Tamaulipan attempt to install slavery.[9]

THE AMPARO PROCESS

In this political and ideological context, the federal judiciary categorically recognized the individual's right to be free from forced labor. In its published opinions, the Supreme Court between 1874 and 1910 never once denied the principle of free labor in the cases that reached it. Until 1899, it always ruled in favor of petitioners who claimed the right to be free from involuntary work. Thereafter, if the Court did not uphold a petitioner's claim alleging some kind of coercion, it did so basically on evidentiary grounds: whether erroneously or disingenuously, the tribunal found that the petitioner had failed to provide sufficient proof. The Court did not qualify the right of free labor doctrinally or legally.

The procedure and law pursuant to which the Court addressed litigation, however, limited the types of cases that could reach it, independent of the local conditions that must have normally affected access to the federal courts. The amparo lawsuit was the principal form in which litigants framed claims for relief by the federal judiciary; in order to obtain an injunctive order or amparo, a violation of the petitioner's constitutional rights by a public authority had to be alleged.[10] The respondent was technically the state actor, not a private employer. The amparo cases citing Article 5 can reflect factual patterns distinct from peonage; many, for example, refer to public service impositions (labor drafts in municipalities).[11] Article 4 also guaranteed freedom of labor, and specifically the affirmative right to work; there are many cases where the federal judiciary either granted or denied an amparo to protect entrepreneurial activity against state regulation, including that of professionals like unlicensed pharmacists, physicians, and attorneys.[12] The focus here, however, is on cases involving challenges to servitude by workers invoking the right of free labor.

The typical factual pattern and legal claim of these amparo cases can be summarized as follows. A laborer employed by a rural estate separated from his employment still owing the employer a debt. The employer sought the assistance of a political authority in his vicinity to jail the ex-employee to pressure him to return to his employment. The employer alleged that defaulting on the debt amounted to a criminal offense. In federal court, the laborer claimed that the jailing political authority had violated his or her rights guaranteed by constitutional Articles 5 or 17, or both. The laborer might deny owing any money to the ex-employer or assert that the debt was of a purely civil character. The federal judge could order the local authority to suspend the action against the petitioner, but issuance of the federal judge's final amparo order to the local authority to end all proceedings against the worker, or release him from detention, would await the Supreme Court's determination.[13]

The review of the federal district court file of one case illustrates the process that a worker had to undertake in order to obtain the support of the federal judiciary.[14] In this amparo case, Rosaliano Limón was an agricultural laborer who left his hacienda in the state of Puebla in November 1894. He was apprehended at a nearby estate and taken before a local criminal judge in January 1895, where he confessed to a judgment for almost 75 pesos rather than go to jail. After another dispute with the hacienda, he abandoned it again in March and was arrested around July 16, 1895. The legal basis for his detention was Puebla's 1880 state statute: "Fraud: servants, day laborers . . . commit it when without just cause, having received an advance they refuse to engage in the promised work."[15]

Limón's wife, María Mauricia, petitioned for an amparo in Puebla's federal district court around July 22, 1895. She signed (and ostensibly wrote) a letter brief. Her legal argument was succinct: Limón's incarceration for a civil debt contravened Article 17. She did not cite Article 5. Her letter stated that merely on the basis of the local criminal court's record, Limón's constitutional rights had been violated. The district court agreed and issued an amparo on September 25. The Supreme Court affirmed it on December 27, 1895. The last document in the district court's file, addressed to the federal judge and signed by the state criminal court judge, is dated February 7, 1896, and says in part: "The order was received . . . transcribing the sentence of the Supreme Court confirming the *amparo* granted by you for Rosaliano Limón. He was left in absolute liberty."[16]

Limón, described as a *peón*, testified to his illiteracy. His wife filed a letter requesting a waiver of court fees due to their indigence. The record does not indicate any organization assisting the peon or his wife, nor the support of a patron. Still, the letters signed by Limón's wife reflect legal assistance. For example, Mauricia cited numerous Supreme Court opinions in her letter brief to substantiate her legal argument. The federal attorney who wrote a brief about the case in effect endorsed her argument, as did the federal district judge. Puebla was not an isolated region as were areas of southeastern Mexico and Yucatán; it is plausible that agricultural workers like Limón and Mauricia could have benefited from this and availed themselves of attorneys for the poor. And while no patron is mentioned in the records, Limón had another employer by the time he was arrested; perhaps this employer supported his litigation.

It is instructive that Limón's wife was able to file the amparo petition within a week of her husband's incarceration and that the federal judge granted the amparo within three months, which the Supreme Court affirmed about three months later. This does not appear to have been an especially slow or cumbersome legal process; and the local authority evidently did release Limón promptly.[17] Nevertheless, one should not generalize from this one case to others where the details of litigation or the social circumstances have not been investigated. In other cases reviewed in this chapter, only the published appellate opinion is considered. Sometimes the opinion provides a fair amount of detail of the circumstances of the case, other times not. The published opinions normally discuss the rationale of their ruling; the opinions aim to justify legally the decision of the Court. They may reflect the relevant social relations sometimes, but rarely is the social context of the underlying conflict fully presented.

In its normally brief labor opinions, the Supreme Court usually applied Articles 5 and 17 without extensive discussion: their meaning did not seem to have been subject to much disagreement. The Court never expounds an exhaustive doctrinal or historical analysis of the right of free labor. In most cases, the justices do not debate the values or policies of each rule or article applied. The respondent local authorities usually justified the detention of the petitioner-laborers by citing local laws. Sometimes they suggested that the worker had been unruly. The federal judiciary, in turn, might express skepticism of the local authority's factual account, hold that the local law was unconstitutional, uphold the principle of the federal supremacy of the constitution and the right of free labor, or find that the local authority had been legally incompetent to arrest the petitioner. In any case, the opinions express the rationale of the ruling tersely.

To reiterate, an examination of the reported cases in the *Semanario Judicial* involving labor issues between 1874 and 1910 indicates that the Supreme Court always supported the laborer against the local authority and hacendado until about 1899, at least if the federal district court had recognized the laborer's petition, that is, if the laborer had been able to file a petition.[18] After 1899, the Court was less disposed to rule in favor of the laborer-petitioner, but it continued to grant amparos enjoining obvious acts of coerced labor. Accordingly, this chapter groups an analysis of cases decided before 1899 and thereafter and concludes by pointing out types of employment disputes that the Supreme Court failed to address. This chapter's argument is, of course, based on the Court's published cases. There are gaps in this record, however: not all amparo opinions were published; and the *Semanario Judicial* failed to appear between 1875 and 1880 (as noted in the introductory chapter).[19] The last amparo identified from the examination of all volumes of the *Semanario Judicial* through 1910 dates to 1908—yet it is plausible that there was more litigation over labor issues thereafter, until the end of the Porfirian regime. Nonetheless, as the patterns discerned here show, it is possible to point to a shift in the Court's decisionmaking happening toward the end of the nineteenth century.

SUPREME COURT DECISIONS, 1880–1899

The following opinions dating between the early 1880s and the mid-1890s exemplify the Supreme Court's decisional or case law during these years. The rulings sometimes explicitly acknowledge the existence of debt peonage. They apply constitutional principles fairly unequivocally and formally. Federal judges rebutted the justifications of the local authorities and construed the pleadings of the petitioner sympathetically. The federal judiciary was willing to hold state law that legitimized debt peonage unconstitutional insofar as it concerned the petitioner's case and assert federal and judicial supremacy in a number of instances. The amparo petitions were initially filed in federal district courts located in various states throughout Mexico: three in Tabasco, others in Coahuila, Tlaxcala,

Campeche, and Puebla. Several other amparo cases arose in Chihuahua and Tamaulipas.

In the amparo of Benito Vicente, the petitioner Vicente alleged that a local justice of the peace in Tabasco violated his constitutional rights, including Article 5 guarantees.[20] The justice of the peace (*juez primero de paz*) had ordered Vicente against his will to continue to work for his employer Armengol on a rural estate, sending police to get him. Vicente himself had initially brought suit before the justice, requesting the rescission of his employment contract. With the counsel of a lawyer, the local justice had ruled against Vicente. The federal judge rejected Vicente's amparo petition, reasoning that since Vicente had asked for the justice's ruling, he had tacitly consented to the decision, hence his continued labor was not involuntary. The district court acknowledged that the normal remedy for a breach of an employment contract was monetary compensation but held that in this case, this remedy was inapposite since Vicente had not offered to pay it, nor had the justice of the peace ordered damages paid. Article 5 was essentially dismissed for being an extreme remedy, which if applied here would undermine the principle of contractual obligations. Vicente's allegation of the police coming after him was dismissed as being too vague, if not a lawful exercise of local authority.[21]

The Supreme Court rejected the federal judge's analysis. Relying on Vicente's factual account, and also on the local justice's report, the Court described a social reality far from one governed by a voluntary contract that the federal judiciary should enforce. During Vicente's employment on Armengol's estate in 1882, the overseer had whipped him. It was for this reason that Vicente decided to quit and asked Armengol for an accounting. Armengol had refused, so Vicente remained in his employment in 1883, subject to more mistreatment. Then Vicente filed the action in the local court of the justice of the peace, only to lose. For the Court, the local justice's decision ordering Vicente to continue working for Armengol until the end of 1883, and instructing Armengol to keep the overseer away from Vicente in order to avoid any further mishaps, confirmed a coercive environment violative of Article 5. In view of the dates of the Supreme Court's final judgment, May 10, 1884, and the expiration of the contract in dispute, December 31, 1883, perhaps the Court's decision was practically ineffective. It nonetheless represented a strong stance of the Court, critical of local, pseudolegal practices approved by the federal district court judge.[22]

In the amparo of Patricio Gómez, the district court judge and federal attorney, or *fiscal*, advising the court sympathized with the laborer's plight and commented on Tabascan social conditions perpetrating debt servitude.[23] The justice of the peace had jailed Gómez at the request of a state judge for the purpose of returning him to his employer. The *fiscal* concluded it undoubtedly violated Article 5 to imprison a person in order to send him back to an estate to work there involuntarily. As the local judges' reliance on the state civil code's provision authorizing the apprehension of fugitives from a hacienda contravened Article 5 and could not provide legal authority for the arrest and prosecution of the petitioner, the judges had violated Article 16, which guaranteed a right against harassment from state authorities lacking the competence to execute the challenged action. The *fiscal* also found infractions of constitutional Articles 17 and 18, as the incarceration was for a civil debt, while Article 18 limited penal sanctions to specific types of criminal acts, certainly not civil ones. Nobody had attributed a criminal act to the complainant.

The federal judge construed Gómez's petition liberally, in accord with Article 42 of the Law of December 14, 1882, and in light of the complainant's social status:

> In conformance with the disposition of Art. 42 of the Law of December 14, 1882, in the present case it follows that judicial consideration should extend to violations, which, although not substantiated in the written complaint, are no less obvious, and are omitted undoubtedly because of the ignorance of the complainant, which convinces one of his status as a servant of a rural estate.[24]

The judge determined there were violations of Articles 17 and 18; the justice had jailed the petitioner for a civil debt: Gómez had, to paraphrase, 'in fact freed himself from masked slavery, in reliance of the most valued constitutional right, that of individual liberty.' The federal district court also considered the article of the state's civil code that the local judges had cited to coerce Gómez. Article 126 of the constitution trumped it: "all judges should adhere to [the Constitution] despite any contrary dispositions that there might be in state laws."[25] It was a strong declaration for the supremacy of the federal constitution over state laws, one the Supreme Court adopted in its unanimous affirmance on the basis of the obvious violation of Articles 17 and 18. The Court reiterated statements about Gómez's liberating himself from "masked slavery," as well as the district court's justification for applying the Law of December 14, 1882, to construe liberally Gómez's petition, since he was obviously an uneducated agricultural laborer.[26]

In the amparo of Crescencio Concepción, the federal judiciary again made explicit references to debt peonage in Tabasco.[27] Both the supreme and federal district courts doubted the version of facts submitted by the political prefect, who had justified Concepción's arrest by calling his conduct scandalous. The district court wrote that evasiveness typified reports of authorities detaining "indebted servants" (*sirvientes adeudados*). It also held that the state law of June 1874, on which the local authorities had relied to press the laborer, was patently unconstitutional:

> In this state the existence of the circumstances claimed here is very frequent, as a basis for the zealous pursuit and apprehension by the authorities of servants called indebted, whose condition differs in nothing from that of slaves, with the end of sending them to work against their will and without fair compensation, when they leave their employment since they no longer wish to continue working. Their legal basis is the local law of June 15, 1874, whose unconstitutionality cannot be doubted; and further, as is known, the same authorities, when an amparo is requested against these acts of theirs, write in their reports if not in brevity then at least with obscurity, with the consequence that it is difficult to discover the constitutional violations for which they are responsible.[28]

Unanimously affirming the district court's amparo order, the Supreme Court alluded to its language approvingly.

In the amparo of Felipe Aguirre, the laborer filed his petition in the state of Coahuila but challenged the state of Nuevo León's law that made leaving an employer without repaying him a fraudulent act and which had been applied against him when he was detained in the first state.[29] The federal district court made a strong pronouncement of federal supremacy and of the unconstitutionality of the state law:

> Whereas: if according to the laws of the state of Nuevo León . . . it is classified as the offense of fraud . . . such a classification cannot be entertained, for being contrary to the prescriptions of the cited Art. 17, and encompassed by Art. 126 of the Constitution, which this, the laws of Congress . . . and all of the conventions made with the President, are the supreme law of the entire Union; the Judges must conform with the Constitution, laws and treaties despite the disposition that can be contrary in the states; the rulings are numerous which grant the amparo in cases like the present one.[30]

The Supreme Court affirmed the district court's ruling, citing Articles 5, 16, and 17. It did not elaborate further an argument premised on the supremacy of federal law, besides in effect incorporating the district court's comments into its opinion. Granting the amparo did signify the prevalence of federal over state law on behalf of the petitioner.

In the amparo of José Corralito, the complainant, a debt peon on the Buena Vista hacienda in Tlaxcala, left it to go to work for another hacienda, defaulting on his employment contract.[31] The first employer complained to the local mayor, who jailed Corralito to pressure him to fulfill his contract. The federal judge stressed that Corralito had been arrested as a fugitive peon while working for his second employer under the state law that sanctioned debt peons. Corralito had defied it, thereby giving rise to the mayor's accusation that he had become disrespectful and disorderly. The district court applied Article 5. The high court affirmed the lower court's decision. As in the case of Aguirre, its judgment largely rested on the holding of the federal judge and the supremacy of the federal constitution over state law.

The opinion in the amparo of Evaristo Luna is lengthier than most and presents enough detail of the underlying contract to give a sense of the legal elements of the employment relationship in the southeastern state of Campeche.[32] Luna had accumulated a debt of 247 pesos when his employer Calderón terminated his employment. Luna offered to repay his ex-employer at the rate of 25 pesos a month, but according to Luna, Calderón tried to assign him, not the debt, to another employer. Luna refused to comply with this intended arrangement. Calderón then denounced him to a local trial judge for fraud, on the supposition that

Luna was going to depart from the area while still indebted. The judge found him guilty under different provisions of the state penal code for fraud and had him jailed. Luna then turned to the federal district court for an amparo.[33]

The employment contract (*contrato de servicios personales*) stipulated the accrued debt, identified the place of work (the estate), the daily rate of pay, and additional task rates. The contract specified that Luna could not separate himself from his employment without liquidating his debt.[34] The *fiscal* applied contractual principles to find it nearly determinative that Calderón, not Luna, had terminated the contract, contending that as a consequence Luna was free to elect how he would repay Calderón. In addition, the *fiscal* suggested that the local judge had violated Article 18, because none of the articles of the penal code cited were apposite. The *fiscal* believed Article 5 also applied: Luna was jailed because he had refused to work for another employer.

The federal judge granted the amparo on the basis that the local authority had violated Article 17: the penal code did not apply, Luna's debt was a civil one, and he had been jailed out of the fear he would abscond. The federal judge did not find sufficient proof that Luna had been jailed to pressure him to work for another employer; hence Article 5 was inapplicable. The Supreme Court agreed with the judge when it affirmed his decision.

The Supreme Court did continue to apply Article 5, however, and granted amparos in at least five more instances between 1881 and 1893 in claims arising in the states of Campeche,[35] Tlaxcala,[36] Chihuahua,[37] and Tamaulipas.[38] The situations out of which the cases arose varied. Three involved groups of workers, but the judiciary regards this litigation as involving individuals not associations of laborers. In the case of José Reyes Ramírez, the federal judiciary construed Article 5 expansively, to cover a minor who had been turned over to an agricultural employer by his mother. After an examination of applicable law, including American law, the Court held that the employer could not force the minor to work. The Court also ruled for Julio Montañez, who refused to follow through with an employment contract to go to Yucatán from Tamaulipas.[39]

SUPREME COURT DECISIONS, 1899–1910

In the late 1890s, the Supreme Court changed its stance toward the litigation of workers alleging coercive labor practices. The first published denial of a laborer's amparo invoking Article 5 or 17 may have happened in 1899, in a case from Tabasco.[40] Alfonso Benito alleged that his apprehension was for the purpose of forcing him to work on an estate. The district court denied the amparo, and the Supreme Court affirmed unanimously: "As the authorities designated responsible for the violative acts denied their occurrence, and the complainant in contrast did not submit any proof that substantiated the violation of rights of which he complains, there is no basis on which to predicate a ruling granting the amparo and therefore this is denied."[41] It is certainly conceivable that Benito did not submit any evidence on which the Court could base an affirmative ruling. But in previous cases coming out of Tabasco, the Court had noted the social realities and conditions that rendered it extremely difficult for the laborer to put together much of a case, scrutinizing local authorities' pretexts. It is possible that in previous litigation the local authorities had lost sometimes because they acknowledged factual allegations asserted by the complainant, while trying to justify them under local laws or practices, and had consequently unwittingly given the Court some grounds on which to rule against them. In Benito the defendant authorities denied outright all of the complainant's allegations. Local officials by 1899 might have learned better how to present their version in federal court.

As recently as six months before the ruling in Benito, the Supreme Court had concurred with the federal judge in Tabasco granting an amparo to Antonio Salvador.[42] He petitioned the federal district court because the Macuspana political prefect had ordered him taken to the finca of San Diego "to furnish personal services against his will." The rationale of the decision granting the amparo hinged on the question of the extent of the jefe político's authority. The prefect indisputably had intervened in the employment and contractual relationship. The Court found this illegitimate, since it was outside the scope of the prefect's duties.[43]

After 1899, nevertheless, it was almost as probable that the Court would deny rather than grant a request for an amparo by a laborer alleging coercion. Of the seventeen cases decided in the period between 1899 and 1910 and examined here, the Court denied eight and granted nine amparos. Is there a pattern to its decisions? As the opinions remain generally brief and nearly conclusory, it is difficult to probe the Court's reasoning. It is noteworthy that the Court never denied a petition if it found an infringement of Article 5 or 17. That is, the rejection of laborers' amparo petitions did not result from legal defenses such as time limitations, "mootness," or claims of immunity. Denials of relief follow from the failure to prove the allegations, according to the opinions, as is the case in Benito.

The amparo petitions arise from disputes in the states of Tabasco, Campeche, San Luis Potosí, Chiapas, Michoacán, Oaxaca, Puebla, Nuevo León, Veracruz, and the federal territory of Tepic. The eight denials are spread across the country, too: Tabasco, San Luis Potosí, Michoacán, Oaxaca, Puebla, and Tepic. They are issued until February 1908. The denials are normally by unanimous vote. The opinions evidence greater preoccupation with the parties' satisfaction of the new federal procedural code promulgated in 1897.[44] The high court's focus on procedural and evidentiary conditions, moreover, surpasses that of the lower federal courts.

The amparo of Ramón Quej illustrates the trend toward framing cases largely in procedural terms.[45] Quej cited Articles 5 and 17, as well as Article 16, because the political prefect of Campeche's capital had sentenced him and his wife to thirty days' imprisonment or a 15 peso fine for refusing to work for a private employer. The Court granted the amparo, but not on the grounds of the alleged constitutional violations.

The political prefect in his report wrote that he had jailed Quej after he became unruly when the former had sought to reconcile the latter with his employer. In the Court's opinion, the prefect had failed to prove satisfactorily his justification for jailing Quej:

> If the executing authority dictated a prison sentence . . . he did not prove in the necessary time the existence of the infraction, nor remit a copy of the order that should have been issued for the imposition of the fine in conformance with the law, nor did he prove that he had issued said order; therefore the imposition of the fine does not appear justified.[46]

The Court's ruling then reviewed the law cited by the prefect:

> In effect the penal code of the state, 1888 edition, in art. 951, establishes that the lack of respect for an authority, attributed to Quej, shall be punished by reference to the applicable, legal or regulatory police dispositions, and that regulation is the one of January 26, 1895, whose art. 112 was violated, according to the political prefect.[47]

It might have seemed that the prefect had been able to justify legally Quej's incarceration. But the Court persisted with its analysis:

> In effect, in conformance with Art. 95 of the cited penal code, violations must be punished by the governmental authority or by justices of the peace . . . and this code, after establishing in Art. 66 that jurisdiction of the violations corresponds to the justices of the peace or political prefects, established in Art. 631 that all the facts and sentence should be consolidated in one act.[48]

This had not been done, so the opinion ended with a critique:

> That in effect . . . when it is not proven with the issued act in the referenced terms the legality of the submissions of the political authority, the infractions that justified the imposition of the fine do not seem to be proven, since there does not exist a document that proves the offensive act and that a penal law or regulation has been infringed; thus lacking in the absolute justification for the acts of the authority designated as responsible, the amparo should be conceded.[49]

The Court then affirmed the amparo for Quej, although only because of the violation of Article 21, that is, for the procedural failings of the prefect: Article 21 required a judge to declare most penal sentences.[50]

In two other cases decided in 1907, one from Nuevo León, the other from Campeche, the Supreme Court similarly ruled in favor of workers for the deprivation of their procedural rights. That is, the Court largely relied on Article 16. The laborers had referenced primarily Article 5.[51] In the amparo of Salazar, the political prefect had detained the complainant for refusing to continue to work as a mason on a hacienda. The Court clearly sympathized with the mason, stretching to find that he had proven his factual allegations.[52] As in other opinions, it discussed how a political prefect lacked the authority to intervene in the employment relationship and had prejudiced the complainant by imprisoning him. Its conclusion also resembles that of Quej in that it is based on the prefect's failure to prove his compliance with procedural requirements, albeit without the detailed review of the regulatory justification published there.[53]

In comparison, not the authorities' defenses but the claims of the complainants were found unsubstantiated by the Court in the following cases: Mariano Arellanes,[54] from Oaxaca; Faustino García,[55] from Atlixco, Puebla, but involving transport to the Valle Nacional in Oaxaca; and Julio Delgado,[56] also involving a consignment to the Valle Nacional. In each of these cases, the defendant public authority refuted completely the allegations, which according to the Court's opinion went unproved. Yet the complainants' allegations were as plausible as any litigation decided before 1899.

In the amparo of Nicolás Mendoza, the opinion of the Court is sufficiently detailed to suggest an alternative holding that would have favored the petitioner.[57] The lengthier opinion, issued in late 1907, may be a result of the lower federal court having granted the amparo and the Court's need to explain its reversal. The lower court's favoring of the worker's claims and the Court's reversal indicate, too, that by 1907 the latter was concerned in such cases with more than the curtailment of the freedom of labor.

Mendoza alleged violations of his rights under Articles 5 and 16, in the federal territory of Tepic by a justice of the peace, Romano, who had also been his employer at a bakery. According to Mendoza, Romano had summoned him, ordering him to work only at his bakery. Mendoza had begun to work for another employer, Zepeda. When Mendoza protested that he was free to work for whomever he wished, Romano called a police officer, instructing him to watch Mendoza and, if Mendoza continued to work for Zepeda or anybody else, to arrest him. Romano disputed Mendoza's vivid statement of threats and the order to the police to pressure him to work in his bakery, yet the local justice's version of the crucial event confirmed some of Mendoza's allegations. Romano largely corroborated the terms of the oral contract of employment outlined by Mendoza, including the stipulation that Mendoza was obliged to work exclusively for him.[58] He also provided a reason why he would have been opposed to the worker leaving his employment, and he acknowledged involving the police officer:

Romano advanced 10 pesos in cash, and later, at Mendoza's request, he gave him various goods, which with the advance, amounted to the sum of 60 pesos, and then it was agreed that he would be paid 62 cents in cash daily for his expenses, and the rest would be added to the account . . . that one day Mendoza did not go to the mill, while the dough was already prepared, for which reason the police officer Fortino Delgado was sent to find him, and when he came, Romano limited himself to telling him about this failing to fulfill his commitment, making him see the prejudice he was thereby causing, and asking him at the same time how he could pay him what he owed, and lastly, advising him at least for that night to work so as not to lose the preparation, and in the contrary case he would expect the results . . . that it is not exactly so that on his part he would have threatened Mendoza in any manner, nor said obscene words.[59]

Despite Romano's statement, the Court concluded that the justice of the peace and employer had not verified Mendoza's allegations and that Mendoza had not submitted evidence to prove his case. The Court reviewed the two claims made by Mendoza, that the local justice had constrained his freedom of labor and that he had been subject to police vigilance. Both of these allegations seem to have been partially corroborated by the report of the justice of the peace quoted above. Oddly, the Court was silent about the direct involvement of the justice of the peace in his own employment dispute, in contrast to other holdings that rebuked the local officials' interference in employment matters and queried their administrative competence. Likewise, the Court was silent on whether the police officer could have had any legitimate role in pursuing the bakery worker.

In contrast to the rulings against Mendoza and other workers, three judgments illustrate the clear relevancy of Article 5 to instances of obvious forced labor. These were cases in which the extent of abuse may have been outrageous. Possibly the Court believed it had no choice but to grant the amparos; two of the three suggest this likelihood. One opinion again is reflective of the Court's concern with procedural requirements.

In the amparo of Demetrio Bustos, the petition was initially filed on August 30, 1905, in Veracruz, against the administrator, or *subregidor*, of Tierra Blanca, alleging violations of constitutional Articles 5, 16, 17, 20, and 21.[60] For a debt of 17 pesos, the subregidor had jailed Bustos for five days, next assigned him street cleaning duties for an additional five days, then handed him over to a labor contractor to be sent to the colonies of Uzumacin for 35 pesos, with ten other individuals who were sold in the same manner. In this case, the defendant government official did not deny the allegations; instead he blamed his predecessor and supplemented the evidentiary record. Indignant justices found a violation of the constitutional articles invoked, unanimously entered an amparo for Bustos, and ordered the federal judge to assign the culpable ex-subregidor to the appropriate criminal court for prosecution.[61]

In Magdalena Vásquez, the amparo petition was filed against a municipal president who had ordered Vásquez to work for a finca to repay her deceased paramour's debt to its owner.[62] Proofs were not submitted in the case, but the municipal president's version of Vásquez's complaint adequately confirmed it for the federal district court to grant the suspension and amparo requested. The high court affirmed the amparo on the basis that the documentation demonstrated that a civil debt had been the basis for obliging Vásquez to work without her consent and without fair compensation, in violation of Article 5.[63]

In possibly the last involuntary labor case decided (and published) by the Porfirian Court before the beginnings of Francisco Madero's presidential campaign, the petitioner Velueta asked for an amparo against a local judge (*juez mixto*) in Palenque, Chiapas, who was detaining him and was going to turn him over to a justice of the peace in Tacotalpa, Tabasco, on the grounds that he had committed theft in that state.[64] Velueta's brief, filed in February 1908, claimed he was really being detained for having left a finca whose owner had mistreated him cruelly, while he owed the owner 100 pesos. Velueta claimed that these actions had violated his rights under constitutional Articles 1, 5, 16, 17, and 18. The local judge responded to Velueta's allegations by remitting to the federal court a certified copy of the documentation of the Tabascan judge regarding the accusation of theft at the finca.

The federal judge denied the amparo, "basing himself only on the fact that the order issued by the responsible authority of Tacotalpa was in the proper legal form, and that therefore the allegedly liable conduct did not violate any constitutional right."[65] The high court reversed the federal judge's decision. It dealt with the issue of the local authority apparently acting lawfully in response to a criminal process by attacking first the form of the supposedly valid documentation presented, then its content. Its analysis of the requirements for a proper extradition order from another state led it to examine the procedural law of both Chiapas and Tabasco. The failure to meet necessary procedural requirements deprived the Tabascan court's request for Velueta's detention of all legal force. The opinion then analyzed the substance of the allegations in the documentation of the theft, concluding that offense could not have been proven, because of its reliance on three faulty and unbelievable declarations. The Court noted, too, the probable motive that the owner and employer had to allege theft. Thus it conceded the amparo, essentially for the violation of procedural rights: Articles 16, 101, and 102 of the constitution, and Articles 745, Paragraph 1, and 850 of the federal procedural code.[66]

Velueta may represent the ideal case decided after the implementation of the federal code of procedure in 1897. It scrutinizes rigorously the local judiciary's actual process and the evidence proffered. It echoes Quej's discussion of the applicable laws on which the respondent prefect tried to rely. Whether this is the result of a direct application of the provisions of the Código de Procedimientos Federales, and the Court's greater adherence to procedural regularity, or of a federal judiciary less sympathetic to workers is difficult to evaluate dispositively. Neither the statement of purpose of the federal code nor its chapter regulating the amparo (Articles 745–762) suggests any intent other than to conserve the amparo action; indeed, the needs of indigent litigants are explicitly recognized.[67] The main ostensible reason for the promulgation of the procedural code was to improve the federal government's powers to collect revenues.[68] Nonetheless, one scholar of the amparo action has suggested that the 1897 amendments to the amparo proceeding, incorporated into the federal civil procedural code, were "chiefly notable for elaborating reasons for inadmissibility of the *amparo* suit and the grounds for dismissing cases in progress."[69]

It is clear that the Court's opinions beginning around 1899 demonstrate, at least on a rhetorical level, a greater emphasis on evidentiary issues and on the legal processes of the defendant authorities. Before 1899 amparo claims were decided mostly on the basis of Articles 5 and 17. Afterward, Article 16, which if applied or invoked earlier had been done generally in conjunction with other constitutional articles, and procedural violations seem more significant. The kind of social criticism of debt peonage found in Gómez and Concepción did not recur in later opinions, regardless of whether the Court applied Article 5. And, of course, the Court began to reject petitions alleging forced labor. If the federal procedural code is a reason for this apparent shift, rather than any public debate about the condition of agricultural laborers, denials of amparo petitions probably did not result from a change in social policy toward debt peonage. Until the end of the Porfirian regime, the Supreme Court continued to rule against the unlawful coercion of labor, as the cases of Velueta, Vásquez, and Bustos illustrate, even as it did not consider industrial forms of labor relations.

CONCLUSION

The federal judiciary under the Porfirian regime did not have much of a direct impact on labor relations. Although the Supreme Court ordered a separate investigation of unconstitutional practices in a few cases, in the context of labor relations spread across vast regions of the country, involving large numbers of workers, employers, government officials, and contractors, these few investigations, if carried out, must have been negligible in terms of their effect. Even if the eventual outcomes of the published cases resemble that of Limón and Mauricia in Puebla in 1895, these cases have to represent a small fraction of the total number of labor disputes implying unconstitutional coercion that arose in the country over thirty-three or -four years. In many instances, a worker who wished to abrogate the employment relationship probably simply left, migrating elsewhere, such as to the United States, a trend about which employers in the northern states complained.[70] Where escape was less practical and hacendados could count on authorities to prosecute or return fugitive workers, such as in the southeastern states, most laborers probably could not access the federal courts to plead their cases, as Mauricia did for Limón in Puebla.

Most parts of the country where involuntary labor has been documented are represented in the cases discussed here—with the exception of Yucatán, where hacendados exploited forced labor systematically by the end of the nineteenth century, as the commercial production of henequen expanded. There is evidently no published Supreme Court case, however decided, of a worker petitioning for an amparo due to labor coercion in Yucatán. One must surmise that in this state agricultural workers lacked access to the federal judiciary, or the federal courts would not consider their petitions. Some combination of the two patterns probably operated, although even if federal judges normally ruled against Yucatecan workers' petitions, the Supreme Court should have received some on appeal and published an opinion of some kind.

The thorough study by Allen Wells and Gilbert Joseph of rural conflict and elite politics in Yucatán between 1876 and 1915 presents an interesting counterpart to the federal cases analyzed here.[71] The study relies in part on state criminal court records, whose dispositions reflect landholders' oppression of the rural proletariat and their strategies to maintain domination. The historians analyze the peonage of agricultural workers and their limited forms of resistance, noting, "existing documentation suggests that the federal government turned a deaf ear to campesino complaints during the Porfiriato."[72] In any case, contemporary critics observed and denounced the prevalence of peonage in the state.[73]

In the 1880s, the newspaper *El Socialista* had despaired about the efficacy of the federal courts in remedying the abuses of debt peonage in a state close to Yucatán, Tabasco. An article published initially in the liberal periodical *El Monitor Republicano* on May 14, 1881, reprinted in *El Socialista* in 1886, referred to the law of 1874 that the federal district court ruled unconstitutional in the amparo of Concepción:

> This law . . . is the state law of June 9, 1874, which was decreed, approved, sanctioned and put into rigorous practice by democrats and liberals. . . . In vain has it been declared unconstitutional by the federal courts in the difficult cases in which those unfortunate ones have managed to ask for an amparo. This has been ridi-

culed as much as possible by those who say that the agricultural sector should be protected.[74]

The same newspaper continued to publish articles denouncing involuntary labor not only in Tabasco but also in Chiapas, as did other periodicals in the mid-1880s. One, *El Partido Liberal*, apologetically proposed that the federal government under the constitution always had the right to end the de facto slavery; what was absent was society's will to do so: "and the Supreme Court can at any time intervene to counter the application of local laws that give to one man complete dominion over another who is burdened by debts. It is imperative that the public conscience awakens and concerns itself with this issue."[75]

In consideration of these public ruminations, the significance of the Supreme Court's decisions upholding the principle of free labor should not be disregarded even if their direct impact was negligible. State laws criminalizing a worker's abandonment of employment must have appeared more suspect in the face of a legal ideology of free labor. In this ideological context, the Court's doctrinal law could have bolstered the arguments of liberal advocates of free labor, including those of the periodical *El Socialista*. Katz defined debt peonage as a "form of forced labor which develops when a number of social and economic prerequisites for bondage in agriculture . . . exist but the state officially refuses to implement bondage while tacitly tolerating and acknowledging it under another name."[76] Debt peonage to the extent it existed was largely a local phenomenon. Under the Porfirian regime, the federal executive may have acquiesced to regional practices, even contributed to servitude when it deported indigenous peoples to plantations in Yucatán. But it did not advocate openly for such a labor system. Tacit official toleration remained tentative, juxtaposed against a legitimate discourse of labor rights, to which the Supreme Court contributed, if with restraint. The federal judiciary voiced the liberal principles of free labor, against local instances of servitude, sustaining ideologically and legally the federal constitution over state and local law, custom, and actual practice.

Debates about servitude among elites continued intermittently, as mentioned; some implicated the nation's leadership as well as local or state powers. For instance, when an agricultural congress convened under the auspices of the governor in March 1896 in Chiapas, to consider reforming the system of peonage in the state, Díaz wrote to the governor, warily advising him against undertaking reforms that might destabilize agricultural production: "'You must believe that if [servitude] exists here it is because I cannot yet remove it; we are still not at the level of education where it is possible to bring such a benefit to the villages.'"[77] When the governor informed Díaz about the closure of the congress, Díaz instructed him to desist from any reform efforts, "'in so much as [peonage] is important to landowners, it would damage your personal prestige and in this respect and if you agree, I invite you to leave it alone.'"[78] Chiapas's governor relented, but the issue of forced labor persisted.

Its persistence in legal and public discourses is surely related to the continued existence and expansion of peonage in the southeastern regions of the country. And in Yucatán, Díaz and his closest advisers collaborated with the state's planter elite in connection with the promotion of economic growth that seemingly necessitated peonage. Díaz himself visited Yucatán in 1906, where he dismissed accusations that masked slavery existed in the state: "'he who is a slave . . . necessarily looks very different from these laborers I have seen in Yucatán.'"[79] The president was insincere, of course, but it is significant that he did not affirm the state's system of forced labor.

As the state's planter elite became more closely associated with Díaz's close advisors, the científicos, this relationship might have further affected Díaz and the federal judiciary's perception of the labor question in the state. The leading científico was José Yves Limantour, the nation's finance minister; one of his strongest cabinet-level opponents was the minister of justice, Joaquín Baranda, who dominated the federal judiciary for nearly twenty years, until he abruptly resigned, in 1901, probably as the result of a contest with Limantour in which Díaz finally sided with his finance minister.[80] Before Baranda's resignation, Limantour had prevailed against him in the reform of the federal civil procedural system and the promulgation of the new code. It would be reductionist to contend that the Court hardened its legal or procedural position regarding agricultural labor cases because of a political contest that did not imply any preoccupation with labor issues. But in fin de siècle Mexico, the científicos were ascendant, if remaining only one faction among ruling groups, and one might conjecture that the federal judiciary for prudential reasons presumed that Yucatán's economic growth should not be challenged and, more generally, that labor cases (among others) after Baranda's resignation needed exacting review. Díaz was indeed hostile to reform of coercive labor systems where it might threaten large landowners' interests. Still, toward the end of the Porfirian regime, hacendados debated the economic attractiveness of a system that required them to invest so much capital in a labor force that constitutionally could not be constrained.[81]

In any case, constitutional and statutory reforms modified the organization and operation of the federal judiciary at the end of the century. Not only were evidentiary standards for evaluating amparo petitions raised; the procedural reforms also devalued the import of jurisprudencia. Whereas before 1897, five consistent Supreme Court rulings were controlling on subsequent, similar issues, after implementation of the 1897 reforms, such case law could be cited only for demonstrative purposes; until further reform in 1908, jurisprudencia would not have again the status of law or any precedential, controlling effect.[82] The objective of this reform probably was to rationalize adjudication—decisions often were seemingly reached inconsistently, and the reportage of them was incomplete and sometimes erroneous.[83] One last judicial reform points to the goals of streamlining federal adjudication and asserting executive power over aspects of it. In May 1900, the public ministry (*ministerio público*) was established to replace the *fiscal* and *procurador* (Court-affiliated attorneys).[84] The Ministerio Público, an office of federal attorneys, would argue cases before the federal courts—on the instructions of the *Procurador General de la República*, a cabinet-level official analogous (to a degree) to an attorney general. As the constitutional reform, initiated by Baranda while still secretary of justice, placed the public ministry squarely under the direction of the federal executive, and the *fiscal* and procurador had been nominally under the control of the high court, the reform surely aimed to consolidate executive control.[85] Whether such reforms actually weakened the judiciary or rendered it more conservative is arguable. One legal scholar suggests that one of the aims of the 1897 reforms was to strengthen the complainant's ability to challenge public authorities, by requiring the latter to adhere more closely to procedural law.[86] This is discernible in a few of the Court's cases, such as the amparo of Velueta. Baranda's ministry of justice was hardly immune to political contests. Although not democrats or liberals in the tradition of the constitution's defenders, the científico lawyers and intellectuals had coalesced in 1893 around the proposal to amend the constitution to remove justices from the electoral process (that is, from Díaz and Baranda's constant political machinations) and ensure them life tenure and thereby a degree of autonomy from the executive power after their appointment.[87] Nonetheless, in combination, the judicial reforms probably had the effect of subordinating the judicial branch further to the executive, even if científico-inspired reform was not formally opposed to judicial integrity.

In view of the reform of judicial procedure, and the president's animus against the disruption of labor systems deemed necessary to the interests of large, commercial landholders, even if unconstitutional, the Supreme Court's affirmation of the rights of free labor is thus notable, for ultimately the Díaz regime was personalist and authoritarian. Since not even Díaz himself could (or evidently wanted to) abolish the constitution or judicial institutions, and the fundamental charter guaranteed the right of free labor and the amparo process, the ideology of free labor remained operative throughout the Porfirian regime and early industrial development.

As explained, the Court was able to defend the right of free labor in part because of the restrictive nature of the amparo process, which allowed judges to decide matters case by case without undermining an entire system.[88] The cases reviewed here illustrate the nature and limits of the process. The Court repeatedly ruled that state and local laws were unconstitutional in connection with their applicability to agricultural workers appealing to the federal judiciary for amparo orders; and the federal judiciary maintained the supremacy of federal over local laws when it found that local legislation legitimized involuntary labor. But its rulings did not result directly in the overturning of challenged state laws or practices. The Court's opinions disputed the justifications made by local authorities; this did not lead to any systematic overhaul of local government practice.

In disputes implying issues other than blatant coercion, the federal judiciary's interpretations of labor rights under the constitution provided little direct support to workers or their organizations. The federal judiciary obviously was not a radical institution. An expansive conception of Article 4 or 5 to include such issues as redistribution of income, premised on a theory of the laborer either retaining a larger fraction of his product (Article 4) or receiving full compensation (Article 5), apparently was never articulated in the federal courts during the Porfirian era, despite some discussion about these implications in the constitutional congress of 1856–57 and among radical liberals thereafter.

Labor conflicts that did not involve the state directly were construed beyond the scope of amparo litigation. For example, in a decision dated September 2, 1874, the Supreme Court ruled against thirty-seven mine workers petitioning the federal court in the state of Chihuahua for relief against their employer who paid them in wooden tokens. The Court held that however distressing was the use of tokens (and Article 111 of the constitution prohibited their issuance by state governments), the amparo action did not implicate the employer, as a private entity.[89]

Most industrial labor conflict in late nineteenth- and early twentieth-century Mexico nominally concerned private actors. Yet employers' reliance on government officials to maintain industrial discipline could have implicated the necessary governmental nexus for an amparo order. Even in instances of government involvement, there are not any published Supreme Court opinions detailing industrial labor disputes.[90] One study examining labor relations in mines in the state of Mexico found a record of an amparo petition by workers being drafted into the army in October 1905.[91] It alleged violations of Articles 5 and 16 by the political prefect of Mineral del Oro; a corresponding published opinion was not found.[92] Whether due to their political sensitivity or because of the contemporary concept of freedom of labor, the Court during the Porfirian era did not decide cases involving industrial workers' rights. Yet if it limited its support of the principle of free labor to cases challenging forms of servitude, to reiterate, this was not altogether inconsequential for a country where agricultural labor relations were extensive, however symbolic or ideological the Court's legal declarations remained.

CHAPTER 3

Porfirian Industrial Relations and the Rights of Labor

INTRODUCTION

The state regularly intervened in labor disputes between 1875 and 1910, notwithstanding liberal and legal doctrine that employers and employees should resolve their differences between themselves, pursuant to agreements reflecting market factors. The hatters' strike was the exception. Government officials normally viewed strikes as if they threatened public order, and they justified regular interference in strikes in terms of their police power to maintain peace. At the same time, employers and workers frequently requested government mediation or assistance. Presidents Sebastián Lerdo de Tejada and Porfirio Díaz, as well as several governors, cultivated alliances with labor groups; these politicians could not condemn workers' protests or demands altogether. Labor associations aligned with government officials contained worker dissatisfaction with governmental approval and support. Actual industrial relations thus qualified the liberal concept of the laissez-faire state.

Liberal ideals lauded by Prieto, Martínez de la Torre, and others nevertheless influenced government policy. The state continued to recognize in principle the peaceful strike as a right of workers, within the narrow terms that legalistic liberals had already outlined by 1875. Liberals' acknowledgment of the right to strike and respect for the autonomy of private property and the right to work, combined with practical state involvement in the resolution of labor disputes, resulted in an ad hoc approach by officials to labor conflict until the collapse of the Porfirian regime. Typically, the federal government or a local governmental office considered each labor dispute in relation to the immediate threat that it posed to social, economic, or political stability, accommodating labor and business interests from one case to another, normally sacrificing the former to the latter. Inaction on the part of the government could mean its appraisal of the weakness of labor to sustain a strike, too, because of the indigence of workers and their frequent inability to set up a strike fund.[1] Industrial relations remained a series of discrete settlements, informal, open to further renegotiation in successive labor conflicts, and sometimes implemented with military force. In particular, the científicos, adhering to a liberal-positivist ideology, failed to articulate a legal doctrine or social theory to justify the state's regulation of industrial relations apart from expressing the need to maintain economic stability in accordance with political economic principles.

One major local government official of the Porfirian era, the jefe político, frequently dealt with labor disputes, sometimes in dialogue with the state governor, or even the president in the case of larger-scaled conflicts. As historians have noted, in many of the strikes that occurred throughout the Porfirian era, employers and workers solicited his assistance.[2] In doing so, employers and workers referenced the law rhetorically. Employers might note the need to maintain public order. Workers petitioning governmental mediation emphasized their rights as citizens under the 1857 constitution with a patriotic flourish, which patriotism Porfirian officials, including Díaz, had celebrated while building relationships with labor groups.

Governmental involvement in labor relations sometimes went beyond the mediation of a dispute. In July 1872, for example, the political prefect authorized the municipal government of San Ángel to adopt regulations for all factories within its jurisdiction in exercise of its police power. The factory rules required workers upon applying for employment to present a certificate of good conduct from any previous factory employment (perhaps analogous to the French *livret*). The municipal rules charged the *junta de policía* with enforcement of the factory rules.[3] Apparently, nobody questioned the constitutionality of the political prefects' frequent intervention in industrial relations, although the Supreme Court had held in forced labor cases that their involvement in private employment matters was unconstitutional. In those amparo cases, of course, the petitioner had complained against the prefect's actions. In the context of factory disputes, workers evidently did not legally challenge the prefect's intervention; more probably they requested or accepted it. And in the context of a collective labor conflict, the prefect's interest was at least partly connected with maintaining public order. Nonetheless, as the federal judiciary's rulings in another context imply, the prefect and state's intervention in labor relations lacked a solid legal foundation.

David Walker has described how Díaz, consolidating his political control over the country in the late 1870s, subordinated to his government labor leaders disposed to collaborate with him, by offering them and their organizations subsidies in the form of support for newspapers, schools, and even minor government offices. In return, such leaders effectively regulated their artisan and labor groups, principally mutual aid associations and, with government officials, frequently mediated labor disputes.[4] These political arrangements began to falter with the onset of modern industry in textile manufacturing, mining, and transport by the 1890s and in particular in the face of crisis and recession after 1906, even as Porfirian politicians attempted to reestablish clientele relationships with a new generation of working-class leaders.[5]

The Porfirian state into the twentieth century continued to use legal rhetoric grounded in the 1857 constitution, while justifying frequent intervention in labor relations mainly in terms of the need to conserve public order. It similarly rationalized persecution of independent labor movements with assertions of their sedition.[6] The revolutionary movement that attempted to organize workers in mining and textile manufacturing, the Mexican Liberal Party (Partido Liberal Mexicano or PLM), did threaten the regime, while affording it the justification for its containment of strike movements. Although the state successfully repressed the PLM and several workers' movements before 1911, ultimately it proved incapable of structuring a stable system, creating new institutions to mediate labor disputes occurring in an industrializing economy or refashioning the dominant liberal ideology. At the same time, labor opponents of the regime, including PLM revolutionaries, barely challenged the pervasive liberal ideology in relation to which the 1857 constitution remained the extant, positive law, even as their practical demands and actions began to transform industrial relations.

This chapter highlights legal issues that arose in connection with major labor conflicts in two strategic economic sectors, textile and railways, in the early twentieth century. It was the sustained strike activity of textile and railroad workers that led eventually to reconsideration of the state's approach to labor relations in subsequent years, even while labor conflict occurred in other economic sectors. Tobacco workers and mine workers, for example, struck frequently.[7] The chapter follows and relies upon the narratives of other historians who have recounted governmental repression of the strikes of 1906–8; but the chapter is especially concerned with the liberal and legal ideology of the regime, as it was expressed by both government officers and union leaders and qualified by the events presented here. Because the conflagration at Cananea of June 1906 provoked a national crisis and was closely associated with the PLM's challenge to the Porfirian regime, affecting ruling elites' perception of the emerging labor movements after 1905, the chapter preliminarily reviews this episode before proceeding to discussions of the major labor conflicts that occurred in the textile and rail sectors between 1905 and 1909.[8]

THE CANANEA UPRISING

Cananea, located close to Arizona, became a booming mining town in the early 1900s as an American entrepreneur organized the extraction of copper ore on a modern (and for the time) gargantuan scale, using both American and Mexican workers. The company paid and treated its American workforce markedly better than its Mexican counterpart, which provoked dissatisfaction among Mexican workers. The PLM, founded in 1905, attempted to foment the creation of small groups of adherents; two formed in Cananea by the spring of 1906. Both cells encouraged workers to protest the company's disparate treatment of them. Neither group espoused the cryptic anarchism of the PLM's leadership, although some of the Cananea leaders advocated overthrowing Díaz. At least one historian has argued that the two local cells differed in strategy, one favoring a legalistic approach for the labor struggle against the company; the other, a strategy of direct action.[9] In any event, the company spurned Mexican workers' demands, probably presented to it by Cananea's municipal president, for the eight-hour day and pay equity. On June 1, workers struck. The strike quickly turned violent, and the company requested Arizona rangers to cross the border to restore order and protect Americans in the mining town.[10] About 275 American rangers, technically as private U.S.

citizens under Mexican command, arrived to Cananea before Mexican troops could be deployed there. The PLM's efforts to lead a mine workers' movement in Cananea and elsewhere failed dismally, as the government quickly suppressed the strike with threats of drafting workers into the army, while arresting most PLM leaders in Cananea who did not escape to the United States.[11] At the same time, the border crossing of American rangers to repress a strike by Mexicans for equitable treatment tarnished the government and any labor policy it might have had. One month later, the PLM announced an extensive social and political program—but which in a detailed section on labor rights was limited to demanding better working conditions and higher wages—nothing that transcended the capitalist system or the 1857 constitution.[12] This was part of the PLM's strategy: it did not believe that an anarchist-communist ideology would prove popular among workers in Mexico.[13] Its revolutionary struggle aimed to overthrow Díaz. The PLM did not consider the immediate transformation of industrial relations.

THE TEXTILE INDUSTRY

Labor conflict in the textile industry had existed since before Díaz deposed Lerdo de Tejada in late 1876; and textile workers had been included in many of the earlier associations of laborers, through the efforts of the Gran Círculo de Obreros (Great Circle of Workers) in the 1870s–1880s. Yet by the 1880s the organization was moribund, and new groups after 1900 had few ties to earlier ones. Modern industrial conditions (large factories utilizing imported machinery) led to the emergence of movements that undertook a number of strikes, which the PLM tried to encourage and which culminated in the employer lockout, riot (or uprising), and massacre of Río Blanco, Veracruz, in January 1907.

By 1903, Díaz personally monitored labor relations in the textile industry. In a letter to Veracruz's governor, Teodoro Dehesa, Díaz expressed his dissatisfaction with the political prefect's handling of a strike at the nation's largest textile factory, in Río Blanco, near Orizaba. In the letter, Díaz flatly dismisses workers' complaints demanding the removal of a supervisor. For him, they were patently unreasonable because they disputed the managerial prerogative of directing industrial operations in the factory. Díaz sought Dehesa's assistance to ensure that the prefect would carry out evictions of strikers from company housing.[14] Dehesa countered Díaz's rigidness, reassuring the president that the jefe político had already informed him of the strike's peacefulness. The prefect had nearly reached an agreement with the company.[15] Significantly, none of the government officials contemplated direct repression of the strike. The issue of strikers' holding over in company housing and their eviction would recur.[16]

In April 1906, textile workers in Orizaba founded the Gran Círculo de Obreros Libres (Great Circle of Free Workers, GCOL).[17] By then, at least two social-political positions existed among workers in the Orizaba region, one of which was linked to the PLM and urged more direct confrontation with the regime.[18] When the newspaper *La Revolución Social,* authored and supported by PLM activists associated with the GCOL, appeared in early June in Orizaba, the government moved to repress the union (notwithstanding the constitutional right of a free press). The recent violent confrontation in Cananea, combined with the PLM's publication of its program in July, convinced the federal government of this party's revolutionary threat. The government thereafter perceived the emerging labor movement around Orizaba as potentially subversive, too, and tried to prevent the PLM from expanding there. In this, it largely succeeded.[19] Key PLM activists in the GCOL's leadership fled on rumors of their imminent arrest. The government detained others, deporting them to the Yucatán peninsula.[20] Meanwhile, local government officials, the political prefect Carlos Herrera and a minor judge in Orizaba, Licenciado Ramón Rocha, supported the GCOL's new, moderate leader, José Morales, believing that this would help ensure workers' moderation—and compliance with government officers' prescriptions—one definition of the law.[21] The pattern of persecuting independent labor leaders and promoting more conservative ones formulated earlier thus persisted.[22] The state—or, rather, multiple state actors at different levels of government, not acting altogether consistently—would tolerate the union, with the objective of avoiding a more militant labor movement. In this instance, as the local judge in Orizaba later explained, the federal district court of Veracruz investigated the union and its members, questioning many, including Morales, who, with his ties to Rocha and Herrera, appeared sufficiently trustworthy to lead the reformed union, pursuant to ideas of "order and morality."[23] (Evidently the federal court did not entertain any amparo petitions of workers asserting their constitutional rights to assemble or control their labor freely under Articles 9 or 5.)

As if to confirm the new relationship with the government and secure its tolerance for workers' associations, Morales sent Díaz on September 16, 1906, a patriotic manifesto affirming the union's loyalty and memorializing the foundation of the union. Morales emphasized the GCOL's adherence to law, order, and other principles necessary for the progress and security of the union, government, and Mexican nation.[24] Morales also lauded the justice of the political prefect Herrera and local judge Rocha and the advice they had furnished.[25] The recital of patriotic ideals along with reassurances of collaboration with local state officials can be construed merely as a supplicant's tactical prudence. Under the civil code and constitution, it should have sufficed to establish legally the organization. Perhaps Morales might have tried to register the GCOL, if the state of Veracruz required this, so that its legal existence could be recognized separately from that of its members; there is no indication that registration was attempted.[26] In any case, Morales had further requested the protection and other guarantees of the supreme government. Another word for "protection" was amparo; the word "guarantees," was associated with the notion of rights: constitutional articles guaranteed rights to citizens and workers.[27] If Morales and the GCOL were not appealing to the judiciary for constitutional protection, they were to the federal government and its chief executive, Díaz.

With at least governmental tolerance, the GCOL quickly set up branches elsewhere in Mexico. In October, the major independent Pueblan labor organization became affiliated with it; like its Orizaban counterpart, the GCOL in Puebla reassured the local prefect of the union's exclusively charitable purposes and desire to refrain from any subversive or political activity (as stipulated in its bylaws).[28] In Tlaxcala, organizing efforts encountered intimidation: the state governor threatened to draft into the army workers affiliating with the GCOL.[29] The GCOL appealed to Díaz, framing its petition with references to its establishment with the knowledge of authorities, including Díaz's, and to the legitimate purposes of the union or *sociedad*, similar to those of mutual aid associations.[30] The petition lastly underscored the GCOL's adherence to order and its respect for authorities and that it would continue to operate under the safeguards and guarantees of the laws and of Díaz.[31]

In the fall of 1906, workers walked out of mills repeatedly in Puebla and Veracruz. They protested their treatment by foreign supervisors and companies' wage deductions or fines for damaging articles and tools, among other issues. Fines and deductions frequently provoked grievances but arguably were lawful under the civil code.[32] In both Puebla and Orizaba, strikers prevailed initially; local officials mediated the disputes.[33] Near Orizaba, the largest strike began on October 26 in the modern Santa Rosa plant, where the GCOL's demands included abolition of fining practices and the reinstatement of workers associated with the union. The company eventually agreed to negotiations mediated by the prefect Herrera. According to one historian, the company finally stipulated to ending the practice of fining workers as well as to a pay increase. During the strike, workers' letters and manifestos appealed to the liberal principles of the constitution, denouncing foreign supervisors who mistreated Mexicans and violated their constitutional rights.[34] Later, in November, Santa Rosa workers backed a GCOL faction led by Samuel Ramírez that nearly toppled Morales from the union's presidency: workers during the strike had found Morales too conciliatory.[35] With the aid of Herrera and the GCOL leader in Puebla, Pascual Mendoza, Morales reasserted control over the union. The influential role of the prefect was manifest: he refused to recognize the new leadership of Ramírez, who was suspected of being tied to the PLM, and had only avoided detention previously with the assistance of legal counsel.[36]

Earlier in September, in Puebla, at one factory, workers wrote a petition stating that they would return to work the moment that the factory owner signed in the presence of the prefect a contract ending all abuses leading to their stoppage and allowed all workers to return without exception.[37] The prefect obtained a broad settlement with affected industrialists. Meanwhile, Díaz stopped Puebla's governor from drafting into the army the GCOL branch president, Mendoza, who was already collaborating with the government. The governor had sought Díaz's advice in regard to drafting him in case he applied for an amparo.[38] Díaz pointed out that among other things Mendoza had done nothing outside of the law until then.[39] By the end of October, the governor warned Díaz, following several minor strikes, of the GCOL's increasing assertiveness. He believed it should be punished as soon as it overstepped any legal limits. Díaz concurred that the governor should "proceed with the greatest severity that the law permits in the case that workers commit some outrageous act; and on that occasion Pascual Mendoza could be made responsible for the actions and punished energetically."[40]

Pueblan textile manufacturers, anxious about the growing strength of the labor movement and possibly also about the government's apparent reluctance to repress it, then organized the Mexican Industrial Center (CIM, or Centro Industrial Mexicano).[41] As the GCOL demanded better working conditions and pay, the CIM posted an industry-wide set of factory work rules, the *Reglamento Interior Único*, around December 3, 1906, at members' factories.[42] The brief set of rules asserted absolute managerial authority over all aspects of production, including the determination of deductions for damage to product or machinery. The rules partly aimed to rationalize production and reduce petty abuses that were prevalent in the factories: the reglamento prohibited kickbacks to supervisors and any kind of physical assault (whether by supervisor or worker). The rules also prohibited the introduction of any reading material, arms, or matches to the factory. Companies reserved the right, moreover, to discipline any action causing them prejudice or disorder and to monitor visitors to employer-provided worker housing. These were surely provisions aimed at barring union organizers from plants and housing. The work rules did not set wage rates but did prescribe hours (twelve per day with ninety minutes for meal breaks), workdays, and paydays.[43]

Workers began to walk out from factories, as of December 3, with the imposition of the *reglamento*. The GCOL prepared a counterproposal within a few days that was lengthier than management's.[44] Although the GCOL's reglamento's form followed the CIM's and was generally moderate, it actually anticipated a new mode of conceiving of industrial relations. It proposed that workers' representatives—the society (one may infer, the GCOL)—would be involved in the industrial relations of the factory. And its final article stated, "the rights of this society are retained, for all time, for any eventuality or impasse, basing itself in all on the laws of our Fundamental Charter." This was not the only reference to the constitution. Company stores that exercised a monopoly were prohibited, in part for their unconstitutionality (a reference to Article 28). Furthermore, "[i]n all the factories of the Republic, the owners, administrators, managers and supervisors should submit themselves to obey, without excuse or pretext, articles 5 and 13 of the Federal Constitution."[45] For the GCOL's leaders, the constitution clearly mattered: while Article 5 guaranteed freedom of labor, Article 13 guaranteed equality before the law; by 1906, workers envisioned that foreigners (and textile factory owners, managers, and supervisors were largely foreign) should also be subject to the laws and courts of the republic, as workers were.[46]

The CIM ignored the workers' counterproposal. Perhaps it had composed its set of work rules as an ultimatum to provoke a showdown with the GCOL. The CIM responded to the strikes that began throughout Puebla and Tlaxcala by locking out all workers employed in its member factories. [47] It is clear that the CIM intended to break the GCOL and the growing labor movement that challenged the managerial prerogatives of the industrialists.

The GCOL appealed to Díaz's mediation. The CIM refused to consider governmental arbitration. Apparently, the federal government initially divided over the labor dispute. In early December, *El Imparcial* reported the demands of the GCOL sympathetically.[48] As textile manufacturers, including, crucially, Orizaba's industrialists, joined the lockout across the country after December 22, the newspaper justified the lockout—by comparing it to the workers' right to strike: "An employer has the same right to close his factory as a worker has to abandon his work. . . . To the workers' strike, employers will respond with 'the lock-out,' their strike."[49] In the same issue, *El Imparcial* dismissed as spurious the GCOL's reglamento that would have set up workers' commissions. The article quoted an anonymous manufacturer who compared the employment contract to a lease in which the tenant accepts the conditions of the landlord and does not impose his terms on the property owner.[50] It appears that the CIM obtained the support of Limantour, who had ties to the Orizaban textile manufacturers as well as to Puebla's.[51] The shutting down of Orizba's factories was crucial to the outcome of the industrial conflict because the largest textile plants were located there, as was the center of the union movement; and GCOL members had been sending aid to their Pueblan associates, enabling them to survive the CIM's lockout. Limantour was especially hostile to the aspirations of organized labor and any alliances it might make with his political rivals, like Dehesa or Nuevo León's governor, Bernardo Reyes.[52]

Not until December 31 did the CIM finally agree to presidential arbitration. Workers had begun to cause disturbances.[53] Or perhaps the GCOL had withstood the lockout longer than employers had anticipated workers could remain unemployed.[54] In any event, by January 3, employers had reached the consensus to accept the president's judgment, after manifesting a threat to disinvest from Mexico if the workers' movement continued to grow and lobbying Díaz to draft an award fully acceptable to them.[55]

Díaz announced his *laudo*, or arbitral decision, on January 4, 1907.[56] The decision clearly had the purpose of precluding the development of the independent labor organization, which might align itself with radical movements, but Díaz did not deny altogether fundamental workers' rights as then recognized in the constitution and civil code. The award largely accommodated industrialists' interests; it did compromise them slightly to concede reasonable points to workers. Thus, the first article stated that work rules in effect at the time of factory closures, or dictated subsequently by owners, would prevail. This meant that the CIM's reglamento was the starting point for Díaz's award, qualified slightly by an allusion to customary factory practices. The third article prescribed a passbook system in which employers would record workers' conduct and industriousness in a notebook, and workers would have to show new employers the book upon being hired. The fifth article stipulated the procedure workers had to follow to make complaints: they had to sign personally any complaint and continue working for fifteen days thereafter while management evaluated it. If workers were dissatisfied with the resolution, they could then separate themselves from the employment. This provision did not ban the strike categorically. The withdrawal from employment could be asserted as a concerted action—a strike. The last article of the award did prohibit strikes but framed the prohibition as an implicit contractual commitment made by the worker not to strike, especially rashly, and referenced the fifth article in connection with the appropriate procedure to follow in a dispute. In addition, the eighth article directed workers to accept prefects' supervision of the censorship of their publications to avoid the dissemination of subversive doctrines or defamation. Díaz did relent regarding the extent to which workers would be monitored in their company housing. And the award balanced the interests of employers and workers in connection with deductions and fines. Child labor was limited, and employers and public authorities were encouraged to promote factory schools. Significantly, the award contemplated an extensive wage system for the benefit of lower-paid workers. With these terms, Díaz's award constituted the first industry-wide collective contract, in effect not just the result of bitter employer and union proposals for an agreement but also the product of the national government's direct participation in industrial relations.

The award should have represented a triumph for the Porfirian regime. As Rodney Anderson noted, it seemingly conciliated employers, reluctant to agree to such arbitration, with a labor movement that had accepted state tutelage, after having been briefly led by more radical leaders, whom the government had successfully marginalized.[57] Order had been maintained without the withdrawal of capital. Or, as one of the leading textile industrialists said in a letter dated January 6, the CIM had approved unanimously "the proposals to which we agreed in the capital with the president of the republic . . . to end the strike . . . [and] thanks to the clauses approved, the authority of owners remains intact, important concessions are made to workers, and the social alarm that the suspension of work had produced is ended, and measures are dictated that tend to suppress the repetition of strikes."[58]

The award actually proved a failure that revealed the regime's incapacity to resolve comprehensively the social question—the incipient challenge to the social order of an emerging working class. If the decision had accommodated the interests of manufacturers and maintained their authority, it left workers dissatisfied. In Puebla and Tlaxcala some workers renewed strikes and Mendoza had to dissuade further opposition to its acceptance.[59] While peace between capital and labor was maintained, it was due partly to Mendoza's temporizing. No such conciliation occurred in Orizaba, where, on January 7, workers repudiated the award violently, rioting until armed forces repressed them in what became a notorious massacre. *El Imparcial* expressed bewilderment about the rioting, concluding that it represented Mexico's confrontation with the consequences of the *cuestión obrera*.[60]

More calculated state persecution followed the violence of January 7. Armed forces sent to Veracruz applied the *ley fuga*—shooting prisoners while they were allegedly trying to escape—along with exemplary executions against the more militant leaders fingered by factory supervisors.[61] Authorities charged 255 people for looting and other violence. The regime probably deported many of the prisoners to labor camps in Quintana Roo; and it suppressed the GCOL.[62]

A few months later, *El Imparcial*'s account of Díaz's congressional message argued that the government was completely impartial, equally attendant to the interests of the employer and worker.[63] The newspaper applauded governmental policy for encouraging and guaranteeing foreign investment, which it insisted benefited the working classes by creating employment.[64] *El Imparcial* said that class struggle existed in other parts of the world due to conditions absent in Mexico, where there were neither socialist nor plutocratic parties. Yet the reality was that the government's ability to reconcile labor and business with more than words diminished as the country's economic situation deteriorated.[65] *El Imparcial* even denied that the conflict in Orizaba had an economic origin: instead, the newspaper reported, it had emanated from disagreements over the internal administration of the factories and had been resolved until the rioting instigated by agitators.[66]

Regardless of how the Porfirian press depicted industrial relations in Veracruz, Díaz's award had become largely inoperative in Orizaba by May 1907. Río Blanco's large factory attempted to implement a new set of rules, which prompted new stoppages. *El Imparcial* ascribed to the dispute a legalistic cause: workers read a provision in the revised company rules to mean that remaining on the job would be construed as ratification of the changes in the contract.[67] The army general assigned to the region provided Díaz supplementary reports. On May 29 he informed the president that the situation appeared peaceful and that seventeen workers had been arrested following some turbulence. The general did not specify the charges against them, writing only that they were among those who were threatening other workers or presiding over the recent disturbance.[68] He confided to Díaz that only this kind of repression would intimidate workers.[69] Indeed, his correspondence with Díaz reflected frustration with workers who, he said, lacked any organization and simply manifested an animus against their jobs. The general dismissed the possibility that they were reacting to the modified rules. Meanwhile, the company had posted notices warning that in accord with its reglamento, it would evict workers from company housing if they did not return to work. The general realized this would exacerbate the conflict but assured Díaz that workers' awareness of certain repression would preclude any formal protest. *El Imparcial*'s correspondent acknowledged, too, the desperate situation, in which if the management withdrew its proposed changes, its authority would be diminished. If it confronted its employees, relations would continue to deteriorate to the company's economic loss.[70] Government authorities did not evict strikers.[71]

The prefect and Veracruz's governor, with the president's advice, instead fashioned a set of rules for the Río Blanco factory that were more amenable to labor.[72] Dehesa assured Díaz that to the extent possible he had drafted the provisions of the proposed reglamento to be consistent with existing state law without prejudicing any interest.[73] Díaz approved these efforts, in a detailed letter suggesting changes to articles covering penalties for defective product and the conditions for the provision of housing.[74] The nation's president pointedly recommended having a third party other than a supervisor or factory director evaluate the appeals from fines for defects, similar to the role played by the jefe político. Díaz believed that having a factory supervisor function as a judge of workers' complaints regarding fines exacerbated tension within the factory. This is significant: it was an acknowledgment on the part of the government of the need for third-party arbitration, in the context of the government actually fashioning the content of the employment contract, subject to industrialists' approval.[75]

Dehesa sent Díaz a revised provision mostly incorporating the latter's recommendations, although he proposed that the third party to determine fines not be the prefect for three reasons: the prefect lacked the expertise to resolve disputes, it was a role inappropriate for his administrative authority, and labor disputes needed prompt resolution.[76] The governor's revision directed that the departmental director and a worker designated by the interested party (the worker being fined) estimate any indemnity for defective work. If the two could not agree, they would nominate a third person; if they could not agree on the third person, a person would be drawn randomly from recommendations made by the director and the worker named by the interested party. In his decision, the person so selected would adhere to the terms and limits previously set.[77] Clearly, state agents were not merely to arbitrate disputes as a neutral third party but contribute to the establishment of an industrial relations system, without, however, elaborating a legal framework or securing a sustainable, peaceful order.

In the end, *El Imparcial* credited the resolution of the strike at the beginning of June to the efforts of the prefect, after having previously referred to the military and governor's involvement.[78] While the governor and prefect's involvement in the revision of the employment contract indicated an expansion of the state's role in labor relations, the prefect retained his police function, manifest in other instances, such as in his report to Díaz about rumors of an imminent strike at another textile factory in Veracruz, the plant in Santa Rosa, toward the end of July. When the management of the Compañía Industrial Veracruzana had approached him with a flyer announcing a strike, the prefect had immediately begun an investigation of the factory, obtaining the names of workers who had distributed it. He ordered their arrest and the posting of *rurales* (rural patrols) in the factory, to avoid any disorder and visibly to communicate to workers his vigilance. The strike did not happen.[79]

INDUSTRIAL RELATIONS AND TRANSPORT

Between 1906 and 1908, major strikes affecting railroads elicited Díaz's direct intervention, selective repression with the threat of further governmental suppression of the right to strike, and the exploration of legislative solutions. Díaz's ad hoc approach to labor relations in the rail sector resembled to a degree his actions toward textile workers; still, the two economic sectors differed in three notable ways. First, railways were especially strategically important to the national economy. If trains stopped running, few goods could be transported efficiently across the country or to the United States. Second, the rail sector and workers' actions were far-reaching geographically as well as economically; local political authorities were thereby generally unsuited to deal with rail conflicts: governors and then the federal government had to resolve them. Third, if many of the supervisors and technicians in the textile industry were foreigners, a larger fraction of workers on the rails were not Mexican. As the railway companies hired Mexicans at comparatively lower wages and refused to employ them in the better positions reserved for foreign employees, nationalist sentiments and resentment over the disparate treatment grew.

The relationships among foreign managers and foreign and domestic workers, during the first years of the twentieth century when the federal government purchased a majority shareholder interest in the main railway lines, further complicated industrial relations in this sector.[80] As one scholar, Lorena Parlee, has observed, the federal government in general tolerated foreign workers' organizations and their strikes if they were peaceful. In contrast, when Mexican rail workers began to organize their separate associations at the turn of the century, the regime watched them closely. During their first work stoppages in 1902, 1903, and 1905, the government followed a pattern of selective repression, sometimes arresting union leaders as well as deploying troops to protect company property.[81]

In July 1906, the Union of Mexican Machinists (Unión de Mecánicos Mexicanos, or UMM) struck the Mexican Central Railroad (Ferrocarril Central Mexicano) as the federal government finalized the purchase of a majority interest in the firm. The strike immediately posed a national crisis, until then the most severe labor challenge to the economy's operation.[82] The UMM composed its strike demands in seventeen paragraphs, to which the company strenuously objected.[83] Most of them concerned employment conditions (e.g., seniority, training, hours) and pay in addition to company recognition of the union. Management concluded that the UMM was calling for a closed shop. The union insisted on equal treatment.[84]

When management refused to compromise with the union, the latter requested Díaz's mediation.[85] The governor of Chihuahua, Enrique Creel, advised Díaz to mediate. Creel commented that the U.S. president had intervened in railway strikes: such action would not appear strange and could have a beneficial effect. The governor's precise argument for Díaz meeting with the workers was subtler. A commission of strikers traveling to Mexico City to solicit Díaz's support would afford everybody a few additional days; and it was possible that Díaz might find a conciliatory solution, providing a service to the company as well as to the workers.[86] Díaz replied ambivalently to Creel, stressing the need for vigilance and severe punishment if necessary, qualifying this by stating, "we could not avoid their action while it was exercised within the laws and peacefully."[87] The president saw UMM representatives privately on August 8 and appeared sympathetic to their claims for pay equity but found their demands for union recognition and changes in employment conditions unjust and impermissible. He further warned the union representatives against continuing the strike. The union ended it.[88]

Parlee argues that Díaz's "unprecedented" meeting with UMM representatives and his support for their claims against discrimination at least partly resulted from a coincidence of interests between the government's objectives of assuming ownership of the railway company and the UMM's nationalist demands.[89] Díaz's mediation and apparent tolerance for the UMM's advocacy of pay equity does contrast with governmental repression of labor movements in mining and textiles about the same time.[90] The regime in the second half of 1906 persecuted liberal political clubs, imprisoned the organizers of the Cananea mine workers' protests and leaders of the GCOL—but also Felix C. Vera, leader of a large railway workers' federation. According to one scholar, the Díaz regime linked Vera to the PLM.[91]

Then, too, the situation on the railways was especially grave: the strike had proven unexpectedly disruptive economically, and the regime could hardly afford to exacerbate the situation. In the aftermath of Cananea and public criticism of the government's repression of the miners' movement at the apparent behest of American interests, Díaz probably wished not to appear excessively harsh. In August 1906, the government was still reaffirming its recognition of the right to strike. Justo Sierra, minister of public instruction, speaking to the closing session of a labor convention, the Congreso Obrero, convened by the tabacco workers' league declared: "the strike is a right, and as such, the government will respect it, but it will not tolerate sedition."[92]

Throughout the strike, the UMM stressed adherence to the law. Initially soliciting the mediation of Nuevo León's governor, Reyes, the union had assured him it would not retaliate against employees who replaced strikers but would try only to persuade replacements to desist from work. The UMM's order of July 25 instructed workers to withdraw to their homes in complete order.[93] Another command issued early in the strike advised that three-person committees should be set up to conserve lawful order and prevent workers from amassing at the work site.[94] The semiofficial press commented about the peacefulness of the strike. The government nonetheless had prepared to contain the stoppage, reassigning troops to Chihuahua, one of the strike centers. Díaz, after his veiled threat to the UMM delegates during their meeting with him, moved to have the UMM leader Silvino Rodríguez arrested. Rodríguez chose to confront the threats and met with company officials, then Díaz, as workers returned to their jobs.[95]

Thereafter, the government continued to arbitrate strikes on the railways, without relinquishing the option of using force. In June 1907, boiler workers (*caldereros*) struck the Mexican Central Railroad. Governor Reyes tried to negotiate with management and striking workers but found them both intransigent.[96] The company requested that Díaz arbitrate the dispute, to which he agreed, with workers' consent.[97] In a telegram to Reyes, Díaz stated that it was urgent to end the strike because industry was at the point of having to suspend production for lack of fuel.[98] In this case Díaz arbitrated.[99]

In contrast, in April 1908, when Mexican rail workers again engaged in a widespread strike led by the Great Mexican League of Rail Employees (Gran Liga Mexicana de Empleados de Ferrocarril), the federal government moved to end the stoppage decisively without offering to conciliate as it had in 1906 or June 1907.[100] The regime had viewed the Gran Liga and its newspaper, *El Ferrocarrilero*, warily since their establishment.[101] Government officials had endeavored to manipulate the league. When rail workers began to organize a chapter of the Gran Liga in Monterrey, Reyes, with his ties to labor, attempted to control the rail workers there and, ultimately, the national organization. The governor wrote to Ramón Corral (then interior minister, vice president, and a major científico) and Díaz to inform them that he had agreed to counsel workers when they indirectly asked him in March 1906 for his advice—provided they amended the bylaws of the league. Reyes contended that this was preferable to letting them proceed independently.[102] Díaz replied that he and Corral concurred that Reyes, like they, should obstruct the Liga as much as possible.[103] Reyes clarified that he aimed to channel the organization so that the law would limit its actions.[104]

In realization of this objective, Reyes had his agent, José María Cantú, a lawyer, named to draft a report and opinion regarding the bylaws of the Liga, which the chapter accepted. The chapter thereupon indicated to the central office that if the latter did not amend its program to remove all language that could justify violence or seemed inspired by anarchism, the chapter would set up an independent association, which would adhere exclusively to the law and exercise its rights duly. For Reyes, the best way to direct this labor group was to interpose trusted agents; and he underscored his belief to Díaz that the union required careful scrutiny.[105] Díaz warmly concurred.[106]

The Gran Liga's bylaws proclaimed as a first principle its obedience to the law and its reliance on it. One provision outlined resort to the strike only in an orderly manner and distinguished such a stoppage from the tumultuous strike, which was unlawful.[107] In April 1906, with Felix

Vera and eighty other members of the union present, one branch of the Gran Liga voted to distance itself from *El Ferrocarrilero*, disavowing that the newspaper represented the organization. The justification articulated was that the branch wished to develop peacefully, independently, and by legal means.[108] Clearly, the Gran Liga had endeavored to maintain a lawful posture and avoid governmental repression. Vera had spent seventeen months in jail between 1906 and 1907 for his editorial stances in *El Ferrocarrilero* (if not for being associated with the PLM), and after his release he wrote Díaz to assure him that the Liga "was mutualist only and concerned primarily with the moral and intellectual advancement of its members."[109] When Gran Liga workers struck in April 1908, Vera, as the league's president, announced that the concerted action would be peaceful and orderly. Indeed, he avoided using the word "strike" (*huelga*) and described the action as a mass resignation, which was intended not to disrupt traffic but rather to protest an injustice.[110] Framing the labor dispute in such terms was in accord with liberal notions of the legality of the strike as the worker's exercise of the freedom to work. Articulated in such terms, it is doubtful that Article 925 applied.[111]

Vera's cautious and legal strategy did not prevent the federal government's manifestation of hostility toward the concerted action. In a meeting with Vera, Díaz had threatened the passage of a constitutional amendment to restrict the right to associate.[112] Díaz may also have insinuated to Vera indirectly the threat of another Río Blanco outcome.[113] Vera took Díaz's threats seriously and desisted from leading the strike. It lasted a while longer, now disorganized. The Gran Liga dissolved. *El Imparcial* opined that a strike was especially pernicious where it involved a public service implicating national interests such as the railways.[114] The federal executive did not introduce any legislation to Congress to curb the right to strike or organize.

In September 1908, Reyes wrote Corral to ask for direction regarding whether to involve himself again with railway workers and the Gran Liga; a group of the more influential machinists in Monterrey had approached him to reestablish the union there and reconnect with other branches. Because it was the largest branch of the Liga, Reyes reasoned that indirectly guiding it could moderate the entire league. He continued to believe it was preferable to engage with the organization to affect it than refuse any cooperation, since then it would proceed altogether independent of his influence.[115] Corral promptly responded after consulting with Díaz that Reyes should indeed exert his influence in the Monterrey branch—to maintain the union's present quietude and prevent it from coalescing into an active force again.[116]

Although the Gran Liga lost the 1908 strike, Mexican rail workers and their organizations persisted in their claims for equal treatment on the country's railways during the remaining three years of the Porfirian administration. As the federal government consolidated its ownership of the country's major rail lines as of 1909, the interests of Mexican rail workers seemingly coincided further with those of the government for the Mexicanization of the rails. Or, at least, it became awkward for the government not to be in favor of a fair policy for Mexican employees on the rail lines that it ultimately owned, even if the management remained under foreign direction. Mexican labor leaders met with Limantour, who as finance minister oversaw the nationalization of the railways, to discuss equitable treatment for Mexican employees. On July 1, 1909, Limantour announced that the nationalized company, Ferrocarriles Nacionales de México (National Railways of Mexico), would pursue, as official policy, the Mexicanization of the labor force, without discharging unfairly foreign workers. A succession of strikes and other forms of pressure by the American-dominated trade unions ensued, as they attempted to defend their privileges. The consequence was that Mexican workers replaced foreign strikers, improving their positions.[117] At the end of the Porfirian government in 1911, Mexican rail workers' associations were growing in size and influence.

CONCLUSION

A couple of months before the April 1908 railway strike, Díaz had told the American journalist James Creelman in a widely publicized interview that his administration was not "an enemy of the working class." He added, "we encourage Mexican workers to form associations to improve their conditions, but we have stipulated the terms under which these unions should act."[118] This was not a completely inaccurate statement of

Porfirian labor policy. The government had encouraged mutual aid associations, and it did attempt to channel union activity, as evidenced by its relations with the GCOL and Liga. During elections it also appealed to workers posturing as their friend. Díaz, however, had failed to resolve the social question, to integrate the working class better into society and the economy. The government refused to acknowledge the social question as an economic and social one requiring more equitable industrial relations.

The científico ruling faction was worried that their political opposition, and not just the PLM, might exacerbate labor unrest and, conversely, that dissatisfied labor would back its opponents, who included governors like Reyes and Dehesa and, later, Francisco Madero.[119] Their concern was reasonable. After the 1908 rail strike, Felix Vera had concluded, "'there is no chance for bettering the condition of labor in Mexico until there is a change in the administration.'"[120] The científicos' rivals began to attract more working-class interest as the presidential campaign accelerated in 1909–10. Reyes posed the most popular and credible challenge to Corral, the científico candidate for the vice presidency, who was linked to the repression of organized labor. *Reyistas* successfully recruited labor support.[121] When Reyes ultimately refused to defy Díaz and the científicos, resigning from the governorship of Nuevo León, working-class allegiance shifted to Madero's campaign, as workers joined anti-reelection clubs.[122]

The clubs invoked political and civil rights in their leaflets to workers.[123] Anderson cites the example of one flier proclaiming that the objectives of the Club Anti-Reeleccionista de Obreros were to overthrow the "tutelage" weighing down the nation and "to secure our constitutional rights, regaining the inherent freedom due every citizen."[124] On May 22, 1910, in a campaign speech to a mostly working-class crowd in Orizaba, Madero promised workers the freedom to organize and press their demands against employers without the state constraining them, as it had on behalf of management in the last decade.[125] This was a more expansive and liberal interpretation of workers' rights under constitutional Articles 5 and 9 than Porfiristas conceded. But it remained within the framework of the constitution, as did Madero's labor platform, revealed at the Anti-Reelection Party's convention in April 1910, which alluded to mutual aid groups and workers' accident insurance.[126] This appeared sufficient to muster labor support; workers, including artisans, became a substantial popular base of opposition to Díaz's regime.[127] Porfirian labor policy had failed to deter workers' turn to the ruling elite's political enemies.

Díaz had managed only to establish a truce with labor. Significantly, the regime had not catapulted altogether the rights to organize or strike that most interested people believed the constitution guaranteed. It had accomplished this by operating extralegally or informally to deter organized labor. Díaz himself had personally warned Vera against persisting in the Gran Liga's 1908 strike. Díaz defeated the strike without exercising tyrannical force but surely with the diminution of his legitimacy: from their perspective, under the constitution, rail workers had been in the right.

Worse (for Díaz as well as for many workers) was the January 1907 debacle. From a legal perspective, it is significant that the regime evidently did not justify its repression of the workers' movement and riot by applying, for example, the penal code's Article 925.[128] The state applied the *ley fuga*, and this was not a formal law. Certainly the military quelled the turmoil effectively and quickly, but again at the cost of the government's legitimacy. The repression was not extraordinary for the regime: indeed it was largely consistent with its labor policies that bordered on extralegality. Thus, rather than regularly threatening application of Article 925 against labor organizers, whether on the rails or in the textile factories, the regime more typically threatened to draft workers into the army or deport them to Yucatán or Quintana Roo. It is possible that in connection with such threats and actions, the federal judiciary did grant amparos—Puebla's governor believed that this was at least a possibility in his correspondence with Díaz—but if this occurred, it does not seem to have been a sufficient deterrent. In the case of Mendoza, Díaz more prudently than the governor believed that the labor leader could be co-opted.

Law did operate minimally as a point of reference under the Porfirian regime for political and social actors—Díaz (and the governors discussed in this chapter) acknowledged it, as did labor organizations such as the

Gran Liga and the GCOL. For the government, the law should have constrained workers' activity: Reyes, for example, imagined that the law could maintain the rail workers' organization within narrow channels under his direction. Díaz threatened to amend the constitutional right to organize if the rail union defiantly exercised that right and tolerated recognition of the GCOL on the condition that it collaborated with political authorities, that is, acted lawfully. But state authorities could not deny altogether the existence of the liberal constitution. This is one reason the regime fell back on the *ley fuga* or the draft to intimidate workers. Meanwhile, the minister Sierra acknowledged the right to strike, and so did obliquely Díaz's laudo. Labor organizations, invoking their members' constitutional rights as Mexican citizens, as the GCOL did in their proposed reglamento, thereby justified their positions, which otherwise were subject to criticisms based on political economic principles and police considerations. The problem with the law was that neither the constitution nor the civil code actually provided the means to structure industrial relations.

The regime had found it necessary to negotiate continually with labor interests, as the country industrialized, although there was hardly a legal or institutional framework apart from the exercise of the police power by the prefects and military for doing so; in transport, the situation was even less amenable to local authorities' routine regulation. The government's mediating role was hardly consistent with the dominant ideological vision of the liberal state voiced by Matías Romero in 1892. It is interesting to reconsider Dehesa and Díaz's correspondence about a reglamento that would have addressed the resolution of fines and deductions satisfactorily for workers in Río Blanco in June, six months after the riot and massacre. The civil code allowed such deductions, but, as noted, they were a constant source of vexation in industrial relations. The president and governor both realized that some kind of third party should arbitrate the disputes that arose around them. Dehesa wrote that the jefe político was an inappropriate official to be so involved. He was correct: as the Supreme Court had ruled in several non-industrial labor cases, prefects who had been closely involved in labor relations for the last decades lacked the necessary legal authority. Nor were they specialists in industrial relations. But there was no obvious state officer who could perform such routine tasks. A legal and institutional underpinning was still lacking, although the practical exigencies necessitated governmental regulation of labor-management relations.

In sum, around Orizaba, for example, during the last decade of the Porfirian regime, numerous government officers had constantly intervened in the industrial relations of the modern textile factory: one local judge, federal district court personnel, prefects, rural patrols, the federal army commanders, the state's governor, the minister of the interior, and ultimately the president. Not only had they been unable to bring more than a smoldering truce to the labor conflict of the region; much of the official participation in the attempted structuring of industrial relations there was suspect. Ideologically, it must have been difficult to justify in liberal terms the drafting of a factory reglamento by the governor and president. Effective specialized institutions for resolution of labor disputes did not exist. Ad hoc arrangements made by government officials ranging from the local prefect to the national president had dealt with labor problems as they arose during the country's initial steps toward industrializing. If this was an industrial relations system, it was not one with much stability or legitimacy. The social question demanded a better answer.

CHAPTER 4

Toward Social Legislation

INTRODUCTION

By the end of the nineteenth century, legal discourse about labor was becoming critical of the doctrinaire liberalism embodied in the civil and penal codes. Law journals published articles discussing the social question and calling for reform, but the discourse extended beyond lawyers. *El Imparcial* presented editorials pointing out the need to resolve social problems ensuing from industrialization and urbanization not only in Mexico but also in Europe. Labor turmoil, the poverty of workers and its consequences—and the challenges posed by more radical or socialist ideologies—led legal elites, mostly in Western Europe, to reconsider some of the premises of liberal legal thought and to propose social legislation. French legal intellectuals pioneered the articulation of this socially oriented law, although the German jurist Rudolph von Jhering's influence was significant; and there were contributors to the new social law in other countries, too. Catholic social doctrine, critical of liberalism, also evolved in response to the social question and the perceived threat of socialism in Europe. Influenced by these new, not altogether unrelated currents in legal thought, and attempting to address multiple social problems, state policymakers in the first decades of the twentieth century began to consider socially oriented solutions throughout the Atlantic world, including in Latin America, although passage and implementation of legislation varied in each country, depending on particular political conditions.[1]

In Mexico, while still under the Porfirian regime, a few state governments haltingly took steps to enact legislation requiring employers to indemnify workers suffering employment-related accidents. The legislation was grounded on a different theory of fault than that found in the civil and penal codes, which were premised on a theory of freely contracting individuals and limited liability to conditions explicitly stipulated. There is a progression in the states' legislative projects, moving from an attempt to construe employer liability more expansively in existing statutory or code duties to holding the employer responsible for employees' injuries regardless of fault. Such legal reform did not proceed very far, but it was reflective of the new paradigm that reformulated liberal presumptions about the free will of contracting parties and the formal equality of employers and employees. Mexican lawyers were receptive to the new discourses partly because dominant liberal legal thought already acknowledged the importance for policymaking of political economy, while Comtean positivism enjoyed widespread influence among the científico elite. In the late nineteenth century, leading jurists believed that sociological knowledge and deference to economic principles were important for law making and that laws should facilitate individuals entering freely into contracts between themselves.

This chapter considers early manifestations of a new social orientation in legal discourse during the last decades of the Porfirian era. It reviews the more significant reformist legislation, coupling it with changes then occurring in legal doctrine largely in Europe and reported in Mexican law journals. The strike movements of the first decade of the twentieth century prompted in part this discourse on the social question in Mexico, but events in Europe and the United States and the reaction to them were also influential. Indeed the transformation of legal doctrine and theory that occurred toward the end of the nineteenth century and during the first years of the twentieth, and which was reflected piecemeal in early legislation (in particular, two workers' compensation statutes), laid the intellectual foundation for the development of labor law in Mexico after 1910. European legal currents influenced the new social orientation of law, but Mexican proponents of labor reform also contributed to the reorientation; and these included PLM, social Catholic, and railway union leaders, whose political ideologies certainly differed.[2] And whether proposals for social and legal innovations—what ultimately led to the making of labor law—were authored by liberal workers' associations, the PLM, social Catholic groups, or members of the Porfirian state's elite, the proposals tended to remain reformist and even comprehensible within an ideology of social liberalism.[3]

EARLY LABOR LEGISLATION

In March 1899, the supreme court of San Luis Potosí, a state with extensive mining operations, deliberated over a workers' accident compensation draft law.[4] Consisting of three articles, it obligated the employer to pay medical treatment and burial costs when at fault for an employee's work-related accident. But only a minimal level of fault was required to impute responsibility to the employer. The enterprise would be liable for an injury resulting from the failure to provide all necessary safety measures or because it had permitted work under dangerous conditions, without taking due precautions.[5] And the proposed law prohibited the enterprise from contracting away its liability.[6] In his accompanying study of the draft law, its author, the lawyer Francisco Pascual García, nearly argued that the employer assumed the risk of injury in the act of hiring the employee, although he still insisted that the employer's responsibility followed from his culpability.[7] The state government did not enact the measure.

On April 30, 1904, the legislature of the state of Mexico passed the first workers' compensation law in the country.[8] The innovation of the new law, authored by the lawyer Francisco Gaxiola, lay in its making the employer explicitly liable for work-related accidents, regardless of fault. Yet it was predicated on Article 1787 of the state's civil code and Belgium's statute of December 24, 1903.[9] The state's Tribunal Superior de Justicia initially objected to its definition of an enterprise, its avoidance of agreements that renounced the right to compensation, and its coverage of agricultural workers when the underlying predicate (Article 1787) did not encompass them. Gaxiola agreed to modify the draft law, still asserting that it dealt with the era's most profound and transcendental social problems.[10] Its mandated benefits were modest: medical costs for three months for injuries or illnesses resulting from work, to be paid by the employer, and indemnification of fifteen days' pay and burial costs in the case of death.[11]

Nuevo León's workers' compensation law, enacted in November 1906, was a separate statute that broke radically from the civil code and previous legal norms limiting employer liability for accidents to explicit contractual provisions. The eminent jurist Jacinto Pallares drafted the statute with the collaboration of Rodolfo Reyes, son of the state's governor.[12] Pallares, in the first paragraph of the statute's statement of purpose, announced the pioneering step that the proposed law represented:

> The attribution of civil responsibility to employers or owners of industrial companies for work accidents is a new juridical creation. It is based on a concept entirely distinct from that which grounds the established one as a consequence of an act or omission contrary to a penal law, since the latter is not applied, as is natural, to the act of the person who suffers the accident. The cases of responsibility prefigured by the penal code . . . have exclusive origin in an infraction of the law, while, for equitable and social-economic reasons, of various nature, the modern industrial movement requires the existence of special dispositions to provide for the indemnification of the worker prejudiced by an unforeseen event, equalizing thus, as far as is suitable, the cooperation of the two elements of wealth: capital and labor.[13]

The statement further explained that modern, mechanized industry increased the risk of injury for which neither the worker nor employer was responsible; hence, for equitable reasons, the enterprise should be charged with compensation. It referred to European workers' accident legislation, centering on the concept of occupational risk (*riesgo profesional*) as well as alternate theories of liability. Significantly, Nuevo León's legislation omitted the main railway companies.[14]

Specific federal laws and contracts covered the railways, without contemplating their industrial relations. Nor did federal courts, despite much litigation that arose from incidents occurring on the railroads that implicated workers. An engineer abandoning a train in transit provoked one exceptional legal discussion in the 1890s regarding the need for federal legislation to regulate the employment of railroad workers. The railway company's legal counsel sought the advice of the Ministry of Communications, which in turn asked the Ministry of Justice and Emilio Velasco if existing legislation provided a sufficient sanction for the engineer's conduct.[15] The Justice Ministry opined that the executive could promulgate a regulation to punish such a worker under the constitution's Article 21. The lawyer Velasco, who twenty years earlier had attracted Guillermo

Prieto's attention with a defense of the right to strike, proposed promulgating a law analogous to the penal code's Article 925. Another lawyer, Rafael Rebollar, did not believe that the abandonment of the train by one worker resembled the situations covered by Article 925 and found that Article 486 of the same code was applicable.[16] No legislation ensued.

More than a decade later, rail workers' organizing successes and strikes led the Díaz administration to begin drafting labor legislation. On April 9, 1907, Limantour wrote Corral about the Gran Liga Mexicana de Empleados de Ferrocarril, which he was closely monitoring (one year before it initiated a major strike).[17] Limantour stressed the Liga's objective of requiring all workers entering into the service of any railway company to join its organization. Anxious about "such exorbitant pretensions that could be so prejudicial to the public service," Limantour had advised the president to charge one or two persons with the preparation of a bill to prohibit this type of organization in the area of public services. He alluded to legislation in other countries that prevented the formation of any association of public employees not related to mutual aid, charity, or recreation. Now Limantour requested that Corral discuss the situation with Díaz and designate the people who could undertake the pertinent studies.[18] Corral replied at the end of the month, mentioning newspaper clippings reflecting questions about socialism and unions of public service employees.[19] He had passed the material to Rosendo Pineda, a key científico adviser of Porfirio Díaz, recommending that he occupy himself with this matter.[20] The federal executive proceeded to draft labor legislation that reportedly would have introduced mandatory arbitration and harshly sanctioned strikes. But it never publicly circulated any labor legislation or submitted it to Congress.[21]

In 1908, the draft revision of the mining law prepared under the auspices of Olegario Molina, secretary of the federal Ministry of Development (*Fomento*), initially subjected employers to limited responsibility for occupational accidents.[22] Foreign interests became alarmed with this proposed reform and the provision restricting ownership of properties in border states. Daniel Guggenheim, a principal in major American mining interests in Mexico, in a letter to Díaz, lambasted the proposed accident compensation provision, threatening that it was "bound to introduce an amount of risk as well as of actual expense far beyond the amount that can be warranted by the profitableness of the business."[23] Molina, in a memorandum, responded to Guggenheim's accusation by pointing out that the draft mining code provision limited liability to where the employer had failed to comply with existing safety regulations and was consistent with Mexican law, European and American workers' compensation statutes, and humane practices.[24] The mining law passed in January 1910 omitted the employer liability provision.[25]

Molina similarly dealt with labor matters in the textile industry that resulted in another indecisive outcome but nonetheless would be a precursor of future developments. The Pueblan labor leader Pascual Mendoza lobbied Limantour in early 1907 for an industry-wide raise in the wage rate to be effectuated through the government's reduction of a textile tax.[26] Then Mendoza met Molina to discuss a new wage rate for workers in Puebla and Tlaxcala, without reaching an agreement.[27]

By 1907, after the strike and lockouts in Puebla and Veracruz, the official Mexican press took note of the growing sentiment for labor legislation to address the social question in foreign countries. Approximating in time Dehesa and Díaz's venture with Orizaba's prefect to fashion a new reglamento in Río Blanco, *El Imparcial,* in an editorial in July 1907, related ongoing discussions in Europe and Argentina to regulate industrial relations, including experiments in legislation, in the face of strikes.[28] The editorial saw Díaz's January 1907 arbitration award, and specifically its regulation of child labor, as the keystone of the new edifice of labor legislation in Mexico. It found promising the *Monterrey News* account of Albert de Mun's proposal for labor councils (*Consejos de Trabajo*), published in *Le Figaro. El Imparcial* explained: "These organizations would be the mechanism by which the labor contract would be transformed from an individual one as it currently is, into a collective one. The council would be in effect the organization that would sanction the contract celebrated today between the employer and employee."[29] It would operate as an institution more sensitive to the needs of both capital and labor in the resolutions of their disputes arising from the employment contract. Lastly, the councils would be capable of determining work rates and the supply of labor in a region.

In the period 1906–8, while *El Imparcial* pondered foreign examples of social reform, various Mexican initiatives for labor legislation were considered, although none was enacted into law. At its convention in July 1907, the Unión de Mecánicos Mexicanos formulated a program that could have served as the basis for labor legislation.[30] Among the nineteen points set out in its "Definitive Program" was the recognition of arbitration as one of the best means to resolve the difficulties between capital and labor. The program retained the right to strike, declaring that the demands of capital and its disregard of labor's interests caused strikes, to which labor resorted for its preservation.[31] Meanwhile, Dehesa charged the highly regarded jurist Silvestre Moreno Cora with the drafting of labor legislation for Veracruz.[32] Nothing, however, was enacted. Similarly, in April 1908, the president of the Academia Central Mexicana de Jurisprudencia, the lawyer Luis Méndez, discussing the social question, suggested the need for a national labor law, particularly a workers' compensation statute.[33]

In July 1906, the PLM published its program outlining a number of minimal demands to address the indigence and exploitation of Mexican workers, both agricultural and industrial. The points, enumerated under the title of "Capital and Labor," called for an eight-hour day and minimum wage, to vary across the country depending on local costs of living. The program also stipulated canceling all debts of agricultural workers, weekly payment of wages, workers' accident compensation, and the prohibition of fines and wage deductions. The program would, lastly, have obliged employers to provide safe working conditions and sanitary housing and proscribed the employment of minors younger than fourteen years of age. It did not mention the labor association or the right to strike or otherwise dispute employers' rights and property interests. The program intentionally remained within a liberal framework, juxtaposing its demands against the Porfirian dictatorship's repeated violation of the 1857 constitution.[34]

LEGAL THEORY AND THE SOCIAL QUESTION, CA. 1895–1907

Twenty years after Prieto emphasized the importance of political economy for law and workers' rights, Emilio Pardo Jr. contended it was a monstrous error to legislate on behalf of workers social and labor regulations that countered the natural laws of political economy. Like Prieto, Pardo believed that political economy and law were intertwined. But for the latter, a lawyer, minister to Belgium, and professor at the prestigious Escuela Nacional de Jurisprudencia in Mexico City,[35] the social question now pressed against the civilized world, along with the threat of socialism.[36]

Pardo dutifully acknowledged the importance of Comtean positivism and sociology, then the dominant ideology among the científico elite.[37] He discerned within sociology the disciplines of political economy and law, proposed that political economy was the most developed of the sciences composing sociology, claimed not to privilege either discipline, and concluded that positive law, or legislation, should adhere to the laws of political economy.[38] Pardo almost recognized juridical principles as natural laws analogous to those of political economy, yet he rejected the conception of an immutable natural law for a historicized account of the evolution of law in a changing social context. Apparently, the historical school of law influenced him. But Pardo did not wish to replace an absolutist standard with a complete relativization of norms nor to collapse legal doctrine into a social science.

Pardo in his essay attacked what he called state socialism, whether revolutionary or "covered in scientific clothing," and it was in reference to this that he examined the social question. Identifying it with the overreaching state, which disregarded the laws of political economy, Pardo argued that the social question had been provoked by two causes, which seemed to result from French experiences: the disenchantment with the promise of the revolutionary tradition and the rebellion of intellectuals and parliamentary members against natural economic laws. He doubted the efficacy of legal regulation of economic relations: "this is to say the disregard for the true relation between law and political economy, and for the rash presumption that positive laws can regulate, modify and alter economic phenomena."[39] But Pardo's criticism of labor legislation did identify the main objects of such regulation: "In employment, regulating its duration, fixing the minimum wage, and inhibiting the freedom of lawful contracts; regarding social security, creating mandatory insurance, without prejudice to the tax burden of payors; in savings, decreeing mandatory reserves to guard against the misery or hunger of old or disabled workers; regarding the association, intending the re-establishment of the guild."[40] Ultimately Pardo contended that positive law should be limited to facilitating the activity of natural laws, ensuring justice and security. Liberty, for this Porfirian liberal, remained the fundamental condition for both political economy and law.

In January 1897, Luis Labastida, professor of political economy at the Escuela Nacional de Jurisprudencia, and *oficial mayor* in the finance ministry, gave the inaugural lecture in the national law school.[41] Entitled "Law and Political Economy," the lecture stressed the importance of political economy for legal practice.[42] Labastida introduced law students to the notion of the close relationship between political economy and legal science, quoting Paul Cauwés. Cauwés was a member of the Paris law faculty and founder of the influential French journal the *Revue de l'Économie Politique*, which helped to spearhead a movement critical of classical liberalism.[43] The bases of law were economic, and the points of contact were liberty and property.[44] For Labastida, realizing this, as well as that political economy was the foundation of the social sciences, would lead to the solution of the major problems of the fin de siècle, in particular the conflict between labor and capital. Economic laws, fixing the price of each factor of production, could resolve the problem of distribution of wealth, the source of major conflict. Labastida did not quite contend that political economy had superseded legal science. Justice still needed to be applied artfully. But political economy could not be ignored: Labastida quoted Emilio Pardo's statement that privileged political economy as one of the sciences within the larger field of sociology. In part, Labastida, like Pardo, insisted that political economic doctrine, endorsing the free play of the factors of production, not be submerged in an amorphous sociology. Students should not dismiss the truths of economic science, as they assumed the responsibilities of the legal profession, in government, industry, commerce, and agriculture.[45]

The salience of political economic doctrine for legal thought at the end of the nineteenth century is further evidenced in other articles published in the leading law journals of the period, the *Revista de Legislación y Jurisprudencia* and the *Anuario de Legislación y Jurisprudencia*. One example is Francisco Pascual García's study of the San Luis Potosí proposal to mandate some medical care to workers suffering accidents, discussed above as an early instance of social legislation. For García the issue of obliging employers to provide care had a two-sided character, one legal, the other economic.[46] In discussing the economic side, he broached the social question and the need for an alliance between capital and labor in order to avoid the advent of socialism or communism. García's criticism of socialism is more measured than Pardo's. And unlike Pardo, he thought there was a need for industrial reform, which he associated with sociology. Political economy nonetheless would provide the legislator criteria "for the defense of the weak and direction of the strong," which, García concluded, accorded with those of Pope Leo XIII.[47]

One further example that presumes political economic theory could answer the social question is the thesis of then law student Justino Fernández, dated June 3, 1896, entitled simply "The Social Question."[48] Fernández began with a defense of the liberal system based on property and contract, which socialism criticized. Political economy provided the evaluative criteria and legitimacy for the existent distribution of wealth, which Fernández posited Articles 2, 4, 5, 27, and 28 of the constitution ultimately endorsed.[49]

Leading jurists also observed the inadequacy of the civil code for resolving the problems of modern reality, as is patent by the lawyer Pallares's comments regarding the shortcomings of a lawyer familiar only with code provisions or in Manuel Borja Soriano's study of the law applicable to mutual aid associations. For both jurists, political economy or historical understanding of the law had to supplement legal practice based on the codes. Prieto and Martínez de la Torre's legal approach in 1875, informed by political economic doctrine, continued resounding one generation later.

Pallares thus disdained the lawyer who did not have historical knowledge of the law in his explanation of the reform of the curriculum of the Escuela Nacional de Jurisprudencia, in August 1889. At the time, the law school required two courses in political economy, which alternated between theoretical instruction and the study of Mexican legislation on finances, taxes, credit, and national statistics.[50] Eight years later Pallares again reviewed the curriculum of the national law school.[51] Pallares reiterated his criticism of the lawyer knowledgeable only about the codes' rules and explained that the codes merely abbreviated a more extensive legal tradition. The law school prepared society's leaders; in order to draft legislation, administer policy, and adjudicate or study the nation's laws and institutions, their education in the sciences associated with legal science was imperative.[52] A competent jurist (*jurisconsulto*) drafting penal laws needed scientific knowledge of anthropology, criminal statistics, and penitentiary systems. The drafting and application of a civil code implied questions of political economy, among other subjects; and controversies of constitutional right encompassed economic problems related to the freedom of labor and the function of capital and wages.[53]

Manuel Borja Soriano's analysis of the law applicable to mutual aid associations, published in 1899, found deficient the civil code dispositions that barely regulated these groups.[54] His is the measured study of a jurist, not of an impassioned champion of trade unions. At the same time, Borja Soriano's study is one of the first in Mexican legal literature to define the union and refer to the manner in which workers or artisans established their associations. Borja summarized the conditions needed to establish mutual aid associations: the preparation of a statement that founding members had convened to establish a society, the election of a directing board, and approval of statutes or bylaws. Mostly, Borja observed, mutual aid societies were concerned with their internal governance, only occasionally entering into legal relations with third parties. Concluding that the mutual aid group must be subject to the rules of contracts of association (*contratos de sociedad*), the lawyer opined that some of the applicable civil code articles would be supportive, others detrimental. Borja then turned to a discussion of political economy, asserting that the "intimate and indissoluble ties linking law with political economy frequently cause phenomena comprehended in the dominion of the first of these sciences to fall in turn under the rule of the second."[55] Political economy, merging with a historical conception of law, ultimately served as a corrective for an inadequate civil code and the means to introduce a discussion of existing social relations.

Seven years earlier, in 1892, the *Anuario de Legislación y Jurisprudencia* had published a lengthy extract of Pedro Dorado's review of developments in late nineteenth-century Italian legal theory.[56] Dorado was a Spanish positivist jurist, and his articles on Italian jurisprudence might have seemed remote to Mexican lawyers. It is therefore significant that the Mexican editors of the *Anuario* devoted extensive space to his work in their legal journal. The extract of Dorado's work shares with Pardo's essay and other contemporary law journal articles the belief that law and political economy are interrelated. In Dorado's piece, however, political economy begins to merge with a sociological perspective more definitively. The social question is raised as implicating in addition to the economic question a multitude of others: religious, moral, legal, political, scientific, and pedagogical. One should study, besides economics, political and criminal law, the philosophy of law, and, above all, sociology, in which all other sciences are grounded.[57]

Economic theory is then examined in connection with the scholarship of Italian political economists, who are classified in respect to whether they are individualists, socialists, or syncretic. Dorado concurs with Italian criticism of Bastiat (whom Prieto had extolled) for his excessive optimism and blind individualism.[58] Dorado identifies three schools of thought opposed to Manchester economics: university socialists (*de la câtedra*), the historicism of Carl Menger (perhaps ironically), and the positivists. And he describes favorably the legislative program recommended by Alberto Zorli to prevent the abuse of property and contract rights; such legislation would encompass state regulation of industrial relations as follows:

> The state can realize this end with its superior power, which is legislative, obliging businessmen and factory owners to be humane with their dependents and promulgating laws that regulate the *hygiene of factories and mines*, that moderate the *work of women and children* and that limit the *hours of work* even of adults, that regulate the *contracts between workers and [factory] owners*. . . . The state should similarly monitor the conditions of housing of workers in order to avoid illnesses, prohibit vagrancy, gambling, and inebriation, create tribunals so that social legislation is complied with, not place obstacles on *workers' resistance associations*, nor prohibit *strikes* which are contained within prudent limits, favor *the participation of workers in the profits of the companies* and societies of

mutual aid, credit and insurance. In a word, the State should intervene, according to Zorli, in economic relations in a mode analogous to the way that the realist school or rather university socialism wish, and are in part achieving it.[59]

Although Dorado generally distances himself from socialist theories, his accounts are respectful of them, and he acknowledges their contributions. For example, he seemingly agreed with a position taken by Napoleone Colajanni in connection with how reorganization of social relations would attenuate the cause of social struggle.[60]

The second part of Dorado's work appearing in the *Anuario* is a critique of the civil code and the French exegetical school from the perspective of contemporary positivist and sociological trends.[61] Dorado signaled the emergence of a youthful group of law professors, not all of whom were positivists or uniform in their approach but who were already initiating new ways of renovating the study of civil law: Vadalá-Papale, Chironi, Cimbali, Ferri, Gianturco, Cogliogo, Gaba, Brini, Salvioli, Polacco, De Filippis, and D'Aguanno.[62] The antecedents to their general sociological orientation are in the historical school of law. Dorado is not the only one who connects the historical school and modern sociological perspectives; he cites numerous scholars who also identified the link explicitly, for example, Bruni, Cogliogo, and Vani.[63]

The practical thrust of the new sociological studies of the civil code was to reform the individualistic legal system to accommodate social and collective institutions. An organic notion of society replaces that of the abstract individual, which further validates a program of reforming civil law for new social institutions, including ones related to production, and to the new conditions of work, more accommodating of the working classes.[64] Dorado recounted sympathetically D'Aguanno's proposals to reform contract law (the law of obligations) to reflect changes in working conditions, among other relationships,[65] and to promote collective institutions, which D'Aguanno had contended evolve in society, arise from social needs, and serve social functions: hence such institutions are not the creation of the state.[66]

Fourteen years after the *Anuario*'s publication of Dorado's piece on Italian legal theory, in 1906, the *Revista de Legislación y Jurisprudencia* published his article "Hacia un Nuevo Derecho Civil," which pointed to the advent of a new civil law, the social law then evolving in France.[67] Dorado argued that it would supersede on principles of necessity and solidarity traditional civil law based on private property and power. While he considered other subjects affected by a new civil law, including property, the law of succession, welfare, and family relations, he devoted about half his essay to the new labor law. He said it was evolving as a result of the efforts and achievements of workers themselves, through their organization into associations and unions. And it was labor law that was establishing new, transcendental principles, such as in the insurance law of work-related accidents and illnesses, which created new social duties and reciprocities and hinged on claims of necessity. The new principles amounted to a subversion or inversion of those in traditional civil law. Labor legislation was completely dedicated to the protection of the weak, in contrast to traditional law's protection of the strong.[68] The analysis reflected the influence of Rudolph von Jhering and the historical interpretation of law. Dorado quoted the German jurist in support of his argument that property rights should be restricted and wealth redistributed or regulated, since the property held by a minority could not be justified in relation to their own contribution to its generation; it was the product of many, in cooperation.[69]

Also in 1906, the Ministry of Development began to publish in one of its journals Paul Pic's *Traité élémentaire de législation industrielle. Les lois ouvriéres* (translated into Spanish as *Legislación industrial*). As with the appearance of Pedro Dorado's essay, publication of Pic's treatise surely indicated the reception of the new social legislation and insofar as readers of these writings were impressed by them, the beginnings of a reorientation of legal thought. Pic's treatise narrated the evolution of labor legislation, culminating in the first statutes recognizing labor unions and the right to strike. One of its excerpts published in the *Boletín de la Secretaría de Fomento* summarized labor legislation at the end of the nineteenth century throughout the European world, as well as in the United States and the British Empire (Canada, the Australian provinces, and New Zealand).[70] Pic contended that legislation was regulating industry more closely and becoming more tutelary toward workers. Noting broad national trends, he classified various laws according to whether they instituted labor departments; recognized labor, professional, managerial, and mixed organizations in order to realize the equality or harmony between labor and capital; monitored industry and commerce, by creating agencies of inspectors; subjected employment contracts to specifications and instructed the judge concerning their interpretation; set minimum standards, including a minimum wage; supported welfare institutions for workers, including housing, savings, or cooperatives; or established special adjudicatory bodies to resolve industrial or collective conflicts. And Pic sketched the principal alternatives to law courts resolving labor matters:

> To organize, with the proposition of resolving collective or industrial conflicts between employers and employees, special jurisdictions, councils of laboring men [*prud-hommes*] or industrial tribunals, committees of conciliation or arbitration courts, jurisdictions composed of employers and workers or employees, in equal numbers and maybe presided either alternatively by an employer or worker or by an arbitrator magistrate or notable independent of the litigation.[71]

It is significant that a state-sponsored journal, that of the Ministry of Development, should publish excerpts of Paul Pic's major treatise—not because this represented any kind of official endorsement but because Pic in France was an important proponent of enacting comprehensive reform legislation to resolve the social question.[72] Pic was one of several academic social reformers, labeled interventionists, many of whom were political economists and held chairs in law schools. Pic himself was professor of labor legislation in the law faculty at Lyons. From their positions in law schools, as political economists the interventionists criticized liberal doctrine and classical political economy during their campaigns to protect industrial workers in the 1880s and 1890s, publishing frequently in the *Revue de l'Économie Politique*, founded in 1886. They undertook empirical studies of industrial relations to demonstrate the fictions of liberal tenets, such as the notion of *liberté de travail* (freedom of labor), used by employers to argue against factory regulation. And they justified the need for reform of labor relations and the amelioration of economic hardship by arguing that exploitive conditions engendered strikes.[73] The interventionists insisted that their objective was social reform, to forestall revolutionary socialism.[74]

From a different perspective, the Catholic Church in Europe also undertook a critique of liberal market relations and proposed a reform agenda to preempt the triumph of socialism among workers. The papacy's social reformism was encapsulated in the encyclical *Rerum Novarum*, published in May 1891 by Leo XIII and soon thereafter republished in the Catholic press in Mexico. *Rerum Novarum* explicitly denounced socialism and affirmed the institution of private property as a natural right. But the encyclical also acknowledged the social question, as such resulting from industrialization and the immiseration of workers; and it proposed fair wages and reasonable working hours. It directed the creation of workers' associations—mutual aid societies. Further, *Rerum Novarum* insisted that class conflict was unnecessary, that a just equilibrium between labor and capital was possible in view of the mutual interdependence of both classes and the organic nature of society.[75] It thereby reiterated several of the points made by legal intellectuals promoting a new paradigm of social law.

CONCLUSION

As labor unrest increased in textile manufacturing and railways, *El Imparcial* reflected the ripples of intellectual currents in sociology and economics. An editorial published in late January 1907, urging workers to cooperate more with industrialists, mentioned the need to consider what economists and sociologists were writing.[76] A piece one month later recounted a speech delivered by the científico Pablo Macedo, then the director of the Escuela Nacional de Jurisprudencia, who had quoted the positivist Gabino Barreda's critique of the traditional lawyer, ignorant of the laws regulating society.[77]

The discussions of both foreign and Mexican legal theorists about the need to supplement the civil law with political, economic, and then sociological theory had their counterpart in reform legislation considered by various states and the federal government. The actual social legislation enacted was undoubtedly inadequate in the face of workers' needs. The federal government seemed incapable of passing any labor legislation.

Nonetheless, a shift in legal perspective was occurring, evident in the legal literature, including the publication of Paul Pic's work, as well as in Jacinto Pallares's workers' compensation statute.

Around the turn of the century, one editorial (among many) in *El Imparcial*, discussing the subject of strikes, dubbed the period "el siglo de las huelgas."[78] Typically, *El Imparcial* found the answer to the social problem in the restoration of equilibrium between workers and employers. In another essay, written during the labor conflict in the textile industry at the end of 1906, the editors opined that if workers' demands were fair, they would be met by their employers, for economic reasons: "The agreement between these two forces, the just equilibrium between capital and labor, demands that one not be the slave of the other; neither tyrannies of capital nor of labor! We believe . . . that if the petitions of workers are just—from the economic viewpoint—employers will accede to them, not only for a humane reason, but because it suits their needs."[79] It was a concept of equilibrium already posited a generation earlier by Prieto, applying a liberal political-economic doctrine that had become only more influential in subsequent years. The interdependence or mutual interest of both factors of production suggested by *El Imparcial* was a proposition accepted by defenders of the regime, like Emilio Pardo, but also by foreign critiques of late nineteenth-century economic liberalism, such as those of Dorado and Pic. Pallares's stress on a historical approach to legal study, which included the subject of political economy, corresponded with the preparation of social legislation, such as Nuevo León's workers' accident statute. Whether advocating the need for social legislation or decrying it, lawyers tended toward concepts of legal or normative rules that acknowledged the salience of social relations.

Thus, Antonio Ramos Pedrueza, a lawyer and deputy in the lower federal congressional house in 1901, criticized government notions of freedom of labor that tolerated the exploitation and abuse of workers. Pablo Macedo defended the government's liberal interpretation of freedom of labor.[80] Six years later (as reported by *El Imparcial*), Macedo would present the positivist critique of the traditional lawyer who had supposedly disregarded economic and social reality. Political economic theory could serve to justify an argument against state intervention in labor relations, as it had for Prieto and more recently for Pardo, but it also, along with the historical school, was facilitating the development of a critique of formal, individualistic doctrine. Paul Pic was a political economist and state interventionist. The new sociological perspective embraced by Dorado was difficult to dismiss by the Cometean-influenced positivists like Macedo. Ramos Pedrueza and Macedo may have differed in the stances they assumed on the social question or in their respective analyses, but they shared in part an ideological and educational foundation increasingly open to sociological interpretations of the economy that provided support for policies entailing a more substantial role for the state in industrial relations.

Meanwhile, the Porfirian científico elite, including Macedo, was obviously failing to respond adequately to the demands of the labor movements in 1906 and thereafter. One can contrast Nuevo León's promulgation of a workers' compensation statute with the frustrated attempt to incorporate an accident compensation provision into the revised federal mining law. Insofar as the Porfirian ruling group, namely, Limantour and Corral, contemplated labor legislation, they seemed largely to have considered it solely as a means to control labor organization. *El Imparcial*'s touting of Díaz's 1907 laudo as labor legislation could hardly have satisfied any call for social reform. The semiofficial newspaper's fleeting interest in labor councils and its coverage of industrial relations in textile manufacturing indicate that even among the ruling elite there was a growing recognition of the need for social legislation to reform labor relations. Pardo and Labastida's defense of a liberal political economy that disdained the social welfare state was faltering, even as their idealized notions of equilibrium between the principal factors of production, capital and labor, would persist among lawyers and legislators.

CHAPTER 5

Legislating Labor Law, 1911–1924

INTRODUCTION

Mexican political leaders enacted most of the major elements of labor law as legislation between 1911 and 1931. The process of making this labor law was interrelated with the events of the revolution that began in 1910. The dominant revolutionary faction in late 1916–1917, the Constitutionalists, drafted the new constitution that included a section dedicated to workers' rights, Article 123. The articulation of measures to protect labor's interests as constitutional rights was a seminal event.[1] Thereafter, Mexican labor law referenced Article 123, as did labor movements. Yet, as noted, the political and social changes that occurred between 1910 and 1920 did not constitute a workers' revolution. Labor participated in Madero's electoral campaign in 1909–10 but did not lead it. As of 1911, workers organized new unions and repeatedly undertook strikes throughout the country and in different economic sectors, but their demands did not normally contest the fundamental structure of capitalism. Revolutionaries did decree the abolition of peonage and higher minimum wages in different regions of the country. Early labor legislation (promulgated before 1917) also aimed to improve working conditions while sometimes affirming the right of workers to organize or strike. Article 123 reflected, or incorporated, many of these measures. Pursuant to Article 123, governors in several states then promulgated statutes favorable to labor, while allying themselves with regional or national labor organizations. But the cumulative result of these endeavors was reformist, not revolutionary. The constitution aimed to reform property and labor relations, not abolish private property; and most political leaders, whether at the national or state level, were not workers. If labor benefited from the revolution and participated in revolutionary and postrevolutionary politics and actions, its "conquests" (the word that union leaders frequently used in the 1920s to signify labor's improved material and social position) were piecemeal, albeit substantial, its position in political and social processes ultimately subordinated to larger political and military contests and the reformed capitalist system.[2]

This chapter outlines the process that resulted in the drafting of Article 123 and subsequent efforts to pass labor legislation. An extensive historiography exists about labor politics and the social movements during the revolutionary era, which arguably extended through the 1930s.[3] The chapter relies on this historiography but focuses more specifically on some of the legal issues raised by Article 123. It begins with the first major institutional change that occurred in industrial relations following Díaz's resignation, the establishment of a federal labor agency and the government's sponsorship of negotiations in the textile sector to try to end widespread strikes and rationalize the sector's wage structure. The chapter then recounts legislative efforts from the end of Madero's administration through the civil war, including—not insignificantly—military commanders' decrees to end servitude. The chapter centers on the drafting of Article 123. Its drafters compromised to pass a set of provisions that ultimately both pronounced and limited the extent of the reformation of industrial relations; this outcome was in part the influence of socially oriented legal thought on the debates that resulted in Article 123.

In the last section of the chapter I discuss how one consequence of the compromises made at the constitutional convention was to generate new questions about federal-state relations, as the central government dealt more regularly with labor matters. Two major revolts, in 1920 and 1923, involving the military, bracketed the evolution of state-labor relations in the postrevolutionary years. Both revolts resulted in the strengthening of the relationship between organized labor and the presidency, but they did not resolve the relationship of the federal government with the states in connection with labor law. By the end of 1924, the concluding point of this chapter, neither the nature of state involvement in labor relations nor the federal government's role had been fully settled or legalized.

ADDRESSING THE LABOR QUESTION

On September 22, 1911, interim president Francisco León de la Barra submitted to Congress a bill (*proyecto*) to establish a labor department.[4] The agency was to collect and publish data about work, serve as an intermediary between agricultural workers and employers when solicited, and arbitrate labor disputes upon request. The bill placed the department in the Ministry of Development, probably the most hospitable bureaucracy for such an agency. As noted in Chapter 4, in 1906, the ministry had published Paul Pic's treatise, which practically served as a blueprint for the establishment of such an office. The ministry already relied upon a network of agencies furnishing it information about labor issues.[5]

The envisioned labor department would be the first state institution devoted exclusively to industrial relations. The project's lengthy statement of objectives (*Exposición de Motivos*) began dramatically by declaring that of all the problems requiring the attention of the federal government, none was of such importance as those related to labor, whether viewed from an economic, legal, or, more comprehensively, social perspective.[6] The exposition justified an increased state role in labor relations on account of the need to deal with disturbances caused by strikes but also because of the public interest in the standard of living of all classes, especially that of the majority. The abolition of slavery was cited as another instance when the state's authority had been exercised similarly to its newly announced objectives. The statement identified the legislative measures being taken in other countries to protect labor: factory inspections, regulation of hours, child and female labor, and compensation for work accidents. In particular, the modern state had created special legislation to improve wages, resolve labor disputes, and establish agencies of conciliation and arbitration. Further legislation envisioned providing labor organizations legal support, assistance to form cooperatives, and pension funds.[7]

The Senate passed León de la Barra's bill on December 11.[8] If the new department constituted a departure from ad hoc Porfirian practices, it hardly represented a revolutionary proposal for the interim president. Existing labor departments in Argentina and Belgium, where León de la Barra previously held diplomatic posts, had impressed him. His biographer describes a "progressive consensus," in favor of some legal social reform that had been coalescing even within ruling Porfirian circles at the time of Díaz's resignation, which endorsed a reduction of the length of the work day and an increase in industrial wages, and which concurred with principles of Catholic social thought in the encyclical *Rerum Novarum*.[9] In July 1911, León de la Barra had indicated his interest in establishing a governmental agency to respond to social unrest. In mid-July, his administration announced it would set up a special office or national chamber of labor to discuss and draft legislation to regulate the length of the work day for men, women, and children and to mediate conflicts.[10]

In the meantime, strikes had begun to break out following Díaz's resignation in May 1911 and continued thereafter into 1912, in transport, mining, the urban trades, and textile manufacturing. Workers formed unions, too, in the mining and transport sectors of the economy as well as in urban centers. In Coahuila, in November 1911, mine workers founded the Unión Minera Mexicana to organize the entire mining sector, while calling for protective labor statutes. In October 1912, the federal government published safety regulations for mining. Shortly thereafter, in late December 1912, the Mexican union of mechanics struck the National Railways of Mexico, leading a movement that involved other rail unions and perhaps altogether 20,000 workers. Their chief demand was the eight-hour day. The union had prepared an extensive set of work regulations and presented it to the labor department. The company had responded by imposing its own set of regulations. The strike resulted in a compromise of a ten-hour day with a 10 percent wage increase and implicit recognition of the union. Telegraph and office rail employees then threatened to strike against the same company, also demanding the eight-hour day; their representatives reached a favorable agreement that was in effect one of the first collective contracts. In these conflicts, the labor department played a secondary role, although it had some influence in the legislative enactment of the mine safety statute: in the rail sector particularly, the unions held a strong position.[11]

In the textile sector, the labor department and federal government's role was more influential. By December 1911, workers were involved in extensive work stoppages.[12] As the labor department started to operate under Madero's administration, in January 1912, the federal government moved to diffuse the strikes. The ministers of development and the interior together sponsored a conference with major textile manufacturers for January 20. The head of the new labor department, Antonio Ramos Pedrueza, a moderate socialist and lawyer who had written on criminal issues besides serving in the Porfirian Chamber of Deputies, also participated.[13] But government officials permitted labor groups to consult with them only separately from the formal sessions of the conference.[14]

Mentioning the extensive work stoppages, the minister of development's opening statement at the conference invited employers to reach an industry-wide labor agreement with the government. The government would raise the agreement to the category of law, submitting a bill to Congress. The minister anticipated stipulations to reduce hours of work and curb child and female labor. He acknowledged that setting a uniform wage rate would prove more complicated.[15]

The manufacturers' lawyer phrased his response in a vocabulary drawn from widespread notions of political economy articulated already by Prieto in 1875 and refashioned in the new fin de siècle legal discourse. Specifically, the lawyer spoke of the need for the government to solve the labor problem by determining the formula "of equilibrium and justice so as not to sacrifice labor or the interests of the capitalist." It was language akin to that of *Rerum Novarum* but also to that of social legal theorists. The lawyer called for guarantees for the textile industry now that the government had created the labor department to protect labor interests: a mediating agency should fill the space in the industrial system, to solve peacefully the controversies arising between capitalist and worker. Noting that such offices in Europe and the United States avoided strikes, he guardedly welcomed the creation of the department. Commenting on how the poor, maize-based diet of workers affected their ability for prolonged labor, he offered that industrialists would accept the ten-hour day, provided unions, possibly represented by the labor department, ended their hostile protests. The question of setting a minimum or uniform salary should be assigned to a commission for further study, in view of regional differences; more specific complaints about working conditions were not appropriate for an industry-wide agreement. The manufacturers' lawyer also proposed a reduction or elimination of the 5 percent federal tax on the textile industry established by the Law of November 28, 1893.[16] The outcome of the conference was a provisional agreement to reduce the workday to ten hours and raise wages by 10 percent in certain cases, while the formulation of a uniform wage rate was studied.[17]

As industrial conflict persisted, and few industrialists implemented the January agreement, the labor department scheduled for July 1912 a second conference to reach a definitive settlement.[18] It began on July 2 in Mexico City. As in January, workers participated only indirectly, the labor department informing their committee of the outcome of daily negotiations between the Ministry of Development and manufacturers.[19] On July 17, Ramos Pedrueza completed an industry-wide agreement or convention (*reglamento*) covering factory working conditions.[20] It was broader and fairer to workers than Díaz's arbitral award of January 1907; still, it lacked the legitimacy of law or a collective contract. No representative of labor had coauthored directly the agreement's writing; and it was legally unenforceable without further state action.

The convention stipulated that it would govern the employment contract between industrialists and workers, which would be deemed accepted by workers on the sole basis of their entering the factory. While confirming the ten-hour day, many of its articles aimed to maintain managerial control against any challenge by labor. In an August circular to textile workers, Ramos Pedrueza, possibly doubtful of whether the department's efforts to establish an industry-wide agreement really could reconcile employees and employers, extolled the benefits of the July document.[21] He emphasized his consultation with the workers' committee, its advances over prior plant agreements, and the advantages of the new wage rate, partly based on the English system (*tarifa inglesa*). He urged workers to disregard agitators and remember that order was the only path of solid progress. The circular's plea suggested the limits of the department's power, when it had kept labor organizations removed from direct negotiations with employers, who did not yet tolerate independent unions. Similarly circumspect, an earlier circular, which had notified employers of workers' complaints of company blacklisting, reminded them that workers had the right to organize under the 1857 constitution.[22]

Madero's administration moved to enforce indirectly the July 1912 textile convention as many industrialists refused to apply its provisions and workers struck for its implementation. In September 1912, the federal executive sent a tax bill to Congress meant to induce industrialists' compliance with the accord, modifying manufacturers earlier proposal. From September 25 to December 1912, the Chamber of Deputies debated the bill. Its major protagonists included the Renovator Bloc (*Bloque Renovador*). Generally supporters of Madero, they were then a progressive faction of reformist deputies who in this matter argued in favor of the state's authority to regulate wages. The Catholic Party, which invoked *Rerum Novarum* and noted earlier debates about the social question among Catholics, also supported the bill.[23]

The Ley Obrera, actually a tax statute, was the only labor bill Congress passed during Madero's administration. In February 1913, General Victoriano Huerta deposed the president and vice president and then had them murdered. However modest the Ley Obrera was, the conferences to establish an industry-wide agreement had posed social issues related to employment contracts, the representation of labor organizations, and the strike, which future administrations would continue to consider, as the country's political edifice crumbled. Notably, the labor department operated under Huerta, its studies and intermediary role contributing to the shaping of labor law.

Three months after Huerta's coup, on May 24, 1913, the Ministry of Development submitted to Congress an initiative to establish federal and congressional jurisdiction over labor legislation. Huerta's administration also issued instructions to governors to form local labor chambers comprised of workers, industrialists, and middle-class professionals, to facilitate governmental resolution of labor conflicts; and the government recommended that states enact measures for Sunday rest and the regulation of child and female labor. Repeating the language of 1912, a bill to raise the status of the labor department and add "labor" to the title of the secretary of industry and commerce declared that the *cuestión obrera* was the problem of the century; state intervention in conflicts between business and labor was necessary in view of the consequences for the nation and its people of excessive exploitation of the worker.[24]

Workers sustained actions following Madero's overthrow. In Mexico City, in 1913, they demonstrated in a march commemorating May Day, urging the Congress to legislate the eight-hour day, compensation for work-related accidents, and legal recognition of labor organizations. In September, the committee representing textile workers petitioned the Chamber of Deputies for, among other things, the amendment of Article 72 of the constitution, so as to place the regulation of labor relations under the jurisdiction of the federal Congress; implementation of Article 9 of the constitution, to protect labor associations and the right to organize; and amendment of the national textile tax to ensure compliance with the July 1912 convention.[25]

The Chamber of Deputies considered other labor bills in 1913.[26] One group of congressional deputies, including *renovadores* José Natividad Macías, Luis M. Rojas, Alfonso Cravioto, Marcos López Jiménez, Jesús Urueta, as well as Pascual Ortiz Rubio, sponsored a set of amendments to the federal commercial code in September 1913.[27] Their bill would constitute one basis for later legislative proposals. At the time, the bill would have amended the commercial code to cover most industrial and agricultural workers as well as commercial employees, regulated working conditions, and made the employer liable for most work-related accidents.

The amendments to the commercial code presumed the framework of the employment contract. For example, they made the maximum workday of ten hours one condition of the contract. Affirmative employer obligations were then listed as following from the contract of furnishing services, such as payment in currency and the provision of healthy and comfortable housing when workers had to live in the country or next to where they worked. A separate set of articles set out the employer's responsibility in work-related accidents, contrasted them with the civil law obligations under which the employer might also be liable, and established an expedited procedure to resolve disputes involving an industrial accident, directing local judges to reach a decision promptly. The proposal also established quasi-adjudicatory labor bodies. Comprised of ten members, half named by workers, half by employers, these agencies would determine the appropriate minimum wage. In addition, they would resolve all other employment disputes, their resolutions having the effect of final arbitral decisions. The bill directed the Ministry of Development to break a tie vote.[28]

During 1913 and 1914, several states passed laws or drafted bills mandating Sunday rest or compensation for work-related accidents.[29] After Huerta dissolved the Congress in October 1913, *renovador* deputies, including José Natividad Macías, joined the Constitutionalists' insurrection against Huerta. The legislative experiments in labor reform initiated in 1912 would continue, spanning the Madero and Huerta governments and various factions in the ensuing civil war. After the defeat of Huerta in July 1914, the labor department in Mexico City and Veracruz would function under either Conventionists or Constitutionalists. The political factions generally shared a vision of a new industrial relations system, with a state institution mediating labor disputes between labor and business, preferably pursuant to social legislation that dictated improvements in the standard of living of the working classes. In contrast, their relations with labor organizations differed according to the circumstances of the moment.

LABOR LAW IN THE PRECONSTITUTIONAL PERIOD

Venustiano Carranza's stance toward labor reform was ambiguous. As mentioned earlier, his Plan of Guadalupe lacked a statement of social reform.[30] The first allusion to the need for social reform may have been his statements in Hermosillo, Sonora, in September 1913; there, Carranza said that once Huerta was defeated, the social struggle for equality would ensue and reform legislation for the benefit of workers and peasants would be essential for the establishment of an equilibrium in the nation.[31] The Pact of Torreón of July 1914, reached among revolutionary military leaders to accommodate Francisco Villa's concerns, stipulated that a revolutionary convention would be held after Huerta's then imminent defeat; it also referenced social reforms.[32] At the time, Carranza sidestepped this avowal. The convention that was finally held, and moved to Aguascalientes, became an arena for the confrontation between Villistas and Carrancistas and resulted in November with the withdrawal of Carrancista generals from Aguascalientes (abetted if not provoked by Villa). The convention declared Carranza in rebellion on November 10, and by December 13 had confirmed a provisional president and a commission to draft a reform program, which would not be completed until April 1915.[33]

As civil war loomed between the Convention forces and the Constitutionalists, Álvaro Obregón committed himself to the latter. In November, Obregón supported within the Constitutionalists a faction, the Confederación Revolucionaria, which included Gerardo Murillo, Alberto Pani, Jesús Urueta, and Rafael Zubarán Capmany.[34] They favored social legislation. Carranza did not object to the group, although Félix Palavicini, around whom a number of renovadores coalesced, did. According to one historian, the Confederación pressed Carranza to consider measures to address the social question.[35] Palavicini's group also set to work on drafting such measures. Thus, in the fall of 1914, as the Convention moved to depose the first chief, and he maneuvered against Villa and the Convention, rallying as many revolutionary generals as he could, Carranza reconsidered social legislation.[36]

On December 12, 1914, Carranza promulgated the Additions to the Plan of Guadalupe. Authored by the renovadores, the decree contrasted Carranza's Constitutionalist movement with the Villista "reaction" that allegedly intended to postpone social and economic reforms.[37] Carranza's preconstitutional government "would be concerned with the expedition and implementation of reforms for which the country had been fighting for four years." The second paragraph of the decree ambitiously set forth a social agenda of reform, promising the expeditious implementation of "all laws, dispositions and measures which will satisfy the economic, social and political needs of the country [and] legislation to improve the condition of the rural peon, worker, miner, and, in general, the proletarian classes."[38]

In view of the political situation in the fall of 1914, it is probable that Carranza issued his December 12 decree both to counter the developing

Convention program of social reform (if not social revolution) and to maintain his leadership of the Constitutionalist movement. Constitutionalist generals in the regions they controlled had already issued orders establishing minimum wages, maximum workdays or prohibiting Sunday labor—and abolishing peonage.[39] By the end of 1914, and thereafter in 1915, these decrees reflected in part the increasing saliency of social issues in the civil war against the Conventionists: many of their preambles alleged that one of the main objectives of the Constitutionalist revolution was social reform.[40] On April 9, 1915, while combating Villa in the pivotal battles near Celaya, Obregón promulgated a minimum wage decree for all workers in the states of Michoacán, Querétaro, Hidalgo, and Guanajuato.[41]

Most importantly, military orders pronounced the end of debt peonage.[42] On September 3, 1914, Pablo González canceled the debts of rural laborers in Puebla and Tlaxcala and of all urban workers in his zone of command.[43] On September 11, in Mérida, Yucatán, Eleuterio Avila declared that since indebted agricultural workers (*jornaleros*) could not enjoy the constitution's individual rights, and one objective of the Constitutionalist movement was to ensure social evolution and extend justice throughout the country, all their debts were canceled, and they were free to remain on the plantations or leave.[44] On September 19, 1914, in Tabasco, the military governor Luis F. Domínguez abolished the system of indebted servitude. He further mandated a minimum wage and eight-hour workday for agricultural workers in language similar to that of Article 5 of the constitution.[45] General Jesus Agustín Castro, governor and military commander of Chiapas, enacted the Ley de Obreros or Workers' Law on October 30, 1914, which proclaimed, "there are no servants in Chiapas."[46] Thus, where the Porfirian federal judiciary had been able to rule against coerced labor only occasionally, in individual cases, revolutionary decrees aimed to end servitude altogether. But it was the same concept of free labor, articulated in the 1857 constitution, which inspired both Porfirian justices and revolutionary generals.

Some of the Constitutionalist decrees verged on more extensive legislation. In Veracruz, General Cándido Aguilar, governor and military commander of the state, issued Decree Number 11, Ley de Cándido Aguilar, on October 19, 1914.[47] Its preamble justified the public power's dictating legislation to establish equilibrium between economic interests in general and individually, on the basis that it was necessary to conserve life, health, and the well-being of workers. The first article limited the workday to nine hours, echoing the prohibition against forced labor of Article 5 of the constitution. Among other prescriptions, the law made employers responsible for sick and injured workers. It proscribed company stores. It also established a mechanism for resolving disputes: boards of civil administration (*Juntas de Administración Civil*) would resolve employer and worker's complaints, while also hearing representatives of trade unions (*gremios*) and associations (*sociedades*).[48]

Subsequently, in October 1915 and January 1916, Veracruz's military governors promulgated legislation to regulate labor unions. Both laws contemplated unions negotiating over the terms and conditions of work and sanctioned employers who refused to negotiate with a union enjoying civil personality. To secure civil personality, the union had to register with the Juntas de Administración Civil and report each semester its financial operations.[49] The January 1916 law justified the right to associate by referencing Article 9 of the constitution and instructed unions not to deny admission to individuals with the same occupation as members.[50]

The most distinctive state legislation reflected the revolutionary process initiated by General Salvador Alvarado. As military commander and governor of Yucatán, he promulgated two decrees within a few months, the second an elaborate statute on December 11, 1915.[51] The statute established a state mechanism to avoid strikes. State dependent unions would complement conciliation agencies and an arbitration tribunal.[52] The freedom to associate was partly predicated on the concept of free labor; statutory incentives encouraged workers to join unions registered with the government. State board arbitration of labor conflicts would prevail over unauthorized strikes by workers not members of officially recognized unions or strikes occurring while a collective contract was in effect.[53]

While Constitutionalist generals decreed, Carranza's civilian advisers wrote labor legislation. Toward the end of January 1915, the Carrancista periodical *El Pueblo* published five bills that together could have formed the basis of a labor code: one amended the commercial code, another concerned the employment contract, yet another was a workers' compensation bill, a fourth directed the formation of local agencies or commissions to set an adequate minimum wage, and the fifth regulated labor organizations. José Natividad Macías and Luis Manuel Rojas, both lawyers, mainly authored the bills as members of the Section of Social Legislation under the direction of Félix Palavicini, then minister of public instruction. Palavicini later wrote that he had set up the section as part of the project to realize the social transformations required by the Mexican revolution: to study and draft protective laws for the proletariat in the cities and country. In addition to Macías and Rojas, the lawyers Alfonso Cravioto, Manuel Andrade Priego, and Juan N. Frías worked with the section.[54] The bills shared similarities with the earlier endeavor of Macías and Rojas to amend the commercial code in the last Congress. Although Carranza did not promulgate the bills, they embodied the same principles that continued to form labor law in the ensuing years; and Macías subsequently invoked them during the debates among delegates in the constitutional congress held in Querétaro in 1916–17.

The amendment to the commercial code extended coverage to more workers, although still describing specific occupations, as did the civil code. Similar to the criticism of the socially oriented French jurists (or Dorado), the bill's introduction said that civil legislation (*legislación común*) governing the employment relationship through the contract, if valid ideally, was marred in reality.[55] The bill, however, still contemplated the contractual framework to regulate employment, and its approach was to limit abuse, not reconceptualize the employment relationship. To end debt peonage, for example, workers were required to repay advances only when they did not exceed one month's wages. The bill in this sense echoed some of the proposals to ameliorate servitude made during the Porfirian era. The workers' compensation bill, in contrast, directed all employers to provide relatively generous benefits in the case of work-related accidents.

The preamble of the project to establish minimum wages by boards of conciliation (*juntas de avenencia*) reflected the understanding of the functions of such administrative organs in 1915. Only with the consent of the interested workers and employers could such boards mediate or arbitrate a dispute. In addition, they should set minimum wages and check compliance with laws protective of workers.[56] The preamble further contended that the collective contract could fix wages more equitably than individual contracts of employment. The last bill closely regulated the union, specifying its permissible purposes.[57] For an association to obtain legal personality, it had to satisfy a number of conditions; and the interior ministry had to approve the articles of incorporation and bylaws. The bill authorized the interior ministry to dissolve an association, if its purpose was altered in a fundamental way or it assumed a religious or political character.

After Macías and Rojas had completed their project, Carranza sent Macías to the United States to study labor law and industrial relations. According to Macías, during his absence from Carranza's side, Zubarán Capmany, then interior minister, persuaded the first chief to assert federal jurisdiction over labor matters.[58] On January 29, 1915, by decree, Carranza amended Paragraph X of Article 72 of the constitution.[59] The decree declared that although the constitution had established fundamental labor rights as human rights, they had become a dead letter before the painful realities of peonage and the exploitation of the worker by an industrial system. The latter did not compensate justly and exhausted the individual and human species with an inhumane workday. This occurred because of the lack of laws implementing Articles 4, 5, and 32 of the constitution and the absence of appropriate organs to make effective their guarantees. The federalization of labor law was necessary because of the nature of such legislation; its impact on the agricultural, commercial, and industrial interests of the entire nation; and the desirability of extending its beneficial effects to all of the inhabitants of the country.

In rivalry with the bills prepared by the section of social legislation, Zubarán also prepared draft statutes, published on April 12, 1915, when the labor department was under his charge as interior minister.[60] By one account, both Zubarán's and Macías's bills were given to Carranza for review, without his reaching a decision to promulgate either legislation.[61] One historian writes that Zubarán drafted his project in response to the demands of the anarchist-leaning Casa del Obrero Mundial, at the time probably the country's largest network of workers' organizations, and in 1915 allied with the Constitutionalists.[62]

Zubarán's draft legislation is more sympathetic toward organized labor than Macías's bills; it is also conceptually more elegant.[63] Using language similar to that of Macías's bills, Zubarán disparages nineteenth-century civil law and appeals to European and American examples of reform legislation. Because of its social importance, this legislation should be justified in terms of public law, requiring the creation of new, completely modern institutions. Like Dorado or French legal reformers at the turn of the century, Zubarán distinguished his position from modern socialism, with whose sentiments he could nonetheless sympathize. Socialism was the threatening alternative to labor legislation; the latter was an attempt to protect the weak, without failing to recognize the rights of capital.[64]

The legislative paradigm was again the contract of employment. Regulation of the workday and minimum wage was justified in terms similar to Macías's analysis.[65] More than Macías's legislation, the Zubarán project outlined how the collective contract would structure industrial relations, commented that the labor movement favored it, and cited examples from other countries, particularly French models. In accord with French legal thought, Zubarán suggested that collective agreements were not actually labor contracts but conventions made between the parties that set the conditions for individual employment contracts. The draft statute also regulated the labor organization, but less intrusively than Macías's project. All collective contracts had to be registered to have legal effect, and all unions had to register with the municipal government. The final chapter directed local judges to resolve disputes arising from the labor contract, contemplating a summary process for claims and arbitration if the parties wished it. Mandatory arbitration ran afoul of constitutional Article 13 (and its prohibition of special tribunals). The legislation charged the labor department with the interpretation and application of the proposed statute.

After disregarding his civilian advisers' proposed labor legislation in 1915, Carranza promulgated on August 1, 1916, a decree nearly suppressing any right to strike. Issued in reaction to the general strike called for July 31, in Mexico City, which threatened to cut off all electrical power to the metropolitan area, the first chief based his actions on Juárez's law that applied the death penalty to treasonous actions, the Law of January 25, 1862. Carranza had the leadership of the strike arrested and tried by a military council. It acquitted the strike leaders. Again Carranza ordered them detained, and a second military council tried them, with the same outcome, although it sentenced one leader to death; he was eventually released from prison, in 1918.[66]

The general strike, although potentially crippling, had been peaceful, its purpose to secure wage increases and protest the spiraling inflation and relative devaluation of wages resulting from the government's issuance of paper currency. Carranza's order, if grudgingly acknowledging the possibility of strikes occurring, asserted that they became illicit the moment they not only pressured the affected employer but also directly prejudiced society.[67] Carranza's decree referred to the strikers' disrespect for the government's currency and denounced the workers as anti-patriotic. Supposedly they had carried out the strike in collusion with the state's enemies who wanted to undermine the government's security; among other things, the strike had allegedly disrupted the production of munitions while the Constitutionalists still were reestablishing order. The first chief therefore commanded that the death penalty would be applied not only to those causing a disruption of order as signaled by Juarez's Law but also to those who "incited the suspension of work in factories or enterprises providing public services" and almost all other workers who knowingly adhered to the suspension. The decree covered physical and property destruction, as well as the use of force and threats to impede workers who tried to continue working. It charged the military authority with trying cases arising from such strikes.[68] Apparently, for Carranza, Article 925 of the penal code was not an adequate deterrent against the mass strike.

THE CONSTITUTIONAL CONGRESS'S DEBATES TO ESTABLISH LABOR RIGHTS

Less than two months after repressing the August general strike, Carranza scheduled elections for a constitutional convention to meet between

November 20, 1916, and January 31, 1917. Carranza and the Constitutionalists, still fighting Villistas and Zapatistas but now the dominant force in the country, had concluded that the 1857 constitution needed amendment. As noted, many Constitutionalist generals, including crucially Obregón, championed social reform, and Constitutionalist propagandists close to Carranza like Palavicini had argued that this was a major objective of the revolution since 1915. Carranza, moreover, needed to legitimize his future presidency in a reestablished national state and wished to strengthen the president's legal powers, which were relatively weak in the 1857 charter. Formal amendment of the constitution was therefore prudent. Constitutionalist military commanders across most of the country were able to hold elections for the convention's delegates successfully on October 22, and the convention opened in Querétaro on November 20, 1916.[69]

The delegates or deputies largely identified with the interests of Carranza or the Constitutionalist generals, if they were strongly committed.[70] Carranza probably expected that his civilian advisers, the renovadores, would dominate the convention. Many of the deputies, disdaining their close links to Carranza and ostensibly their congressional service initially under Huerta's regime, balked at their machinations and pretensions and rallied around their opponents, sometimes labeled jacobins and probably inspired at least partly by (the never present) Obregón. The renovadores lost control of a key constitutional commission at the congress and, after losing a major contest over the extent of permissible religious education, compromised on such social issues as labor rights.[71] The congressional debates themselves indicate a division between Carranza's legal advisers (many of the principal renovadores were lawyers) and the deputies who first expressed the need for more constitutional protections for labor. Still, despite personal animosities, ideological differences at the convention were not as significant as once reported.[72] The deputies who expressed themselves on the labor question mostly shared an ideological view about workers' rights, consistent with the military commanders' 1914–15 decrees and labor laws and not altogether inconsistent with the renovadores' social liberalism. In this context, it was possible for José Natividad Macías along with other Carrancistas to guide the constitutional debate toward the adoption of a program closer to their more legalistic views about industrial relations. They thereby avoided the more radical implications voiced by a few of the delegates and proved partly successful.

Carranza presented the constitutional congress with a draft charter that barely altered the labor-related provisions of the 1857 constitution. Similar to his January 29, 1915, decree and Zubarán's April 1915 project, the draft constitution gave the national Congress authority to legislate on labor matters. Carranza's inaugural speech suggested that the federal legislature would then be able to establish all of the institutions of social progress beneficial to the working class—and mentioned specifically a minimum salary, limiting the workday, employer liability for occupational accidents, and insurance for old age and illness. Carranza was silent on any right to organize or strike.[73] The constitutional commission of five delegates, all leftists according to E. V. Niemeyer, added a few items to Carranza's proposed Article 5, including a requirement of mandatory judicial service for lawyers and a directive to punish vagrancy.[74]

The addition of several protective measures at the end of the commission's version of Article 5—limiting the workday to eight hours, prohibiting night work for women and children, and prescribing a day of rest—resonated with the earlier decrees issued by Carranza's generals. The commission's report justified its measures as limits on the *libertad de trabajo* for the interests of future generations, to prevent the exhaustion and waste of humans caused by excessive, debilitating work.[75] The freedom of labor embodied in Article 4 now operated to defend employers' power to impose the contracts they wished on individual workers, instead of forbidding restrictions on workers' rights to quit work. These were the same justifications for the state's curtailment of the workday stated in Zubarán's project or the Ley de Cándido Aguilar.

The commission adopted its few labor protections on the initiative of Veracruz's delegates: Cándido Aguilar and Heriberto Jara, both generals, and Victorio Góngora, an engineer. Their draft had also proposed pay equity, compensation for occupational accidents and illnesses, and the resolution of conflicts between labor and business by conciliation and arbitration committees. The commission's report said the latter proposals should be deferred until the deputies discussed congressional powers.[76] This was consistent with Carranza's aim to delegate jurisdiction over labor law to subsequent federal legislatures.

Deputies or delegates critical of the failure to incorporate sufficient reforms into Article 5 doubted that any federal legislature would enact labor statutes and criticized jurists and the formal, legal viewpoint that deemed it inappropriate to include regulatory measures in a constitution. Jara complained of lawyers who argued that a constitution should not encompass legislative provisions.[77] Héctor Victoria, Yucatán deputy and self-identified worker, also criticized legal thought that precluded detailed regulation in the constitution, decrying the "perfidious labor in the detriment of public liberties carried out by academics, intellectuals and, in a word, the jurisconsults."[78] Victoria especially supported state arbitral tribunals to adjudicate labor disputes under state laws; he called for reforming Article 13 to facilitate the establishment of such far-reaching labor tribunals, a radical proposition.[79]

In the December 27 session, Carlos L. Gracidas, labor leader and Veracruz delegate, uttered a viewpoint as radical as Victoria's. Gracidas delivered an expansive reading of Article 5 that emphasized the rights of full consent and just compensation, equating these with the ideals of the international labor movement and labor's struggle for the eight-hour workday and higher pay. Alluding to labor conflicts in Veracruz, Gracidas contended that acceptance of the pay offered by employers did not amount to fair compensation because of a voluntary agreement.[80] For Gracidas, fair compensation under the constitution included profit sharing with the capitalist, and he linked the rights of full consent and fair compensation to the August general strike and its repression, reinforced by the amplification of the Law of 1862.[81] Gracidas's interpretation of Article 5 differed radically from its nineteenth century reading by liberals like José María Lozano, but it was still a plausible construction within a liberal framework—and it contributed to scuttling the Carrancista draft article.

In the face of the constitutional congress's rebuke of a parsimonious Article 5, the renovador deputies recalled that they had promoted social legislation and workers' rights since their congressional service in 1913.

Alfonso Cravioto, an intellectual and lawyer, introduced fellow lawyers José Natividad Macías and Luis Manuel Rojas, who had not only previously written labor legislation but also were mainly responsible for the writing of Carranza's draft constitution.[82] Cravioto asserted that the renovadores, as progressives, had developed a position between liberalism and socialism. The labor norms Carranza and Macías embraced had not been crystallized into constitutional reforms because they were regulatory. Cravioto concurred with an earlier proposal to withdraw all amendments to Article 5, in order to formulate a chapter in the text dedicated to labor, acknowledging the deputies' preference for the inclusion of more regulatory provisions in the constitution.[83] He effusively proclaimed that the Mexican convention would articulate the rights of workers as the French Revolution had established the rights of man. Cravioto conceded, however, that the renovators would accept keeping these measures in Article 5.[84]

Macías's tendentious speech then tried to persuade the assembly of Carranza's sympathy for labor and social legislation.[85] Although rhetorical, it was more programmatic than deputies' objections to alternative versions of Article 5 and encompassed practical ways to incorporate an extensive set of labor reforms into the constitution. It also presented a telling commentary on the state of legal thought on labor in Mexico at the end of 1916 and the legal issues implied in any legislative plan. Lecturing the deputies, Macías outlined the various laws that needed to be enacted to address the labor problem; these dealt with employment, accident compensation, insurance, and social welfare. He probably wished to underscore thereby the complexity of the necessary reforms; in any event, his enumeration reflects an early national appraisal of the elements that comprise labor law, the influence of European social legislation on the labor question, as well as a reiteration of his earlier draft projects.[86]

Macías devoted part of his address to explaining the significance of the novel administrative labor board of conciliation and arbitration, composed of industrialists and workers' representatives. It would function mainly to conciliate divergent labor and business interests relating to the wage rate, by calculating it in accord with relevant economic and equitable factors. He rejected the proposal of modifying Article 13 to configure labor organs as law courts: as tribunals they would be "more corrupt and harmful for workers than the courts that have existed in Mexico."[87] The lawyer deftly appealed to the animus against lawyers and the legal system of many deputies, who believed that courts were unsympathetic to workers and were excessively formalistic.[88] Tribunals applied the law, which prejudiced workers. Administrative bodies would operate with the consent of the parties, and conciliate the interests of the worker with capital.[89] Since most strikes resulted from wage disputes, Macías posited that administrative labor agencies could also channel and reconcile strike activity. He carefully avoided denying the right to strike altogether: his legislation recognized it as a "social-economic right."[90] The same labor agencies determining wage levels would regulate the strike.

Macías's conception of the social function of the collective labor contract was also ambitious. The union and employer would sign this agreement: "the individual worker disappeared, the personality of the worker was not considered, consequently the union committed itself to provide a certain number of workers daily, during the specified period of time, and it mattered little [who they were], provided they were able and could perform satisfactorily their labor." Macías thus suggested that through the implementation of collective contracts, conditions would be normalized: "in this manner the same salary, workday, and work would be obtained, and the worker's interests would be made entirely comparable with those of the employer, which would be impossible in a system of individual contracts." The individual worker would be free to abandon his work, too, without obligation to complete his contract. This would resolve the tension posed by Article 5, between the right of free labor and the requirement to fulfill a contract.[91] It was a point that had troubled liberals since the 1856–57 constitutional convention when Juan Morales Ayala had voiced his opposition to the article.[92]

Macías expanded on another issue, federalization of labor law. He claimed to have objected to the promulgation of Carranza's 1915 decree to have the national Congress legislate on labor matters, conceding that labor law should be enacted at the regional level, since working conditions varied across the country. Macías hardly defended the assignment of this power to the federal legislature by the draft constitution. Rather, he said that at his recommendation Carranza had agreed to let the constitutional deputies determine whether the states or the federal government should have the relevant jurisdiction.[93] Macías and Carranza clearly relented over the issue of the federal government controlling labor legislation. There was vocal opposition on the part of Yucatán's deputy Victoria to federal determination of labor reform.[94] Other states' delegations where labor legislation had been passed already, namely, in Veracruz and Sonora, or where there were strong labor movements, championed the inclusion of labor rights in the constitution but probably were wary of the federal legislature assuming control over the process of reform and possibly overturning state legislation. One quantitative study of the voting patterns of constitutional deputies found close correlations with left or jacobin positions, the delegations where the labor movement was strong or labor statutes were in effect, including Sonora, Veracruz, and Yucatán, and issues about the centralization of state authority.[95] Support for the states' jurisdiction over labor matters surely also followed from such governors' alliances with labor and the resulting power they wielded.[96] In any case, Macías never argued for federalization of labor law at the convention, insisting only that any constitutional directive to the states on what to legislate should not be inserted in Article 5, which dealt with individual rights; this would only be theoretically confusing and destructive and would not protect the working class.[97]

Upon concluding, Macías proposed that deputies gather with Pastor Rouaix to draft an alternative article outlining the principles for labor legislation.[98] The president of the constitutional commission, Francisco Múgica, defending its draft, said that the commission had found it too problematic to include a provision establishing the minimum wage, in view of regional variances in economic conditions throughout the country. The commission retained the same language of "just compensation and full consent" already in Article 5 without further elaboration, in view of the difficulty of defining these ideas, "which constituted until now the problem of socialism."[99] Otherwise, Múgica could not rebut Macías's arguments and program; and deputies postponed the vote on Article 5.[100]

In his personal retrospective, Pastor Rouaix, minister of development in 1916, describes how he, Macías, Rafael L. de los Ríos (a secretary in the Ministry of Development), and Lic. José Inocente Lugo, then the chief of the labor department (and not a constitutional deputy), formed a nuclear group that largely wrote the labor chapter in approximately ten days in early January 1917, as members of a committee designated by the commission and constitutional congress.[101] This nuclear group began its task by gleaning from Macías's legislative projects fundamental points in order to form a preliminary outline based on the questions raised in the constitutional debates. Additional recommendations made by deputies in the following days were refashioned and incorporated by Macías, Lugo, de los Ríos, and Rouaix at night. Macías mostly prepared the introduction to the group's draft. The deputies who attended most frequently and contributed most to the regular meetings of the group included Victorio Góngora, author of the first initiative to expand Article 5, Esteban B. Calderón (a PLM leader in Cananea in 1906), several colleagues of Rouaix who had collaborated with him in Durango, the workers Dionisio Zavala and Carlos L. Gracidas, and the lawyer Lic. Rafael Martínez de Escobar.[102] Rouaix confirmed the importance of Macías's early draft statutes as the basis for the committee's proposal, as well as Carranza's endorsement of Macías's work.[103]

On January 13, 1917, the debate over workers' rights resumed openly in the congress as Rouaix's group presented the new labor chapter and revised Article 5. The introductory statement to the proposal termed the constitutional bases of the new chapter, Article 123, economic.[104] Hence, they were not concerned with the type of individual rights articulated in the first articles of the constitution, such as in Article 5. The statement justified the proposed labor provisions by pointing to foreign examples, where social legislation supposedly had promoted industrial growth. Further, they would "fill the vacuum in the codes, defining exactly the nature of the labor contract, in order to maintain the desired equilibrium in the legal relations between workers and employers, subordinated to the moral interests of humanity in general and the nation in particular, demanded by the conservation of the species and the improvement of its culture under conditions of welfare and security."[105]

The Rouaix draft of Article 123 actually represented an attempt by the renovators to conserve the Carrancista objective of deferring the enactment of labor legislation to subsequent legislative bodies (if not the federal legislature), by compromising with the deputies in Querétaro who wanted the constitution to incorporate workers' rights. Carranza's civilian advisers accomplished their objective by outlining an extensive set of norms to which state legislatures would have to adhere when enacting labor statutes at some later time. Crucially, these social and economic norms would not be self-executing; that is, state legislatures would have to pass statutes to implement these norms; only then would they become enforceable law. The lawyers' argument for the separation of the section of the constitution that enumerated individual rights—which were self-executing—from those they termed social and economic (such as the right to strike) was certainly consistent with Macias's reading of social law and nineteenth-century legal liberal tenets. It was probably also reflective of Macías's and other Carrancista lawyers' reasonable belief that social legislation was a subsequent legal development, following chronologically after the recognition of fundamental individual rights, even while they embraced the reform agenda with its conceptualization of social relations, as adumbrated earlier by Pedro Dorado or Paul Pic, among others. But the legal perspective of Carranza's civilian adherents also had a strategic component, and the draft of Article 123 presented by Rouaix would not have guaranteed workers' collective rights to the extent that the constitution affirmed individual rights.

In any event, the constitutional commission over which Múgica presided amended the Rouaix-Macías draft in a few important ways. It added a transitory article, which allowed for the self-execution of the principles outlined in Article 123, in the absence of state legislation, thereby blunting the thrust of Macías's circumscription of social rights.[106] It similarly strengthened the right to strike by narrowly delineating what could be defined as an illicit strike; otherwise, the Rouaix draft would have limited the right to the pursuit of an equilibrium between capital and labor. It also added a provision establishing the right of workers to share in businesses' profits; and, not least, it tightened the mandate requiring the states to enact labor statutes.[107] That Rouaix's draft was more conservative than the commission's revision of it, which became Article 123, is patent.[108] Deputies finally passed the constitutional commission's revised

Articles 5 and 123 in the second session of January 23, 1917, unanimously.[109] Carranza signed the constitution on January 31; it was promulgated, with the labor articles, on February 5, 1917.

THE CONSTITUTIONAL ESTABLISHMENT AND LIMITATION OF LABOR RIGHTS: ARTICLE 123

Perceived and frequently lauded as representing a progressive, even transcendental, development in law by contemporaries and scholars, Article 123 did accord a constitutional status to numerous demands that workers' movements had made during the preceding ten years, some of the social reform initiatives that had remained unrealized, and revolutionary military decrees.[110] But the multiple provisions of the chapter or title that comprise the article hardly amounted to a transformation of law in themselves.[111] Article 123 left the contractual employment relationship largely intact and did not replace it with a concept of a collective or social contract. The constitutional congress established the state's obligation to ensure the terms and conditions of employment. But Article 123 barely adumbrated the state institution that would regulate such standards; instead, it displaced the federal government from legally and comprehensively regulating industrial relations. As to Article 5, the new constitution largely reiterated the language of the 1857 charter; absent from its text was the draft proposal that would have punished vagrancy.

The provisions of Article 123 are articulated in thirty enumerated *fracciones* (or paragraphs).[112] The first ones largely incorporated the kinds of protective measures decreed by military commanders, and which the constitutional commission's draft of Article 5 had encompassed: the eight-hour work day, restrictions on night work, and on the labor of women and children. The fourth paragraph mandated a day of rest; the fifth restricted the work of pregnant women and guaranteed postpartum leave. These tutelary standards reflected general sentiments at the time, including not only those of social liberals, workers, and revolutionary generals but also those expressed in the encyclical *Rerum Novarum* and the PLM's program; yet neither social Catholic activists nor PLM leaders were present in Querétaro. One rail union did send a complete program of reform to the convention, to demand the eight-hour day, prohibition of child labor, retirement and accident benefits, affordable housing, the right to strike, and the creation of labor boards.[113] If Article 123 adopted some of these points, however, it was not because of the success of direct lobbying by the union.

Other provisions of the article afforded workers more legal protections. Paragraph VII announced the principle of equal pay, regardless of sex or nationality, thereby affirming Mexican workers' demands for equitable treatment vis-à-vis foreign workers. Paragraphs VIII, X, and XI dealt with wage compensation, including overtime pay. With these provisions, the state was assuming a larger, paternalist role but not a distinctly new one. Similarly, Paragraph XII, which obliged employers to provide housing at a minimal rent, in addition to other services, remained consistent within a paternalistic system already becoming evident in the last years of the Porfirian regime when the Chihuahua state government had passed a law for workers' housing, or even with Díaz's 1907 laudo that recognized workers' interests in their company-provided housing (however grudgingly).

More radical was the requirement of profit sharing with workers, directing state commissions to calculate the rate; this implied a redistribution of income, a new property interest, and a new, regulatory, state entity. Article 123 combined this requirement with the provisions for setting an adequate minimum wage, in the sixth and ninth paragraphs. The fourteenth paragraph made employers responsible for work-related accidents and occupational illnesses; the fifteenth instructed employers to adopt adequate health and safety standards to prevent accidents and organize production to guarantee to the maximum extent possible the health and lives of workers, consistent with the nature of the business. The possible implications of these requirements for businesses were profound; the mandated reorganization encroached on the presumed property rights of the business. But they were not altogether novel, as Porfirian governors had promulgated the first accident compensation and hygiene or safety laws.

Paragraph XVI guaranteed workers, like employers, the right of organization but with little elaboration. (The twenty-second paragraph did protect workers belonging to unions from discharge: the employer who dismissed a worker without a justified reason was obliged, at the election of the worker, to complete the contract or indemnify him with the sum of three months' salary.) Paragraph XVII declared that the laws would recognize as a right of workers and of employers the strike and lockout. Paragraph XVIII actually qualified the right to strike: "strikes shall be licit when they have as an objective the attainment of equilibrium between diverse factors of production, harmonizing the rights of labor with those of capital." The subsequent sentences instructed public service workers to give a ten-day notice to a board of conciliation and arbitration and exempted from the paragraph's entitlement workers in munitions factories. Paragraph XIX also qualified employers' right to lock out workers; it limited the lockout to instances where overproduction necessitated the suspension of work in order to maintain prices within the range of input costs and directed employers to obtain the prior approval of a board of conciliation and arbitration. These restrictions on the exercise of the lockout and strike created the potential for a substantial role of state regulation. Paragraphs XX and XXI, in addition to the ninth, also referred to boards of conciliation and arbitration. Paragraph XX directed the submission of labor conflicts to a tripartite board composed equally of labor and employer representatives plus one from the government. Paragraph XXI stipulated the consequences of disregarding a board determination.[114]

Several provisions aimed to outlaw peonage in agricultural labor and to end abusive practices present in factories during the Porfirian era, such as the retention of wages as fines, mandatory use of the company store, or an inhumane workday.[115] The 1917 constitution, in effect ratifying the decrees of military commanders that abolished peonage, superseded the free labor judgments of the Porfirian Supreme Court. But in 1917, after years of revolutionary civil war, these provisions against peonage hardly appeared central to Article 123. Other parts of the article either provided more protection to individual workers or aimed to promote institutions other than unions for the workers' welfare. The twenty-ninth paragraph stated that the establishment of social funds for old age and life insurance, the involuntary termination of work, accidents, and other similar ends was socially useful. The federal government, like every state government, should promote the organization of such institutional funds, to instill social security.[116]

Article 123's entitlements or benefits for workers seemingly lack an overall thematic structure. They do not embody a unified scheme or paradigm of social law or a revolution in property or contract rights, however influenced they were by legal trends since the late nineteenth and early twentieth century. One major early work in labor law explained the aggregate character of the article as partly the product of draftsmen who were not legally trained, seemingly disregarding the role played by Macías and others.[117] Another leading specialist of labor law in his seminal treatise *Derecho Mexicano del Trabajo*, first published in 1938, in order to fashion a coherent concept of Article 123, regrouped its various paragraphs under the categories of individual contracts of employment, international law, the collective organization of labor, social welfare, protection for the family of the worker, and governmental authorities (the conciliation and arbitration boards).[118] Only one of these categories dealt with the subjects of the law of labor organizations, collective agreements, and strikes. The deputies did not elaborate the concept of collective rights: Article 123 said nothing explicitly about the collective agreement, which was already then becoming the focal point of industrial relations and about which Macías had expounded provocatively. The successive paragraphs of Article 123, in part, evidently track the discussions that resulted in its eventual form.

LABOR LAW, 1917–1924, AND THE FEDERAL QUESTION

The constitution became effective May 1, 1917. Article 123 immediately signified the raising to a constitutional level many of the demands that labor had made during the preceding years: this was of symbolic and ideological importance and could serve to empower labor's ongoing struggles. But the constitutional article could not mean much in a legal and positive sense until states enacted implementing legislation. Between 1918 and 1928, states did pass more than ninety laws and decrees related to the constitutional article.[119] Application of labor laws did not necessarily follow from enactment, of course.[120] State enforcement of legislation to implement Article 123 depended on the relative strength of labor movements and their relationships with public authorities, including the states' governors.[121] At the same time, Carranza, lawful president after quickly held elections, remained hostile toward an assertive labor movement.

Two states that pioneered labor legislation after May 1917, Yucatán and Veracruz, had preconstitutional labor laws as well as governors allied with popular or labor movements. Yucatán's legislation created a state-dominated system with powerful labor tribunals.[122] Veracruz enacted more liberal labor legislation, which served as a model for most other state laws.[123] Promulgated in January 1918, the labor code resembled in form Zubarán's project.[124] Both laws as legislative conceptions of labor relations went further than Article 123. Still, in both laws the employment contract largely framed the regulation of industrial relations.

The Veracruz code required union registration with municipalities and prohibited unions from coercing workers to unionize, engaging in political or religious activity, or accepting into the organization agitators or individuals propagating "dissolvent ideas."[125] The provisions governing the strike only faintly echoed those of Article 123. Significantly, they defined the strike as the suspension of the employment contract and stipulated that the employer could not enter into new employment contracts while strikers' contracts were suspended. The code limited permissible objectives of a strike to contractual disputes and the support of licit strikes. Since the labor contract encompassed the entire employment relationship, the permissible strike objectives could be interpreted broadly. Or, since the contract by custom specified relevant conditions, it could serve to limit permissible strikes. Veracruz's law also procedurally conditioned the right to strike. Article 158 required that workers furnish their employer with a written set of demands and notify the municipal president. The statute contemplated the possibility of binding arbitration, detailing the institution of conciliation and arbitration boards, setting up both municipal boards of conciliation and a central board to arbitrate. It defined them as administrative authorities dependent on the executive power with a tripartite membership of labor, business, and government representatives.[126]

The economically and politically important federal district, namely, Mexico City, remained without any comprehensive labor statute. The Chamber of Deputies considered two bills providing compensation for work-related accidents in October 1918, and in 1919 the Chamber discussed another labor bill, modeled on Macías's earlier work.[127] The president hardly controlled the federal legislature.[128] Carranza's government by decree did establish the Ministry of Industry, Commerce, and Labor (Secretaría de Industria, Comercio y Trabajo, or SICT) in December 1917, which would intervene in labor disputes and attempt to regulate unions and employer associations, and under which the federal labor department would thereafter operate.[129] Labor boards were also instituted in the district by a decree in November 1917, which encompassed the regulation of the company lockout.[130]

Soon thereafter, in 1918, Carranza's labor department wrote legislation to relax the limits placed on the lockout and to restrict severely the right to strike.[131] The bill's exposition argued that Article 123 tacitly acknowledged the principle of arbitration. Linking the right to strike with the right to work, the exposition observed that all human rights had legal limits.[132] The bill subjected strike leaders to arrest for not furnishing advance notice of a strike to a board, reiterating this condition for strikes in strategic industries such as electrical power and railways. It prohibited a group's imposition of the strike on anyone, thereby providing a more repressive tool than the penal code's Article 925. In addition to fines and imprisonment, the draft legislation allowed for the dissolution of a union that ignored a decision of the arbitration tribunal.[133]

It does not appear that Caranza's labor department wrote legislation to subordinate the labor organization to the state, as had Yucatán or Macías's 1915 bills. Carranza did attempt unsuccessfully to dominate the labor movement when union leaders formed a national federation. After unions failed to establish a federation in March 1916 and again in October 1917, Gustavo Espinosa Mireles, the governor of the state of Coahuila and an ally of the president, sponsored a convention to meet in Saltillo in May 1918.[134] Carranza could not forge a strong relationship with the federation that emerged out of the convention, the CROM. The convention elected Luis N. Morones as its general secretary, and under his leadership, the CROM pursued politically feasible policies, termed "multiple action," to distinguish its strategy from the direct action of anarchists. It grew steadily, the major labor organization in Mexico City affiliating with it, as well as groups in the textile industry, especially in Orizaba. But the CROM's relationship with the federal government had deteriorated by 1919.[135]

In June 1919, the most powerful rival to Carranza, Obregón, announced his candidacy for the presidency. As mentioned earlier, in August 1919, CROM leaders signed secretly a pact with Obregón. The pact called for the creation of a separate ministry of labor, headed by somebody sympathetic to the CROM; and the legal recognition of the CROM as the representative of all labor groups in the country, in addition to the executive's promulgation of a labor statute once it had been passed, among other things.[136] In late October 1919, major strikes paralyzed the textile industry in Orizaba. Unions sought the closed shop. Textile manufacturers in the end had to accept the mediation of the new minister of the Secretariat of Industry, Commerce, and Labor, Plutarco Elías Calles, who favored the unions. The resulting collective contract acknowledged union control over hiring.[137] Calles resigned a few months later, in February 1920, but the violent shift of power from Carranza to Obregón that year augured well for organized labor and the CROM. Under Obregón's presidential administration, the CROM dominated the federal labor department, including, importantly, the section charged with the federal district's labor boards.[138]

Between 1920 and 1924, CROM union membership increased, as did initially the frequency of strikes, many of which ended in victories for organized labor.[139] The number of victories suggests a readjustment of management-labor relations. The incidence of strikes also indicates the difficulty of achieving any consensus with employers regarding the acceptable norms of industrial relations. Businesses accepted Article 123 very reluctantly. The National Confederation of Industrial Chambers (Confederación Nacional de Cámaras Industriales, or CONCAMIN), the major federation of industrialists that formed in December 1917 in part to present a united employer front against labor, openly opposed Article

123.[140] Collaboration between Veracruz's state governments and organized labor led employer groups such as CONCAMIN to advocate the federalization of labor law, which also would have created the opportunity to amend the substantive protections in the constitutional article.

When Veracruz's governor on two occasions, in July 1921 and June 1923, sided with labor and promulgated legislation that extended the benefits promised by Article 123, employer threats of lockouts and recourse to the federal judiciary for amparos to suspend the implementation of the state laws provoked political crises and confrontations between the president and governor. The conflict ultimately became entangled with the military rebellion nominally headed by Adolfo de la Huerta in December 1923. In the meantime, the labor and political struggles impressed the president with the need to federalize labor law.

A recalcitrant national Congress stymied presidential attempts to pass legislation. During his presidency, Obregón especially wished to replace Article 123's requirement of profit sharing with a social insurance program that would have been less invasive for businesses. His labor insurance law (Ley Sobre el Seguro Obrero), sent to Congress November 20, 1920, died there.[141] On July 5, 1921, the state legislature of Veracruz enacted the Law Regarding Participation in Profits or Ley Sobre Participación de Utilidades, known commonly as the Ley de Hambre (Hunger Law), which mandated profit sharing. Employers, arguing that the law infringed their individual rights and managerial prerogatives, immediately lobbied the state government to block its application and threatened to close their factories. Neither approach alone proved effective in stopping the legislation. Employers' filings of amparo actions to enjoin the application of the statute did stop its implementation. Obregón's support of the employer petitions, as evidenced by the endorsement of the Ministerio Público of the suspension of Veracruz's statute, may have been the determinative factor for the federal judiciary's stance against it.[142] In the meantime, Obregón himself pressed the governor to abrogate the law, in favor of his proposal for insurance.

While the federal judiciary granted amparos against the Veracruz law in August, in November the Puebla legislature also passed an extensive labor code with a provision for mandatory profit sharing. The

Puebla-centered employer federation, the CIM, threatened a lockout; again, the federal judiciary practically enjoined a labor statute.[143] Puebla's statute, coupled with Veracruz's, renewed employers' latent interest in the federalization of labor law. At the CONCAMIN's fourth convention in September 1921, the agenda called for national legislation.[144] Federalization also appealed to Obregón; in December 1921 he included a provision to federalize labor law in his project for insurance, amending an earlier bill. Congress overall remained intractable.[145]

Veracruz's labor conflicts over legislation again led to political and federal crises in the summer of 1923. In order to settle a series of strikes by a labor movement demanding employer coverage of workers' occupational and ordinary illnesses, the governor, Adalberto Tejeda, promulgated two decrees instructing employers to provide assistance.[146] This time Obregón was less supportive of the position of employers, who had argued that the state legislation went beyond Article 123. Apparently, Obregón communicated instructions to have agents of the Ministerio Público appeal any amparos granted by the federal judiciary in Veracruz.[147] Employers began filing amparo petitions in July, most of which the federal judge denied. In August two amparo orders were granted to a major employer, but appeals ensued.

The political situation for Obregón deteriorated in late summer and fall in Veracruz and throughout many regions in the country, as opposition grew to his presidential nominee, Calles, who was closely associated with Tejeda as well as the CROM. Under these circumstances, Obregón tried to calm labor in Veracruz and rein in Tejeda. Then, Veracruz's military chief, friendly with industrialists and hostile to Tejeda and the CROM, joined the uprising in December against Obregón and Calles. The CROM immediately rallied to the federal government. As the insurgency was contained in the following months, the balance in industrial relations shifted markedly toward labor and particularly the CROM.[148]

In June 1924, Veracruz completed the drafting of a comprehensive workers' compensation bill, the Ley Sobre Riesgos Profesionales (Law on Occupational Risks).[149] In July 1924, the federal executive prepared a bill to establish a national labor law, which aimed to resolve regional labor conflicts with their political ramifications, such as in Veracruz.[150] It proposed a constitutional amendment to make the national Congress exclusively responsible for labor law. It also would have replaced the Article 123 requirement of profit sharing with an alternative form of insurance, under the administration of the federal government and funded by a tax on employers.[151]

Obregón's draft address to the Chamber of Deputies, attached to the bill, and alluding to the recent crises in Veracruz, analyzed industrial relations and labor law since 1917. Obregón justified a more substantial role for the state as the crucial intermediary in labor relations, referring to the precepts of Article 123. These precepts signaled to the state "the unavoidable duty of seeking the social equilibrium based on the integral improvement of the country's working classes, creating a new legal order that protects a complete category of acts not regulated in our present law, as are the organization and development of the capitalist and working classes and all the activities of their life in relation and mutual interdependence."[152] Mentioning Carranza's constitutional proposal for the federalization of labor law, Obregón emphasized the economic necessity of having the same legal conditions for industrial and commercial development throughout the country; indeed, labor legislation was central to the production of wealth. The uniform industrial and commercial system adopted by the constitution was broken when each state legislated in labor matters, producing unequal conditions for industry and commerce as well as legislative competition. Furthermore, the subjects covered by Article 123 were nationally the largest social class, comprised of workers in industry, cities, and in the country. Obregón therefore proposed replacing Article 123's language that described what kinds of occupations were covered by the article with two terms, employer and worker (*patrono* and *trabajador*).[153]

Obregón lamented the actual state of labor law in relation to the achievements of workers in their struggles. Workers had obtained more through their own efforts than on account of the laws enacted by the states, many of which had not passed legislation yet. No legislation had realized satisfactorily the social reform pronounced in Article 123, and the laws most favorable to labor had not been implemented fully, "out of fear that the affected industries would migrate to states where dispositions more liberal for capitalism operated."[154] Obregón expected to have his draft project circulated through the press and Congress, to elicit commentary.[155] Too divided, Congress did not pass the proposed legislation.[156]

CONCLUSION

Article 123 might have been a remarkable achievement, but its significance in 1924 was partly symbolic and ideological: labor could invoke the article and legitimize its claims as constitutional, lawful, and just; but it was more difficult to apply a rule derived from the article or have it enforced. Insofar as Article 123 was a legal benchmark, its significance was more complex and problematic. Many of its provisions, such as those concerning the nature and powers of the boards of conciliation and arbitration, hence their social function and limits, were ambiguous or vague. The implication that Article 123 contemplated an expanded state was equivocal. The operation of labor boards necessitated a state more active in industrial relations. Yet if the boards' actions were dependent on the consent of interested parties, the power of the state in connection with their activity would be more questionable. And Article 123's delegation of jurisdiction of labor matters to the states actually functioned to weaken the federal government's power.

Obregón may have prevailed over regional authorities much of the time, such as Veracruz's governors or military commander in 1923–24; these outcomes, however, were not because Article 123 had granted him federal supremacy in labor relations. Article 123 would serve to legitimize a stronger central state eventually. This scarcely happened during Carranza's administration; and insofar as it occurred during Obregón's presidency, it was partly a consequence of his informal and intermittent alliance with the CROM and his political and military aptitude. By 1924, when Obregón proposed amending Article 123 to federalize labor law, he clearly was arguing for the necessity of the state to govern industrial relations nationally and for a stronger state, in the aftermath of severe political and social conflict in Veracruz (and to varying degrees in other states with labor movements close to powerful governors).[157] Carranza would have preferred to control from the federal seat of the presidency labor relations, too, but he had to relent on this point in Querétaro.

Article 123, indeed, was the product of a revolution whose outcome in 1917 was uneven and problematic. The provisions of the article reflected in a cumulative sense the struggles of labor movements since the Porfirian era (their "conquests") and revolutionary leaders' responses to them. The most insistent advocates for a detailed set of labor rights were precisely the delegates from states where governors (many also military commanders) collaborated with labor, such as in Veracruz and Yucatán, and had enacted labor legislation already. Politically, they preferred the federal government not to assume control of labor legislation. In the ensuing years, many of the same states continued to attempt to assert control over industrial relations. There would normally be a legal facet to the contests that occurred among the federal government, unions, employers, and the state governments, one articulated with reference to Article 123.

The language of Article 123, however, was the product not only of the revolution but also of the concepts associated with social and legal reform since the late nineteenth century, beginning with the affirmation of the freedom of labor, which had been central to the liberal discourse of labor rights during the Porfirian era. Article 123 ratified the rights of free labor—it essentially prohibited any form of peonage—but the labor chapter went further than a recapitulation of nineteenth century liberal rights. For example, its eighteenth paragraph permitted the strike if its objective was to obtain equilibrium between the factors of production and harmonize rights between capital and labor. This language resembled some of Prieto's liberal vocabulary in 1875 predicated on political economic theory yet it was closer to later social reformers' premises about the organic, interrelated nature of society. The eighteenth paragraph actually embodied Macías's concept of a social economic right, which was clearly influenced by notions of social legislation. The constitutional convention had distinguished the right to strike from an individual right, qualified it, and envisioned its regulation by administrative organs. The right to strike was no longer justified as an expression of the freedom of labor or as the worker's exercise of a property interest, ideas that had also influenced

Prieto's discourse and that of other nineteenth century liberals. New social legislation—as well as jurisprudencia—would elaborate the nuances of any rights associated with the strike. Much of this elaboration would be articulated by the administrative boards that Article 123 simply referenced, and which were a central element both of social-legal thought and the Mexican state's efforts to institutionalize its role in industrial relations, as of the establishment of the labor department in 1911.

Neither state nor federal administrative organs, however, were in a legal or constitutional position to interpret or implement adequately and nationally the principles of Article 123 and related norms. And in this period, the federal legislature proved incapable of passing national legislation that might have accomplished such a task. Indeed, the one federal power or branch that was in a legitimate position to address constitutional questions related to labor was presumably the weakest one, the federal judiciary. Nonetheless, its consideration of the legality of state laws and administrative labor boards and, later, federal experiments short of constitutional amendment and national legislation would lead to the outcome that federal and labor issues would be articulated in legal and constitutional language.

CHAPTER 6

The Supreme Court and Labor Law, 1917–1924

INTRODUCTION

On March 5, 1918, a strike of 7,000 to 15,000 workers in the textile industry began in Puebla when negotiations over wages broke down.[1] The governor attempted to mediate a solution, but employers and workers were intransigent. The industrialists refused to raise wages more than 60 percent above the 1912 level, and workers insisted on a minimum increase of 80 percent.[2] The strike spread. In the city of Puebla, striking workers demanded legislation to implement Article 123.[3] The governor spoke to some of the demonstrators, assuring them of his sympathy and of their right to strike.[4] The same day a commission of state legislators met with strikers to discuss passing a supportive law; on March 7, the state congress passed a statute directing the establishment of special commissions to set a minimum wage not less than the 80 percent increase demanded by workers and also to provide for profit sharing.[5]

Puebla's textile industrialists denounced the March 7 law as unconstitutional and turned to the federal judiciary for relief.[6] They filed amparo petitions, and on March 15, the federal district judge in Puebla suspended implementation of the new statute. The state legislature appealed the suspension to the Supreme Court.[7] In the suspension proceedings of Hijos de Ángel Díaz Rubín, a major industrial crisis, which had assumed political and constitutional proportions, confronted the justices. Since the Court had been reestablished only recently under the new constitution, it had published few opinions concerning labor law. The judge's suspension of Puebla's labor statute in this case had a larger impact than any single dispute yet heard by the Court. It resolved this litigation in narrow, procedural terms against labor.

The justices openly divided on whether to affirm the suspension order; only after several days of discussion in the Court's public conferences, on April 18, did they vote, 9–2, to affirm it. The justices faced an awkward procedural problem: the district judge had entered the order defectively; he had not specified which acts were to be suspended. As a general legal principle, an amparo action should not be used to declare state laws unconstitutional. The March 7 law had required employers to nominate representatives to the commissions (so that they could begin to determine wage and profit rates) and threatened sanctions if they did not. Industrialists chiefly objected to this requirement, complaining that the legislative mandate to raise the minimum wage by 80 percent contravened the provision of Article 123 that directed special commissions to set the minimum wage.[8] The legislature contended that the underlying amparo action was inappropriate (*improcedente*) because there were no pending actions in need of restraint. The Ministerio Público agreed with the legislature and recommended revoking the suspension order.[9]

The Court's judgment tersely rejected the argument of Puebla's legislature that since the underlying amparo was inappropriate, the suspension should not have been considered, but the justices themselves had debated the issue heatedly.[10] The opinion placed aside these doubts, emphasized the threat of fines if employers refused to name representatives, and deemed this threat irreparable.[11] The Court then analyzed whether the suspension would affect social and state interests as it was required to do so by the applicable legal standard.[12] It found there would be no such impact, notwithstanding the Ministerio Público's analysis, which posited that laws should carry out socially beneficial wealth distribution and help to consolidate the state. The Court based its analysis on the liberal principle that laws should protect individual rights, and laws indirectly affecting society could be suspended without prejudice to societal interests. More specifically, the Court declared that the Pueblan labor law of March 7 regulated only the employment contract, in relation to a specific social class, hence did not prejudice all of society or the state.[13] One of the dissenting justices, Alberto González, disagreed with the majority opinion and argued that society was represented by the many striking workers in Puebla and the governor. The social interest workers embodied should not be disregarded because of their indigence or humbleness; nor should the state interest as embodied in the governor be rejected.[14] González, however, could not persuade the majority. He and José María

Truchuelo voted against affirming the suspension order.[15] Both had been constitutional deputies in Querétaro.

That almost all of the briefs came from employers disquieted González. Their absence in support of labor's interests indicated workers lack of legal counsel, which led González to urge the justices to articulate their reasoning carefully.[16] But workers did not lack legal representation altogether: *Excélsior* published on April 4 an interview with Lic. Sánchez Ponton, whom the conservative Mexico City newspaper described as the authorized representative of the Sindicatos Obreros de Puebla.[17] Two weeks before the Court ruled, Sánchez Ponton had articulated a legal analysis for labor: the Pueblan legislation was lawful; it merely implemented Article 123's directive to establish special commissions to determine the minimum wage and profits to be shared.[18] The substantive question of the constitutionality of the law may have been important in the abstract, and Sánchez, like the justices, referred to it. But the immediate, pressing question was a procedural one and remained whether the action for an amparo, and more specifically a suspension order, was even cognizable. Sánchez, like González, thought the suspension was inappropriate. There had not been a violation of any constitutional right. The industrialists were in effect challenging the constitutionality of the decree, for which the procedure referred to in Article 105 of the constitution was more appropriate than an amparo action.[19]

The Court disregarded these legal arguments. To cure the federal judge's overly broad order, which had entailed ruling against the legislature, when it was not clear whether the lawmakers had done anything outside of their constitutional power to legislate, the Court narrowed it to a suspension of the law's requirement to name representatives.

The justices thereby resolved the appeal from the suspension order. They did not solve the labor conflict so directly. At the time the Court reached its decision, workers in the city of Puebla persuaded the municipal president to try to arbitrate the labor dispute. Apparently nothing came of this. The Court's judgment provoked new threats of a general strike extending beyond the textile industry. On May 1, a demonstration was cruelly repressed. The governor distanced himself from the strikers. They sought the intervention of Carranza, who delegated responsibility for mediating a resolution to his minister of labor and industry. He in turn concluded that the labor dispute was, under the constitution, a problem for the state government. By May 28, factories began to readmit workers, without the wage increases sought, under police guard. On July 11, newspaper stories pronounced the end of the strike.[20]

The Supreme Court's evaluation of Puebla's statute in the context of a major labor conflict is astounding. During the Porfirian era, the federal judiciary never overtly intervened in a major industrial dispute, much less did it overrule and set aside, in effect, a labor statute. The Court's involvement in labor legislation after 1917 represents a novel development for the federal judiciary as well as for the evolution of labor law. That such involvement proceeded largely through amparo litigation is itself noteworthy, in view of the strictures against the general applicability of amparo orders. Yet under the 1917 constitution, the federal courts would repeatedly grant amparos or issue orders suspending (that is, enjoining) the implementation of labor legislation or the actions of state labor authorities.

One may posit that the Court's justices, adhering to liberal tenets, were hostile to the insurgent and reformist labor movements and their championing of the norms incorporated in Article 123; or that the federal judiciary was subject to the will of the presidency. The latter point is actually more difficult to sustain, in view of the relative weakness of the federal executive in the period following the effective date of the new Court (June 1917), the nominating process for justices, and the nature of amparo litigation. Certainly, in a number of specific instances, one can conjecture that the presidency pressured the high court to reach determinations it favored. Thus, in another large-scale labor and political crisis discussed in Chapter 5 and analyzed below, Obregón publically through the Ministerio Público (and perhaps privately, too) exerted pressure on the Court to enjoin application of Veracruz's Ley de Hambre between 1921 and 1923.

Political, including executive, pressures certainly affected judicial decision making. The process, however, was complex and not simply a system of hierarchical ordering from the presidency down to judges.

Contemporaries critical of the high court's positions against organized labor recognized this: Lombardo Toledano criticized, in 1926, the Court for adhering to nineteenth-century liberal principles adverse to the evolving labor law and the union movement that promoted it; General Salvador Alvarado, the radical governor who had initiated social reforms in Yucatán, made comparable comments in 1919.[21] Neither suggested, however, that the federal executive must have directly determined the Court's adjudication of cases; political factors had normally conditioned the judicial process differently.

The case-by-case decision making of the federal judiciary between 1917 and 1924 that, most importantly, considered the nature of administrative labor boards was a function not only of political but also of legal processes. Generally, the cases that the high court reviewed involved mostly individuals; still, the litigation produced incessant pressure. Whether the Court ultimately would define, in particular, the legal import of the decisions of the boards of conciliation and arbitration would depend on the persistence of board actions, which in turn depended first on the growth of the organized labor movement that resorted to the boards for resolution of workers' disputes with their employers, and second on employers who appealed board resolutions to the federal judiciary in the absence of other responsive political institutions. These, too, were the social and political factors affecting the legal process. Conversely, legal processes would shape industrial relations. The federal judiciary's initial refusal to recognize the administrative boards' application of new labor norms tended to delay the development of labor law. At the same time, the turn to the courts also meant that employers and employees were continually framing their conflicts in accord with different legal principles, encompassing nineteenth-century liberal ones predicated on individual rights and newer ones associated with notions of social legislation. Procedurally, petitioners and respondents had to consider their problems in terms of litigation before various forums. Judicialization and the legalization of industrial relations resulted.[22]

The Supreme Court's case-by-case approach to the status of the boards of conciliation and arbitration was, in sum, both politically and legally significant in several respects. Labor boards were the principal day-to-day state agency for the application of labor law. They were in the position to make law by resolving disputes or ratifying outcomes, which included the signing of collective contracts. If the determinations of such labor boards lacked legal effect (because of the Court's refusal to recognize that they were legally enforceable), then the boards—which were government institutions—could be disregarded to a certain extent. Further, while labor statutes throughout the 1920s were products of the state legislatures, it was through the Court's final judgments regarding such statutes that the federal legal imprimatur was made. In specific instances, the president or a federal ministry might intervene and arbitrate a major conflict. But it remained by its nature an ad hoc resolution. Even when a Court's judgment technically had applicability only to the immediate case before it, because of the form of legal decision making—written statements of law, with expectations of their consistency and uniformity—the federal judiciary's role in the construction of the legitimacy of the administrative labor boards tended to matter.

This chapter reviews the Supreme Court's adjudication of labor cases between 1917 and 1924. It argues that the Court's political stances, insofar as they were shaped by external political determinants, were more generally affected by the changing membership of the high bench but that in any event the Court's own decision making in an institutional context of litigation contributed to the form and determination of its judgments. Politics and law intertwined. The chapter accordingly considers the process of nominating justices and the especially important course of development around the question of the nature of the boards of conciliation and arbitration. It begins with an examination of judicial determinations of the constitutionality of state statutes—where, as in the case of Hijos de Ángel Díaz Rubín, its role was extraordinary.

LEY DE HAMBRE

Veracruz's Ley de Hambre in July 1921 required employers to share their profits—retroactive to 1917. As mentioned in Chapter 5, employers immediately filed amparos to block the law's implementation. The federal court in Veracruz obliged. By one count, it granted 126 amparos on

August 11, 1921.[23] Nearly two years later, in April 1923, the high court affirmed the lower court's amparos in two published decisions.[24]

In the interim, the Supreme Court refused to ratify the district court's practical suspension of the Ley de Hambre.[25] Of course, when it heard the appeals from the suspension orders, on February 10, 1922, five entire months had lapsed since the federal district court had made its rulings. Some justices still wished to postpone deliberation of the matter, as employers wished, but the majority, in a vote of 8–2, chose to hear the appeals then. González said that the delay was prejudicing unions and prolonging the crisis; he referred to a similar situation in Puebla.[26]

The set of questions that the Court had to consider in the litigation was whether the acts complained of were sufficiently imminent and nearly irreparably prejudicial for the employers to warrant their suspension. The alleged concrete act was the formation of special commissions for the fixing of profit shares. The board of conciliation and arbitration was directing the summoning of employers, in order to have them prepare lists of representatives to form the commissions (workers would also join them). The process stalled at this stage, employers claiming that once the commissions were established, subsequent acts, infringing their rights, would follow.[27]

The federal judge had suspended implementation of the law with some support from the Ministerio Público. Others in the ministry opposed the suspension, believing that the complainants were not really harmed by the statute, the amparo was inappropriate or contrary to law, and state interests actually would be damaged because the law would effectuate the purposes of the constitution. Finally, justices proposed reversing the federal district court's suspension order but differed initially as to how to phrase the opinion: should it signal to employers that they could move again for a suspension order if any further act occurred, or would doing so amount to advice for one party?[28] González criticized adopting any language that would indicate officious judicial timidity and a desire by the Court to ameliorate the decision with hopeful language for the complainants. Employers with their lawyers would know about their right to renew their motions for relief. It was a point not lost on the

Court, in view of the language it was tending to adopt. Another justice persuasively commented that the Court's denial should not be justified on the basis that the suspension would prejudice the state's interest as the Ministerio Público advised. To recognize a prejudicial effect would foreclose the possibility of suspending any future action, because even if it were not too remote, it still would harm the state. This too apparently persuaded the justices, who voted 9–1 to deny the suspension on the narrower basis that the petition was premature. Only one justice would have granted the suspension request, finding a series of actions already initiated and about to culminate in the demand to inspect companies' accounting books. Although he conceded the social interest in the resolution of labor's problems, he stressed the constitution's protection of individual rights.[29]

More than a year passed before the Court finally ruled on the substantive matter of the amparos filed to prevent application of the Ley de Hambre. In Cervercería Moctezuma, S.A., the employer's complaint against Orizaba's municipal president and the state's central board of conciliation and arbitration alleged actions similar to those considered in the suspension proceedings. For the Court, these represented sufficient concrete acts warranting an amparo, if any of the company's rights thereby had been violated.[30] A transitory article of the statute requiring employers to share profits generated since February 5, 1917, that is, prior to the law's enactment, afforded the employer its winning arguments. Article 14 of the constitution prohibited among other things the retroactive application of a law. The central board countered that Article 123's establishment of the right of profit sharing belied the allegation that the state law was retroactive. The Court nevertheless held that the transitory article upset the company's rights to its profits in violation of Article 14. The date of the constitution failed to rescue Veracruz's legislation: Article 123 merely outlined the bases that states should follow when they enacted legislation. González alone dissented from granting the amparo.[31]

Two weeks after issuing its opinion in Cervercería Moctezuma, in essentially a companion case the Court applied the same rationale and holding in Cía. Agrícola Francesa.[32] The one notable difference in the two holdings was that in Cía. Agrícola Francesa the federal judge's amparo was modified to the extent that future acts alleged by the employer and enjoined by the judge, and notably the possibility of having to open the company's financial books in violation of the commercial code, were deemed too remote for the amparo and so were dismissed. González objected to the entry of the amparo; eight other justices endorsed it; while the vote to dismiss the remaining claims was carried by seven justices against two.[33]

The justices discussed the profit-sharing cases in conference on April 14 and 28, 1923.[34] They devoted more time to another companion case of Cervercería Moctezuma, Luz Bringas contra la Junta de Conciliación y Arbitraje de Veracruz y del Presidente Municipal de Orizaba, Ver., but the issues were the same.[35] All except González found that the transitory article was an unconstitutional, retroactive law. One justice, however, said that the Veracruz law would not have been unconstitutional had it not directed profit sharing to begin February 5, 1917. This certainly implied that the special commissions were constitutional. González concurred with this proposition, but he alone then inferred that the nomination of members to the commissions could not be the subject of an amparo action. It was pointed out that the Court recently had been considering actions in Puebla to suspend the requirement of naming employer representatives to administrative boards. These actions were distinguished. In the Pueblan cases, the boards would consider a myriad of disputes. In Veracruz, the commissions were charged solely with the calculation of profits since 1917.[36] This was as far as the Court would go: solely because the transitory article called for a retroactive application would it be found unconstitutional; the special commissions were constitutional.[37]

In contrast to Hijos de Ángel Díaz Rubín and the Veracruz cases, in Zorrilla y Miaja, the Supreme Court affirmed the federal judge's denial of an employer's request for a suspension of an award of the state of Oaxaca's Junta Central de Conciliación y Arbitraje.[38] The state board had ordered the company to pay each worker of a textile factory, Fábrica de Hilados y Tejidos, "La Soledad de Vista Hermosa," forty-five days' wages due to a shutdown stemming from overproduction. The opinion is noteworthy for its discussion of the historical relationship between law and society and its analysis of the standard for issuing a suspension order pending final review of the amparo, the same standard applicable in Hijos de Ángel Díaz Rubín but here interpreted radically differently. After outlining the standard of review, the opinion narrated a brief history of labor law, from a social perspective, noting that labor law had become a branch of public and constitutional law:

> It is a juridical axiom in modern science that law in its broadest sense follows the multiple and various phases of civilization, because, the product of social life, it is consecrated to regulate men's relations, relations that change with time and space. It can be affirmed, without breaking with the severity of a judicial decision, that the relations between capital and labor have experienced their juridical evolution, passing from slavery, raised to a social institution, to the regulation of the civil code . . . to private law, in order to reach the present moment . . . in which work is no longer a social force, within the economic conceptions of the epoch, but rather has been socialized in law, forming a part of the constitutive precepts of a people. Consequently, the juridical controversies between labor and capital, at least in our present constitutional structure, have passed from private law, in which the State and society are interested indirectly, to public law, as constitutional law is a branch of this, in which they have a direct interest.[39]

Labor law insofar as it implied determining the rights of business and workers would thus amount to constitutional and public law and not just the determination of private rights between the two parties. The opinion stretched farther, concluding that just about any strike or lockout would affect the tranquility of any region of the country where it occurred and social and state interests; therefore, the requested suspension order would be inappropriate.[40] Even though the opinion acknowledged that the denial of the suspension petition might prejudice the company's interests, it minimized their importance.[41] Seven justices voted to deny the suspension, while three dissented.[42]

In Ortiz Borbolla, the Court revisited the claims of an employer being required to name a representative to one of Puebla's newly constituted conciliation and arbitration boards, a result of Puebla's labor law effective December 2, 1921.[43] On this occasion, the Court reversed the amparo, finding most of the alleged constitutional violations to refer to future acts. It recognized that the requirement of naming a representative to the board was an actual, present event, for which there would be a fine for noncompliance. Now the Court held that this requirement could not violate the individual rights of the employer, since it was in accord with Article 123. Indeed the constitutional article required states to enact statutes to establish such boards. The reversal was unanimous, although only six justices voted to dismiss (*sobreseer*) the employer's remaining claims for being premature. Two, including González, would have denied the amparo on these claims.[44]

THE POLITICS OF LAW: THE NOMINATION OF JUSTICES

The successive renovation of the Supreme Court between May 1917 and July 1923 contributed to the shifts in its positions on labor matters, as reflected in the divergent opinions in the cases of Hijos de Ángel Díaz Rubín, Zorrilla y Miaja, and Ortiz Borbolla. In this period, the Congress elected three cohorts of justices, in accord with the 1917 constitution. With the purpose of introducing life terms for justices gradually, Article 94 prescribed that the first generation of justices would serve two years (1917–19) and the second generation four years (1919–23). As of 1923, the third generation elected would be removable only for misconduct. Article 96 directed Congress to elect justices by a majority vote of at least two thirds of both houses from a list of candidates named by state legislatures.[45] The official legislative record, the *Diario de los Debates*, and Mexico City periodicals indicate that either state legislatures or their delegations in the federal legislature named candidates whom the latter body as an electoral college then elected.[46]

The constitutional election of justices did not mean that the executive power was altogether uninfluential or that political factors were absent from the process. The first cohort of justices generally approximated the political views of Carranza, while the election of the last cohort under Obregón's presidency provoked a political crisis. Yet newspapers and even congressmen normally avoided discussions of the ideological positions of the judicial candidates, even when they were lambasting egregious politicking by deputies and senators. Elite views, as expressed between 1917 and 1924 in *Excélsior* and another major newspaper publishing in the capital, *El Universal*, attempted to separate legal from political discourse, including the politics surrounding the realization of the putative goals of the revolution. Legislators, including constitutional drafters, had written the law, and judges were supposed to apply it faithfully and carefully.

In its reports of the election of justices in May 1917, *Excélsior* thus emphasized that the major congressional blocs concurred on their criteria for selecting justices: they would consider only the honor and professional capacity of the candidates.[47] Congress had avoided nominating candidates pursuant to any political criterion. In the words of the newspaper:

> All the probable candidates appear to have kept their distance from the political conflict of the last few years, and, according to our informant, this will be the principal reason for their probable election, since in accord with the criterion of most members of the Congress, the Supreme Court justices should be upright men . . . who without preoccupying themselves with the course of politics dedicate themselves only to fulfilling the high duties that the esteemed office imposes on them.[48]

In a subsequent piece, the same newspaper acknowledged the existence of some debate, with some congressional members favoring candidates with values consonant with revolutionary principles: "the opinions are divided, as some argue in favor of men versed in law and completely honorable, even if they are not revolutionaries, and others ask as an essential requisite that they have worked for the people's cause." The congressional blocs agreed that the nominees should be of "an affiliation clearly liberal."[49]

As lawyers educated in law schools during the Porfirian era, the new justices had much in common.[50] Several had held midlevel positions in the Porfirian bureaucracy or had been law professors. But they were not drawn from the elite Porfirian legal establishment of Mexico City. Three had been constitutional delegates: Alberto M. González, José María Truchuelo (as mentioned), and Enrique Colunga. González and Truchuelo frequently dissented from the majority opinions in labor cases. During the constitutional convention, they had advocated for the popular election of justices, a radical-liberal position dating to the nineteenth century.

González had participated on the reporting committee of Article 123.[51] In contrast, Colunga had been a law associate of Fernando Lizardi, one of the major figures identified with the more conservative Carrancista wing of the constitutional convention. One might surmise, then, that many of the new justices were not apolitical. Neither were they military or popular leaders born of the revolution. Most surely shared much of the liberal and elitist culture of civilian officials, some of them also lawyers, who served the Carranza administration.

The election of new justices in May 1919 produced a cohort not very different from the first, in a congressional session that *Excélsior* described as "one of the most tormentous that has happened during this period."[52] By the middle of 1919, Carranza's influence in the Congress had dissipated substantially, as legislators rallied around the more popular Obregón, when he announced his presidential ambitions in June.[53] One legal scholar has suggested that by then the major congressional bloc had elected a cohort closer to the more progressive views of Obregón.[54] Lobbying occurred for judicial candidates by the Mexico City bar, which advocated unsuccessfully for at least one sitting justice, Victoriano Pimentel, who was renowned for his legal knowledge.[55] *Excélsior* reported how "propaganda flyers in favor of determinate candidates" were hung over the desks of congressmen on the day that elections were held in Congress.[56]

Legislators reelected González, whose labor sympathies by then had attracted publicity.[57] In contrast, some of the other new justices had held positions in the executive branch or evidently adhered to the more conservative politics of Carranza. Antonio Alcocer was head of the legal department of the Ministry of Industry, Commerce, and Labor at the time of his election. Benito Flores was originally from Coahuila, Carranza's home state, and had been in various public offices since the Porfirian era. *Excélsior* described him as a lawyer "of the principal capitalists and most renowned banking and industrial institutions of the Laguna [a region partly in the state of Coahuila]."[58] Ernesto Garza Pérez, then thirty-five years old and employed in the foreign ministry, had held a government position in Coahuila when Carranza was governor of the state. Reputedly he also had been a member of the PLM and had been jailed in

1903.[59] *Excélsior* reported that Patricio Sabido collaborated with Alvarado's radical project in Yucatán, figuring in the local agrarian commission and the Tribunal Revolucionario. Enrique Moreno, reelected to the high bench, had been a government secretary at the side of Calles during the preconstitutional period in Sonora. José María Mena enjoyed a "brilliant reputation" in Veracruz and at the time was president of the highest court of this state.[60]

The renewal of the Supreme Court in 1923 provoked a major political crisis in Congress, resulting in a rupture between the Senate and the Chamber of Deputies. New justices did not assume their positions until late July 1923, almost two months after the designated June 1 starting date. The dominant party in the lower house had tried to promote its list of candidates but was stymied by a group of sixteen dissident senators, who denied Congress the necessary quorum to elect nominees by absenting themselves from the joint sessions. President Obregón exercised limited power in the federal legislature by then; rather, the main political blocs dominated, the Partido Nacional Cooperatista (National Cooperative Party, PNC) in the Chamber of Deputies from January until the end of 1923.[61] Congress was able to elect a new generation of justices only after the Chamber reached a compromise with the dissident senators. The executive branch probably brokered the final terms of the compromise, which guaranteed the Senate the nomination of five justices, the Chamber designating six. This compromise required the PNC to withdraw a number of its proposed candidates.[62]

The periodicals *El Demócrata*, *Excélsior*, and *El Universal* condemned the PNC for its attempt to elect partisan lawyers to the high bench, as it had done at the end of 1922 in connection with the election of local judges in the federal district. But even the most acerbic accusations refrained from using language that explicitly denoted a candidate's political ideology. If senators and media accused the PNC of attempting to control the judicial branch, or of proposing candidates who were unqualified, they still did not fault or endorse candidates for their conservative or progressive positions. Likewise, Emilio Portes Gil, then president of the PNC bloc in the Chamber, had accused the dissident senators of being Partido Liberal Constitucionalista (Constitutional Liberal Party, PLC) obstructionists; what their politics meant in reference to policy went unspoken.[63]

In general, the new cohort of justices was somewhat younger than its predecessors but not overtly more ideological; the new justices had also graduated from law school during the Porfirian era. Clearly, all three cohorts more than other contemporaneous political groups had been formally educated in a nineteenth-century elite liberal system; but the justices in 1923 also assumed their seats on the bench six years after the constitution they were charged to uphold had gone into effect. Before their election, *El Universal* had opined that two justices, Leopoldo Estrada and Jesús Guzmán Vaca, were lawyers lacking the necessary experience. It faulted Gustavo Vicencio and Garza Pérez for having sat on the preceding, slighted high court. In comparison, the newspaper lauded Salvador Urbina, among others. Urbina was relatively young, thirty-eight at the time of his nomination, and had taught political economy and criminal law at the national law school, subjects associated with progressive developments and labor, that is, social law. *El Universal* wrote that Urbina was "illustrious, and of rare probity." The newspaper added that Ricardo B. Castro, then a senator, was "not a jurisconsult of great imagination, but did know the science of law; and his honorableness had not been placed in doubt."[64] These latter two would pronounce the strongest rationales for the reversal of the Court's jurisprudencia in 1924. The Chamber of Deputies had selected Castro as one of its candidates; the Senate, Urbina.[65]

THE EVOLUTION OF JURISPRUDENCIA AND THE CONCILIATION AND ARBITRATION BOARDS

As adumbrated in Chapter 5, Article 123 declared, in two paragraphs, the twentieth and twenty-first, that state bodies, the boards of conciliation and arbitration, should resolve conflicts between capital and labor.[66] Although the constitutional language suggested that boards were not law courts, it failed to specify the types of disputes that the boards should conciliate and arbitrate, such as collective or individual conflicts. Nor did the text of the article unequivocally establish the nature of the boards' decisions: were they to be arbitral determinations binding on the parties or advisory ones that could be disregarded? Constitutional delegates inconclusively had debated the nature of the boards, as discussed earlier. To recapitulate, one group of delegates, including Veracruz's, had urged the establishment of conciliatory mechanisms, using as a model its state's agencies. Yucatán's delegation, including Victoria, supported the creation of tribunals that would in effect form a labor court system, as had been established under the revolutionary government of his state. The language of these two paragraphs could be utilized to propound either model.

The twenty-first paragraph of Article 123 was especially ambiguous. One possible meaning was that the parties to litigation before a labor board could disregard its determination (and possibly be sanctioned for a maximum penalty, as the paragraph indicated). Or it could be interpreted to indicate that its awards were binding, and parties to it would suffer the full liability arising from a dispute, the worker's liability limited to the termination of his employment contract. The Supreme Court interpreted the paragraph both ways, over time.

Given the posture of most of the cases that reached the Court, it had to focus mostly on the status of the labor boards and the character of their determinations in light of their lawful authority. Under constitutional principles and the amparo procedure, it was difficult for the federal judiciary to consider other aspects of the labor law emerging in the states. Cases such as Hijos de Ángel Díaz Rubín or the amparos challenging the Ley de Hambre were atypical, and in any event decided normally in connection with procedural law. Still, labor law was quickly and practically phrased in constitutional terms, not only because of the provisions stipulated in Article 123 but also because of the amparo lawsuit. The nature of Article 123 had raised workers' demands to the level of constitutional right, but that necessitated implementation by employers, labor organizations, and different state bodies. At the same time, the scope of judicial review allowed the federal courts to exempt employers successfully petitioning for amparos from the awards of labor boards applying or fashioning the new labor law. An employer who sought to avoid a decision by a labor board normally asserted that such a decision was only advisory, not obligatory, and any attempt of the board to enforce its decision violated the employer's procedural rights guaranteed by Articles 14 and 16, which largely carried over from the 1857 constitution into 1917 text, and are described briefly in Chapter 1. Employees and unions rejoined with arguments that invoked the rights of Article 123 or referenced state labor statutes. Despite the federal judiciary's largely conservative role in industrial relations, at least until 1924, capitalists and workers thus began regularly to resort to legal language and judicial institutions. Both the recourse to the federal judiciary by employers who invoked their individual constitutional rights and a legal, labor-oriented culture ambivalent about the role of the judiciary tended, ironically, to promote the judicialization of industrial relations—while detaining the positive development (and effective implementation) of labor law.[67]

Outlining the evolution of the Supreme Court's case law between 1917 and 1924 in relation to the three successive cohorts of justices suggests several tentative conclusions. First, the nomination of justices influenced the direction of case law, but not in a simple manner. The first cohort who presided between 1917 and 1919 tended to interpret the text of Article 123 more formally and to view labor boards more suspiciously than would succeeding generations. A discernible change in relevant case law occurred in mid-1921, two years after the second cohort of justices had replaced the first; the marked reversal in case law happened in early 1924, several months after the third cohort had assumed office. Explaining the evolution of judge-made law still requires one to examine factors in addition to the renovation of the membership of the high bench. Clearly, the political and social environment between 1917 and 1924 had changed: by 1921, the federal judiciary had to consider amparo petitions of employers in a context of a labor movement that asserted its positions in various state and federal governmental agencies, including labor boards; moreover, organized labor had begun to articulate its interests through the then novel *derecho industrial* or labor law.[68] The Supreme Court, however, normally dealt with these changing social and political conditions only indirectly, case-by-case. This process was one in which the Court had to evaluate both earlier published opinions of decisions and precedents (jurisprudencia) and increasingly the practical consequences of its decisions. The actual process of judges deciding cases and rationalizing their judgments implicated legal doctrine and procedure.

Soon after it was reestablished in 1917, the federal judiciary began to entertain amparo petitions from employers in Yucatán. The state was among the first to enact a labor statute implementing Article 123, on July 28, 1917, and its radical leadership, first under Salvador Alvarado, from March 1915 to November 1917, and then under Carlos Castro Morales and Felipe Carrillo Puerto, pioneered the establishment of labor tribunals, from as early as 1915.[69] Carranza strongly opposed these innovations. As Carrillo Puerto publicly endorsed Obregón's presidential aspirations in mid-1919, the president authorized the repression of the socialist party that was under Carrillo's direction.[70]

The newly elected Supreme Court judges shared the federal executive's hostility toward the reformist experiments of the state government inYucatán. They consistently ruled against the Yucatán labor institutions in the amparos that reached the high tribunal. The cases resembled one another: administrative decisions supported managerial, supervisory, or skilled employees who had brought complaints against their companies over salaries accrued some time before the initiation of the action. If between 1917 and 1920, Yucatán's *juntas* resolved disputes concerning laborers, rural workers, or urban wage employees, the high court did not issue opinions about these matters. According to Gilbert Joseph, Alvarado's populist and social reforms did not initially result in the organization of rural workers.[71] The cases that the federal judiciary considered are consistent with this observation. Circumstances atypical of most labor situations—involving higher-status employees with individual, not collective, claims for relatively large sums owed for contracts fully executed—influenced the evolution of the case law between November 1917 and August 1918, when the Court made a definitive judgment that in large part remained the manifest federal law on labor institutions until February 1924.[72]

The Court consolidated its legal doctrine regarding labor boards when it granted an amparo to Lane Rincón Mines Incorporated in August 1918.[73] Although its ruling as jurisprudencia would remain dispositive until early 1924, it was not a unanimous decision, and the lower court judge, with the recommendation of the Ministerio Público, had denied the amparo requested against the central board of the state of Mexico, even fining the employer for filing a petition.[74] The solid legal bulwark against the administrative bodies had fissures from inception. Once again the original complainant was not a laborer but a supervisory or managerial employee, given his relatively high salary, while his claim was for past wages for the period between 1914 and 1916. Lane Rincón refused consistently to recognize the competency of the board to hear the employee's complaint.[75] Furthermore, there was no state legislation implementing the provisions of Article 123, which might have afforded some substantive legal authorization for the board's actions. The state of Mexico had merely enacted a law to regulate the boards of conciliation and arbitration in January 1918.[76] The Court consequently had several bases on which to grant the amparo, in view of its recent Yucatán trilogy. It also had a rationale, had it wished for one, for not granting the amparo and avoiding the matter, merely by accepting the lower court's ruling.

The Court preferred to write an opinion that nearly resembles a short treatise, by presenting a set of rationales to justify its amparo against the board, at least four of which continued thereafter to undergird similar rulings. First, the Court held that an amparo could be brought against a board resolution. It was not a trivial point to make. If board resolutions were merely conciliatory recommendations, as Yucatán cases had first suggested, then it was not evident that they needed to be enjoined, or could be, as two justices had reflected aloud in the conference discussing one such case. The opinion, however, did not explain its reasoning in these terms. Instead it discussed the status of the boards by referring to the classification made between public and private law (private parties sometimes agreed to arbitration). The Court surmised that resolutions of labor disputes by administrative boards were instances of public law decision making. Their decisions were subject to the amparo action.

Second, and most important for subsequent labor cases, the Court declared that the board lacked *imperio*, the power and legal authority that courts had to adjudge disputes with binding effect. The Court reasoned that in view of Article 123, the board was not a law court but a public law institution charged with the policy of avoiding large-scale social turmoil that was upsetting to public order and the organization of industry, turmoil that resulted from the sudden suspension of production by workers or employers. Third, pursuant to the twentieth paragraph of Article 123, the boards should consider only labor conflicts and not other matters stemming from the employment contract. Fourth, the opinion reiterated the interpretation from an earlier Yucatán case, that Article 123's twenty-first paragraph evidenced the intent of the constitutional drafters to limit the scope of the boards' review to existing contracts. The rationales of the opinion thus comprised a judgment consistent with earlier rulings, but the justices still differed among themselves about the nature of the boards. González voted against granting the amparo in a separate statement contending that amparos should not apply to board resolutions. Truchuelo dissented with González from the majority's amparo, because he believed that the boards did have the power to indemnify workers as the board's award had ordered.

If Lane Rincón represented a definitive judgment, it failed to quell altogether the trend of boards taking up worker and union complaints against employers. Although one labor scholar observed that "the boards were slow to get underway," in the next five years the federal judiciary had to continue to rule on employers' applications for relief from board rulings.[77] Some labor boards refused to assent to the judicial limitations imposed by the judgment in Lane Rincón and persisted in subjecting companies to administrative proceedings with arguably binding outcomes. In the face of employer appeals and such stubborn board activity, the Court's case law, while seemingly adhering to the rationales of Lane Rincón, began to give way point by point. Parties posed one issue after another in ongoing litigation. When workers were the original complainants in state administrative processes, their employee status could hardly be challenged successfully; still, companies tried to do so. Likewise, companies attempted to assert that Article 123 should apply only to large-scale conflicts; the Supreme Court rejected these contentions fairly easily. More troubling was the case of an individual worker recently discharged: did his or her claim relate to a completed employment contract outside the scope of board review as jurisprudencia suggested, since the matter concerned a completed or executed contract? And if the administrative bodies were lawful public institutions, charged with the hearing of employment contracts, in what sense were they not competent: what effect could their resolutions have if they lacked imperio?

Initially, at least before the Supreme Court's membership began to change, it appeared that the federal judiciary would be able to dispose of these questions consistently under Lane Rincón, even augment the legal bases for curbing board rulings in a series of amparos pleaded from only a few states. The Court remained especially adamant that the boards lacked any juridical capacity.[78] In the amparo of Martínez, the Court may have attained its most extreme stance, rejecting board pretensions to decide an employment dispute.[79] The opinion began its legal analysis with a flat statement that Yucatán's board had violated Article 13 of the constitution (prohibiting special courts for privileged individuals or entities).[80] González and another justice dissented from the majority of seven.[81]

Twelve days after deciding Martínez, however, the Court issued its ruling in Victoria y Anexas, S.A.[82] It, too, constituted a repudiation of the boards' capacity to adjudicate a labor matter, but the ruling did not apply Article 13. The Court merely held that the central board of the state of Mexico lacked imperio, its opinion reiterating language from Lane Rincón regarding the board's conciliatory function.[83] A bare majority of six justices voted for the amparo, which entailed reversing the federal judge's denial of the employer's petition. The board had tried to apply the commercial code, which both the mining company and justices deemed the province of the law courts and beyond the competence of a labor board. At the same time, the Court had concluded of Article 123 that it held that boards needed to perform a function in industrial relations, a point not denied by the opinion of Lane Rincón. The federal judiciary, even after Lane Rincón, remained unsure of what the boards should do.

TOWARD LA CORONA

As recounted, in June 1919 the composition of the Supreme Court changed.[84] New appointees to the high tribunal facilitated modifications of the case law, although the replacement of justices from the first to the second Court does not coincide neatly with the development of precedents, evidenced by the split decision in Victoria y Anexas. There was a more notable alteration in the Court's position toward labor boards only in June 1921. Why would there have been such a shift then? One can surmise that political conditions had continued to evolve: Carranza's government had given way to Obregón's more progressive and populist politics in May 1920, while organized labor had begun to exercise more influence in several states. Persistent amparo appeals from labor board actions required the justices to continue to rule on the nature of these state organs.

In any event, in the amparo of La Blanca y Anexas, S.A., both the federal judge and the high court denied the mining company's petition for relief from the award of the Junta Especial de Arbitraje de Pachuca, Hidalgo, which had ordered either the reinstatement of a worker or compensation in the sum of three months' wages.[85] The company had argued among other things that the board's actions violated Article 13. The federal judge had rejected this argument, reasoning that the same constitutional text had also directed the establishments of labor boards. The Court essentially agreed with the federal judge and rejected the notion that any activity of the boards entailed a violation of Article 13, in one passage stating that even if the boards were not tribunals, if the award itself conformed with Article 123, it would be justified and could not violate individual rights guaranteed by constitutional Articles 13, 14, and 16.[86] In this case, there was no account of a state agency attempting to enforce the award, so the mere declaration of it did not contradict the notion that compliance with the board's determination remained voluntary.

One year after deciding La Blanca y Anexas, the Court marked a clearer break with past case law, without overturning any rulings. In Las Dos Estrellas, another mining company asserted that a board to be set up under Michoacán's state labor code to hear the claims of four discharged workers would violate its rights under Articles 13 and 14.[87] It was by then a standard argument of employers: the boards were actually impermissible special tribunals in contravention of Article 13. But under the Michoacán labor law, the board would have been authorized only to make a determination; enforcement of it would proceed in a law court.[88] The Court rejected flatly the assertion that Article 13 could have been implicated by the board's decision making, even if it had acted as a special tribunal, which the opinion hastily qualified boards were not. The second cohort of justices thus refused to entertain the theory that the boards were unconstitutional special tribunals, one that the first had briefly adopted. But the ruling in Las Dos Estrellas still rested on the premise that the boards lacked the power to effectuate their determinations, which was in this case bolstered by the legal framework of the Michoacán labor code.

The justices found more problematic Las Dos Estrellas's invocation of jurisprudencia denying the boards the competency to hear disputes about terminated contracts, as the underlying dispute involved four ex-workers of the company. Rather than overturn its precedents, the Court found the four workers to have had existing employment contracts at the time they filed their complaints. To do so, it relied on the conditions necessary for termination under the Michoacán labor code. Only one of the parties, the employer, had sought to terminate the contract, and under the state code this was insufficient.[89] One justice in the public conference queried the state law's coherence and maintained that the contracts had been terminated consistent with the Court's precedents.[90] To apply prevalent case law in this case, however, would hinder the boards from even considering what Article 123 clearly encompassed. Doubting such limitations, delineated in earlier opinions, the Court now held that boards could hear most disputes arising between an employer and employee, citing La Blanca y Anexas.[91]

This highest federal tribunal, now composed by the second cohort of justices, was thus moving toward recognizing a larger role for the labor boards. The limit on boards only being able to hear disputes arising from contracts in force was not holding if Las Dos Estrellas and La Blanca acknowledged that most labor disputes were cognizable. Still, the Court continued to restrict boards to an advisory capacity.[92] If the award had been deemed mandatory and about to be executed, then the amparo would have been merited. For greater clarity, in an atypical move the Court proceeded to restate its ruling.[93] Only one justice dissented from the majority's denial of the amparo. González wrote a separate opinion, as did a colleague. In it, González focused on the need to recognize the authority of the administrative boards to decide labor cases adequately and insisted that acknowledging this would not violate Article 13.

González distinguished between unconstitutional special tribunals, which treated people differently and unequally, and courts with particular jurisdictions, of which the boards were basically an example. The latter maintained the liberal principle of equality before the law. González also rejected the emphasis on the notion of imperio. For him, jurisdiction was the crucial element of an authority charged with the capacity to resolve disputes.[94] González's opinion thus presented an alternative frame of legal analysis, one the Court was not ready to adopt.

Following its ruling in Las Dos Estrellas, the Court's judgments in connection with board resolutions were more divided. The Court continued to maintain that its set of earlier rulings about the competency of the boards to hear only existing contracts constituted controlling law. It granted the employer an amparo in the Texas Company of Mexico against Veracruz's central board in a narrow decision largely for procedural reasons.[95] The Court reaffirmed its case law that board decisions did not have the character of definitive legal judgments and were mere administrative resolutions. Narrow as the ruling was, and as settled as the opinion's language seemed, the vote split six to three, González with two other justices opposing the majority's amparo.[96] Similarly, the justices divided in another amparo decided on the same day. In Sansores, the employer, an estate owner, had appealed from a decision of the Yucatán Tribunal de Arbitraje to the federal district court.[97] A supervisor had complained to the state's board in April 1917 for unpaid wages accrued between August 1917 and March 1918. Justices again applied established case law in upbraiding the board for having acted outside of its competence. They reiterated the doctrine that the constitution restricted boards to resolving disputes arising from existing contracts. They thus affirmed the amparo granted by the district judge—but only by a margin of five to four.[98]

LA CORONA

On May 19, 1923, the Supreme Court ended its session, closing until July 27, when a new cohort of justices assumed its place on the bench. On January 24, 1924, they adjudicated the amparo of Díaz Ordaz. It was the first major appraisal of the legal authority of the juntas that the recently elected cohort made in a published opinion.[99] Did Díaz Ordaz represent a new stance of a new Court?[100] The opinion at first reading does not seem very remarkable. But it is another step toward the full legal recognition of the determinations of labor boards.[101] Not coincidentally, the case involved the central labor board of Veracruz, one of the more active and persistent at the time. As pointed out, and similar to Yucatán, Veracruz had been among the first states to enact labor legislation. Since 1917, the municipality of Orizaba in Veracruz had become a center of labor radicalism under the control of the CROM.[102] And in the early 1920s, the governor was advancing the state's increasingly powerful labor interests against various large industrialists operating there.

In this context, the case of Díaz Ordaz was an old one—the federal judge denied the petition for an amparo in 1918—and an odd one in that Veracruz's board had ruled against the employee's claim of wrongful discharge. The employee had requested the Court to set aside the board's award so that he could proceed into a state court. The Court refused. This is significant. Essentially the Court was ruling that the board's determination should be binding. Its rationale was based partly on the theory that the employee had consented to the board's decision. Normally employers indicated that they were not submitting to a board's jurisdiction; there was an awareness of the possible implications of tacitly agreeing to boards' processes. Nonetheless, generally administrative board decisions were not supposed to be binding. Now ten justices disdained undermining the board's competency, supposedly conceded by the parties.[103]

One week later the Court issued its seminal opinion, La Corona.[104] La Corona, an oil company, had filed an amparo petition with the federal court in Veracruz against an award of the state's central board declaring it liable under state law for the work-related injuries of a laborer. Consistent with the arguments of other employers in earlier cases, La Corona contended that the board had again defied controlling law and adjudged the matter as a court, arrogating to itself the status of a special tribunal, in violation of the company's constitutional rights. The federal judge had granted the amparo against the board due to the violation of Article 13, in December 1922. The Court overturned the amparo. Its opinion was broader than necessary: instead of dismissing the amparo petition, as Veracruz's board had requested on the basis of the petition being procedurally defective, the judgment denied it altogether. The high court unequivocally rejected the lower court's ruling that the boards were special tribunals in violation of Article 13: "Nothing more erroneous than this concept because the Boards of Conciliation and Arbitration are not special tribunals."[105] Different provisions in the same legal text, as a hermeneutic principle, had to be read together to create a consistent rule. From a more policy-oriented perspective, and reminiscent of González's earlier reasoning in dissenting opinions, the Court noted that tribunals with jurisdictions over specific subject matters already existed. The states had created them in the proper exercise of their authority to ensure more rapid justice. In this case, Veracruz's legislature had lawfully established the board. The Court concluded unanimously that its award had not violated the company's rights.[106]

The justices reviewed La Corona in their public conference on February 1, then went into a private, secret session.[107] Castro dominated much of the discussion during the public conference. He first tackled the issue of whether the board was a special tribunal violating Article 13. This it was not, he said emphatically: "A special tribunal establishes a privileged court of exception."[108] A second issue disposed of quickly was the fact that only one individual was involved in the dispute. Castro argued that individual disputes often expanded into group conflicts, and the two were intimately related.

The pivotal issue that the Court had to resolve remained: whether administrative boards should have the legal authority to make enforceable determinations, or did they have imperio? If they were not special tribunals, could their awards have binding effect? The company had relied on the standard reading of Article 123's twenty-first paragraph. Castro simply inverted the interpretation of this paragraph.[109] In doing so, the Court had to address its earlier jurisprudencia; Castro explicitly broke with precedents by distancing himself from the first Court that had formulated the basic rule that the boards lacked imperio:

In other decisions the Court did declare, immediately following upon the promulgation of our Constitution, in the first Court, from 1917 to 1919, that the Boards of Conciliation lacked *imperio*. The truth, for me, is very strange that that Supreme

Court that had just come out of the revolution and which was born from the same Constitution, just after its promulgation and which was composed in part by three constitutional deputies, came to declare that the Boards could not and should not have *imperio*.[110]

The Court would have to oveturn its controlling precedent, in order to implement the intent and policy of the constitution, according to Castro:

> The truth is that if the authority and *imperio* of the boards were denied . . . we would have to conclude that the constitutional congress did nothing to avoid the conflicts between capital and labor in the Mexican republic; but it appears that now our opinion changes in the sense of conceding their authority—and on my part the *imperio* of these boards.[111]

Although no justice explicitly refuted Castro's main point that the boards had imperio, two who had also sat on the earlier (second) Court, Gustavo Vicencio and Garza Pérez, objected to this conclusion and argued that since the judge's amparo had enjoined only the board's declaration of the award, which had not been enforced, they could overrule the judge, without addressing precedents interpreting Article 123.[112] Their argument failed to dissuade the Court.

La Corona and similar decisions upset employers and their lawyers.[113] A major association of businesses, the Confederation of Industrial Chambers (Confederación de Cámaras Industriales), organized one response in the middle of February, an essay-writing contest to examine—and criticize—the Supreme Court's new case law.[114] Prestigious jurists and intellectuals sympathetic to business interests presided over the contest: Miguel Macedo, director of the Escuela Libre de Derecho; Manuel Gómez Morin, director of the Escuela Nacional de Jurisprudencia; and Carlos Díaz Dufoo. The main legal theories presented by participants demonstrated that board awards could not be obligatory.

Narciso Bassols authored the prize-winning essay.[115] It distinguished the purposes of boards from those of courts largely on the basis of the constitutional debates that arguably reflected the intent of the drafters of Article 123. Bassols pointed out that the constitutional convention had rejected the idea that the boards should be tribunals. According to Bassols,

Macías had influenced the drafters of Article 123, endorsing the Veracruz proposal for conciliatory mechanisms against Yucatán's system of arbitration courts; and Paul Pic's classification in turn had influenced Macías, which Bassols argued distinguished the system of mandatory arbitration operating in New Zealand from those of conciliation in Belgium and the United States. New Zealand's arbitration tribunal had not served as a model for the Mexican boards; subsequently, the justices had not understood the distinctions among foreign models as it had fashioned the case law now under attack. As a solution to the current legal and institutional inadequacies, Bassols recommended the creation of labor courts to adjudicate individual conflicts and coexist alongside administrative boards.[116]

The Court responded to Bassols in its public conference on August 21, 1924, when in the case of Cía. de Tranvías, Luz y Fuerza de Puebla, S.A., it overturned the amparo that a federal judge had granted against Veracruz's board in 1919.[117] The case had involved a widow of a worker killed in an industrial accident. The published opinion consolidated the ruling in La Corona; contemporaries found it exemplary of the Court's new jurisprudencia.[118] The Court's ruling rested largely on policy and pragmatic grounds. The opinion justifies the binding power of board decisions by noting the contrary situation: workers would have to sue in law courts, even though the constitutional and statutory purposes for establishing the boards had been to afford labor an alternative to the dilatory procedures of the civil law system, ultimately in order to avoid social disturbances. The boards had to be, in effect, legitimate tribunals charged with resolving all questions related to the employment contract, whether concerning an individual or a group.[119]

During the conference, Urbina pointedly rebutted the criticisms that the Confederación de Cámaras Industriales and Bassols had leveled against his interpretation of the intentions of the constitutional delegates.[120] The disagreement between Urbina and Bassols hinged on how each contextualized Macías's statements regarding administrative boards. Where Bassols placed Macías's references in a framework about the dispute resolution mechanisms of foreign administrative agencies, Urbina tried to relate Macías's position more to the domestic evolution of the labor organization and the auspicious transformation of the employment contract.

According to Urbina, Macías had acknowledged the appearance of the union as an intermediary in the institution of the collective labor contract; and for him the union and the collective labor agreement were the fundamental premises of Article 123's provisions that directed the establishment of conciliation and arbitration boards.

Urbina further deflected Bassols's criticism of the shift in case law by stating the practical consequences of the Court's decisions. Justices had concluded that otherwise revolutionary, constitutional principles would be undermined and that what Macías had sought to avoid would occur: workers having to litigate in courts. The administrative boards had to function as tribunals, in fact, to resolve disputes in accord with principles of fairness and conscience, although they were not courts of law ("no son tribunales de derecho, sino de hecho").[121] Urbina even insinuated that the failure of the national Congress to legislate labor courts or reform the civil law had required the Court to intercede. But he stepped back from the radical assertion that the Supreme Court had enacted law.

The author of the opinion in Cía. de Tranvías, Luz y Fuerza, Manuel Padilla, also spoke in the conference and related his arguments closer to contemporaneous legal theories around the individual contract of employment. Padilla did not declare the advent of the new labor law of the union and collective agreement as boldly as Urbina. Disputes between individuals regarding their employment contract were definitely civil law issues, but Article 123 had assigned them to the labor boards. Padilla conceded that the boards' politicized nature, which he described graphically and which Urbina had abstracted, was unsatisfactory in practice but added, "we should not analyze nor do we have to analyze this point; it is a vice that probably with time will be corrected, as have others, such as when the Executive nominated judicial functionaries and removed them freely."[122]

CONCLUSION

The judicial resolution of the nature of labor boards in 1924 mattered in several respects. The actions of the boards at the time posed questions about the extent to which the state should regulate or structure industrial relations, in the face of the emergence of strong labor movements and unions, some of them close to factions of federal and state governing circles.[123] In institutional terms, the federal judiciary's adjudication of amparo petitions placed the courts in the position of either undermining or affirming the establishment and operation of the boards. In legal terms, the Supreme Court's belated acknowledgment of the boards' competency to preside over labor disputes contributed further to the judicialization of industrial relations—even as the decision of La Corona deferred to the boards' decision-making capacity. One reason for the establishment of the agencies, both detractors and proponents of them agreed, had been to provide workers an alternative forum for disputes with their employers. One might accept Urbina's formula that the boards should be "not tribunals of law rather of fact," but workers and employers would still present legal or quasi-legal arguments and counterarguments before the boards that cited norms and rules.[124] As mentioned, the constant appeal of board awards to the federal judiciary implied the regular framing of labor issues in the constitutional language of Article 123 and individual rights. The federal judiciary, having tried to deny the boards' legal authority for several years, nevertheless had considered perforce legal appeals about them and then sanctioned them as constitutionally and legally legitimate administrative bodies capable of adjudicating employment matters: industrial relations were thus judicialized at a formative moment in their evolution.

Around February 1, *Excélsior* did not carry a front-page story on the Court's seminal judgment. The military rebellion of Adolfo de la Huerta in Veracruz and elsewhere received front-page status.[125] The two events—a shift or reversal in the Court's jurisprudencia, the military rebellion affecting Veracruz as well as other regions in the country—of course have been linked. Contemporaries acclaimed or decried the Court's turnaround in 1924, and scholars since then have noted the reversal in case law in that year.[126] Legal treatises dutifully refer to the shift in jurisprudencia in 1924 but normally without any analysis of the evolution of doctrine occurring between 1917 and 1924, while historical scholarship has assumed, not implausibly, that the high court responded to political pressures, indeed that organized labor's support for Obregón's government led to the Court's change of direction.[127] The Court's judgment in La Corona does bear markings of a political decision. Garza Pérez and Vicencio were right: an alternative, narrower holding could have disposed of the case. And the justices went into a private, confidential session after the public conference: one can speculate about what they said. Castro's statement regarding how it appeared, in 1924, that the Court would revise its earlier case law can be read as connoting a degree of resignation or detachment in the face of a different social and political situation. Triumphantly, the new jurisprudencia was hailed later in 1924, in an expression of solidarity, by a more explicitly political body, the Cámara de Diputados.[128]

The judgments in La Corona and related amparos, however, were not only political but also legal decisions and comprised not so much a dramatic and capricious reversal in the Court's position as an impending development resulting from the pressure of persistent litigation and the case law that the Court fashioned in response. Castro also had mused that the decision of La Corona, in narrow, legal terms, was not as abruptly radical as it then seemed. Indeed, earlier decisions had already rejected legal arguments that attempted to strip boards of all authority or contended that they were impermissible special tribunals contravening Article 13. The Court in Las Dos Estrellas in June 1922 had not only expanded the types of workers' complaints boards could entertain, building on La Blanca; it also had approved of Michoacán's labor code's scheme for enforcing board awards, which directed how they should be presented to a tribunal. This was one step away from La Corona, even as the Court had hastened to add then that the boards did not have imperio. In addition, González's separate opinion in Las Dos Estrellas already had prefigured the eventual turn in the case law. And the case Díaz Ordaz held, in effect, that the board's decision was mandatory. The shift in case law arguably had begun even as early as 1919–21, as the second generation of justices replaced the first. As quoted, Castro himself had commented about the change in the composition of the Court from that of the first one, in 1918, to that of the one presiding in 1924.

Although it is definitely possible that Obregón reached an understanding with the Court about the need to recognize the authority of the boards, it also appears that the Court's decision making was affected by changes in its composition in July 1923.[129] As of the date the new judges joined the high court's bench, its position had become increasingly sympathetic to organized labor, as the August 1923 case of Gambú, for example, suggests. Gambú is noteworthy because the justices flatly rejected the employer's complaint that she had suffered harm from the requirement of having to name a representative to an administrative board—the kind of prejudice to an employer's interests that the Court had found only a few months previously in a set of decisions effectively nullifying the Ley de Hambre. In contrast to its final ruling on Veracruz's profit-sharing law, or Puebla's minimum wage law in 1918, the Court in Gambú revoked the order granted by Puebla's federal judge on January 12, 1922, which had suspended the formation of a central conciliation and arbitration board pursuant to the state's labor legislation.[130] The Court now held that the state interest was served by the implementation of the labor statute.[131] This was not such a novel interpretation of the balance of interests implicated in the review of a suspension order. Zorrilla y Miaja had already equated labor rights with the public interest. And in Ortiz Borbolla the Court had already upheld the requirement of Puebla's law that employers nominate representatives. The trend of the Court by 1922 (the year of the decisions in Zorrilla y Miaja and Ortiz Borbolla) was toward accepting the operation of administrative labor bodies. Gambú, however, was a simple, unequivocal decision reached unanimously by all eleven justices—and most were new to the Court.[132]

By 1924, the Court justified its rulings favoring labor or the boards' authority by reference to public policy, the historical and social realities of the time, and the consequences of its decisions. Its opinion in the case of Zorrilla y Miajas had sketched a historical progression in the law affecting industrial relations from private to public law. The opinion reiterated social-legal notions and the importance of the public interest. The 1924 opinions underscore the social and political purposes of the constitutional provision requiring that boards resolve employment disputes, although without disregarding the text of Article 123. The Court alludes to the consequences of not recognizing the boards' imperio. To reiterate,

Urbina tried to show how the labor boards had to reflect the social realities of the time: the labor movement and the law being created through collective contracts between unions and employers. The Court's evolving labor doctrine thus indicates a policy-oriented form of legal reasoning concerned with the objectives of reformist government programs and the conditions they addressed. The case law was shifting from a narrower, more formal kind of legal reasoning preferred by the first cohort of justices. The new jurisprudencia was more politically sensitive, regardless of whether it was the result of immediate political pressures.

In any event, jurisprudencia was in the first instance a product of the decisions of the Supreme Court's judges, whose views differed. Moreover, the justices' views varied more decisively as successive cohorts assumed their positions on the Court. Surely, the nominating process for justices and the composition of the Court had to encompass political considerations. Yet contemporary public opinion, indicative of the broader legal culture, as expressed in major newspapers or by public officials, tried to deny that policy-oriented or ideological factors should influence the justices' nomination.

One reason for establishing labor boards had been to circumvent the judicial system, which was seemingly unsympathetic to workers' needs. Such belief reflected not only a "revolutionary" animus against judges. It also assumed that an alternative forum was better suited to dealing with modern industrial problems[133]—this, because it was presumed that courts ideally applied the law narrowly, without reference to political criteria. In contrast, labor boards, as lay mediating bodies, could entertain nonlegal factors in their determinations, but pursuant to a legal-cultural tradition still evident in the early 1920s, they were not supposed to issue orders that could deprive parties of their rights: this was the prerogative and function of the law courts, applying the law correctly. The Court's decisions in 1924 holding the boards capable of issuing binding decisions in part eroded this conceptual separation between legal and political decision making, which had been breaking down through constant legal challenges and because of changing social and political circumstances. In the end, labor boards would become politicized courts in all but name.[134]

Already in 1924 the Court's case law regarding the authority of the labor boards reflected a growing politicization of adjudication, that is, a form of legal reasoning by the justices more concerned with the policy implications of their decisions. In this legal and political context, the further judicialization of industrial relations would contribute to the greater politicization of law.

CHAPTER 7

Labor Law and Supreme Court Decisions, 1925–1931

INTRODUCTION

After overturning the amparos in La Corona and Cía. de Tranvías, Luz y Fuerza de Puebla, the Supreme Court consistently held that labor boards had imperio, reversing amparos granted by federal judges before 1924 under prior jurisprudencia.[1] The federal judiciary finally would recognize the binding quality of board awards. Beyond 1925, few opinions even mentioned this issue. But litigants involved in board proceedings continued to appeal to the federal judiciary for relief from administrative actions. After 1924, much of the Court's case law on labor relations addresses the normative and practical limits of the administrative boards' decision-making authority. As now construed by the Court, Article 123 had charged conciliation and arbitration boards with the adjudication (and hence often the application) of workers' rights in the first instance. The institutional framework henceforth would be one in which the Court in the last instance set the parameters for the boards' decision making.

This framework was in part possible because of the absence of overarching federal legislation. As long as the national Congress could not enact labor laws (except for the federal district and territories), the state labor boards remained the chief agencies applying whatever legal norms existed in their respective jurisdictions, subject only to the amparo appeal procedure. The federal government attempted to expand its administrative reach in industrial relations both formally and informally after 1924, but its endeavors were constitutionally and legally suspect. It was consequentially an unstable system that began to emerge; it was one, however, in which the Court perforce had a significant position.

The Supreme Court was surely aware of its relatively weak position in an authoritarian, if fledgling, state, yet in a number of instances its rulings seemed to belie its political vulnerability. This chapter examines several important cases that the Court decided between 1925 and the enactment of comprehensive federal legislation in August 1931. The cases concern the Court's evaluation of the implications of the boards' newly legalized status and that of their decisions. They also reflect the justices' grappling with the developing labor law, to which their opinions were contributing, and the issues the new field of law posed, as they tried to integrate some of its disparate elements while organized labor was becoming a powerful actor. Some of the cases involve the authority of the federal executive as it established an industrial relations system during this period. It became imperative to solve within the framework of the federal system problems raised by economic activities spanning state boundaries, now subject to state administrative regulation through board decision making—especially when state boards contravened the interests of the centralizing, federal government or those of large businesses. A major labor conflict in 1925 in the oil industry in Minatitlán, Veracruz, again raised questions about the judiciary's role in the field of industrial relations, when the CROM was influential in the federal government. Then the 1926–27 railway workers' strikes challenged the administrative system of regulation, prompted the creation of the federal labor boards, and underscored the need for federal labor legislation.

This chapter focuses on these major conflicts that were judicialized, including the railway workers' strike of 1927, in which the Supreme Court found the executive branch's administrative reaction to it in violation of the constitution. It also reviews a case in which the Court queried the constitutionality of the system created by the federal executive to regulate the textile industry. In this period, 1925–31, the Court's opinions still contained references to principles of nineteenth-century liberal law (especially as to contractual notions or individual rights) as well as discussions of social law. The chapter analyzes judicial presumptions in Court opinions about the importance of the contract of employment, which sometimes were in tension with notions of collective interests, in addition to noting affirmative statements about the new labor law. The chapter's conclusion reiterates the point that in toto, as illustrated by the cases reviewed here, the Court's adjudication mattered for labor law, industrial relations, and the politics of the late 1920s.

Obregón was surely concerned about the Supreme Court's decision making and its relative autonomy. Among the major constitutional amendments that he had marshaled through the Congress as he anticipated returning to the presidency was one modifying the Court's structure. As earlier mentioned, one amendment added five justices to the bench and divided the high court into three chambers so that justices could specialize in different legal areas. This presumably would enable the Court to review amparos arising from labor board decisions more quickly, knowledgeably, and efficiently. As of December 1928, the president would select the justices, the Senate ratifying the nominations. Clearly this would augment the president's power over the justices. It was a reversal of the policy that constitutional delegates had instated, to distance the Court from the president's influence; and it actually resembled earlier proposals of the científicos during Diaz's rule. Furthermore, the amendment required that all current justices—who had lifetime tenure—resign in December, so that the incoming president, Obregón, could nominate a new cohort.[2]

Obregón's death in July 1928 probably prolonged the relative autonomy of the Supreme Court. Although the constitutional amendment passed in May 1928, the president who actually selected the new cohort in late December was Portes Gil, whose term was limited to one year. Calles was then trying to consolidate his informal power; he would emerge as the jefe maximo (chief boss or maximum chief). The period 1929–34 would be called the Maximato, as three presidents served during the six-year term, each of them to varying degrees vulnerable to the pressures exerted by the chief political boss. But it is doubtful that Calles was directly involved in the nomination of the justices. In his memoirs, Portes Gil said that he prepared the lists of eligible candidates and was proud of the names he proposed to the Senate: they were selected for their legal and professional qualifications, not for their politics or personal affiliations.[3] Whether Portes Gil was candid or not, *Excélsior* lauded his choices; it interviewed numerous prestigious lawyers, some of whom were clearly moderate or conservative in their political and ideological views, for example, Manuel Gómez Morin and José María Lozano. They also rhapsodized about the interim president's choices, declaring that the new justices were not necessarily the most distinguished jurists but that they were generally nonpolitical, honorable, and highly qualified, more so than the preceding generations.[4] The Senate quickly ratified the president's nominations, a move that was in contrast to the contentious congressional debates of 1923.[5]

It is difficult to discern whether the new justices (very few were reappointed from the preceding Court) or the division of the high bench into specialized chambers changed the orientation of the Court. The 1928 cohort of justices was clearly more sympathetic toward organized labor than was the first cohort of 1917, as evidenced by the shift in case law. An avowed critic of the CROM was responsible for the nominations to the 1928 Court. But at the time Portes Gil also leaned toward the left and labor apart from the CROM.[6] Meanwhile, Calles had distanced himself from the CROM and in September 1928, as noted earlier, declared his intention to steer the nation toward institutional and lawful rule. Amparo orders notoriously went unenforced in this period; but presidential preponderance over, or interference with, the decision making of the Court—by political accident (Obregón's death) as much as by political circumstance (Calles's informal status as the ultimate wielder of power)—was less pronounced than after 1934, with the exception of a few notorious cases. By 1931, the Court may have enjoyed some approval from organized labor.[7] These political conditions, however, hardly ensured either a rule of law regime or a Supreme Court able to apply the law consistently and fashion it systematically.

THE LEGITIMATION OF THE BOARDS OF CONCILIATION AND ARBITRATION

After 1924, Supreme Court decisions bolstered the state administrative and quasi-adjudicatory activities restrained or nullified previously, including not only the enforcement of awards but also, for example, the convening of local boards and administrative commissions. In 1925, the Court rejected numerous appeals by Pueblan employers for relief from the state's requirement that they nominate representatives to such bodies. In Vega, the Court held that Article 123 called for the naming of representatives to the boards.[8] A notice to nominate did not violate an individual's rights; and allegations regarding the unconstitutionality of the labor statute, or what the administrative board might do in violation of the petitioner's rights, were premature. An amparo against a law would be issued only if the law had begun to be implemented.[9] Two weeks later, in Villar, the Court overturned an amparo.[10] The governor, in response to the employer's petition, had suggested that the requirement of nominating representatives to the boards was a right conferred on capital and labor. The justices disagreed, holding flatly that it was an obligation mandated by Article 123, hence a legal requirement that could not violate any right of the employer.[11] In Vélez, the Court rejected the employer's argument that Puebla's labor statute was unconstitutional.[12] The opinion cited Hijos de Ángel Díaz Rubín for the proposition that in such a case an amparo was appropriate only if it mandated the petitioner to do something immediately.

More judgments rebuking employers' avoidance of labor laws or board decisions followed.[13] In an 8–2 vote, justices overturned the amparo in Tomás Ruiz y Cía., which had been granted to stop profit sharing under Veracruz's Ley de Hambre.[14] No mention was made of the Court's earlier amparos predicated on the theory that the law was retroactive. On this occasion the Court found the employer's argument speculative. The Court also dismissed an amparo to stop the determination of Chihuahua's minimum wage, since the mere promulgation of a provision could not prejudice anybody.[15] Nor could a board declaring its competence,[16] or requiring a party to submit to its jurisdiction, harm an employer.[17] Parties, too, should address their differences to a labor board before petitioning the federal judiciary for an amparo.[18] A number of published opinions held that the petitioner had consented to the board's competency and hence should not raise this issue.[19]

THE SUSPENSION OF BOARD AWARDS

Ruling that board awards were binding sharpened the issue of whether courts might still order the suspension of the execution of an award as part of the routine amparo procedure. Employers had of course already effectively used this temporary remedy. The case of Hijos de Ángel Díaz

Rubín and the challenges to the Ley de Hambre initially reached the Supreme Court as appeals from suspension orders issued by lower court judges. If the federal judiciary normally ordered a board to suspend its enforcement of a decision, board determinations would again become ineffective. Even if the Court eventually rejected an employer's amparo petition, the postponement of the execution of the award could render the initial administrative ruling largely meaningless when workers normally lacked the resources to litigate indefinitely or survive in the meantime. The authority and very legitimacy of administrative decision making could be corroded as a practical matter if board awards remained unenforceable.

El Águila's case, decided by the Supreme Court in January 1926, probably was the most celebrated litigation involving the suspension of a board award in the mid-1920s.[20] The case arose from a strike at El Águila's refinery in Minatitlán, Veracruz, in which the British company first had tried to avoid a collective contract that stipulated a union security agreement or closed shop (*cláusula de exclusión*) and then dismissed workers mostly belonging to one union. The Court opinion and extensive discussions by the justices during two days of public conference did not make law in the strict sense of establishing binding precedent. But the case reflected then current notions not only about the cláusula de exclusión but also about the right to strike, the lockout, and the applicable standard for granting an order of suspension. And the case was politically significant, for the CROM (and its patron, President Calles) and Veracruz's governor, Heribero Jara, as it involved a major foreign oil company.[21] An *Excélsior* headline termed the case a transcendental matter. Workers, labor leaders, and lawyers expectant of the Court's judgment packed its public conference.[22] To pressure the justices, unions threatened a general strike in Mexico City. The steering group, the Consejo de la Federación de Sindicatos del Distrito Federal, when canceling the strike announced that "labor organizations in the federal district had absolute confidence in the justices of the Supreme Court and expected that they would know how to impart justice in this case so transcendental for the labor movement in the country."[23] Different unions had engaged in solidarity actions against El Águila, while the CROM, attempting to increase its influence in the oil sector, counseled striking workers and organized a boycott of El Águila's products.[24]

Interunion rivalry had vitiated industrial relations at the refinery.[25] When the company discharged employees at the behest of the Unión de Obreros de Minatitlán, with which it had made the collective contract stipulating the closed shop, other unions complained to Veracruz's governor. Then the refinery reduced its production and discharged one shift of workers, most of whom belonged to the Unión de Obreros. This union was able to rally a coalition of workers' groups at the refinery (the league or *liga de agrupaciones obreras*) to support its position and demand the company's strict adherence to the collective contract and its extension to the coalition, as well as the reinstatement of the discharged workers, among other things. The company refused to accept the demands, contending that the contract was unconstitutional (because it established the closed union shop, violating the right to work). Workers struck on September 5, 1925, basically seeking the reinstatement of the 149 discharged workers.[26] The company opted to submit the dispute to Veracruz's central labor board.[27] The coalition of striking workers received advice from the CROM, including through the SICT.[28]

On October 27, Veracruz's central board ruled against El Águila on six main points. First, the strike was lawful. Second, the collective contract was valid (the implication being the validity of the cláusula de exclusión). Third, the discharge of one shift of workers in one department was approved as of the date of the board's decision. Fourth, the company had to pay workers wages until the date of the board's award because it had not obtained the agency's prior authorization for the partial lockout. Fifth, the company was to pay wages for the duration of the strike to the Unión de Obreros and other affiliated groups. Sixth, workers were afforded fifteen days to return to work.[29]

On November 9, El Águila petitioned for an amparo and a preliminary suspension of the execution of the board's resolution alleging the violation of its rights under Articles 4, 14, and 16 of the constitution. A federal judge issued the suspension order, and the central board appealed it to the Supreme Court. The Court considered the applicable legal standard (whether suspending the award would prejudice the state or society; and whether without the suspension order the petitioner-company would suffer harm difficult to repair).[30]

The justices felt the pressure being exerted on them. The justice who presented the opinion at the public conference, Jesús Guzmán Vaca, began with the assertion that he would fully explain his position, "without fear of any kind and without letting the possible epithets about [his] ideas affect him."[31] The attention focused on the Court appeared to have encouraged justices to articulate their positions carefully. Guzmán Vaca said that the amparo regulatory statute was not appropriate for labor matters: the amparo was created to protect individual rights and was reflective of the triumph of individualism. In contrast, the present constitutional regimen distanced itself from individualism; the 1917 constitution had taken into account the transformation that had occurred especially in public law. Article 123 posed the contradiction between individualist and socialist principles. Guzmán Vaca hardly defined the latter; rather, he alluded to what socialism was not, Soviet law. He reiterated that Article 123 was completely opposed to individualism. Given that the amparo suit was instituted to protect individual rights, it was difficult therefore to adjust it to labor law, which earlier Guzmán Vaca had opined remained incomplete, both as to case law and legislation.[32]

More precise were the qualms the justice expressed about the applicability of the suspension standard to labor matters. Guzmán Vaca found the legal standard completely inadequate for resolving El Águila's suit. His was a straightforward acknowledgment of the discretion the justices had to determine an outcome: "These articles, we know very well, are conceived in a completely ambiguous form, and they lend themselves as much to deny as concede the suspension, giving opportunity, ultimately, for the Supreme Court to resolve as it wishes, which is contrary to the constitutional regime."[33] The consideration of individualism, Guzmán Vaca added, was a Pandora's box, as the federal judiciary used it, especially in connection with the standard of irreparable harm. Furthermore, the collective contract, the new legal institution, could not fit into the framework of the old law—and here the reference was to the closed shop clause that affected third parties, that is, nonunionized workers: "And one asks: how does one want to adjust a labor contract to the old framework, if there are phenomena which produce effects against third parties . . . in the collective contract, there are clauses that affect third parties who have not had anything to do with it."[34]

Guzmán Vaca did not settle the questions he posed. He did justify upholding the suspension order against the central board's determination on the fourth point, which instructed El Águila to pay workers laid off due to the partial lockout until the company had obtained the board's approval for the layoffs. It was in the public interest for the board to adhere to labor law. Neither Article 123 nor the state labor law afforded monetary compensation to workers locked out. Still, the public interest in the resolution of strikes justified refusal to suspend the board's order on the fifth point, which had ordered strikers paid.

Challenged in the conference by one justice who voted to revoke entirely the suspension order, Guzmán Vaca emphasized that the determinative criterion was whether suspension of the award would affect the social interest. Again he said that the irreparability of the harm caused one individual or the other was secondary.[35] Guzmán Vaca less successfully responded to the justice's skepticism that the substantive remedy to pay strikers their wages had any textual or legal foundation. He fell back on a policy argument, one based on a contractual notion that the strike was a suspension but not the termination of employment: "Since the moment that the Constitution has permitted workers to declare themselves on strike, they are defending a right of which they can make use, and this right would be nugatory if they came to lose the right to the payment of their wages . . . but if the strike has been declared licit they can return to complete their work without this being terminated; this is the reach that they have, it is what all writers on labor matters indicate."[36] Guzmán Vaca acknowledged that otherwise, there was no legal source for the conclusion that wages of strikers should be paid; as for the company's termination of jobs, the justice was more sympathetic to the position of the company; from his perspective, there had been not a lockout but rather justified layoffs—which the board had implicitly acknowledged in its award.

During the second day devoted to El Águila, Francisco Modesto Ramírez, Garza Pérez, Padilla, acting as president of the Court, and Francisco Díaz Lombardo spoke in the public conference. The same issues predominated. Ramírez argued that the lockout was illicit until the company obtained the approval of the board, conjecturing that the contrary ruling would make it easier for employers to lock out workers and avoid their compensation. He further suggested that the order to pay workers in the interim merely posited that they remained employed until the board issued its finding, analogizing the situation to that of workers entitled to pay while striking lawfully.[37]

Garza Pérez concurred with Guzmán Vaca, underscoring the importance of the case, not for the pressure being exerted on the Court by both El Águila and labor organizations, which he mentioned, but because it was the first case in which the federal judiciary was considering suspending a board's resolution of a major strike. The effect of suspension of the award would be to prolong the strike.[38] For Garza Pérez, cases that involved only one worker did not affect the social interest; in contrast, the strike clearly affected society, and the justice elaborated what he believed was obvious, referring to the social interest in "harmony between the factors of production."[39] He stated the precedential value of El Águila, even if alone it did not amount to binding case law:

> Consequently, I believe that this case is very distinct from previous ones and they cannot be compared. It is an entirely new case, and the resolution that the Court pronounces will establish a precedent that will naturally be received attentively by the entire nation; but principally by those interested in this class of conflicts and by the federal district judges, who will have to take into account the resolution that the Supreme Court pronounces in this case so that it serves them as a norm to apply, if they so esteem it convenient, while there is no *jurisprudencia* over the particular, in the same sense.[40]

Garza Pérez added that the only really determinative criterion for refusing to grant a suspension order was whether it implicated the social interest.

Padilla voiced the alternate theory that even the suspension of board orders concerning just one worker affected social interests. According to him, society was keenly interested in all people having employment. He emphatically favored overturning the federal judge on all points. Granting a suspension, even in the case of individual disputes, effectively denied the rights of workers. He realistically noted that employers could sustain an amparo action until its completion but that workers barely subsisting could not. In this respect, he returned to Guzmán Vaca's initial comments of the previous day regarding the inadequacy of the amparo and civil law to realize the aim of Article 123, to guarantee workers the rights affecting their very life. Society had an interest that the worker and his family not suffer.[41]

Díaz Lombardo, the last justice to speak before the vote was taken, as well as the only one who had sat on the high bench before 1917, disputed Padilla.[42] Society had an interest in the amparo remaining available as an effective remedy; and if suspensions were disallowed, the amparo often would be rendered ineffective. The law was simple: the judiciary should enter the suspension order whenever the petitioner risked incurring harm difficult to repair, unless the order would cause prejudice to society or the state.[43]

The judgment was fractured after two days of open discussion, but the Court ultimately denied the order of suspension except as to the fourth point of the board's award.[44] The CROM claimed victory.[45] Strikers actually languished after the Court's decision, receiving only a fraction of the retroactive pay indicated by the Court's judgment. SICT minister and CROM leader Morones reached an agreement with El Águila compromising the amount to be paid. The CROM probably pocketed most of this sum.[46] One of the strike leaders soon thereafter was assassinated, and many workers, dispirited by the outcome, departed from Minatitlán.[47] The political equation of the Minatitlán strike was complex: in 1926, Calles and Morones were sensitive to the extent that they could press a major oil company; in turn the oil companies were capable of influencing directly or indirectly the federal judiciary.[48] The state governor Jara was then an ally of labor (he had been one of the strongest advocates of labor rights in the constitutional convention as a delegate from Veracruz), as was generally the board of conciliation and arbitration in the state. The CROM had supported the governor and his predecessor; but they also became rivals and antagonists; and Calles was interested in asserting his control over a powerful governor. In this case, the CROM's influence was manifestly more visible and successful.[49] But the justices' assertions of their position need not be discounted as epiphenomenal; indeed, they acknowledged the pressure exerted by organized labor and then proceeded to address the difficulties inherent in deciding a case such as the suspension order entered against the state labor board in favor of the oil company. And the rules that they articulated as to the payment of wages while workers were on strike, or regarding the consequences of a lockout, as well as to the limits of board decision making, would remain operative, and continue to evolve, throughout the decade. In this case, as one leading industrial relations scholar has noted, the Court had implicitly recognized the legal validity of the union security agreement (or closed shop), to which El Águila had been strongly opposed and which by the end of the litigation benefited the CROM.[50] If the judgment was not an explicit ruling on this legal point, which would continue to trouble the Court, the issue surely had concerned the justices, as Guzmán Vaca's ruminations about the labor contract reflect.

In any event, despite the attention that El Águila received, the judgment did not settle the specific question of when to issue an order suspending a board award in amparo litigation. Justices remained divided in subsequent decisions, a bare majority tending to rule against suspending board determinations.[51] Some opinions stressed the theory that suspensions of awards would prolong labor conflict, even where a single worker had made the initial claim, and that there was a social interest in the quick determination of workers' claims.[52] Others said that the public interest favored workers receiving their awards in view of their pressing needs; not paying them would cause extreme prejudice.[53] Suspensions against similar awards by the federal board, once established, were denied, too.[54] Using the same rationales, the Court denied suspensions requested against board orders to reinstate workers.[55] Through 1931, the case law generally disfavored the suspension of orders to pay wages. On September 26, 1931, the Court refused to suspend a board order to pay wages to a professional employee, citing its case law.[56] But a counterposition existed among the justices; in three separate dissenting opinions, one severely criticized prevalent doctrine.[57]

In American Smelting and Refining Co., a slim majority of the Court held that the suspension of an award, in this case to pay one worker, caused grave prejudice to society.[58] A single worker's livelihood affected not just his interest but larger ones, too, beginning with the union to which he belonged, since suspending the board order would encourage employers to act similarly toward other workers and their families, the unit integrative of the social organism. The opinion mentioned the new orientations of legal doctrine to support the proposition that an individual's personal interest implied the larger interests of the class to which he belonged. The rationale that the social and collective interest disfavored suspension of an award for basic sustenance would recur in subsequent cases.[59] The Court similarly declined to suspend awards in workers' accident cases.[60] These decisions were to be distinguished.[61]

In Welch, the Court tailored its position, restating points made in the case of El Águila and advancing a principle it deemed relevant to the new labor law, the privileging of group rights.[62] A dispute between a single worker and capitalist did not implicate social and state interests. A group conflict and a board order resolving a strike, as in this case, obviously did: "and above all, when it is a sentence that puts an end to a strike that is challenged, one cannot negate that society is interested in the execution of the award."[63] The board award had instructed the employer to pay 50 percent of the wages accruing during the strike, admit to the factory all strikers, pay workers their salaries if there were a lack of work, and, last, restart production within three days of the notice of the award. After recounting the employer's arguments and the legal standard, the Court countered with the principle that the group's rights prevailed over the individual's: "It is indisputable that in the conflict between rights, those of the larger entity should always prevail and this character corresponds in every case to collective ones before individual ones."[64] It was not a position shared by all justices; they divided in a 6–5 vote denying the suspension order.[65]

In March 1930, the Court overturned a judge's refusal to suspend the federal board's decision directing a telephone company to sign a collective contract.[66] The high tribunal now asserted that all individuals and collective entities, such as a corporation, equally enjoyed constitutional rights and affected the social and state interest. Another judgment issued in June 1930 concluded that although the case law had favored the enforcement of board awards in conflicts between capital and labor, the operative principles differed where the dispute was between two unions and there was a public interest in the economic regimen of the company—such as Ferrocarriles Nacionales de México.[67]

Differing stances toward suspensions were evident in three published opinions dated between the middle of 1930 and March 1931. In one the Court held that suspension of a board order was inappropriate when the board had instructed the company to reinstate workers, as the company was not prejudiced.[68] In Cinco Minas, the Court amended the federal judge's decision and suspended the board's order in respect to a wage increase but upheld the recognition of the union since the state interest favored the organization of workers.[69] The application for a suspension order failed in La Suiza, where the board order was for the wage payments during a strike.[70] Consistent with the opinion in El Águila, the Court surmised that a resolution ending a strike was in the public interest and should not be suspended.

The Court further modified case law regarding board awards for the payment of basic wages to individuals or, in the case of accidents, medical expenses. It initially tended to refuse petitions to suspend such awards; then its decisional law became more porous.[71] Many judgments did not attempt to distinguish the result from prevalent case law, or they did so very tersely.[72] The alternate position of the Court sympathetic to the suspension of board awards was already prevailing sometimes by the end of 1927. Opinions were qualifying earlier categorical statements in favor of the execution of awards for workers. The number of published decisions approving the suspension of awards increased in 1930 and 1931. Many of them involved the national railway company and the federal board created in September 1927. Only awards clearly providing sums for necessary sustenance largely remained immune from a suspension order.[73]

In two cases involving Ferrocarriles Nacionales de México, the Court distinguished the presumed impact of the board orders it suspended from the kind of destitution its case law had aimed to avoid.[74] In one, the employees would remain employed, receiving some wages to cover the costs of sustenance. In the other, the Court said each case had to be evaluated on its facts to ascertain if precedents applied. One more judgment involving the railways distinguished between the order to pay wages owed, which could be suspended, and reinstatement, which did not harm the company.[75] Suspensions of wage payments remained in principle inappropriate,[76] unless deemed unnecessary for sustenance.[77] The Court affirmed the suspension of orders to terminate employment that boards probably issued at the behest of unions intent on maintaining the closed shop.[78]

Suspensions in a number of cases reflecting different factual patterns evidence new considerations. An award by the Veracruz central board relating to vacation was believed to cause sufficient prejudice to the employer and, outside the case law favoring workers, to warrant its suspension.[79] In Cía. Tra[n]scontinental de Petróleo, S.A., the opinion said that the presumption of denying suspensions because labor law was in the public interest was rebuttable.[80] In this case, the Court found that the federal board should have had jurisdiction over the labor dispute, since it affected the oil industry. Here the public interest favored granting the suspension and a federal board hearing the matter. Another case, Vásquez, related to a lockout by the employer; the Court analyzed the labor law on this subject and suspended the award.[81] The partial suspension in Sindicato Revolucionario de San Bruno concerned the reinstatement of workers.[82] In Oteiza, the Court suspended the Oaxacan central board's determination that a strike was lawful.[83] Awards affecting third parties only indirectly implicated in the labor disputes might be more easily distinguished from the prevailing legal standards, although such actions could affect a worker's pay.[84] Resolutions of the federal boards involving interunion conflict and a union security deposit were also suspended at the end of 1931.[85] By then the case law was pointing toward suspending board resolutions on the application of employers.

THE SOVEREIGNTY OF THE BOARDS OF CONCILIATION AND ARBITRATION AND ITS LIMITS

The federal judiciary's recognition of the imperio of board decisions repeatedly led to questions about the deference that should be accorded to their evaluation of evidence, in the framework of the amparo proceeding.

The case law established that boards as administrative bodies were not subject to the same exacting standards as law courts. Boards should try labor matters as tribunals of conscience, applying notions of equity. They had the "sovereignty" to evaluate the evidence submitted to them. Hence the judiciary should defer to the boards and their resolutions, at least when they did not impinge constitutional rights.

Six cases decided in late 1927 and early 1928 exemplify these notions. In each one the Court confirmed the federal judge's denial of the amparo. In Cía. Ltda. de Tranvías de San Luis Potosí, it said that boards needed only to adhere to their regulating statute and decide in accord with their conscience.[86] In Limón it held that the boards in the federal district had the discretion to reach their decisions on the basis of conscience and equity in a way that courts could not.[87] In Real it stated that awards were immune to revision, were not legal judgments, and an amparo would be appropriate only when an award violated an individual's constitutional rights.[88] Mackeprang held that the state labor law, not the civil procedural code, should supply the relevant standard of proof.[89] Even where the state labor law referred to the procedural code, as in Yucatán, justices concluded that administrative boards did not have to judge as a court, since the constitution indicated only that they conciliate on the basis of conscience and equity.[90]

In 1929, in United Sugar Companies, S.A., the Court upheld the award for a union in connection with a strike and its aftermath ultimately on the basis that boards were sovereign; that is, administrative boards could make factual determinations.[91] In decisions involving the major foreign companies Asarco and the Texas Co., the Court ruled that the boards had the discretion (sovereignty) to evaluate proof according to their conscience and equity and therefore judges could not substitute their appraisal for the boards' nor were the latter subject to the same rules as courts.[92] In accord with these principles, in Gallardo justices held that the standards of investigation and the prescriptive period for filing a complaint differed between a board and a law court.[93] In Morrison, they adjudged that a complaint of death of a worker did not have to be legally specific for a board award.[94] Faya, decided on the same day as Morrison, held that it was unnecessary to establish formally the familial relationship before the central board of

Durango.[95] The Court denied an amparo to the oil company El Águila, finding an article of the state labor law in Tampico unconstitutional since its direction to have law courts enforce board awards deprived them of their sovereignty to resolve labor conflicts.[96]

Deference to board discretion regarding evidence occasionally extended to the fashioning of remedies, even substantive law.[97] In Fernández del Valle, the Court held that when neither Article 123 nor state law specified the just causes for discharge, boards could.[98] In Wisburn, the Court accepted Chihuahua central board's decision that the discharge of a worker who refused to work overtime was unjustified; boards had the discretion and power (sovereignty) to decide such questions.[99]

Although the language of many judicial opinions now rationalized the legal authority of the labor boards, the federal judiciary also was regularly granting amparos against their resolutions. While the case law altogether appears inconsistent, the recurring principle applied by the Supreme Court was that the boards had to adhere to fundamental procedural standards and could not infringe the constitutional rights of the parties in their proceedings, notwithstanding the boards' acknowledged discretion to resolve matters pursuant to their conscience and sense of equity.

For example, in an amparo brought by El Águila, the Court held that the remedy afforded two of several workers violated the company's rights under Article 14 because one worker had desisted from the litigation and the second had not asked for any indemnification.[100] The Court reasoned that no labor conflict had transpired between the company and these two employees; therefore, the board had not met the requirements of the state labor law. The amparo nullified the board's award solely as to these two workers and not to others. Similarly, in April 1925, an amparo enjoined the Guanajuato central labor board's indemnification of a worker who did not plead the remedy. Boards could not go beyond claims made or relief requested in the complaint.[101]

In González, the Court stated that boards had to receive proof and hear the parties' allegations; it also outlined the requirements that an enforcing board needed to follow.[102] In Collado, the amparo issued against the Veracruz central board declared the necessity of an award's strict adherence to the state's labor law to avoid violation of Articles 14 and 16 of the constitution.[103] Boards must still follow procedural safeguards, wrote the Court in Sloan, when it granted the amparo against Guadalajara's central junta.[104] One party's failure to establish legal personality before Guadalajara's board was cited as the reason for the amparo of Fuller.[105] The federal judiciary also had to consider the problem of prescriptive periods, time limits within which a complaint had to be filed with a board, as more awards involved contracts already concluded. The Court inconsistently decided board awards that relied on state law.[106]

Between 1930 and 1931, the Court continued to relieve parties from state board decisions.[107] A few opinions contained language that seemingly further limited the scope of their determinations.[108] The Court did not let stand board decisions in which a party (the employer in these cases) had not been summoned or heard.[109] The opinion of Reynés declared that while the boards had sovereignty to weigh evidence, they could not disregard facts apparently proven.[110] Ochoa said that the boards, in this case Michoacán's, should apply the relevant law and only in the absence of a relevant provision should they rely on their conscience.[111] Huasteca Petroleum Co. emphasized the two-step process of mediation and arbitration as requisites for the Veracruz board to reach a binding decision.[112] Carvajal concluded that Yucatán's board could not refer to state law when Article 123 was silent on the matter.[113]

THE AMPARO OF THE CTC AND THE ESTABLISHMENT OF THE FEDERAL LABOR BOARD

As the Supreme Court recognized the authority of the boards of conciliation and arbitration to adjudicate labor disputes, it sought to bar other governmental bodies from doing likewise. In July 1924, in the case of Gracia Nemesio, the railroad company Ferrocarriles Nacionales de México (FNM), then managed by the federal government, pressed the issue of whether a federal district court or the administrative labor board of Nuevo León should have jurisdiction over the claims of two dismissed workers.[114] If the railroad company were deemed a federal, governmental entity, then the federal judiciary would have direct jurisdiction over matters affecting it under Article 104 of the constitution. The Nuevo

León labor board objected to the federal district court trying the case, so the board and court appealed to the Supreme Court. With one justice dissenting, it ruled for Nuevo León's central board, reasoning that the company's nature remained fundamentally that of a private organization; as such its labor relations were subject to Article 123, therefore to conciliation and arbitration boards, not law courts.[115] The opinion discussed the question of whether a state board could exercise its jurisdiction over a federal respondent, yet nobody seemed especially preoccupied with the possibility of such an administrative body adjudicating a federal matter such as a labor conflict unfolding across state boundaries.[116]

Analogously to Gracia Nemesio, in amparo actions decided in the next few years, the Court held that determinations made by authorities without the legal power (*facultad*) to resolve labor conflicts violated constitutional guarantees. In Cía. del Ferrocarril Sud-Pacífico de México, justices unanimously granted the railroad company's amparo against Jalisco's state authorities.[117] The central board there had relied completely on the papers filed with the state department of labor. This violated Article 123, Paragraph XX, because the labor department and not the board had effectively adjudged the complaint.[118] In Cía. Minera "Maravilla," Hidalgo's governor had resolved a labor dispute dating back to 1918 between the mining company and one worker.[119] The labor board simply ratified it. Again, justices held that Article 123 required labor boards to determine fully such matters, in a split vote of 7–3.[120] In 1927, the Court rejected an attempt of Sinaloa's highest tribunal to overturn a labor board's determination.[121] Even when both parties to a dispute had agreed to private arbitration, the Court maintained that the boards had exclusive jurisdiction to resolve such disputes.[122] It also ruled that a labor board's power to determine a question about wages due trumped a law court's bankruptcy proceeding.[123] Decisions through 1931 restricted labor matters to labor boards and repudiated the intervention of other governmental authorities, including a municipal president of Veracruz, the state governor of Mexico, and a minor judge of the federal district.[124]

It was in this legal context that the federal judiciary considered the major railway workers' strike of 1927, led by the Confederation of

Transport and Communication Workers (Confederación de Transportes y Comunicaciones, or CTC). By then, the newly reconstituted private management of FNM (in which the federal government still had a majority ownership interest) was attempting to downsize its labor force and curtail the strength of militant unions affiliated with the CTC. At the time, CROM unions were expanding in the railway sector, with the encouragement of the federal government. In late 1926, FNM's management began to dismiss machinists and otherwise to discriminate against them while favoring CROM workers. The machinists' union (Unión Mexicana de Mecánicos, or UMM) threatened to strike in December. Morones, in his official capacity as minister of the SICT, tried to arbitrate the conflict between the UMM and FNM. His decision upheld the company and the UMM struck. By February, CTC workers, in solidarity with the UMM, also struck. Many of the union leaders of the CTC's affiliates, however, did not endorse the strike even as union locals participated in stoppages. Morones declared the CTC's strike illegal and illicit (as he had the UMM's stoppage).[125] FNM fired most workers engaged in the strike (about 20,000): it was now legally able to do so, because the government's declaration of the illegality of the strike implied that the strikers had abandoned their employment unjustifiably. The strike nonetheless spread, and the government deployed troops and tried to repress it. In early March, the General Confederation of Workers sponsored solidarity actions, reflecting the anti-CROM animus of segments of organized labor. Meanwhile, reports of sabotage and violent confrontations between strikers and replacements abounded. By April, the CTC was losing the strike.

In this context of a broad but fluctuating strike, repressed by a government visibly allied with the CROM, the CTC had petitioned for an amparo against the SICT's declaration that the strike was illicit on March 4, alleging that the state (the SICT and President Calles) had impeded workers' exercise of their constitutional right to strike.[126] On May 3, 1927, a federal judge in Mexico City (*Juez Tercero Supernumerario de Distrito*) granted the amparo.[127] Although he avoided ruling on the president's violation of the CTC's members' right to strike, the judge held that Morones's declaration was unlawful and lacking in legitimate authority.[128] The provisional judgment, however, did not order the reinstatement of workers or provide them any other practical assistance. The amparo did threaten the government and FNM: the latter because it might have to compensate workers or reinstate them and the former because it might be deprived of a fundamental mechanism to regulate strike activity.[129] The labor conflict in any event had become a legal dispute.

The SICT appealed the judge's amparo to the Supreme Court. On September 17, 1927, as it became apparent that it would consider the judge's ruling, President Calles created the federal board of conciliation and arbitration (Junta Federal de Conciliación y Arbitraje) to adjudicate labor disputes that the federal government had determined should be under its jurisdiction.[130] It was doubtful that Calles had the legal authority under the constitution to federalize the adjudication of labor (since Article 123 directed the states to enact labor legislation). He had failed earlier to obtain legislation establishing such a federal board.[131] But at least the presidential decree would establish the kind of forum—a tripartite, administrative labor board of conciliation and arbitration—that the Supreme Court had held in its case law was necessary to decide labor disputes. Indeed, on October 4, 1927, the Court ruled that the SICT had lacked the authority and competency to declare the CTC's strike illegal.[132] Its judgment stated unequivocally that the constitution authorized only a labor board to reach such a decision about a strike, and that where the labor conflict implicated a federal matter, it had to be a federal labor board.

The judgment, moreover, explicitly recognized that a strike had occurred and that the SICT had violated the constitutional rights of members of the CTC who had struck. The SICT had raised the issue of whether the CTC had the legal personality to litigate the amparo action on behalf of strikers. As fifteen of the eighteen member groups of the confederation had disavowed the strike ultimatum and FNM's management had withdrawn its recognition of the federation in February, it was not a spurious issue. In the 1920s, interunion rivalries, the absence of industrial unions, and the formation of straw labor groups had accentuated problems related to the bona fide representation of employees. Did the CTC represent a striking workforce in the amparo proceeding? The Court concluded that in fact it did, that there were striking workers affected by the declaration of the SICT, and that locals of the member unions whose officials had disavowed the strike supported and recognized the confederation. The Court opined that some labor groups had not supported the strike while others had and that this was sufficient to recognize the CTC's legal capacity to represent the aggrieved individuals who had applied for the amparo. The judicial opinion was a powerful statement of workers' rights to organize and strike and a stinging repudiation of the attempt of the SICT to declare a strike illicit.

The SICT tried desperately to avoid the Supreme Court's judgment. It had assigned the railroad case to the newly created federal labor board, which precipitously conducted a hearing and made a determination finding the strike unlawful on October 3, shortly before the Court issued its judgment. The CTC had refused to participate in this administrative proceeding, citing procedural irregularities, and had petitioned again for an amparo. As the Court pronounced its decision, the federal board indicated that it would set aside its award and proceed anew with the matter; and so it did.[133]

It was an inauspicious beginning for the federal labor board. From its inception, its dependency on the executive power and the SICT minister was manifest. The president of the newly created board was the same head of the labor department who had decided against the CTC recently and who not coincidentally was also a CROM leader. One of the representatives of capital on the special board set up to hear this first case was a managing officer of the National Railways; one labor representative was associated with the CROM and had contracted with the FNM to supply it with replacement workers during the strike. The presiding representative of the government had been involved in the investigation of the strike by the SICT's labor department and also had CROM ties. Just one of the board members, Donato Muñoz, was independent of the juggernaut fixed against the CTC.[134]

The outcome of the federal labor board's deliberations was predictable. The CTC pleaded for the reinstatement of all strikers, without any loss of their seniority and with compensation and damages.[135] Such a remedy theoretically followed from the evolving law of the employment contract and strike (already evident in the justices' public deliberation in January 1926 over Veracruz's central board's award in El Águila): a strike suspended individuals' employment contracts; it did not terminate them. So upon cessation of the strike, workers were entitled to their employment under their same contracts. Employers could not replace their employees without incurring liability for breach of contract, unless a labor board explicitly ruled that they were relieved from having to reinstate them or the workers did not return. The federal labor board rejected the arguments of the CTC. In its decision of December 8, 1927, the board ruled that FNM did not have to reinstate the confederation's members nor compensate them in anyway: the strike had been illicit—and, indeed, had not constituted a strike at all. The set of rationales to justify this decision are actually astounding. The federal board found the ten-day strike notice provided by the CTC inadequate, as the federation had phrased the notice in discretionary terms. The board reasoned that the disturbances caused by a strike of a public service were incalculable and strikers could not arrogate the power to strike when it appeared opportune to them, once the ten days had lapsed. Instead, they should initiate their action precisely at the expiration of the tenth day. The notice to strike was dated February 7; the strike began approximately on February 18.[136] The board held in addition that the strike had been illicit, because a majority of the strikers had carried out violent actions. Although the board's opinion described acts of sabotage and assault, it did not indicate or detail how a majority of strikers had engaged in them.

Perhaps cognizant of the weakness of its conclusions based on existing law, the board hinged its decision on a novel argument at the time: that the strike had never involved a majority of FNM's workers, hence it had been an abandonment of work by some employees. The board theorized that a majority of a firm's labor force had to endorse the strike in order for the government to recognize it; conversely, a concerted action of a minority of the workforce was not constitutionally protected. The board grounded this theory in part on a CROM-backed statute (the Organic Law of Constitutional Article 4 in Relation to the Freedom of Labor) that was enacted in December 1925 for the federal district, and had as one of its purposes the protection of strikes undertaken by a majority of a firm's labor force, when some employees attempted to continue working.[137] Although the statute was inapposite to a walkout of a minority of a company's employees, the board construed it with the developing doctrinal principle in labor law that privileged the rights of the majority against those of minorities, such as the collective agreement over the individual contract. However specious or creative was its reasoning in construing that the concerted action of thousands of workers had not amounted to a strike as stated in the constitution, the board was clearly engaged in a legal evaluation. Yet the opinion phrased this argument as a factual matter: "thus this disturbance in the work of the Railways does not have the character of a strike and is a simple abandonment of labor by those who attempted to put the Railways on strike." And, to buttress its depiction, the opinion asserted explicitly that the board had made a careful study of the evidence, in accord with general principles of equity and in good conscience (and insofar as relevant law did not exist)—precisely the regulatory standard for the deliberations of such administrative boards. [138] This was important, because pursuant to case law, factual evaluations of administrative boards were entitled to substantial judicial deference: labor boards were sovereign in the evaluation of relevant evidence, although not in the application or creation of law.

Nearly a year and a half later, on May 30, 1929, the Supreme Court in effect affirmed the federal labor board's award, grounding its judgment largely on the legal doctrine that the board's factual evaluation was unassailable, as the board had the discretion to evaluate the proofs of the case and ascertain its facts.[139] It was a long opinion, but one in which the Court made very little positive law: it recounted at length the reasoning of the district court, which had adopted the federal board's rationales. The high court did not go this far; its own rationale was narrower and said nothing about the theory derived from the 1925 statute privileging concerted actions by a majority of a firm's employees or about the board's discussion of the new labor law. These were legal issues, after all. Instead, the Court applied its principle of deference to the boards in factual matters and took the federal board's finding that a majority of workers had not supported the strike to mean factually that there had been no strike and that consequently there had been an abandonment of work, for which there could be no constitutional remedy for the CTC's members.[140]

One might attribute the apparent inconsistency in the Court's position to the change in the membership on the high bench, in accord with the constitutional reform of the Court effective December 20, 1928.[141] If this is a factor in a possible shift of the Court's stance (toward the federal executive, for instance), it is not a simple one, as it was Portes Gil who nominated the new Court justices, and (as mentioned earlier) he was hostile toward the CROM, which after 1928 lost much of its earlier notable influence in government.[142] By the time that the Court ruled on the labor board's determination against the CTC in 1929, the political balance between the CROM and other unions had changed, and the CROM had lost its privileged position in the federal government.

Indeed, in the shadow of the Court's negative judgment, the CTC obtained a political resolution as a result of the change in the nation's political balance. CTC leaders and activists awaited the Court's 1929 ruling vigilantly at the end of May. There were about 100 striking workers or supporters along with three members of the strike committee present at the Court's public conference when justices pronounced the judgment against them. In protest, they announced a hunger strike and refused to leave the court building. The next morning Portes Gil summoned strike leaders to his office and made an agreement with them for the reinstatement of strikers, with seniority rights—essentially what the CTC had sought from the federal labor board and judiciary since 1927. Following the president's directive, FNM issued Circular 64—which led to further litigation but did allow for reemployment with some of the rights lost in 1926–27.[143]

The federal labor boards, and administrative labor boards in general, however, remained the state agencies primarily charged with the resolution of labor disputes. By 1929 it was becoming evident there would be federal legislation to frame their operation. In this context, the May 1929 decision can be interpreted as an instance in which the Court, consistent with its earlier 1927 decision, took the position that labor boards, not the SICT minister—and not the federal judiciary—should resolve labor disputes, including a strike. If this is a plausible reading of the Court's decision making, it was a prudent (and probably necessary) position for it to have adopted: justices surely avoided having to challenge the federal executive as frequently as would have occurred had the federal judiciary actually scrutinized the determinations of the federal boards.

Following the Court's judgment against the CTC, a number of published opinions reiterated the same basic principle of sovereignty in relation to amparos sought against federal board awards. Other rulings afforded federal boards a degree of discretion to reach their resolutions.[144] The Court denied amparos against the federal board in two cases involving the national railways, where the main issue was the interpretation of the provision for the retirement of workers in the company's reglamento (which approximated at the time a collective agreement).[145] The opinions reiterated the complete sovereignty of the boards to evaluate the facts of a case. The reglamento was not law; rather, it posed a factual question, and therefore the board, not the judiciary, should interpret it.

By 1930, however, other opinions were overturning resolutions of the federal labor board, echoing the Court's concerns expressed about state labor board proceedings. One decision on February 18, 1930, which enjoined the award to the Sociedad Ferrocarrilera, held that since the boards essentially operated as law courts, notwithstanding their status as administrative bodies, they should adhere to certain limits related to the nature of the complaint before them.[146] In two cases involving Ferrrocarriles Nacionales, the Court again ruled against the federal board. Where the award was based on a single provision of the reglamento, which was not proven, the amparo was warranted, since the federal board had an obligation to resolve the conflict on the evidence submitted.[147] Nor should the board enlarge its remedies from the initial resolution. This violated Articles 14 and 16.[148] A further step was taken a few months later, when the Court began to rule that the federal board lacked the authority to estimate the consequential damages resulting from the national railways' contractual violations. Toward the end of 1931, the Court enjoined federal board decisions on the grounds of their providing remedies not demanded in the initial complaint,[149] for misinterpreting the reglamento,[150] as well as on the basis of the limited scope of their sovereignty.[151]

The federal judiciary, moreover, continued to doubt the legitimacy of the federal government's executive powers in the area of industrial relations after its first CTC decision. In the May 1930 amparo of Cía. Industrial de Orizaba, the Court queried presidential decrees that had federalized the regulation of industrial relations in the textile sector.[152] Veracruz's central labor board had ruled for a worker suffering from tuberculosis, which state legislation deemed an occupational illness. The company petitioned for an amparo to put aside the board's award on the basis that the industry-wide textile agreement approved in March 1927 by presidential decree had delegated the state labor boards' jurisdiction to the SICT and, once the federal labor boards were established, to them. On October 29, 1929, the federal judge granted an amparo, agreeing with the company. Within the framework of the amparo action, the Court could not go so far as to declare unconstitutional the presidential decrees. It did, however, overturn the amparo and hold that Veracruz's board remained competent to hear the complaint of the textile worker's illness. The Court explicitly added that the presidential decree of March 15, 1927, ratifying the textile convention, insofar as it assigned to the SICT jurisdiction over disputes arising in the textile industry, contravened basic constitutional precepts:

> Upon the President of the Republic resolving, in his aforesaid accord [of March 15, 1927] that the Secretary of Industry, Commerce and Labor will take cognizance of all labor conflicts of the textile companies in the republic, it is incontrovertible that in addition to legislating in labor matters, without being authorized to do so and against the express text of the first paragraph [of Art. 123], [he] invaded the sovereignty of the States, that, in accord with said precept, had expedited their labor laws, ordered by the same, giving jurisdiction to the local boards to take cognizance of the expressed conflicts. In addition, upon instructing that the Secretary of Industry, Commerce and Labor would take over the repeated conflicts, [he] violated flagrantly the twentieth paragraph of [Art. 123] that expresses in part: that the conflicts between capital and labor will be subject to the decision of a Board.[153]

The Court stated that at least part of the presidential decree creating the system of federal labor boards also contravened Article 123:

> By the Presidential Decree [of September 17, 1927], a Federal Board of Conciliation and Arbitration was established to resolve conflicts between employers and workers, directing that said Board would intervene, amongst other cases, when by written agreement the majority of the representatives of industry and of workers in a branch had accepted the jurisdiction of the Federal Government. Here, as in the agreement of [March 15, 1927] the Executive of the Union legislated over labor matters, without being legally empowered to do so and against what is directed in the first paragraph of [Article 123].[154]

This was a remarkable ruling in that it disputed, at the very least, the legality of the president's executive decrees establishing the federal labor board and the comprehensive regulatory system of industrial relations in the textile sector fashioned after years of negotiation among manufacturers, the federal government, and CROM-affiliated unions. The Court probably had misgivings about accepting the creation of federal boards in 1927 but had thought it worse that the SICT should be operating in lieu of such boards. As federal legislation became more certain, perhaps the Court concluded that it could assert a more critical position regarding the executive's unconstitutional insertion in labor matters (especially since after 1929 it was clear that the federal boards were not to exercise jurisdiction in the textile sector).[155] In any event, the Court suspended wage increases that the textile convention called for on January 24 and March 14, 1931, in response to company petitions in the cases of Tomás Urrutia and Sociedad "Alfredo Sordo, Sucres."[156] Together, these decisions underscore the limits of lawful executive authority: the presidency could not establish a lawful industrial relations system absent constitutionally framed federal legislation. Further, they suggest that the federal judiciary could not be counted upon to adjudicate as a dependent branch of the executive power in all cases or to legitimize the presidency or any other government's actions in labor relations.

TOWARD EL DERECHO OBRERO: FROM THE EMPLOYMENT TO THE COLLECTIVE LABOR CONTRACT

As the Supreme Court confirmed the powers of administrative labor boards, its opinions generally bolstered the principle that an employment contract had to exist as a jurisdictional requirement for the exercise of the boards' powers. For example, although the main issue in the 1924 amparo of Cía. Limitada de Luz, Eléctrica, Fuerza y Tracción de Veracruz related to the competency of labor boards to hear disputes involving only an individual worker and his employer, the Court's opinion presumed that a contract of employment must be the underlying governing relationship between the parties.[157] The unanimous decision overturned an amparo granted on May 26, 1919, which had enjoined a determination of Veracruz's central board favoring a discharged machinist, the federal judge reasoning that the board could hear only group conflicts. The Court still seemed to have in mind the 1924 *convocatoria* sponsored by the Confederación de Cámaras Industriales.[158] It cited the French treatise by Georges Bry entitled (as given in Spanish) *Las leyes del trabajo industrial y de la previsión social* for the argument that the labor boards could hear individual claims as law tribunals and not just group conflicts as mediating bodies.[159] In the public conference, one justice, drawing from Bry, said that individual conflicts were encompassed by the capital-labor relationship expressed in Article 123—provided they originated in the contract of employment.[160]

The Court's rejection of the persistent employer assertion that labor boards could consider conflicts only arising from employment contracts still in force also presumed the existence of a contract.[161] If this employer argument tended to diminish as a major contentious issue, as late as 1929 the Court still had to restate the rule that boards had the power to hear almost any matter arising from an employment contract, whether or not it remained in force.[162] Initially the opinions awkwardly construed the contract in question as remaining in force, sometimes stating that a single party, the employer, could not terminate the agreement alone, because if that were possible then employers could easily circumvent the jurisdiction of the boards.[163] After 1926, several decisions reiterated that Article 123 did not distinguish between existent or concluded contracts.[164] The Court, in any case, assumed that the employer and employee had made a contract of employment at one time. As it rebutted one legal theory favored by employers, litigants and justices continued to articulate the employment relationship in contractual terms.

The employment contract could be construed liberally to expand board jurisdiction. Or if a contract was not found to exist or had been terminated lawfully, then the implication might be that the individual claimant (a worker) was left without a remedy, due to the absence of any right, regardless of whether the labor board could entertain the claim. That is, the question of an employment contract could have substantive and not only jurisdictional ramifications. The case law rarely expressed the concept of the *contrato de trabajo* in these precise terms. Normally an employment contract had to be established for the board to be able to hear a dispute and for the worker to invoke a right to relief. In Sota, for example, Veracruz's central labor board recognized the oral agreement of employment of two workers.[165] The employer, an agricultural estate, filed an amparo petition alleging the absence of a contract because the workers had refused to sign one. The parties had never perfected the contract. The Court upheld the board, pointing out that the state labor law permitted oral contracts.[166] In another amparo case involving El Águila, the Court dealt with the factual situation of a worker who had been employed by two companies jointly when he was killed in a work accident.[167] The justices' discussion centered on what comprised employment under Article 123; the legal outcome largely depended on whether an employment contract had been effectuated. As one justice said: "in conformance with the law, the Constitution, [the complainant] does not have a right to receipt of that indemnification that the board of conciliation and arbitration believes should be paid, because this does not deal with a worker subject to a contract of employment. . . . [T]he fact that the company gave him a payment does not establish a contract of employment."[168] In 1926, in Orozco, the Court asserted that Article 123 encompassed in general everybody who entered into an employment contract. [169] In Pernet, justices granted an amparo; their decision depended in part on their perception that no contract of employment had been formed.[170] The Court found that Veracruz's central board had made a determination without establishing the existence of a contract; the worker had to prove there had been such a legal agreement.[171] The Court found insufficient a letter suggesting some relationship between the complainant and the manager of Pernet's estate; without proof of the contract, the board's order had violated Pernet's rights.[172] Similarly, in 1927, the Court affirmed an amparo holding that the requirement of weekly rest applied to those protected by Article 123—not to those who lacked an employment contract.[173] Some statutory labor matters, however, were not articulated in contractual terms; or the contractual analysis was peripheral.[174]

After 1924, when the Court considered the appropriate court for an individual obviously not a worker, its opinion normally hinged at least partly on its perception of the relevant employment contract.[175] The contract might reflect the existence of a relationship covered by the commercial code and for a civil court to adjudicate. One 1931 amparo case, La Compañía Mexicana Molinera de Nixtamal, evinces the justices' categorization and conception of labor law, their perception of the function of labor boards, and the limits of both, in relation to the interpretation of the employment contract.[176] An employee had filed a complaint against his employer with the federal district's labor board while a lawsuit was pending in a civil court. His claims were essentially for back pay, other compensation owed, including sales commissions, and the three months' wages normally awarded for discharge. The company denied that he was a worker subject to the board's jurisdiction and especially disputed that it should compensate him for sales commissions. The Court agreed on this point and granted an amparo against the board's order to pay the employee 6,000 pesos. Otherwise, it let the award stand. The decision attempted to separate two legal fields, in order to limit the board's jurisdiction in the matter:

> This Supreme Court has already established in diverse cases that the controversies caused by reason of acts related to labor cannot be regulated by laws of a civil character, rather only by laws that regulate labor, [and] one should note that such a thesis is founded in the consideration that labor law and civil law are two

branches of legal science completely independent, and it cannot be admitted, consequently, that the latter can be supplemental of the former, nor that civil law precepts can have an application in issues of labor and by the labor tribunals, nor, therefore, that they can be infringed upon or applied inexactly by said tribunals.[177]

The opinion maintained as in other cases that the boards were to resolve simple disputes according to their conscience, while law courts should decide more legally complicated matters:

The objective that the constitutional deputies proposed . . . on creating in Article 123 . . . [and] the boards . . . was that these authorities . . . resolve the difficulties that arise between employers and workers. The members of these boards, which do not constitute a law tribunal, decide in conformance with their conscience and in accord with what their prudence counsels, because of this class of issues, because of their nature and simplicity, do not call for legal knowledge to resolve them; but when there are questions in which it is indispensable *to apply the laws that regulate the contracts from which the conflict emanates or arises,* the boards should not be considered capacitated . . . to resolve such difficulties, rather the civil or federal courts should take cognizance of them . . . comprised of judges and magistrates, who should be people versed in legal science.[178]

Applying this reasoning to the case, the Court removed part of it from the board's jurisdiction. For the Court, one factor that distinguished the different legal fields was the nature of the employment contract; and what necessitated a court's review of the case was the need to apply laws about which board officers lacked the necessary expertise. When interpretation of the legal nature of the contract from which the conflict arose was in issue, a law court should adjudicate.

Contractual notions only sometimes informed the Court's ambivalent stance toward aspects of labor law that expanded union power (such as the closed shop) or restricted employers' managerial discretion (such as limitations on shutdowns or lockouts). Its suspension order enjoining implementation of the industry-wide textile convention, in La Sociedad "Alfredo Sordo, Sucres," for example, was justified in terms of contractual rules. The mandated increased wage rates pursuant to the textile agreement, according to the Court, deprived the employer of the benefits of existing contracts with employees.[179]

The Court's denials for relief from board rulings that employers' shutdowns were unlawful mostly referenced Article 123's nineteenth paragraph.[180] An alternative analytical framework existed based on the notion of the employment contract. A company might terminate its contracts with employees for justifiable economic reasons and not be engaged in a lockout. El Águila had attempted this approach in 1925–26. In 1930, Max Camiro, a leading employers' attorney, elaborated the argument in a law journal.[181] Camiro had made the same point before the Court years earlier.[182] The Court at that time rejected his analysis finding a shutdown governed by the requirements of Article 123. But one justice had said that boards were competent to hear such disputes arising from the contract of employment.[183]

The Court accepted the closed shop in collective contracts reluctantly. Its stance was sometimes articulated with reference to contractual notions, but it also predicated rulings on other principles, such as a due process right to have a board consider the worker's complaint.[184]

In the amparo of Velasco, the opinion acknowledged the employer's argument justifying a worker's discharge pursuant to the collective contract (and exclusion clause, stipulating the closed shop).[185] Nonetheless, the Court stated it was not for the parties to contract such a condition, as it was a matter of public law.[186] The Court applied Article 5, which it rarely referenced any longer, explaining in part its ruling in terms of the right of free labor, which was violated by obliging the worker to belong to a union, under penalty of the loss of his employment.[187] In the amparo of Méndez, the decision's rationale was based on a concept of a property right in the job.[188] The Tamaulipas central board had directed the company to fire a worker. In his amparo petition, the worker invoked a right under Article 4 to engage in his work, which the federal judge endorsed. The judge also reasoned that the worker had a property interest in the job, of which he should not have been deprived without a hearing. The Court sidestepped the Article 4 liberty of work theory, in effect only upholding the property right in the job. That property interest, to the degree it existed, followed from the unstated premise that the worker had a contract with the employer. The opinion contrasted the property theory with the union's plausible argument that the individual worker's right to the job depended on the collective contract and union membership. Hence, the worker leaving the union ended his right to employment with the company. The opinion did not rebut the argument directly, stating that it was for the board to consider when it gave the worker a hearing. The Court thereby avoided, as in Velasco, basing its ruling explicitly on a theory of the employment contract, when the issue was the interplay between the individual worker's rights against those of a union that had entered into a collective contract with the employer.

Contractual notions are more evident in the case of the Orden de Maquinistas y Fogoneros.[189] In this conflict between unions, the Court dismissed the amparo in a close vote. The Orden had requested the amparo against the federal board's recognition of the Unión de Conductores, Maquinistas, Garroteros y Fogoneros as representatives of the majority of FNM's relevant railway personnel. Both unions as well as Ferrocarriles Nacionales had been present at the proceedings of the federal board—FNM, however, not as a party to the litigation. This was a crucial factor for the majority of the Court: it decided that the board's award had not prejudiced the Orden, since it could still enter into a contract with the employer, who had not been bound by the determination. The underlying premise was less viable within a framework of collective labor agreements, but it was comprehensible within the terms of contractual law and due process: it was for the employer to decide with which of the labor organizations it would contract, since it would be obliged to satisfy the terms of the contract.

Arturo Cisneros Canto's dissenting opinion argued that the majority should have voted to deny, not dismiss, the amparo petition.[190] The board had determined the dispute correctly. In support of his position, Canto referred to the evolving labor law instead of the contractual framework of the majority opinion and of the Orden. Canto argued that the board had made a careful, factual evaluation of which labor organization represented more workers and could represent them better. As the evaluation of facts was within the scope of the board's powers, the Court should have respected its decision. Second, the board's determination of the majority status of the Unión had resulted from applying elementary principles of labor law (*el Derecho Obrero*). In contrast, the Orden had contended that its members had the right to enter into a contract with the company. Such a theory, according to Canto, harkened to an earlier, individualistic, conception of contract law and would only undermine the policies of the ascendant labor law, which centered on the labor organization's entering into a collective contract. Canto emphasized that the collective contract would replace individual employment contracts. It followed, too, that more employees joining the union would strengthen it, with the employees better protected. Accordingly, the federal board's study and evaluation of the relative strength of the Unión over the Orden had been appropriate and had not violated any rights, from the viewpoint of the evolving labor law and the majoritarian principle.

Canto's analysis was that of a dissenter. The majority opinion had elected to address the interunion dispute on narrower procedural grounds within a contractual framework. The novel principles of labor law or *el derecho obrero* propounded by Canto had not yet prevailed in the federal judiciary. The Court's labor decisions between 1924 and the promulgation of the federal labor code in 1931 reveal that the law associated with labor relations was in flux: contractual notions articulated in nineteenth-century civil codes overlapped with social-legal doctrines—already expressed in 1916, in Querétaro, and earlier, during the Porfirian era, but in 1931 not yet fully determinative.

CONCLUSION: A JUDICIAL DETERMINATION OF LABOR LAW?

When the federal judiciary granted the amparo requested by the CTC against the SICT, a consensus was in the making that boards of conciliation and arbitration were the appropriate governmental bodies to adjudicate labor conflicts. By 1930–31, the Supreme Court had largely ratified the nature and status of these administrative organs. In a perceptive article published in 1930, Bassols examined the Court's accomplishments.[191] Like his 1924 essay, it was largely a critical evaluation of the Court's case law. Now conceded is the law-making role of the federal judiciary in the constitution and delimitation of the labor boards:

In this matter, as in no other in Mexican law, the role of federal case law is most important, for as we have seen it has been the *jurisprudencia* that acting as a source of law—even apt to destroy the juridical application of the Constitutional texts in force—created the jurisdictional power of the boards in labor matters, imposed them as tribunals and even marked the essential forms that the procedure followed by them should satisfy.[192]

This role or function of case law had resulted from the legislature's failures to enact the necessary legal framework; the law making had happened through the Court's case-by-case review of amparo actions, which was inherently unsystematic. In 1924, Bassols had urged the creation of a special labor court separate from the administrative board. In the intervening six years, the Court's case law had created a fait accompli contrary to this. Bassols believed it would be foolish to try to reverse the trend. He proposed completing the transformation of the administrative boards into labor courts of law.

The larger issue was how to reconcile the status of labor boards as lay bodies charged with resolving disputes according to their sense of fairness, with a need for regular accountability. Law tribunals had to adhere, in theory, to applicable legal norms, but boards did not. The Court had applied constitutional notions of procedure and evidentiary fairness in many amparo actions, but the amparo process was hardly capable of comprehensively remedying the problems that Bassols observed.

Bassols identified organized labor and its political allies in state governments as the main force opposed to refashioning the labor boards as law tribunals:

On the other hand, always opposed with marked resistance to any intention to organize completely the boards and regulate their procedures, is the force of workers and the labor governments, which with the best of faith and with justification drawn from what the civil and penal tribunals operating in Mexico teach, have an aversion already instinctive, for all that signifies judicial proceedings, procedures, recourses, paperwork, the intervention of lawyers, and in general, a system of tribunals as we have in our view.[193]

For Bassols, the pressure of organized labor thus contributed to some of the incoherence of the Court's decisions related to the character of the boards and procedural labor law.[194] Bassols was at least partially correct in his appraisal. Lombardo Toledano had accepted the fundamental political nature of the boards in an essay published in 1930, which Bassols cited.[195] The frequent legalistic overturning of the boards in the amparo process must have dismayed labor interests, as articulated by the CROM. Yet Bassols was confident that the full legalization of the administrative labor boards would benefit the working class by making these tripartite bodies less dependent on the determinations of government representatives, at a time when the latter were beginning to side more with business interests.

As Lombardo Toledano observed (in late 1926), the Supreme Court's case law mattered as doctrine.[196] Practical enforcement of amparos was another matter in the authoritarian politics of the 1920s; disobeying such injunctive orders was notoriously frequent.[197] The amparo lawsuit could enable the Court to nullify executive decisions, but it did not constitute a process by which rules or rulings were assuredly enforced. Yet even if judicial commands were disregarded, and the meaning of law or the *estado de derecho* weakened thereby, the role of the Supreme Court in shaping both labor law and industrial relations is noteworthy. The Court's opinions served not only to legitimize positions adopted by employers, unions, and state authorities. Its insistence after 1924 that only administrative boards could decide labor disputes in a quasi-judicial manner, combined with its later deference to the federal board and still later its query concerning the board's constitutionally suspect origin, certainly contributed to the trajectory of labor law and industrial relations. Furthermore, the Court's affirmation of the underlying relevance of the employment contract and of contractual principles in labor matters helped structure discourses on the exclusion clause (if individual contracts existed between workers and their employers, it was more untenable to dismiss some at the prompting of a union holding a collective contract with the same employer); on the right of a majority union to a collective contract (such as in the amparo the Court dismissed in La Orden de Maquinistas y Fogoneros de Locomotores); and, not least, on the right to strike under Article 123.

Article 123 recognized that workers had the right to strike, but it did not mandate the legal and administrative incidents attendant to the stoppage of work that had become part of the law of the strike by the late 1920s. Some of these followed from the language of Article 123's relevant provisions (e.g., workers striking a public service had to provide ten days' notice), and some clearly did not. Thus, workers' entitlement to reinstatement with pay for the period of the stoppage is not specified in any paragraph of Article 123. One can infer some of the legal elements of this labor law that referenced the constitutional article, but this is the point: the law was crafted from premises that workers had contracts with their employer and that a strike suspended the contract for the duration of a strike, rather than terminating it. This is a plausible argument (as reasonable as Prieto and Martínez de la Torre's in 1875), but it was dependent on several premises: the boards' function in conflict resolution, the constitutional right to strike, and the employment contract. The law evolved through a process of labor struggle, state labor board decisions, and state legislation. By 1926 the Supreme Court had accepted most of its parameters, as the suspension case of El Águila attests, when justices ratified Veracruz's board's analysis and decision, quibbling more on the point of the alleged lockout than on the remedy for the strikers. And by 1929, the Court accepted the federal labor board's argument as to whether a strike had happened. The federal board and the CTC, in turn, accepted that striking workers had enjoyed contracts with the FNM—until the abandonment of work (or strike) occurred. Contractual principles combined with novel labor law doctrine, which adjudicators (in this instance, as in many, labor board members) were fashioning—and which the Court was, in effect, ratifying. Justices did not normally make law *sua sponte*. They responded, first, to parties' arguments and requests (such as the CTC's petition for an amparo) and, second, to the many circulating legal and political arguments relating to an issue that was framed through litigation. Yet their decisions surely carried more weight as an expression of the nation's law than an opinion of one labor board or another.[198]

In a more practical sense, the Court's decisions mattered, too. Its refusal to accept the SICT's determinations of a strike's unlawfulness and insist that a federal board had to perform this governmental function, coupled later with the refutation that the president had the legal authority to create such federal labor boards, underscored the urgency for the nation's political, business, and labor leaders of enacting federal labor legislation, a project that had languished throughout most of the 1920s—until, not altogether coincidentally, 1927–28. The Court's ratification in 1929 of the federal board's decision signaled that the federal judiciary would normally accept the decisions of labor boards in their regulation of strike activity. Its subsequent judgments repudiating applications of the textile convention, however, continued to highlight the unlawful quality of the federal government's endeavors to rationalize industrial relations across state boundaries and outside the scope of state board jurisdictions. This was not a contrarian or solitary position (even if it disputed executive authority), of course: clearly, in the political context and within the legal tradition of Mexico, federal labor legislation was necessary.

CHAPTER 8

The Enactment of the Federal Labor Law, 1925–1931

INTRODUCTION

Mexico's Congress enacted the *Ley Federal del Trabajo*, the federal labor law, in August 1931, ostensibly to implement the provisions of Article 123 uniformly across the nation.[1] State governments appeared incapable of effectively regulating the labor relations of the country's larger industries, some of whose operations crossed state boundaries.[2] The constitutional compromise of granting the states jurisdiction over labor matters was clearly failing. By 1931 a consensus existed within the national political leadership, seconded by major labor and industrial groups, for the federalization of labor law. Yet both labor and capital publicly denounced the legislation as the government promulgated it, while the federal government was quite fragile. Despite the economic and political problems then besetting Mexico (the Great Depression and an informal political arrangement presided over by the jefe maximo, Calles, who ruled indirectly through a dependent president lacking popular support), the federal executive was able to maneuver its legislature to vote for a manifestly ambitious bill against the overt opposition of the major interested parties, labor and industry. Perhaps the legislation finally passed because as weak as the central authority was, so were industrialists and organized labor. Circumstances suggest that the federal labor statute, as a compromise bill, garnered the tacit support, or resignation, of the more important interests of both labor and business, despite their visible postures. It did, in any event, set out a comprehensive legal framework for the regulation of industrial relations in most sectors of the economy, one grounded in political and legal developments that had contributed to the formal rules of labor relations until then.

Five points are emphasized in this chapter. First, enactment of the federal labor law was a state project. Second, many of the important officials directly involved in the writing of the 1931 legislation (but not all of them) were hostile to the CROM and close to managerial interests. Nonetheless, in order to ensure passage of the bill, the federal executive power had to compromise with congressmen and the CROM on several provisions consequential to the consolidation of powerful unions, which, in conjunction with the overall scheme of the law recognizing labor organization, dismayed Mexican business interests. But, third, the 1931 labor law did not alienate major U.S. business interests. Fourth, apart from its ambitious objectives to legalize and institutionalize industrial relations across Mexico, the statute was specifically concerned with legitimizing the federal government's already existing regulation of strategic economic sectors, such as the railways. Fifth, the federal labor law was part of a process of institutionalizing industrial relations, whose legal and intellectual origins antedated the 1910 revolution.

This chapter begins with a consideration of the attempts in 1925 to pass federal labor legislation by the major labor organization then aligned with the president, the CROM, and business ambivalence toward these legislative efforts. It reviews the attempts of Calles and Morones to regulate labor relations in strategic, economic sectors, including the railroads—which were shaken by the CTC's strike in 1927. Indeed, the rail workers' strike led to the establishment of the federal labor board, whose suspect constitutionality surely underscored the urgent need of federal legislation. The chapter proceeds to recount interim president Portes Gil's attempt to pass a federal labor code, as the CROM lost much of its political influence, then the promulgation of legislation under the presidential administration of Pascual Ortiz Rubio. The chapter concludes with a comment about the principal actors affected by the 1931 law and reiterates the argument that this legislation reflected legal concepts under discussion since the late nineteenth century.

EMPLOYER AND CROM PREFERENCES FOR THE FEDERALIZATION OF LABOR LAW

In April 1925, a few months after the inauguration of Calles's administration, U.S. Ambassador James Sheffield reported a long conversation conducted with the Mexican president about labor problems.[3] The ambassador mentioned how labor disputes prejudiced American business interests. Calles replied that "much of the labor difficulty" was "due to the absence of Federal legislation regulating article 123 . . . in the Federal District and the territories." He said that a labor bill would be submitted to Congress when it next convened in September, to implement the provisions of the constitutional article there. Also under consideration was the expediency of enacting a federal law to regulate Article 123 nationwide, preempting state laws. Calles "intimated that in view of the disparity in labor conditions in various parts of the country, the passage of Federal legislation applicable to the whole country was not likely."[4]

One embassy official opined that the absence of appropriate laws to regulate Article 123 contributed to labor conflict and arbitrary state action. When the Mexico City Tramway Company tried to lay off employees, the federal district government interpreted Article 123 to prohibit dismissals. The official concluded that "this controversy, like so many others, may be said to be due in the last analysis to the absence of legislation regulating article 123 of the Federal Constitution, and in the meantime this British owned enterprise like many others, including American, is exposed to arbitrary interpretations of the Constitution with all their attendant uncertainties."[5] American businesses, like other employers, sought to avoid the jurisdiction of state labor boards, such as the federal district's and Veracruz's. For example, the American embassy reported in June 1925 how the Huasteca Petroleum Company in Tampico, facing a dispute between rival unions, hoped that since its operations crossed state lines federal authorities would take cognizance of the conflict. In any event, it contemplated refusing to submit to the jurisdiction of the Veracruz board, deemed too sympathetic to workers' interests.[6]

Making the national Congress responsible for labor law could provide a way to circumvent the perceived hostility toward business interests of specific state boards, such as Veracruz's. Morones, both as secretary of the SICT and as a CROM leader, also supported federalization, if with distinct motives. Huasteca Petroleum's local representative told the American chargé d'affaires that Morones had calmed him about the possibility of Veracruz's labor board hearing the union's complaint, alluding to the possibility of federalizing labor law: "Morones said further that the state legislatures were already being canvassed with regard to the possibility of amending article 123 . . . so as to permit exclusively Federal regulation of that article." The chargé d'affaires realized the discrepancy with Calles's recent comments on the difficulty of implementing labor law on a national level. "Señor Morones, however, replied [to Huasteca's representative] that he was ready to defend the expediency of passing a Federal law to regulate article 123 against the suggestion that owing to differing conditions in various states Federal regulation was extremely difficult. [The Huasteca representative] further understood from Señor Morones that a Federal law regulating article 123 would be on the statute books by the end of the current year."[7]

The federal government's assumption of jurisdiction of labor disputes faced opposition from state governments. In the Huasteca Petroleum case, deputies from the Veracruz legislature personally complained to Calles that the company disregarded state law and asked whether the federal government would continue to handle the matter. Calles assured them that he had placed it in the hands of the state government and would respect the sovereignty of the states.[8] Meanwhile, oil companies worried that the state governments of Tamaulipas and Veracruz would not concede completely their jurisdiction over labor conflicts, even after enactment of a national labor statute:

> Officials of the large oil companies . . . are wondering whether the proposed Mexican National Labor Law will, if passed by the Mexican Congress, take precedence over the labor laws of the States of Tamaulipas and Veracruz in cases where the provisions of the aforesaid local laws are at variance with the provisions of the National Law. Several of these officials are of the opinion that the State governments of Veracruz and Tamaulipas will attempt, in specific cases where the two laws are at variance, to enforce the provisions of the State labor laws, regardless of the existence of a National Labor Law, when such a procedure is calculated to result to their advantage politically or otherwise; and that the situation thus brought about will result in greatly increasing the number of legal controversies in the Mexican courts at the expense of the oil operators.[9]

Veracruz's labor laws and boards in particular remained throughout 1925 the foil against which some business interests, or their allies, touted federalization.[10] Sheffield in late October referred to an editorial published in *El Universal*, which advocated federalization of Article 123 to counter the anti-capitalist and populist labor laws of the states.[11] The editorial, anxious about the radical potential of a federal law, mentioned Veracruz's recent accident and occupational illness insurance statute, vociferously resisted by the state's textile industry. Sheffield read the editorial to reflect a public opinion in favor of federalization consistent with Morones's earlier statements predicting passage of a statute.

The Chamber of Deputies passed a bill to implement the provisions of Article 123 in the federal district and territories in November 1925.[12] The CROM probably authored the bill, but the Senate stalled it. Opponents of the draft statute tended to believe it would serve as a dangerous precedent for the federalization of labor law in a manner inimical to their interests, such as Veracruz's statutes, even if the act would apply only in the federal district and territories. Many other states would regard the labor law of the federal district a model to copy, as its civil and penal codes had been. CROM proponents of the bill believed that with a slight modification, the addition of one article, the draft law could assume a national scope of coverage.[13]

The CROM clamored further for the pending bill and federalization of labor law. Its general secretary congratulated members of the Chamber of Deputies over their vote for the legislation, in a statement dated November 11, 1925, and "begged" them "to bring about the reforms corresponding to Article 123 to federalize the labor legislation" as well as the creation of a separate labor ministry.[14] During the November 29 demonstration protesting the federal judge's order suspending Veracruz's labor board's award against El Águila, the CROM also urged the Senate to pass the bill.[15]

One view in the U.S. embassy conflated the Chamber of Deputies' passage of the bill and the ongoing replacement of agrarians with labor governors in several states as cumulative evidence of the ascendancy of the CROM.[16] Probably an exaggerated viewpoint, it reflected how business interests found the bill ominous and excessively pro-labor at a time when they perceived the Mexican government as too close to the CROM. The president of the mine owners association mentioned meetings between Mexico City's industrial associations and congressional deputies, in which the parties pored over each article of the labor bill. The industrialists' representatives failed to persuade the deputies.[17] If the same source is credited, Calles had initially instructed senators to approve the bill. Mining companies objected strenuously while business interests in general were "much alarmed" and lobbied the Senate "to introduce modification which will make it possible to continue to do business in this country.[18] In addition, employers appealed directly to Calles.[19] Ambassador Sheffield believed the Senate would vote for the labor bill, disliked it, and concluded it remained within the scope of Mexico's internal affairs.[20]

One year later, the Senate continued to impede passage of the bill. On December 13, 1926, the upper house postponed voting on an amended version drafted by a Senate committee. Sheffield wrote, "the Senators opposed to rushing the bill through the Senate argued that in a matter of such complicated character longer study of the proposed legislation was necessary and it so happened that the members who were of this opinion were in the majority." The ambassador added: "It does not seem altogether unlikely that the general political situation and especially the international position have for the moment made the Government less insistent upon enacting this legislation. It is generally conceded that, should the president of the Republic use his influence affirmatively to assure the passage of the bill, it would pass."[21] CROM labor deputies Lombardo Toledano and Ricardo Treviño denounced the Senate's failure to vote on the labor bill. Treviño was especially virulent in his attack against the Senate and referred to the "capitalistic tendencies" evident in the session coming to an end.[22]

The draft statute languished in the Senate until 1927. Anticipation of a renewed effort to vote on it in that year led to the formation of an association of employers who had opposed the statute in 1926. Mostly British, American, and French industrialists, they sought to ameliorate its provisions. Sheffield did not express any great optimism that they would be successful, as the CROM-backed draft law headed for passage.[23] He concluded a letter as follows:

> It is hoped to complete the organization of the association and have it in working order prior to the commencement of the next session of the Mexican Congress, at

which time it is anticipated that the labor elements in Congress will make a determined effort to pass a bill regulating Article 123. . . . The C.R.O.M. has already announced its intention of pressing for this legislation and for this purpose it will, of course, be able to enlist the active support of President Calles and the Minister of Industry, Señor Morones. Employers of labor, I understand, are hopeful that with the authority of a strong organization such as is being created they will be able at least to modify some of the more impracticable and drastic features of the proposed Mexican legislation on this subject. Whether such hope is justified remains to be seen.[24]

The ambassador could have been more optimistic, although his pessimism was understandable: the CROM appeared to predominate in government, in the operation of the labor boards of Mexico City, and many places elsewhere.[25] Hence it seems paradoxical that the CROM failed to pass laws to legitimize or consolidate its power. But the CROM did not control the Senate.[26]

THE ESTABLISHMENT OF THE FEDERAL LABOR BOARDS

As legislation floundered in the Congress, the executive acted by fiat to try to regulate labor relations in the rail, mining and oil, and textile sectors of the economy. A circular dated April 28, 1926, directed governors to let the federal labor department assume jurisdiction over labor disputes on the railways. The circular justified this on the basis that industrial conflicts affected more than the immediate site of the incident, national interests were implicated, and unions had located their offices in the federal district. The circular could not base the federal executive's attempted assumption of control over labor matters on any lawful or statutory basis; and essentially it so conceded. One year later, on March 5, 1927, the SICT extended its attempt to exercise jurisdiction in labor matters to mining and petroleum. The argument was similar to that made in the railway circular, stressing necessity and national interest. As noted in Chapter 7, in the textile industry, the SICT under Morones had undertaken extensive negotiations with manufacturers and unions during 1925–27, in order to establish an industry-wide collective contract; on March 17,

1927, Calles had ratified the accord by decree, directing the SICT to resolve disputes arising under it.[27] In the meantime, the railroad strikes of 1926–27, combined with the amparo granted to the CTC by the federal judiciary, had called into question the legality of the SICT's arbitration. As described previously, Calles responded by issuing another decree in September, creating the federal labor boards to hear labor disputes in the railways but also in other strategic industries.[28] The decree papered over Calles's inability to have the Congress enact such legislation.[29] Without authorizing legislation, the September decree would be especially suspect constitutionally, as the Supreme Court concluded in later rulings querying it, the March 17 decree, and even the federal labor boards' legal remedies.[30] The need for federal labor legislation was now urgent.

THE OBREGONISTA ALTERNATIVE: THE PORTES GIL PROJECT

One day after the Supreme Court's ruling against the SICT, joint legislative committees reported to the Chamber of Deputies a draft bill to amend Article 123, to permit national labor legislation.[31] As the need for federal legislation to implement Article 123 had become more apparent for the ruling faction in the federal government, however, other political factions and employers remained concerned about CROM-supported legislation. Obregón, then planning his ineluctable reelection to the presidency, opposed the CROM bills and indicated that he would sponsor his own legislation upon becoming president at the end of 1928. His candidacy constituted a direct threat to the political arrangements and privileges of the CROM and augured the decline of its political influence. The labor federation's proposed legislation was an attendant casualty.

In September 1927, the Spanish chargé d'affaires, Dupuy de Lome, still worried aloud with his American counterpart that the upper house would approve radical amendments to the lower house's pending legislation. The Spanish diplomat, receiving his information from a Mexican senator, surmised that Calles intended to reward the CROM for its reluctant endorsement of Obregón's presidential campaign and to maintain the labor organization's support. Another possibility existed: to give the CROM their law before the political balance completely changed and it could no longer be promulgated. Dupuy de Lome predicted that the Senate would pass the bill within a few days and worried that its requirement of employing Mexicans would hurt Spanish employers, a concern the American chargé d'affaires, Schoenfeld, shared.[32]

Schoenfeld followed up his discussion with Dupuy de Lome by consulting F. H. Mifflen, secretary of the employer group the Association of Industrial and Commercial Enterprises. Mifflen said Morones had recently intimated to him that when the deputies again took up the labor bill, recommendations of the employers' group would be considered—perhaps a new draft of the law. The employers' group set up two committees to rewrite several chapters of the bill and revise those parts of it that the Senate had approved in general at the end of 1926. Mifflen expected not that their version of the bill would be accepted without modifications but that it could be used to reach a less objectionable statute than the one under discussion in 1926. Mifflen feared the possibility of proponents of a more radical bill rushing it through the Senate, despite assurances by senators and CROM officials that the bill would be postponed until 1928. Schoenfeld meanwhile was informed of the weakening influence of Morones, as Obregón's campaign gained strength. He wrote, "General Obregon is reported to me to have stated privately that the Law regulating Article 123 . . . will not be passed until President Calles goes out of office, although it is understood that when arrangements were made with Mr. Morones for the backing of the Labour Party in support of Obregon's candidacy no agreement was made to postpone the Labor Law."[33]

On October 19, 1927, two weeks after the committees of the Chamber of Deputies had submitted their report on the bill to amend Article 123, the American embassy reported "the existence of considerable conflict in the Mexican Congress regarding this legislation."[34] By then the Senate majority sympathetic to Obregón opposed the CROM-backed bill, on the basis that it contravened the states' concurrent jurisdiction in labor issues.[35] Instead, Obregonista senators wished to vote for a bill submitted by Obregón on December 9, 1921, when he had been president, to create a workers' insurance fund. Meanwhile, Labor Party (i.e., CROM-affiliated) members in the Chamber of Deputies released a statement maintaining the importance of the federalization of labor law. They contended that only a few states had implemented the mandates of Article 123, with scant enforcement of the statutes. And they pointed out that Obregón's insurance bill could not be "lawfully considered" unless Article 123 was amended. Schoenfeld believed that the outcome of the standoff depended on what Calles would do, qualifying this opinion by noting that the president could not disregard entirely the wishes of Obregón. In turn, he thought that Obregón's "obligations" to the CROM complicated his position, despite his antipathy to the organization and his strong preference for a workers' insurance scheme.[36]

One week later Schoenfeld wrote that the conflict between Obregonista senators and Labor deputies had "markedly increased."[37] The Obregonista bloc wanted to vote for the workers' insurance legislation but not for a national labor statute. The Labor congressmen insisted on the immediate passage of the acts to federalize labor law. To support them, the CROM issued a public statement, published in *Excélsior* on October 27, calling for rallies throughout the country to counter senatorial opposition. The CROM's insistence, consistent with resolutions taken at its sixth and seventh conventions, precipitated a breach within the Obregonista bloc in the Senate, embarrassing Obregón.[38]

Congress finally rejected the CROM's demands. In May 1928, the CROM, and its related Labor party, appealed to the congressional permanent committee to consider the bill to regulate Article 123 during its special session. The permanent committee denied the request on May 16. The federal legislature reflected Obregón's influence. Schoenfeld opined:

> It is of interest to report that from the discussion which resulted in rejecting the appeal of the Labor Party and the CROM for consideration of the bill regulating Article 123 . . . it appeared that General Obregón himself now has in preparation a bill of his own to regulate this important article. . . . It was indicated in the discussion yesterday that this bill would be introduced in the regular session of Congress beginning September 1, next, and that it would include the scheme of workers' insurance, the substance of which has already been reported to the Department, and in which . . . General Obregón is particularly interested.[39]

The denial of the CROM's appeal demonstrated the overwhelmingly Obregonista composition of the Congress, while the legislators affiliated with Morones's party were no longer as amenable to his direction.[40]

Shortly after Obregón won the presidential election in July 1928, a close associate of his, José Aspe Suinaga, told the American embassy that the president-elect had indicated "it was his intention, when Congress convened on September 1, 1928, to submit two bills to that body, the first dealing with insurance for labor, and the second, regulating Article 123 of the Federal Constitution." Aspe added that given the composition of the Congress, "these bills will undoubtedly be enacted and that the texts thereof are such that when given the force of law the political power of the CROM and its regional leaders will be reduced to unimportance."[41]

The assassination of Obregón in July 1928 delayed only briefly Obregonista plans for federal labor legislation. Upon his nomination to be interim president, Portes Gil convened a conference of labor and capital representatives to discuss the draft code that he had prepared, still in his capacity of minister of the interior. On October 20, 1928, his announcement of the legislative project to the press invoked the memory of the deceased president-elect:

> A few weeks before the last trip of General Obregón to this capital, I received a letter from him in which he manifested his wishes that I formulate a project of a regulatory law of Article 123 in order that, as soon as he arrived to Mexico City, we would have an exchange of ideas, as much as in respect of said project as in respect to what constituted his most legitimate aspiration during the last years of his life, that is, the Labor Insurance Law. With the indication of General Obregón, I began to elaborate said projects, which will be completed by the first fortnight of next November.[42]

At the time, Portes Gil contrasted his commitment to enact a labor statute, which he claimed paralleled similar legislation promulgated in 1925 in Tamaulipas when he was the state's governor, with the CROM's failure to have done so during its years of greater influence.[43] In view of the CROM's repeated frustrated efforts, Portes Gil's criticism of the confederation appears politically motivated, reflective of his antipathy for it.[44] The incoming presidency signaled the end of the obstructed CROM-backed labor bill: "in the Senate there has existed for some time a bill for a Labor Law and [Emilio Portes Gil] will duly take up with that Chamber a request to suspend decision thereof since it is believed that this bill is untimely, defective and incomplete."[45]

The convention of labor and employer representatives, or Convención Obrero-Patronal, met between November 15 and December 8, 1928. Among the more important business and labor groups, only the CGT abstained from attending the convention.[46] The CROM participated fully until it verbally attacked Portes Gil, in a self-defeating political move.[47] Before this occurred, Portes Gil stated in his parting message to the convention, as he assumed the office of the presidency, the objectives of enacting a federal labor law. The legislation should be practical, not a useless, idealistic law; it should encompass the rights achieved by workers, that is, their conquests, while considering the relationship that should exist between capital and labor. Put differently, the legislation should recognize the needs of capital, too.[48] These points would reverberate in ensuing debates around passage of the federal labor law.

Portes Gil's legislation was a comprehensive legal code meant to encompass most aspects of industrial relations and covered most issues arising from the employment contract while promoting the collective contract. It outlined a hierarchy of factory commissions, local (municipal), state, and federal boards to adjudicate labor disputes and a national council to determine other economic issues.[49] In view of the CROM's recent collaboration with the state, it outlawed any political activity by unions. Along with the regulation of the strike, the code implied extensive state intervention and supervision of industrial relations.

At the convention, Lombardo Toledano presented the critical positions of the CROM, still the main labor federation in the country. Lombardo affirmed two points Portes Gil conceded in his parting statement, the same ones repeatedly championed by labor and acknowledged at least rhetorically by governmental leaders as they pressed for the federal legislation. First, any statute should implement the rights established by Article 123. Second, it must incorporate the progress achieved by workers due to collective contracts and state laws—in other words, their conquests.[50] The CROM, Lombardo insisted, had supported the federalization of labor law and still did. Lombardo did object to Portes Gil's proposals for regulating union activity, contending that the legal personality of the union derived from Article 123 and was not a privilege to be accorded by the state.[51] Yet while Lombardo criticized provisions for monitoring labor organizations, his argument allowed for state supervision of union conduct, provided governmental intervention was limited to general prescriptions.[52]

On December 21, 1928, Portes Gil presented the Senate his initiative to amend constitutional Articles 123 and 73, Paragraph X, so that Congress could pass labor legislation applicable to the entire country.[53] The interim president justified the constitutional amendments mostly on economic grounds.[54] To appease state governors, Portes Gil compromised the future legislation: while labor law would be nationally uniform, state governments would enforce and apply this law in industries not specifically under the jurisdiction of the federal labor boards. Portes Gil acknowledged that the federal government had already created the federal labor boards because of the "need . . . so widely felt" and "in order to try to limit to one regulation the labor difficulties which were presenting themselves in these industries throughout various States of the Republic," thereby alluding to the major conflicts that had occurred in the railway and other important sectors of the economy.[55] The federal labor boards' jurisdiction would be restricted to these sectors. Although the Senate quickly approved the constitutional amendments, some chamber deputies opposed them because they believed amendments did not protect the states' jurisdiction over labor matters adequately. The final language of Paragraph X of Article 73 was as follows:

> The enforcement of the Labor Laws shall correspond to the authorities of the States within their respective jurisdictions, except when it is a question relating to railways or other enterprises of transportation, operating under Federal concessions, mines or hydrocarbons, and, lastly, labor performed at sea or in the maritime zone, in the form and manner which the regulations shall fix.[56]

Excélsior, on August 4, reported one more compromise reached between the president and Congress: to leave the textile industry outside of the jurisdiction of the federal labor boards. Portes Gil initially had wanted to place the industry within their scope.[57] The amendments to Articles 73 and 123 became effective on August 31, 1929.[58]

THE PROYECTO DE CÓDIGO FEDERAL DE TRABAJO

The Escobarista military rebellion and the inaugural convention of the National Revolutionary Party (PNR), sponsored by Calles, both happening in early March, delayed Portes Gil's completion of the draft federal labor code, or *Proyecto de Código Federal de Trabajo*, until July 1929.[59] Consisting of 639 articles, in addition to eight transitional ones, compiled into four books or parts, it remained as ambitious as the draft circulated at the convention in late 1928. A lengthy statement of purpose (*Exposición de motivos*) by Portes Gil adumbrated the main themes covered by the code, in the order of their appearance in the text.[60] A legal code, it was conceived as "a systematic and logical classification of general and mandatory dispositions corresponding to a unitary subject doctrinally and philosophically." It was meant to be a "legal organism."[61] The exposition said that the code should definitively establish the rights and obligations of workers and employers as well as the role and coordinating function of the state, meeting the "urgent" and "palpable" necessity for national legislation.[62]

The Portes Gil code's purpose to ensure social peace and order at the site of production was to be achieved by affording workers security in their employment and employers security in their investments, while directing them to recognize unions, closely regulated by the state.[63] Employers had to enter into collective contracts with unions. Unions had to limit themselves to representing workers in connection with economic issues; they could not engage in political activity. The code severely circumscribed the right to strike and aimed to replace it with arbitration by labor boards. The code would limit the boards' discretion through its detailed rules encompassing most aspects of labor relations. The code protected business' most important interests: it transformed the constitutional right of profit sharing into a savings scheme, and it conserved managerial prerogatives regarding investment and disinvestment by clearly distinguishing suspensions of production or reductions in operations from the lockout.

The code's structure posited as a premise of labor relations the employment contract, modified and elaborated by the state; or, as the exposition put it:

> The matter in the present case is labor economically considered. This develops and manifests itself within human will as a natural product of the relations between men in the contract of labor and as a product also of the force and will of the State, which balances and orients individual and collective activity or activities. That is the object of the Code: to establish the juridical norms that regulate these relations and set the conditions in which work should be realized.[64]

The code's organization sets out, first, the rules to govern the individual contract; second, the *contrato de equipo*, or labor contractor's agreement (an institutional innovation of the code); and, third, the collective contract.[65] Echoing Macías's valuation of the collective contract in his speech to the constitutional convention in December 1916, the exposition emphasized that it was the most important institution encompassed by the code. Not only were larger employers obliged to sign one; it would not be legally effective until filed with the relevant governmental authority.[66] The code further posited the *contrato ley*, or contract law, as an industry-wide agreement (similar to the textile convention) that would follow from collective contracts entered into by specific companies and their workers, and which the government could impose under certain conditions. Portes Gil ultimately justified its imposition by suggesting that the constitution recognized not only the individual person but also the collective.[67]

The code contemplated quelling acrimonious interunion rivalries, which had plagued industrial relations in the 1920s, by privileging the majority union exclusively.[68] Portes Gil rejected Lombardo's main criticism of mandatory union registration, namely, that the state might thus be attempting to suppress an already existing organization; the state would have little discretion to deny registration. More theoretically, Portes Gil asserted that the labor organization was a public or semipublic entity.[69] The code balanced the constitutional right to strike against prescriptions also in Article 123 directing the resolution of disputes through arbitration. The exposition made a convoluted interpretation of the tension between the right to strike and the establishment of arbitration boards:

> How is it possible that on one hand workers are permitted the right to strike, in order to obtain the realization of right[s], and on the other hand, the State intervenes with its force to obtain the same end? Therefore the right to strike is useless and unnecessary. Constitutional arbitration as further ahead we shall see is a semi-mandatory arbitration, and the strike in itself is not a right, rather a means of coercion that the Constitution recognizes, and accords it juridical process to obtain right[s].[70]

Code provisions actually narrowed procedurally and substantively the range of permissible strikes.

Organized labor guardedly subscribed to Portes Gil's project. The ad hoc workers' association, the Alianza de Uniones y Sindicatos de Artes Gráficas para el Estudio del Código Federal del Trabajo, convened a conference to formulate amendments to it as a unified labor front. The Convención Pro Ley del Trabajo met between August 15 and August 20, 1929.[71] Almost all major labor organizations, except the CGT, attended it. The CROM criticized the project systematically while the communist Confederación Sindical Unitaria de México (CSUM, the Unitary Mexican Union Confederation) labeled it fascist. The organizing committee for the convention remained more conciliatory.[72] Attendees recommended changes to the draft code as corrections that would reestablish rights already attained (*conquistas logradas*).[73] The proposals could be quite specific—for example, elimination of the *contrato de equipo*,[74] which, according to Lombardo, made the union a labor contractor "the most hated figure" of the working class and restricted its presence in a plant.[75]

The convention tacitly accepted the state's intervention in the internal affairs of unions, although it strenuously objected to the prohibition on political activity, reasoning that in practical terms union activity often assumed a political character without overstepping a defensive function of protecting members' interests. The prohibition, too, contravened constitutional principles. As a compromise, the convention suggested limiting the prohibition to electoral activity. After the convention, labor groups demonstrated for their amendments and a federal labor law.[76]

Excélsior, which was then linked to the powerful group of Monterrey industrialists, published capital's concerns about the pending legislation.[77] Business groups initially adopted a guardedly sympathetic stance toward Portes Gil's project, applauding the constitutional amendments enabling the federalization of labor law, then became critical of many of the code's provisions, lobbying publicly for far-reaching modifications. The industrialists' rhetoric reiterated that the needs of production, the economy, and foreign investment required legislation reconciling the interests of labor and capital. The rights of capital needed assurances; if the code upheld labor's rights under Article 123, it should not extend them. An open letter of the Grupo Patronal (Employer Group) published in *Excélsior* in late July described Mexico's economic crisis and said that the only viable solution was to attract foreign capital. Since the potential for investment was affected by conditions in other countries, burdening production costs any further would discourage investment and worsen the depression. The federal labor law had to ensure capital's right of property and managerial discretion to direct enterprises and select personnel, from foreign countries if necessary.[78]

An editorial in *Excélsior* in mid-July, denouncing union *líderes*, an allusion to the CROM, opined that laws covering industrial relations must stimulate production. To realize this purpose, the legislation should conciliate both the worker and the entrepreneur's interests; preferring one at the expense of the other harmed both.[79] Another editorial in early August applauded Congress's enactment of the constitutional amendments authorizing federalization and criticized defenders of the more "advanced" labor legislation in some states. The editorial approved of Portes Gil's proyecto conditionally. Congress, it asserted, should legislate for all, not just workers; the radicalism of "advanced" laws implied the ruin of industrial enterprises, breaking the equilibrium that ought to exist between capital and labor. The legislature, like the judge, should accord each its own, guaranteeing the rights of capital and labor.[80] This was a liberal argument: it formally resembled Vigil's, Prieto's, Martínez de la Torres's, and Lozano's, to a degree.[81] But whereas they, in the 1870s, had contended that labor was the equal of capital in order to advance labor's position, now the argument was deployed to curb labor's pretensions for more.

The Chamber of Deputies began consideration of Portes Gil's project on September 2, 1929.[82] An article published in *Excélsior* on September 11 reported employer complaints, such as indefinite or "perpetual" employment contracts, mandatory, collective contracts, "forced unionization," and the recognition of the solidarity strike as licit. Too burdensome for industry were obligations regarding rest periods, paid vacations, housing, as well as third-party liability.[83] Portes Gil personally tried to placate the Monterrey industrialists. He failed.[84] An extensive memorandum presented by the Convention of Industrial Delegates (Convención de Delegados Industriales de la República), filed with the Chamber of Deputies on September 20, and summarized by *Excélsior*, recommended multiple changes to the code.[85]

The memorandum argued that freedom of contract should be consecrated in an absolute form in labor legislation for industrial progress and to facilitate foreign investment. Invoking constitutional Article 4, and construing Articles 4 and 123 together, the memorandum asserted that the only qualifications of contractual freedom should be those stated in Article 123. Under the same rubric of freedom of contract, the memorandum attacked the labor code's privileging of the union, that is, "forced unionization." Recognition of the union should not infringe employers' statutory or constitutional rights, such as the right to direct and administer their business and contract freely. The union, the memorandum further argued, was a spontaneous product of the class struggle. The objectives of the code were to eliminate the struggle and establish stable relationships. "Forced unionization" would maintain class struggle, impede the collaboration of employers and workers, and produce results contrary to those envisioned. The memorandum then cited twenty-nine articles requiring deletion or modification. It conceded Article 123's right to strike but juxtaposed Article 17, prohibiting taking justice into one's own hands, to construe the worker's right narrowly, and limit it solely to "obtaining the equilibrium between the factors of production, harmonizing the rights of labor with those of capital." To distance administrative boards from political pressure, the judiciary should designate the government's representatives on them. Additional commentary discussed indemnifications for discharge and accidents, payment of overtime, rest and vacation periods, and

Article 139, which required employers to provide housing. Since this last provision actually implemented a mandate of Article 123, the industrialists suggested reducing fines for noncompliance to a *de minimis* sum.[86]

Combined with their objections to the labor code, business associations urged the Chamber of Deputies to prolong its deliberations of the draft legislation. Congressional deputies proved receptive; they were divided over the bill. On September 9, the Chamber agreed to hold public debates on the proyecto and give interested parties until September 20 to comment about it.[87] In view of the short tenure of the interim president, prolonging study of the draft legislation froze it. Furthermore, the withdrawal or suspension of investment, especially foreign, and in particular American, was a constant threat to its passage. To illustrate, on September 10, *Excélsior* reported that General Electric, which had plans to invest one million dollars to manufacture light bulbs, "suspended all [related] activity, declaring that if the labor code were promulgated in its present form, it would desist from carrying out its projects." Likewise, American Smelting, which had completed arrangements for the investment of eight million dollars in a refinery in Rosita, Coahuila, awaited the outcome of the legislative process.[88]

Ford threatened, too. On August 17, the *New York Times* reported that Henry Ford was contemplating a reduction of his planned investment, issuing instructions that the proposed extension of the company's assembly plant not begin until he had finished his study of Portes Gil's draft law. In the context of his initial decision to expand, which had been perceived as a promising indication of future development, the possible reduction was described as "providing substantial material for reflection, for general industrial conditions pending uncertainty as to in what form Emilio Portes Gil's proposals will reach the statute book, are sufficiently depressed without further notices such as that cited."[89] One month later, Ford's manager in Mexico City, Adrián René Lajous, submitted comments critical of the Portes Gil proyecto to the Chamber of Deputies, highlighting Ford's concerns with provisions on mandatory collective contracts, housing, and the requirement of paying additional indemnification for an employee's discharge. Lajous said that mandating collective contracts in violation of the freedom to contract would lead to litigation and the Supreme Court's determination of the constitutionality of the relevant provisions, creating uncertainty for all concerned, including the public and the fisc.[90]

The *New York Times* had observed in the meantime, "deputies are making slow, almost inappreciable progress in their work and some sources consulted . . . do not think it probable that the new law will be enacted before Emilio Portes Gil ends his provisional term in the executive office."[91] The Chamber of Deputies formally endorsed the code, in general, on September 25. This did not ensure passage of the legislation.[92] President-elect Pascual Ortiz Rubio, too, was signaling dissatisfaction with the draft code and his disposition to prepare an alternative.[93] In the end, the legislature adjourned on December 30, 1929, without enacting the code.[94]

THE LEY FEDERAL DEL TRABAJO

Congress could not vote on labor legislation again until September 1930, unless the president convened a special session. The federal executive did not reintroduce Portes Gil's proyecto. Ortiz Rubio, now president, set up a technical commission comprised of officials from the Ministry of Industry, Commerce, and Labor and the Ministry of Interior to revise the code. Aarón Sáenz, who had been the preferred presidential candidate of Monterrey's industrialists to succeed Portes Gil, was charged with supervising the redrafting process of the legislation and marshalling it through Congress.[95] He was generally regarded as being a partisan of business interests and an adversary of Portes Gil. Delegating to Sáenz the responsibility of ensuring passage of a labor statute evidenced the federal government's aim to reassure business interests that had strongly opposed Portes Gil's project.[96] Promptly, a draft version of the revised law was given to Ortiz Rubio, who held several cabinet meetings during January 1931 to review it. "All the ministers of Government and the heads of the several independent departments of the Government . . . attended these meetings."[97] They reputedly reached a consensus endorsing the draft with few alterations.[98] The permanent congressional commission received it on March 12, 1931, with a request for a special congressional session. Before official release of the draft, press rumors insinuated that "the most radical provisions" of the Portes Gil proyecto had been eliminated.[99]

Sáenz asked Eduardo Suárez to assume responsibility for drafting the language of the legislation.[100] Suárez had occupied the chair of labor law at the law school of the national university and presided for a brief time on the federal district's labor board. In his memoirs, which briefly sketch his role in the redrafting of the labor law, Suárez wrote that his position on the board had been difficult because of the CROM's attempts to outflank him when he held against union affiliates. They presented their cases before the "omnipotent" minister Morones, who in turn took their complaints to the then president Calles. Calles would summon Suárez eventually to meet with him to present the reasons for his rulings. At these audiences with the president, Calles normally agreed with Suárez, requesting only that the latter state the rationales of his decisions broadly.[101] Suárez assumed for these reasons that Sáenz had requested his participation on the drafting commission. Besides Suárez, the commission consisted of Aquiles Cruz, Cayetano Ruiz García, and Alfredo Iñarritu, all of whom had ample experience on the labor boards.[102] Iñarritu had been a member of the Portes Gil drafting committee.[103]

The commission worked "arduously" on the draft law every night till dawn. Sáenz regularly joined the working sessions. According to Suárez, upon its completion the draft was aired immediately to obtain the comments of labor and business. Sáenz then gave it to the council of ministers. The council deliberated over it for several days. Genaro Estrada, secretary of foreign relations, General Joaquín Amaro, secretary of defense, and Manuel Pérez Treviño, secretary of agriculture and development, approved the labor code. Manuel Puig Causaranc, then head of the department of the federal district, and Octavio Mendoza González, subsecretary in the Ministry of the Interior, objected to the proposed law. Ortiz Rubio equivocated.[104]

Initial public reactions of employer and labor groups to the proposed legislation were measured. The employer association the Grupo Patronal, in April 1931, completed an analysis of the draft law, with proposed modifications.[105] The analysis juxtaposed the Grupo's revisions with the disputed articles of the bill; each one was introduced with a brief statement. The approach was legalistic and technical. In effect, the Grupo accepted the overall structure of the Sáenz bill as well as its basic premises. In the face of governmental determination to enact a comprehensive statute, the CROM, at least in January 1931, also assumed a cautious position, as evidenced by articles published in *Pro-Paria*.[106] The lead editorial on January 14 noted that the president of the permanent congressional commission had just declared that this time the revised labor code would be sent to Congress without being sidetracked in debates. The editorial outlined how Sáenz would shepherd the project through the legislative process. Another article, dated January 17, inquired whether the bill would be revealed to interested parties before the legislature deliberated on it.[107]

By May the CROM had formulated a stance more critical of the draft statute. *Pro-Paria* announced the formation of the Frente Unico (the single front), which was set up to pressure the government to improve the Sáenz project. The same paper added that the draft statute had provoked profound uneasiness among all labor groups and was in absolute discordance with Article 123, and that it had failed to take into account the evolution of labor's customary rights arising from labor board decisions or contained in collective contracts then in force.[108]

The U.S. embassy reported that the press depicted the Chamber of Deputies divided over the proposed statute, "a minority group being composed of those in favor of very radical labor legislation, and a majority group being composed of so-called Moderates."[109] In anticipation of receipt of the draft bill, the PNR's bloc in the lower congressional house, encompassing "the great majority" of deputies, had already held a meeting regarding it and had appointed two committees of twelve to study the draft. The two committees "divided themselves into eight groups of three members each, in order that each of these small groups might study one chapter of the proposed law." The president of the PNR bloc, General Melgar, promised to hold a special session of Congress to ensure a sufficient amount of time for the committees to study the draft. They would begin their discussions of it on March 23. Meanwhile, the PNR bloc in the Senate said it would meet on March 13 to appoint committees to cooperate with their lower house counterparts.[110] The SICT released the draft statute on March 18, 1931.[111]

The special congressional session opened on May 22, with the draft legislation (*Proyecto de Ley Federal del Trabajo*) formally presented. Ortiz Rubio's brief preamble, introducing the project, and Sáenz's longer statement of purpose (or exposition of reasons) are more prosaic than the rhetoric of Portes Gil's exposition. Tracking the draft project, the Sáenz exposition provides brief justifications for its main provisions, generally by balancing the need to promote or sustain national production with the need to conserve the achievements of labor and rights established by Article 123. Ortiz Rubio's introduction to the project makes three observations. First, legislation should be enacted expeditiously in order to initiate a regime clearly defining the conditions for furnishing labor so important to the national economy. Second, the law is urgently necessary because the constitutional amendments of 1929 rendered it impossible thereafter for states to legislate on labor matters or remedy the deficiencies of their labor tribunals. Third, the project is an indispensable complement of the president's political program: practically, it would create security for workers and employers and signal the possibility for investments and new sources of employment.[112]

The exposition mentioned the precursors of the bill: principles drawn from state laws, customary practices, and case law (jurisprudencia), including board rulings, draft legislation for the federal district (probably a reference to the 1925 bill), and Portes Gil's project, as well as foreign models. The last provided a basis only for comparison.[113] The exposition then took up the main themes delineated in the draft statute, in the following order: the state as employer, sources of law, the collective contract, the *contrato de equipo*, the employment contract between individuals and its regulation, labor organizations, strikes and lockouts, occupational accidents and illnesses, and the peaceful solution of conflicts. Like Portes Gil's project, the Sáenz draft made the collective contract mandatory with a union that represented a majority of the workers in a firm and underscored its social function both as the mechanism to ensure peaceful industrial relations and as the embodiment of the achievements of labor. Unlike the Portes Gil proyecto, it extended coverage of the collective agreement to all workers regardless of their union status.[114]

Significantly, the Sáenz project recognized the lawfulness of the *cláusula de exclusión* in a collective contract. Article 48 permitted this clause only in connection with the hiring of workers; it did not make it mandatory, and it exempted workers already employed at the time of the signing of the collective contract from having to belong to the relevant union. The exposition explained the *contrato ley* as a means to establish uniform conditions for an entire industry and eliminate one of the most important, presumably debilitating elements of competition. The exposition defended the *contrato de equipo* against criticism by labor groups. And it seemingly tried to persuade employers to accept unions. They improved labor relations, through the collective contract, "a formula for permanent peace between classes." The union movement had reached such a state of development that it was senseless to disregard or fight it.[115]

The exposition emphasized Mexico's tradition of liberal constitutionalism: whereas in some nations unions had been subordinated to the state, transforming them into public law entities (*organismos de derecho público*), a different solution had been reached within Mexico's political framework. The labor organization was considered to be a civil (private) institution, with a legal personality, simultaneously characterized by public aspects.[116] In accord with Portes Gil's code, the Sáenz draft law prohibited unions from engaging in political, business, and religious activities.[117]

The Sáenz project also aimed to regulate the strike. Given the existence of legal mechanisms to resolve industrial conflicts, it deemed the strike a secondary recourse permissible only when the constitution expressly authorized it.[118] Like Portes Gil's project, Sáenz's draft defined the strike as the suspension of the employment contract. Lawfully striking workers were therefore entitled to their jobs upon returning to work and were required to execute indispensable tasks to maintain the plant during a work stoppage. The strike was obligatory for all workers once a majority had declared it; and for legal recognition, a majority of the workforce had to favor it. The exposition justified this by invoking the Ley Orgánica of Article 4.[119] The exposition recapitulated the following conditions necessary for the state's support of a strike: it had to be undertaken essentially with the objective of harmonizing the interests of the employer and worker, declared by the majority of workers, meet (administrative) procedures, and not violate the terms of the collective bargaining agreement.[120] If it did not satisfy these conditions, the appropriate labor board could impose civil sanctions and order workers back to their jobs under the threat of the termination of employment. The Sáenz project, without so stating in its exposition, thus incorporated the arguments asserted by the federal labor board and tacitly ratified by the Supreme Court in the amparo cases of the CTC. This, in the late 1920s, along with other labor board decisions and several state statutory provisions, had become the actual law on the right to strike but without the definitive and comprehensive imprimatur of federal legislation.

THE AMENDMENTS OF CONGRESSIONAL DEPUTIES

Labor leaders' increasingly strident denunciation of Sáenz's project and government figures, accusing them of betraying workers' interests, put the PNR bloc in the Chamber of Deputies publicly on the defensive. The ruling group's response was twofold and lacked consensus. First, PNR leaders, like Melgar, attacked the CROM, asserting that the legislation was in the public interest.[121] Second, the deputies charged with reviewing Sáenz's bill (not all of whom were in accord with Sáenz) amended the project, significantly strengthening union power.[122]

El Universal, whose editorial stance was not inconsistent with the views of government leaders at the time, propagated the argument that the solution to class conflict lay in the normalization of industrial relations and the correct interpretation or application of law:

> After fourteen years of endeavors and of attempts in every direction, the issuance of the law to normalize relations between workmen and capitalists, seems to be definitely in the course of accomplishment.
>
> One might truthfully assert that 99.9 percent of the difficulties and conflicts which have arisen in the country since the definite triumph of the Revolution, are due to the lack of harmony occasioned by the application, interpretation and execution of the much maligned Article 123.[123]

This editorial detailed the shortcomings of laws in Mexico, echoing complaints long heard of their irrelevancy to social realities and the inadequate drafting and utopian expectations on the part of legislators:

All our laws, above all the fundamental ones, have suffered from the defect of vagueness and lack of precision. Our legislators seize upon the most recent Utopia, the most fashionable idea, the most glittering technical phrase. . . . The difficulty lies in the application of these flamboyant and most novel theories. There arises the necessity of regulating them and as the regulations can have nothing to do with the desiderata written into books but deal rather with naked, cruel and inexorable realities, said regulations are hardly ever written, or if they are they need others to explain, clarify and expound them. The already dead Constitution of 1857 will not give us the lie, as practically all of its precepts remained without regulation, especially those which constituted guarantees or confirmed rights; and it must be remembered that that constitution did not have to deal with the complexities, details and intricacies of the present one.[124]

El Universal alluded to the willingness of both sides to compromise, and to Melgar's presentation of "a balanced and sensible understanding," in which the conquests of the Revolution and Article 123 were respected, while national industry and investments received protection and due guarantees.

The editorial, like Melgar's statements, was more concerned with employers' needs: "the employers feel that this law will have to be of such nature that it will not raise the cost of production and increase the gravity of the problems which are exhausting the economic life of Mexico." It concluded that "the life and prosperity of Mexican industry which today is languishing" depended on the work of the legislators.[125] An earlier editorial in the same newspaper had emphasized the importance the draft law would have for foreign investment. "Everything which directly or indirectly contributes to the entry of foreign investments should be considered as beneficial to the country. Such a thing would be a just and reasonable Labor Code which, while supporting the interests of Labor, would make secure those of Capital. The Code will dispel the doubts which are cherished by the investor and will persuade him to establish himself in the Republic, which is at the threshold of a great industrialization."[126]

While the government presented the Sáenz project as an institutional innovation in the public interest, labor organizations, mainly the CROM, lobbied the government.[127] On May 14, Ortiz Rubio met with representatives of the Alianza de Agrupaciones Obreras y Campesinas de la República, or Alliance of Labor and Peasant Groups of the Republic, which had coalesced in opposition to the draft legislation.[128] Lombardo Toledano, on behalf of the Alliance, asserted that the legislation disregarded many of labor's achievements and was contrary to the letter and spirit of Article 123. Labor groups objected especially to provisions denying the right to strike under certain circumstances and standards that might overturn labor contracts then in force. Unions suspected that employers were using the economic crisis as a pretext to force the legislation through Congress.[129] The critical position of labor organizations evidently affected the president. He seemed to entertain modifying the draft law, publicly assuring labor that workers' advances "won by the revolution" would be consolidated, not undermined.[130] This development "greatly exercised" Sáenz. After meeting with Ortiz Rubio, Sáenz issued his public response to the Alliance: the draft law had the approval of the president. The Alliance rebuked Sáenz in another public letter, stating that it would refuse any further discussion with the SICT.[131]

Sáenz already was trying to line up the support he needed. Possibly on the day Ortiz Rubio spoke with members of the Alliance, leading government officials in the afternoon convened in Chapultepec Castle to discuss the draft law. Ortiz Rubio, Calles, Colonel Riva Palacio, then interior minister, Sáenz, and the PNR congressional committees studying the draft bill reportedly attended. Sáenz had called the meeting so that Calles, as jefe maximo, "might impress upon the senators and deputies the necessity of passing the project substantially as it was drafted."[132] Suárez recounted attending one such conference with Calles, among others, without dating it. From his description, this closed meeting could be the same one Sáenz scheduled; in any event, Calles gave his crucial endorsement.[133] An unpublished transcript of the meeting at Chapultepec evidences a desire on Calles's part to reach a viable solution of the existing differences over sections of the draft bill and incorporate the modifications of the congressional deputies and their labor allies. It also indicates some distance between Calles and Sáenz. Ortiz Rubio remained mostly silent at the meeting.[134]

As summer came, the president of the congressional committees indicated that the bill would be promulgated into law by September 1. *Excélsior* predicted that Congress would approve without debate those provisions not under challenge, that is, most of them. The secretary of the Association of Industrial and Commercial Enterprises informed the American embassy of his apprehension that "a law very burdensome to employers will be passed."[135] In contrast, representatives of two large American enterprises said, "they have been assured by the Minister of Industry, Commerce and Labor that the law will pass substantially as drafted originally by that Ministry." Further, "one of these men had been informed through one of his sources that the report as prepared by the committees of the chamber of deputies will be substituted by the original project with a few amendments before the final passage of the bill." The representatives of American businesses worried about the amended provisions relating to collective contracts and the inclusion of tuberculosis in the list of covered occupational diseases; "the project otherwise if passed as indicated by the Ministry of Industry, Commerce and Labor, will be quite satisfactory."[136]

While Congress apparently ignored the Grupo Patronal's suggestions and accommodated some of those of organized labor, the employer group sent the legislature another memorandum dated June 8, 1931. It referenced the national economic crisis and within this context argued against the committees' amendments dealing with labor contracts, indemnities for occupational diseases, particularly tuberculosis, and "especially the tendency of the project as amended to favor the working class as opposed to the interests of the rest of the country."[137] Complementing the statement of the employers' group and attacking the committees' amendments, the Monterrey chamber of commerce wrote its own statement, urging enactment of legislation benefiting not just one class at the expense of the country as a whole.[138]

On July 10, the legislative commissions published their report in the *Diario de los Debates*, with their amendments. The report reflected the commissions' full awareness of the economic crisis affecting the country and the unspecified economic implications of the labor law. It conceded the surfeit of sentimental arguments available to enhance the benefits or rights of workers but added that the commissioners had not let themselves be persuaded by such arguments; it recommended to the Chamber of Deputies the same stoic resolve. Workers' rights that were recognized in the course of modifying the draft law were either basic ones or reflective of achievements already attained. The report rejected the free play of market forces and classical liberalism as guiding legal principles. It adopted the position that the federal labor law should promote unionization as the best means available for workers to defend their class interests. The report declared that it had gone beyond merely tolerating or recognizing the union, as in the Sáenz proyecto, to "strengthening the organization, stimulating its development, and creating new unions."[139]

The commissions made minor changes regarding the obligation to contract with a union, the collective agreement, and its termination. On the basis of Ortiz Rubio's representation that the executive would prepare a separate civil service statute, they deferred coverage of public employees.[140] The commissions added Article 13, a transitory provision, to protect workers covered by collective agreements stipulating more favorable conditions than those prescribed in the legislation.[141] They deleted the contrato de equipo, concurring with labor's complaints that employers would use it to avoid collective contracts and to combat unions.[142]

Importantly, the commissions extended the cláusula de exclusión to allow collective contracts to stipulate the discharge of workers not belonging to a union (and not merely to require union membership at the time of hire).[143] The closed union shop was legally authorized. The modifications also broadened the definition of the union so as to permit it more activities and narrowed the bases for canceling union registration.[144] The commissions reintroduced the solidarity strike as a legitimate objective. They also further regulated the internal affairs of unions by specifying more requirements for the bylaws, among other minor changes.[145]

Sáenz accepted the amendments made by the congressional advisory commissions and then launched into an attack against the CROM, accusing it of decrying the federal labor law in order to protect its own interests.[146] Ortiz Rubio weighed in at the end of July to rebut labor criticisms of the proposed legislation. The issuance of the labor law was designated a "national necessity."[147] Supporters of the legislation rushed it through the congressional houses. On the last day of voting, the Senate approved 450 articles in two hours. The American embassy speculated as follows:

> After leaving the Senate it was impossible to obtain a copy of this law, and no one has seen it since it left the Senate and was signed by the President. It is thought by some of the prominent business men in Mexico City that rushing it through the Senate, and the secrecy, were to facilitate certain changes in some of the drastic provisions, by higher authority, similar to the case of the Petroleum Law which was changed after it had been passed by both Houses of Congress.[148]

The outcome was formal promulgation of the federal labor law, on August 18, 1931.[149] On August 28, the law was published in the official daily publication of the government and went into effect.[150]

DISSATISFACTION WITH THE FEDERAL LABOR LAW

After the lower house passed the labor law on August 4, *Pro-Paria* condemned it, referring to attacks by Sáenz on the CROM and congressional deputies and to Ortiz Rubio's threat ("the government will proceed with an iron fist").[151] The Alianza persisted with complaints about the legislation, on August 15 protesting to Ortiz Rubio the Senate's approval of the bill and objecting to elimination of coverage of public employees from the law.[152] The Alianza pleaded that the transitory articles be changed: "So as to guarantee as far as possible, the existing collective labor contracts and the conquests which the proletariat has already obtained. Particularly as regards the subject matter of transitory Article XIII [w]e call attention to the danger which threatens the arbitration of the Conciliation and Arbitration Councils through the fact that collective contracts can be modified in an arbitrary period of time."[153] One CROM leader objected to the failure to make the closed shop obligatory and not just permissible, warning that the requirement to contract with a union would encourage employers to collaborate with their minority company-dominated organizations. He castigated the requirement that unions provide advanced notice of a strike and the envisioned role of the labor boards during a strike and termed the federalization of labor law a myth.[154]

Publicly, employers' groups reacted lividly to the congressional amendments and the enactment of the labor law. *Excélsior* published the dire appraisal of the Grupo Patronal, which categorically declared that Congress had disregarded the Grupo's recommendations. Instead of reasonable legislation to achieve the "desired equilibrium between the factors of production," the employer group said that the labor law was a class-biased code. The employer group would "continue to fight to the end that the application of this law be made to conform to the precepts of the Constitution.[155]

In contrast to the shifting positions of the Grupo Patronal and the CROM, the Mexican communist party's periodical, *El Machete*, consistently analyzed the Sáenz project as a governmental strategy to subordinate the working class to the state on behalf of national and employer interests.[156] In February the underground newspaper had reported a recent statement of Sáenz, condemning the leaking of a complete copy of the draft statute; the paper suggested there were factions within the ruling PNR who might try to posture as more "revolutionary" (than Ortiz Rubio and Sáenz), namely, Portes Gil or Tejeda.[157] In March the newspaper alleged that capitalists had participated personally in the drafting of the labor bill; and it noted Sáenz's business proclivity, his sugar interests, and links to the Monterrey industrialists. The newspaper wrote that the chapter of the statute concerning railroad workers was formulated in the offices of the Ferrocarriles Nacionales.[158] Both the proposed labor law and the debt treaty (*Convenio de la Deuda*) were part of the government's strategy to reconstruct the nation on a firm capitalist base.[159] The paper dismissed CROM threats of a general strike: the labor confederation was attempting to bargain for a better price to sell out.[160] It depicted as a virtual charade the employer offensive against the bill and the deputies' rally against it.[161] *El Machete* concluded toward the end of July that the amendments were superficial, the fundamental provisions of it were left intact, including mandatory arbitration, governmental intervention, and regulation of unions.[162]

Soon after promulgation of the federal labor law, *Pro-Paria* reported instances of employers seeking to renegotiate collective contracts and reduce benefit levels where the standards of the new federal law were lower than those in existing agreements.[163] One labor scholar writing in the early 1930s commented about such attempts by employers to revise contracts, and labor opposition to them.[164] *El Machete* advocated both resistance to the new federal statute and use of it when tactically convenient, without acceptance of its premises.[165]

CONCLUSION

The declamatory posturing of labor and employer groups against the newly promulgated federal labor law is not inconsistent with the government's attempts to accommodate both labor's and business's interests. Ortiz Rubio's administration tried to placate the concerns of business as it prepared the labor statute, and it compromised with organized labor (or congressional deputies sympathetic to labor's interests) so that Congress would pass the legislation. This compromise, in turn, failed to satisfy labor fully, while provoking a strong reaction from business groups. Both business and labor disputed important elements of the new statute. Organized labor was genuinely apprehensive that businesses would reduce their workforces and apply to labor boards for releases from contractual requirements on the basis of the lower standards of the federal legislation; these events did occur. Employers feared the consequences of union closed shops and the further state subsidization of organized labor, as would develop in the ensuing years. The criticisms of the federal labor law by capital and labor nonetheless can obscure much of the significance of its passage.

The governmental coalition that promoted the law's enactment aimed to structure industrial relations so as to ensure that business could prosper in Mexico; this meant, in particular, guaranteeing conditions for the management of investment and production. Portes Gil and his project had failed to secure the confidence of industrialists, including the Monterrey group and foreign capitalists. Ortiz Rubio and Calles behind him would attempt to reassure business by scaling back some of the provisions of the Portes Gil code but, equally important, by signaling that under the new law businesses would be able to invest and disinvest more freely and by delegating the legislative project to one of industry's more trusted allies, Sáenz.

At the same time, Ortiz Rubio's administration could disregard neither Article 123 nor the country's labor movements, even though the latter were divided and, in 1930–31, weakened by the economic depression. The very legitimacy of the federal government depended on its character as a revolutionary state, and its revolutionary character was closely linked to the realization of Article 123. Article 123 may not have been fully realized in 1931, but its symbolic importance was substantial—and in view of the existence of labor movements that invoked it recurrently, its symbolic promises required a measure of fulfillment. Among policymakers within the government (not least the jefe maximo, Calles), some incorporation of the achievements of organized labor since 1910 was imperative. Significantly, the federal labor law had to obtain the consent of both capital and labor to a degree if it were to be viable; indeed it could not be passed by the legislature or presented to it without the inclusion of labor's rights.

The legislation, however, aimed to be more than an affirmation of Article 123 or a set of guarantees to capital's property interests or a compromise encompassing both. The federal labor law was a project to institutionalize labor relations so as to supplant politicized labor conflict with a system of precise legal rules that would serve as norms to be applied to resolve (or circumvent in the first place) disputes in a rational and equitable manner. Government drafters and proponents of the legislation may have truly believed that institutionalization at the federal level of the collective labor contract and union subject to the premises of a private production system could transcend the divisiveness of labor conflict tied to political struggle that had threatened production throughout much of the 1920s—even before the beginnings of economic depression toward the end of the decade. Their rhetoric certainly suggests as much, as does the articulation of the federal labor law and its major antecedents, the Portes Gil code and 1925 CROM bill: all are extensive, and the code and 1931 law are comprehensive in their attempt to regulate all aspects of industrial relations.

The legal antecedents of the federal labor law date back to earlier state legislation, such as Veracruz's, and ultimately to the conceptualization of social law as a transformation of liberal legal doctrine and principles. All of the parties who contributed to the formulation of the legislation referenced liberal and social liberal concepts that had circulated in the Atlantic world since the late nineteenth century. The conceptual framework and its outline in the exposition introducing the federal labor law are clearly immersed in this discourse of social law. The Grupo Patronal relied more in its analyses of the draft labor law on liberal notions of freedom of contract and labor (embraced by workers in Mexico in the latter part of the nineteenth century) and on the liberal political economic concept of the equilibrium of the factors of production, while Lombardo Toledano, as one major public intellectual and legal advocate of organized labor, articulated forcefully the concept of collective rights that Macías in the constitutional debates of December 1916 had already presented. That is, regardless of the social or economic interest being furthered or defended, the interlocutors in the debate over the enactment of the statute were using a similar and overlapping legal and ideological language.

In the debates over the passage of federal legislation, all of the major parties accepted and furthered the legalization of industrial relations. They accepted that government agencies would regulate industrial relations and adjudicate labor disputes to some extent. They disputed the degree to which government should be involved, but none, except perhaps the waning anarchist CGT, dismissed governmental intervention or participation in the system—and that this governmental activity, along with that of unions and businesses, should be articulated in legal terms. Interestingly, even the communist party advised using the new law (but without accepting its ideological justification). The irony that the state finally promulgated comprehensive labor legislation when workers' movements were relatively weak can be explained in reference to the political situation at the time. It is perhaps as ironic that the CROM, which not only had benefited from its special relationship with Calles until 1928 but had also furthered its position in extralegal (or racketeering) ways, presented such a legally strong appraisal of Sáenz's draft law, while largely politically debilitated; or that Ortiz Rubio's administration compromised with some legislators to incorporate provisions to the draft law that substantially strengthened the position of organized labor.[166]

The leadership of the federal government, ultimately, ensured that federal labor legislation was enacted: it needed such legislation. In the middle of the country's deep economic depression, led by a volatile political alliance, the central state had to assert its authority in labor relations that affected the entire country or strategic regions of it. Calles already had taken a major step when he decreed the establishment of the federal labor boards. The federalization of labor law had to follow if such boards were to operate legitimately and if the federal government was to exercise a degree of influence in the national economy. Otherwise Calles would be simply a boss ruling through decree, deals, and force, which may have been close to social and political reality frequently but was patently unstable in the face of other (if less powerful) bosses and chiefs. Calles must have realized this in his September 1928 address announcing that Mexico subsequently would be governed through institutions lawfully. The presidencies of the Maximato (1928–34) may have been to varying degrees weak, but their instability could be only greater in the absence of the legal institutionalization of important aspects of social and economic life, not least of which concerned industrial relations. The federal labor law affirmed this aspiration to institutionalize and legalize industrial relations. Much more than Article 123, it outlined a system in which unions would sign collective contracts with employers, which could stipulate control over hiring by the unions, but which otherwise would largely defer to managerial authority in relation to questions of production. The state through administrative labor boards would closely regulate the strike, insofar as it was permitted.

Indeed, the state would preside over the industrial relations of unions and employers: to the degree that the law fully recognized unions and afforded protections to labor, the union would exist conditioned on its recognition by state agencies. Such legislation in a narrow sense envisioned inhibiting the operations of such a powerful political and social organization as the CROM had become in the 1920s. More broadly, the lawyers who drafted the legislation and its precursors accepted (or believed) that labor organizations, capable of carrying out strikes but regulated by state labor boards, could not be deemed private agents altogether. They implicated the public interest. Labor law and the social question it addressed transcended the separation of private and public law, central to the liberal vision. It was a point about the elements of new law with which the Supreme Court had grappled since its first decisions under the 1917 constitution, case by case (even as it had endeavored to deny imperio to the administrative labor board). And it was an issue with which the drafters of Article 123 had also dealt, albeit less comprehensively and successfully than those of the federal labor law of 1931. The corollary of a stronger "revolutionary" state legally empowered to regulate industrial relations was a labor law that encompassed both private (contractual) and public elements.

Conclusion

THE FEDERAL LABOR LAW of 1931 from one perspective was the culmination of a process: that of the evolution of labor law. Contemporaries perceived it in these terms: both Emilio Portes Gil and Aarón Sáenz in the introductory statements to their respective projects said that the authors of the proyectos knew about foreign models, customary practices, earlier legislation, and judge-made law. As these sponsors of the legislation acknowledge to a degree, however, the development of labor law was hardly a uniform, detached evolution of ideas. Organized labor insisted that the legislation incorporate its *conquistas*, conquests wrested in struggle. The ruling circle of generals and politicians between 1929 and 1931 repeatedly reassured organized labor that they would respect the achievements of the revolution sanctified in Article 123.

Article 123 had not comprised a full statement of labor law or a radical transformation of legal doctrine. The former was the accomplishment of the 1931 statute. The latter resulted more from the litigation in the federal courts (and the sometimes grudgingly conceded opinions of Supreme Court justices) and the debates surrounding the projects to enact comprehensive legislation that occurred in the 1920s. Perhaps the constitutional drafters might have achieved a transformation of law, but the final version of Article 123 instead adopted a skeletal list of some of labor's demands, with terse instructions to the states to establish boards of conciliation and arbitration, among other points. In contrast, Macías in the constitutional congress had sketched a vision in which administrative labor bodies would closely regulate industrial relations by determining wages according to economic and equitable criteria and in which the collective contract negotiated by unions would normalize and equalize working conditions: this was a utopian vision evocative of currents in social legal thought circulating since the turn of the twentieth century. Yet Article 123 omitted any mention of the collective contract and scarcely referred to labor organization, curiously, since Macías was one of the main contributors to the labor chapter. Although its directions to the states to establish labor boards were not inconsistent with Macías's proposals, the constitutional language was too vague to ensure the character that the boards should assume. Macías's description of an industrial relations system was impracticable and perhaps even insincere in view of the events of 1916. Likewise, Gracidas's allusions to the clause in Article 5 guaranteeing fair compensation for voluntary labor in its simplicity was too radical for either the constitutional convention or existing industrial relations (in the absence of social revolution). So Article 5 remained in the constitution substantially in its earlier (1857) form, largely unelaborated; and if Article 123 incorporated many of the provisions of the military commanders' decrees, regarding the abolition of peonage or the minimum wage, and multiple demands of labor, it failed to supplant the fundamental conception of the employment relationship, expressed in contractual terms. It was certainly novel to raise labor's program and military decrees to a constitutional level, and the thirty paragraphs of Article 123 were a militant pronouncement. Together they would come to constitute a major ideological symbol for both organized labor invoking the power of public authority and governments endeavoring to legitimize themselves as popular, pro-labor, and heirs of a continually reinterpreted revolution. But Article 123 in itself did not constitute a transformation of law.

Article 123, moreover, initially legally weakened the federal government insofar as it delegated the enactment and enforcement of labor law to the states. Obregón's proposal to amend the constitution and federalize labor law in July 1924 addressed this point and justified the need for a stronger federal state to regulate industrial relations more effectively nationally. But between 1917 and 1930 the federal legislature remained too divided to enact labor legislation—even when the executive supported it. Although the federal labor department became an important participant in industrial relations, as of 1912, and through most of the 1920s, when it was closely allied with the CROM, it lacked the legal authority to ensure that its decision making would be recognized as legitimate. Significantly, the federal judiciary then responded to employers' pleas to enjoin state actions in labor matters through the early 1920s. The Supreme Court, largely pursuant to the amparo proceeding, thereby engaged in constitutional rule making in industrial relations. This case law considered among other issues the important question of the nature that the administrative labor boards should assume. It was not the only element shaping their development. But the case law and its authors, the justices, had to be taken into account.

For both the governments that military commanders began to reestablish in different regions of the country by approximately 1916 and the federal government under the reformed constitution in 1917 strove for legitimacy; and the new rulers along with the politically active classes, still mostly influenced by liberal ideologies, esteemed a constitutional and legal order as the legitimate form of the state. The Court's judgments rebuking the declarations of the Ministry of Industry, Commerce, and Labor regarding disputes arising in strategic economic sectors, such as in the 1927 amparo of the CTC, could only have underscored the tenuous legality of the ministry's jurisdiction over labor matters.

It is noteworthy that the Supreme Court held the ministry's actions unlawful and insisted that the constitution required the establishment of a federal board of conciliation and arbitration to adjudicate labor disputes, as it is notable that it failed to uphold the CTC's right to strike two years later and basically deferred to the federal board's determination of this right. There were limits to its law-making ability in the social and political context of the period. Yet political and social struggles were in part expressed through the federal courts, as they were also regularly expressed through the boards of conciliation and arbitration. Employers who were not going to adhere to a state law could threaten a shutdown of their operations; but they also petitioned for amparos. By 1927 an independent labor organization such as the CTC also resorted to the federal judiciary in the course of a major strike. In view of the constitutional and legal order that Obregón and Calles sought to establish, one that confirmed the prevalence of private enterprise but also acknowledged the aspirations of a mobilized working class, the institutions and doctrinal language of law were important. Even though the Court was subject to social and political pressures, and the legal system suffered from corruption, law mattered. It was not completely reducible to any other social process between 1875 and 1931.

The constitution of 1857 had guaranteed the right of free labor as one of the essential rights of the individual at a time when coercive and semi-coercive employment practices existed widely in some rural areas and before industrial expansion engendered the formation of a large working class. Subsequently, mainly French social theorists and political economists developed the intellectual and doctrinal underpinnings of modern labor law. In Mexico, new doctrines and theory were already being debated among lawyers and political leaders before the resignation of Porfirio Díaz in May 1911 and the inauguration of the federal labor department. The social legislation drafted in 1915 by Macías and Zubarán Capmany, among others, reflected this theoretical influence. This earlier discourse and related social legislation, more than the actual language of Article 123, are the beginnings of a transformation in law. When the Supreme Court started to operate again in June 1917, novel legal notions of labor rights were circulating along with beliefs grounded in the rights of free labor. The Court, however, was to address these new legal concepts—and the parties posing them—largely with institutional, procedural mechanisms formulated before the revolutionary interregnum and by reference to a liberal ideology only partially qualified by the evolving labor law.

The result of the Supreme Court's institutional and procedural approach to labor issues, informed by a mix of doctrinal notions, was a jurisprudencia that shaped the developing labor law mostly in a negative sense. In contrast to its affirmative, consistent pronouncements in support of the right of free labor in the nineteenth century, at least until the mid-1930s the Supreme Court's case law did not project a unified legal ideology. The case law refracted the tensions and conflicts evident in labor struggles in society and in the contending doctrinal notions manifested in litigation. Too often the Court undermined the new labor law as promulgated or applied in the states. Its judgments actually tended to immunize initially employers from the application of the new, substantive law. Judicial decisions usually limited rules, rather than creating or recognizing new entitlements or arrangements. When the Court considered broader legal ideas voiced in the labor disputes it adjudicated, it continued to consider fundamental liberal institutions, such as the contract, as the basis of the employment relationship. And justices generally did not speak of the premises of property law as they applied to labor relations, unless it was to protect existing expectations such as to avoid the threat of profit sharing by Veracruz's Ley de Hambre.

In part because of the context in Mexico between 1875 and 1931—that is, a legal tradition that circumscribed judicial decision making, and the experience of a succession of authoritarian and sometimes violent rulers who tried to concentrate their power in the executive branch of government—it is implausible that the federal judiciary could have countered more effectively the executive power of the state. Ultimately, the Supreme Court's decisions served to extend state power, putatively on behalf of labor. From 1917 through most of the 1920s, neither the federal legislative nor executive power could effectuate a centralized, lawful labor policy. In this situation, under the mandate of Article 123, the Court had to decide significant labor matters, in a way that it had never done under the Porfirian regime.

The Court, in particular, had to rule on the nature of the boards of conciliation and arbitration. Even when it nullified their determinations, the Court found that they were public authorities, issuing awards in matters that affected the public interest, not only relations between individuals. The Court breached the wall separating public and private law, to the detriment of the latter. In litigation and jurisprudence, labor law tended to merge the two spheres of law, in accord with social legal theory but also in a manner that justified the expansion of the state into the regulation of industrial relations. When the Court insisted that Article 123 charged solely administrative boards with the resolution of labor disputes, after 1924 held that such boards should be quasi-courts (in that their awards would be binding on the parties litigating before them), and after 1927 ruled that a federal labor board had to resolve labor disputes of a federal nature, it thereby affirmed one of the ways that the central state could extend its authority over segments of the national economy. The Court also had to consider the scope of the decision making of such boards and by 1929 had largely deferred to them. It thus gave its legal approval to a new form of state organization that operated with such discretion that its determinations frequently appeared capricious or went beyond normative expectations. Justices had to resolve what was legally cognizable under Article 123 and concluded finally that it was almost any matter that arose from the employment relationship, if it could be described as a contract. They determined who were protected individuals and groups pursuant to Article 123 and finally provided a broad definition of the worker and his or her association. The Court continued, meanwhile, to try to read exclusion clauses in collective contracts narrowly. These issues, as articulated in the Court's opinions and rulings, resounded in the federal labor law of 1931, which contemporaries imagined would begin to settle them more firmly than could jurisprudencia, built on case-by-case proceedings.

The promulgation of the Ley Federal del Trabajo did express the federal government's aspirations to legalize and institutionalize industrial relations uniformly and nationally, as the Supreme Court had necessitated after 1927. The legislation that Calles, as the maximum political chief, had Sáenz maneuver through Congress surely represented a compromise among the major interests at that time concerned with industrial relations, one that would ensure an environment for the protection of capital, including, significantly, foreign investments. The correspondence of the U.S. embassy tracking efforts to pass federal legislation tends to confirm this latter point. But the denunciations of the labor law, even if public posturing to some extent, underscore the absence of a consensus between capital and labor interests about the legal system of industrial relations, despite government attempts to reach accommodations with both and establish a system in which it would preside as mediator and final arbitrator. The narrative of the enactment of the statute reflects that the federal executive endeavored to pass legislation satisfactory to business interests but then, to ensure rapid passage, had to compromise with congressmen and organized labor interests, especially in connection with the issue of the exclusion clause; these compromises, in turn, upset businesses. In the end, the law outlined an industrial relations system in which unions, employers, and the federal government would interact, formally and institutionally, through labor contracts and labor boards, while the prerogatives of management and private property, in particular private profit taking, would predominate. It was a system in which the strike was ambivalently recognized and thoroughly subjected to state regulation.

In view of the enactment of comprehensive labor legislation, one might assume that the Supreme Court's extensive decision making in connection with labor law would diminish, with justices assuming a role of merely applying the statutory law in simple, unequivocal terms, perhaps like proverbial bureaucrats with rubber stamps. An examination of a sampling of Court cases decided between 1931 and 1934 suggests otherwise.[1] The published opinions reflect a nuanced legal approach to industrial relations. Many of the Court's decisions were divided, indicating the failure of a consensus among the justices themselves. The length of many of the opinions also indicates that the questions the Court faced were relatively novel. The Court construed the federal law in a number of instances creatively. In engaging in polemics about various issues of labor law, the Court not only interpreted the statute but also continued to speculate about labor law broadly and to apply Article 123. Federal labor legislation had not entirely displaced reference to the constitution's labor chapter. That is, labor law was still deemed to be evolving; and the Court's decision making did not entirely conform to the modest role of merely applying already established, positive legislation. Policy objectives seemingly guided the Court's reasoning in a number of cases. The Court definitely supported labor interests in this period. What is further evident about the cases is that workers' interests (such as interunion rivalries expressed in litigation about the exclusion clause) were not always unequivocally presented before the adjudicatory bodies. Justices, moreover, manifested their preferences, such as their hostility toward the exclusion clause. On this point, as mentioned, they shared a view with the drafters of the 1931 law, if not with the CROM or the labor organizations that had prevailed on the statute's recognition of it.

Recurring judicial language as well as the text of the 1931 legislation still paralleled the legal proposals to reconcile harmoniously as factors of production the interests of capital and labor that liberal intellectuals Prieto and Martínez de la Torre had made in 1875, although by 1931–34, in the Supreme Court's published opinions, it was on the basis of legal and political economic theory stressing the importance of collective interests. Urbina's references to a new majoritarian principle in the developing labor law justified the contractual possibility of the closed or union shop that the new code recognized. But language derived from political economy, conceiving and positing as both natural and normative a point of equilibrium between the factors of production, subsisted from 1875 through 1931, as the language of Article 123 guaranteeing the strike, reiterated in part in the 1931 code, evidences.

The relationship between the state and labor organization would continue to evolve after 1931, importantly in informal and political terms. The 1931 federal legislation, however, has been the most authoritative, formal accomplishment in the process of the making of labor law in Mexico, a point that does not minimize the symbolic or political significance of Article 123. The statute ratified and specified a formal normative structure of industrial relations, even as informal arrangements would persist among the major actors (capital, labor, and government), sometimes with reference to the normative system, sometimes without. More than Article 123, the federal labor law outlined in detail the role of the state in industrial relations; indeed, it was this that most distinguished postrevolutionary labor law from its nineteenth-century liberal antecedents. Both may have imagined parity between the factors of production, but whereas nineteenth-century liberals sympathetic to labor had believed that parties could, through the contract alone, regulate their relations satisfactorily, by 1931 most of labor's advocates believed that the private contract was inadequate, actually masking an unequal exchange (as the social law theorists had argued), and that collectivist solutions were necessary, realizable through state action.

After 1934, the status of the Supreme Court suffered marked change, if not demotion. In that year, Lázaro Cárdenas, the presidential candidate for the PNR, proposed constitutional amendments to replace the life tenure of the justices with terms of six years to run concurrently with the president's, as well as the creation of a fourth specialized chamber (*sala*) dedicated exclusively to labor cases. Congress passed the amendments even before Cárdenas's inauguration, providing a constitutional basis for the subordination of the federal judiciary to the presidency.[2] The change surely facilitated the executive's power over the high court, although interestingly it continued to rule occasionally against the federal government in *juicios de amparos*.[3] If, in any case, the Court thereafter demonstrated greater dependency on the executive power, the legal condition stemmed largely from the political context of 1934, affirmed in constitutional reform. As the Mexican polity stabilized in the decades after 1931, the Court's role in fashioning legal rules and doctrine may have diminished or assumed a position reminiscent of the later Porfirian era in its relationship to the executive power (when it nonetheless upheld the right of free labor in accord with liberal-legal beliefs). But in the period between 1917 and 1934, the Supreme Court's contribution to the making of the legal rules of labor relations was significant.

Reference Matter

Notes

INTRODUCTION

1. Scholars, like contemporaries, have long accepted the proposition that lands were privatized and consolidated in large estates, a process that created a landless population of agricultural workers; the proposition continues to be restated: see Moreno-Brid and Ros, *Development and Growth in the Mexican Economy*, 63 and citations therein. The process of privatization, however, varied throughout the country, as more recent scholarship has shown: see, e.g., Kourí, *A Pueblo Divided*, and "Interpreting the Expropriation of Indian Pueblo Lands in Porfirian Mexico." Generalizations about the process are problematic.

2. Nickel, "Peonaje e inmovilidad de los trabajadores agricolas en México, La situación de los peones acasillados en las haciendas de Puebla-Tlaxcala," 9, originally published in German under the title "Zur Immobilität und Schuldknechtschaft Mexikanischer Landarbeiter vor 1915" in *Saeculum*.

3. See Keesing, "Structural Change Early in Development: Mexico's Changing Industrial and Occupational Structure from 1895 to 1950."

4. Cf. Tomlins, *Law, Labor, and Ideology in the Early American Republic*, who underscores the importance of labor law for the development of law and the American polity, xii–xiii, citing several other legal and social histories that also suggest its significance.

5. In Mexico, Mariano Otero's *Ensayo sobre el verdadero estado de la cuestión social y política que se agita en la república mexicana* was published in 1842; but the phrase becomes extensive throughout the Atlantic world and again in Mexico with distinct connotations at the end of the nineteenth century.

6. See Kennedy, "Three Globalizations of Law and Legal Thought," on which much of the paragraph is based; on the notion of the social question elsewhere in Latin America, see, e.g., Zimmerman, "Intellectuals, Universities and the Social Question," and Morris, *Elites, Intellectuals, and Consensus*. More recent scholarship discussing the social question has focused on aspects of it not directly related to labor. See, e.g., Rosemblatt, "Charity, Rights, and Entitlement: Gender, Labor, and Welfare in Early Twentieth Century Chile"; and Bliss, "The Science of Redemption: Syphilis, Sexual Promiscuity, and Reformism in Revolutionary Mexico City."

7. See Womack, "The Mexican Revolution" (narrating the revolution as primarily political conflict); and Knight, "The Mexican Revolution."

8. Knight, "The Working Class and the Mexican Revolution."

9. Molina Enríquez, *Los grandes problemas nacionales*; Kourí, *En busca de Molina Enríquez*.

10. Cf. Middlebrook, *The Paradox of Revolution*; Haber et al., *The Politics of Property Rights*; Carr, *El movimiento obrero;* Bortz, *Revolution Within the Revolution*; and Córdova, *La ideología de la revolución mexicana*.

11. See the introduction in Salvatore et al., *Crime and Punishment in Latin America*. Since the publication of this work in 2001, more modern Latin American legal history has

been written in English; see, e.g., Pérez-Perdomo, *Latin American Lawyers*; Mirow, *Latin American Law*, and his "Marbury in Mexico." On labor law adjudication from a historical perspective, see James, "Liberal Jurisprudence"; and Schjolden, "Sentencing the Social Question." One historiographical review of Mexican legal history is Peter L. Reich's "Recent Research on the Legal History of Modern Mexico." A more extensive historiographical essay is Pablo Mijangos's *El nuevo pasado jurídico mexicano*. In Mexico, under the auspices of the Supreme Court, Lucio Cabrera Acevedo directed a multivolume, quasi-encyclopedic history of the Supreme Court in the nineteenth and twentieth centuries.

12. "El Informe Rendido por el Licenciado Guzmán Vaca," *El Universal*, 20 December 1928, p. 1.

13. "La Autodefensa de la Suprema Corte," *El Universal*, 21 December 1928, p. 3.

14. See L. Meyer, *México y los Estados Unidos en el conflicto petrolero*, 173–75, 271–72; and Haber et al., "When the Law Does Not Matter."

15. Gruening, *Mexico and Its Heritage*. Scholarship on corruption in Mexico includes Morris's *Corruption and Politics in Contemporary Mexico* and Lomnitz's *Vicios públicos*.

16. The respective categories and terms of contract and property law differ in the civil law tradition from those of the common law, of course. Thus, the law of obligations corresponds approximately to contract law. See Zamora, *Mexican Law*, chapter 17.

17. Hale, "The Civil Law Tradition"; Merryman and Pérez-Perdomo, *The Civil Law Tradition*; Butte, "Stare Decisis, Doctrine, and Jurisprudence in Mexico and Elsewhere."

18. Carpizo and Madrazo, *Derecho constitucional*.

19. The amparo lawsuit is more complex than this brief summary; for example, it has been used routinely to appeal from state court judgments; but this use of the action and others are not relevant to the cases discussed in this study. See Baker, *Judicial Review in Mexico*, chapters 5–7, for a broader overview of the amparo lawsuit.

20. Baker, *Judicial Review in Mexico*; Burgoa, *El juicio de amparo*.

21. See generally, Burgoa, *El juicio de amparo*; Baker, *Judicial Review in Mexico*, chapters 5 and 6; and Fix-Zamudio, *Ensayos sobre el derecho de amparo*.

22. Since the enactment of constitutional reforms in December 1994, the Supreme Court has been able to undertake general reviews of legislation pursuant to Article 105c of the constitution. But the individual or particular nature of the amparo action has been retained. See Domingo, "Judicial Independence"; and Jorge Carpizo, "Reformas constitucionales al Poder Judicial Federal y la jurisdicción constitucional, del 31 de diciembre 1994."

23. Most of the amparo cases after 1917 are thus entitled "Amparo Administrativo en Revisión," or if the case is a review of a suspension order entered by a federal district court, it might be entitled "Amparo Administrativo. Revisión del Auto de Suspensión."

24. See Baker, *Judicial Review in Mexico*, 234 (the applicable constitutional provision is Art. 107); Burgoa, *El juicio de amparo*. In the cases reviewed in this study, suspension orders became central to much of the litigation after 1917. See Chapters 6 and 7. But this interlocutory remedy was available before 1917, too. See Moreno, *Tratado del juicio de amparo*, chapter 4.

25. Baker, *Judicial Review in Mexico*, 42–45 and 52–56; Fix-Zamudio, *Ensayos sobre el derecho de amparo*. Cf. Zamora, *Mexican Law*, 259, regarding backlogs and judicial responses to them more recently.

26. See Articles 147–149 of the Ley Reglamentaria de los Artículos 103 y 104 de la Constitución Federal, reprinted in Suprema Corte de Justicia de la Nación, *Historia del*

amparo en México. This law was promulgated in 1919 and is frequently referred to as the Ley de Amparo of 1919. See Baker, *Judicial Review in Mexico*, 52. The technical requirements and scope of jurisprudencia or controlling case law have varied over time, both in the nineteenth and twentieth centuries; this is a simplified, introductory account; see also Serna de la Garza, "The Concept of *Jurisprudencia* in Mexican Law," for a discussion of *jurisprudencia*.

27. See Serna de la Garza, "The Concept of *Jurisprudencia*," 141, for the definition of *tesis*: "a written expression in an abstract form of the criteria used to interpret a legal norm which was applied to solve a specific case."

28. See Cabrera Acevedo, *La Suprema Corte de Justicia* [1901–1914], citing *El Libertad*, 26 August 1914.

29. Constitución Política (1917), Articles 103–7, and 94.

30. See Domingo, "Judicial Independence." Supreme Court judges in the period of this study are usually called *ministros* or ministers and sometimes *magistrados* or magistrates; in this book, the term *justice* is used to distinguish Supreme Court members from lower court judges.

31. Fix-Zamudio, "La Suprema Corte de Justicia y el juicio de amparo," *Ensayos sobre el derecho de amparo*, 545.

32. Unger, *Knowledge and Politics*.

33. See generally Kennedy, *A Critique of Adjudication*.

34. Lombardo Toledano, *La libertad sindical*.

35. See Carpizo, *El presidencialismo mexicano*.

36. See generally Casar and Marván, *Gobernar sin mayoría*.

37. Suarez-Potts, "The Mexican Supreme Court"; Domingo, "Judicial Independence"; González Casanova, *La democracia en México*.

38. Cosío Villegas, *La constitución de 1857*; see also Arnold, *Política y justicia*.

39. See generally Cabrera Acevedo, *La Suprema Corte de Justicia* [1877–1882] and [1882–1888].

40. Ibid.; cf. Mirow, "Marbury in Mexico."

41. See, e.g., "Versión taquigráfica del discurso pronunciado por el Lic. Vicente Lombardo Toledano en el mitin celebrado en la Alianza de Ferrocarrileros Mexicanos el día 24 de julio de 1931," published in the magazine *CROM* 15 November 1931, and reprinted in Lombardo Toledano, *Obras completas*, 7:160. Cf. Córdova, *La ideología de la revolución mexicana*, chapters 4–6.

42. Suarez-Potts, "The Mexican Supreme Court." Cf. Sieder et al., *The Judicialization of Politics in Latin America*, regarding recent political-legal developments in the region; and Unger, *Law in Modern Society*.

43. Lombardo Toledano, "Las fuentes del derecho industrial."

44. Dawson, *The Oracles of the Law*.

45. See Fisher et al., *American Legal Realism*; Gordon, "Critical Legal Histories"; and Kennedy, *A Critique of Adjudication*.

46. Bassols, "Que son, por fin, las Juntas?"

47. I also read transcripts of public Supreme Court conferences in which justices discussed their legal positions. These transcripts are bound in volumes and held in the Court's historical archive (Archivo Histórico de la Suprema Corte de Justicia de la Nación), which is located in Mexico City. These unpublished transcripts (Versiones Taquigráficas) date from 1917.

48. Cf. Middlebrook, *The Paradox of Revolution*, who quantified administrative federal labor board decisions for a later period than that covered in this book.

49. A presentation that used explicitly a discursive vocabulary could prove illuminating, too; there is scholarship with Foucaldian overtones, especially as to developments in criminology in Latin America occurring in the same time period as this study. See, e.g., Piccato, *City of Suspects*.

50. See Beatty, *Institutions and Investment*, 13, citing Sikkink, *Ideas and Institutions*, and North, *Institutions*.

51. Law can be described more broadly, of course, than this positivist conception of it. See, e.g., essays in Salvatore, et al., *Crime and Punishment in Latin America*.

52. Kennedy, *A Critique of Adjudication*, chapters 2 and 7.

53. Translations are mine unless otherwise noted. Generally, when possible, the book uses already existing translations.

54. Hale discusses the problems of legal terminology and translation in connection with Mexican law, in "The Civil Law Tradition," 261.

55. Madero, Plan de San Luis Potosí, 5 October 1910, reprinted in Tena Ramírez, *Leyes fundamentales de México*, 732–39.

56. Cabrera, *Obras completas*, vols. 3–4. Cabrera was a young lawyer and brilliant dissident journalist when he wrote his essays criticizing the científicos. He later served in the Twenty-Sixth Congress and become Carranza's close adviser.

57. Knight, "The Working Class"; Ruiz, *Labor and the Ambivalent Revolutionaries*, Bortz, *Revolution within the Revolution*.

58. Ruiz, *Labor and the Ambivalent Revolutionaries*, 37–38.

59. Lear, "La XXVI Legislatura."

60. Plan of Guadalupe, reprinted in Córdova, *La ideología de la revolución mexicana*, 444.

61. Knight, *The Mexican Revolution*, vol. 2.

62. Ruiz, *Labor and the Ambivalent Revolutionaries*, 39–41.

63. See Carr, "The Casa del Obrero Mundial."

64. Dulles, *Yesterday in Mexico*; Womack, "The Mexican Revolution."

65. Haber et al., *The Politics of Property Rights*, 70–71.

66. See Benjamin, "Laboratories of the New State," 72; Womack, "The Mexican Revolution"; Haber et al., *The Politics of Property Rights*, chapter 3.

67. See Rocha Bandala et al., *La competencia en material laboral*; and Middlebrook, *The Paradox of Revolution*, 56–62.

68. The statute has been amended, as has Article 123, since 1931; see De Buen Lozano, *Derecho del trabajo*.

69. Clark, *Organized Labor*, 186–90; Bortz, "Legal and Contractual Limits," 278–81.

70. Haber et al., *The Politics of Property Rights*, chapter 3.

71. J. Meyer, *Estado y sociedad con Calles*, 57–198.

72. Ibid.

73. Cabrera Acevedo, *La Suprema Corte de Justicia* [1924–1928].

74. Ibid. See also Clark, *Organized Labor*, regarding the demise of the CROM. She dates its decline to 1927, see p. 127, and generally pp. 127–47.

75. "Informe rendido por el C. Gral. Plutarco Elías Calles, presidente constitucional de los Estados Unidos Mexicanos ante el H. Congreso de la Unión, el día 1 de septiembre, 1928," reprinted in the *Diario Oficial*, 10 October 1928.

76. See Haber et al., *The Politics of Property Rights*, 63–65, citing Weldon, "Political Sources."

77. J. Meyer, *Estado y sociedad con Calles*, 126.

CHAPTER 1: THE RIGHTS OF FREE LABOR, 1875–1910

1. Coatsworth, "Obstacles to Economic Growth in Nineteenth-Century Mexico"; Beatty, *Institutions and Investment.*

2. Beatty, *Institutions and Investment*, 5–6; Margadant, *Introducción a la historia del derecho mexicano*, 190–91.

3. See Rosenzweig, "La industria," 420–21, quoting Matías Romero. The translation is largely based on the editors', in Jaffary et al., *Mexican History*, 257–58.

4. Art. 1, Constitución Federal de los Estados-Unidos Mexicanos, Sancionada y Jurada por el Congreso General Constituyente el día 5 de febrero de 1857, reprinted in Tena Ramirez, *Leyes fundamentales de México*, 607. The quotations and summaries of the constitutional articles are drawn from the 1857 constitution as reprinted in this volume. Regarding the social grounding of the constitution's individual rights, see Womack, "Luchas sindicales," and Reyes Heroles, *El liberalismo mexicano*, vol. 3.

5. Lozano, *Estudio del derecho constitucional patrio*, 166–67.

6. Cf. González Navarro, "El trabajo forzoso," 591–93, describing state-level delegations to private entities of the power to punish before 1857.

7. Ibid., 595–96.

8. Estatuto Orgánico Provisional de la República Mexicana, 23 May 1856, Art. 24 (III), in Tena Ramírez, *Leyes fundamentales de México*, 502.

9. For an overview of the period, see Bazant, "From Independence to 1867."

10. Zarco, *Crónica del Congreso Extraordinario Constituyente*, 18 July 1856 session, 277, and, generally, 276–78. See generally Reyes Heroles, *El liberalismo mexicano*, vol. 3, regarding Ignacio Ramírez's social liberalism.

11. See Zarco, *Crónica del Congreso Extraordinario Constituyente*, 21 July 1856 session, 281; and 22 July 1856 session, 290 (regarding the vote tallies). Another issue was debated in connection with the article: whether it would prohibit the state, including municipalities, from drafting its citizens for public work projects (see 276, 280). Generally, the advocates for the article said that it would apply only to labor relations between individuals. Initially, the provision was enumerated as Article 12 and was later renumbered Article 5.

12. The original language was expansive: "The liberty to exercise whatever kind of industry, commerce, or labor that is useful and honest cannot be constrained by law, nor by the authorities, nor by individuals with title to property." Proyecto de Constitución, 16 June 1856, reprinted in Tena Ramírez, *Leyes fundamentales de México*, 556.

13. Zarco, *Crónica del Congreso Extraordinario Constituyente*, 453.

14. Ibid., 455. See generally Reyes Heroles, *El liberalismo mexicano.*

15. Zarco, *Crónica del Congreso Extraordinario Constituyente*, 457.

16. See, e.g., Código Civil. The civil code discussed here applied to the federal district and territories and also served as the paradigm for most other state codes that were subsequently adopted. A few states had attempted to promulgate their respective civil codes earlier in the century. State codes could differ from the federal district's code as to specific provisions, including a few dealing with the employment relationship. The federal government amended the code in 1884, changing provisions regarding testamentary powers,

among other things—but certainly did not draft any sections on labor matters. For a brief history of the codification of Mexican civil law, see Zamora, *Mexican Law*, 450–52; and Margadant, *Introducción a la historia del derecho mexicano*, 184.

17. Merryman and Pérez-Perdomo, *The Civil Law Tradition*.

18. Código Civil, 114–15.

19. Código Civil, Arts. 2565 and 2582.

20. Código Civil, Título decimo tercero.

21. Código Civil, Art. 2569 (applying to servants).

22. Ibid., Art. 2587 (applying to day laborers).

23. Illades, in *Hacía la república del trabajo,* discusses in detail the formation and operation of artisanal and labor associations under the civil code and the provisions mentioned here, among others. In brief, Illades underscores the fluidity of such associations, and the minimal requirements that the civil code established for their constitution, in contrast to the hierarchical requirements set or ratified by corporatist authorities of the colonial era.

24. Código Civil, Libro primero, De las personas; Titulo tercero, De las personas morales; Libro tercero, De los contratos, and Titulo undecimo, Del contrato de sociedad.

25. Ibid., Arts. 43–5.

26. Código Penal, Art. 925. The criminal code was enacted on 7 December 1871 and went into effect on 1 April 1872. It too served as a model for other state codes and applied to federal matters across the country, remaining in effect technically until promulgation of the 1929 and 1931 codes (the former not being implemented). See Margadant, *Introducción a la historia del derecho mexicano*, 184–85; Speckman Guerra, "Justice Reform and Legal Opinion," 225–49, 228, 235, 242.

27. Womack, "Luchas sindicales," 424–25.

28. Código Penal, Art. 331.

29. See Articles 922, 928, and 926 of the Código Penal, respectively.

30. Taibo, in *La huelga de los sombrereros*, has collected contemporaneous articles about the strike published in the artisan newspaper *El Socialista*, as well as providing a factual summary of it. The account presented here is based on his work. Illades also analyzes the strike and contends that it represented a watershed in an evolving discourse around labor relations. See *Hacia la república del trabajo,* 158–67.

31. See *El Socialista,* 25 July 1875, no. 134, for the tie between the newspaper and the Gran Círculo. See generally the articles collected in Taibo, *La huelga*.

32. "Huelga" by V. C., in *La Firmeza*, 5 June 1875, no. 22, reprinted in Taibo, *La huelga*. An article in *El Socialista*, 30 May 1875, mentions that the employer Zolly indicated he would negotiate with a representative of the workers; they then nominated Prieto. See Taibo, *La huelga*, 46.

33. Ibid., 50.

34. See Reglamento de la Sociedad Reformadora del Ramo de Sombrerería, published in *El Socialista*, 30 May 1875, no. 126, reprinted in Taibo, *La huelga*, 32–44.

35. Cf. Chapter 1, Art. 3 of the *Reglamento de la Sociedad Paz y Unión en las Artes para Auxilios Mutuos* (where the objective of the society is to promote the physical and moral protection of members in the event of necessity).

36. Ibid., 34, 37–38.

37. *La Firmeza,* 5 June 1875, no. 22, reprinted in Taibo, *La huelga*, 53.

38. *El Socialista,* 1 August 1875, no. 135, reprinted in Taibo, *La huelga*, 105.

39. See Prieto, "El Colegio de Abogados, el Liceo Hidalgo y la cuestión de las huelgas," in *Revista Universal*, 8 August 1875, p. 1, reprinted in Prieto, *Obras completas*, 25:139. For the early national history of the Colegio de Abogados in Mexico and its origins in the colonial era, see González, "El Ilustre y Real Colegio de Abogados de México," and Mayagoitia y Hagelstein, "De real a nacional."

40. See Martínez de la Torre, "Las huelgas," 5.

41. Prieto, "El Colegio de Abogados."

42. Ibid.; Martínez de la Torre, "Las huelgas." See also "La naturaleza, historia y condición de la huelga, disertación leída en el Colegio de Abogados," 25–26 September 1875, reprinted in the pamphlet as "Breve estudio sobre la cuestión de huelgas de obreros leído en el Colegio de Abogados de México por Guillermo Prieto" and published in Prieto, *Obras completas*, 25:143.

43. Martínez de la Torre, "Las huelgas," 6–8.

44. Ibid., 8.

45. Ibid., 14–15. The phrase *estado de derecho* is analogous but not quite identical to the term "rule of law."

46. Prieto, "La naturaleza." For a discussion of Prieto's address, see González, "Testimonios."

47. Prieto, "La naturaleza," 145.

48. Ibid.,145–46.

49. Ibid., 148–58, 164.

50. Ibid., 158–160, 161, 163.

51. Ibid.,168.

52. See Prieto, "El Colegio de Abogados," 141.

53. Lozano, *Estudio del derecho constitucional patrio*, 150.

54. Ibid., 162.

55. Estatuto Orgánico Provisional de la República Mexicana, 23 May 1856, Art. 22 and Art. 24 (III), reprinted in Tena Ramírez, *Leyes fundamentales de México*, 501–2.

56. Ibid., Arts. 31–34, p. 503.

57. Ibid., Arts. 62, 63, p. 507.

58. Steinfeld, *Coercion, Contract, and Free Labor in the Nineteenth Century*.

59. Ibid., 5, 10. Article 1780 of the Napoleonic code proscribed courts from ordering employees to return to their former employers from whom they had separated before completing their employment contract. See Sonenscher, *Work and Wages*, 367. Dunham, *The Industrial Revolution in France*, 201–2, minimizes the effectiveness of the *livrets* as a means of monitoring workers. In *Coercion, Contract, and Free Labor in the Nineteenth Century*, Steinfeld cites both Sonenscher and Dunham, 243.

60. Cf. Illades's argument regarding the seminal quality of the hatters' strike and the exercise of liberal rights of free association as outlined by the constitution, in *Hacia la república del trabajo*, 199–205.

61. See Díaz, "The Satiric Penny Press for Workers in Mexico."

62. Cf. Anderson, *Outcasts in Their Own Land*, 322–26.

63. The phrase "social liberalism" is, of course, drawn from Reyes Heroles, *El liberalismo mexicano*, as reinterpreted by Womack, "Luchas sindicales."

64. Lozano, *Estudio del derecho constitucional patrio*, 201–4.

65. Ibid., 393–95.

66. Gallardo y Rionda, "Las huelgas," in *El Socialista,* 27 September 1875.

67. Vigil, "La cuestión de huelgas," in *El Siglo Diez y Nueve,* séptima época, T. 54 (12 September 1872).

68. Ibid.

69. The concepts encoded in 1870–71 were, of course, part of liberals' legal discourse by the mid-nineteenth century.

CHAPTER 2: FREE LABOR AND THE FEDERAL JUDICIARY, 1875–1910

1. Knight, "Mexican Peonage."

2. Katz, "Labor Conditions on Haciendas in Porfirian Mexico." The description of labor relations here is mostly drawn from Katz's and Knight's articles.

3. Thus, Bauer argues that in many instances the form of indebtedness should not be construed to mean that estates employed workers against their will. He acknowledges that in some regions, such as Yucatán, the evidence indicates forced labor. See "Rural Workers in Spanish America."

4. Both Knight and Katz describe the different patterns of recruitment and employment: see "Mexican Peonage," and "Labor Conditions," respectively.

5. Cf. Wells and Joseph, *Summer of Discontent, Seasons of Upheaval,* chapter 6, which lists the methods estate owners used to maintain their coercive labor systems.

6. Katz, "Labor Conditions," 21, 38, n. 108; see also Knight, "Mexican Peonage."

7. See González Navarro, "El trabajo forzoso en México," and *El Porfiriato: La vida social,* 220. In connection with Sonora, see Article 10 of the Sonoran statute, reprinted in *El Socialista,* 17 February 1882, p. 1. Other state statutes are also mentioned in the judicial cases discussed below.

8. Katz, "Labor Conditions," 37, citing González Navarro, *La vida social,* 220.

9. González Navarro, "El trabajo forzoso," 602, and *La vida social,* 220–21; Katz, "Labor Conditions," 32, n. 94.

10. The Introduction discusses the amparo suit in more detail.

11. See Lozano, *Estudio del derecho constitucional patrio,* 169, citing the Supreme Court's case law through 1875, which found public service impositions unconstitutional, despite the position of Ignacio Ramírez, then a justice. See also the constitutional convention debate in connection with Article 5 described in Chapter 1.

12. See, e.g., the Amparos of Sandoval y Bulle, 29 January 1881, *Semanario Judicial de la Federación* (hereafter SJF), 2d época, vol. 1, p. 166 (shipowners impeded from operating pursuant to a regulation but amparo denied because the regulation was lawful); Ramon Padilla, 22 June 1885, SJF, 2d época, vol. 8, p. 729 (amparo granted to merchant selling maize); Toribio Ruíz, 2 October 1890, SJF, 3d epoca, vol. 3, p. 604 (amparo granted to petitioner incarcerated for unlicensed practice of medicine); Ignacio P. Rodríguez, 25 March 1895, SJF, 3d época, vol. 10, p. 203 (amparo granted to individual penalized for unlicensed practice of law).

13. The published opinions of the Supreme Court normally contain a perfunctory order.

14. The records examined here were located in Caja No. 60, Expediente No. 43, of the federal district court collection, Primer Juzgado, held in 1998 in the Archivo del Estado de Puebla, Puebla. The opinion of the Supreme Court was published as "Rosaliano Limón," 27 December 1895, SJF, 3d época, vol. 10, p. 1262.

15. Ley de Agosto 10 de 1880, Libro 3, Tit. 1, Capitulo 2 y 5, reprinted in *Disposiciones Complementarios del Código Penal del Edo. de Puebla*, 16–18.

16. AEP, Caja 60, Exp. 43.

17. Cf. Charles Dickens's (fictional) account of English judicial process in *Bleak House*.

18. All of the relevant Supreme Court's published opinions in the *Semanario Judicial de la Federación* between 1874 and 1909 were reviewed to identify rulings on laborers' petitions for relief from coercive labor practices. No denials of an amparo petition dated before 1899 were found. Cases were selected for a more careful reading on the basis of the extent of their opinions. The conclusions reached in this chapter depend largely on an analysis of twenty-six such cases spanning this period. For an explanation of the approach used here, see the Introduction.

19. Indeed it would be an interesting and possibly fruitful exercise to probe if the process of publishing decisions was merely haphazard or if there were particular reasons to explain publication. In the last years of the Porfirian regime, it is possible that decisions reached after 1908 were not published as events in 1910 and 1911 began to overshadow the Court's routine operations.

20. Amparo of Benito Vicente, 10 March 1884, SJF, 2d época, vol. 7, p. 39.

21. Ibid., 39–41.

22. Ibid., 41–42.

23. Amparo of Patricio Gómez, 1 March 1890, SJF, 3d época, vol. 1, p. 209.

24. Ibid.

25. Ibid.

26. Ibid., 214.

27. Amparo of Crescencio Concepción, 23 July 1892 SJF, 3d época, vol. 6, p. 225.

28. Ibid., 227–28.

29. Amparo of Felipe Aguirre, 3 September 1881, SJF, 2d época, vol. 3, p. 314.

30. Ibid., 317.

31. Amparo of José Corralito, 31 March 1884, SJF, 2d época, vol. 7, 112.

32. Amparo of Evaristo Luna, 24 November 1893, SJF, 3d época, vol. 8, p. 951.

33. Ibid., 956–57 and 958.

34. Ibid., 952.

35. Amparo of Isabel Nahal y Socios, 1 June 1881, SJF, 2d época, vol. 1, 227.

36. See Amparo of Euologio Chico, 12 November 1881, SJF, 2d época, vol. 3, 759; and Amparo of Jose Reyes Ramírez, 17 November 1881, SJF, 2d época, vol. 3, 823.

37. Amparo of Epitacia Santa-Anna, 28 August 1884, SJF, 2d época, vol. 7, 531.

38. Amparo of Julio Montañez, 5 October 1893, SJF, 3d época, vol. 4, 694.

39. Ibid.

40. Amparo of Alfonso Benito, 25 September 1899, SJF, 4th época, vol. 4, p. 513. This is the first amparo decision holding against a laborer claiming he was being forced to work, which I found in the *Semanario Judicial* in a search through the indices of the accessible reporters published up to 1909.

41. Ibid., 513–14.

42. Amparo of Antonio Salvador, 10 March 1899, SJF, 4th época, vol. 3, p. 174.

43. Ibid., 175.

44. Código de Procedimientos Federales.

45. Amparo of Ramón Quej, 9 February 1900, SJF, 4th época, vol. 5, p. 200.

46. Ibid., 202.

47. Ibid.

48. Ibid.

49. Ibid.

50. Ibid., 203. As was normally the case in this period, Articles 101 and 102 of the constitution, and Articles 818, 819, and 828 of the Federal Procedural Code were also cited. See Art. 21, 1857 Constitution, reprinted in Tena Ramírez, *Leyes fundamentales de México.*

51. Amparo of Francisco Rodríguez Gómez, 21 October 1907, SJF, 4th época, vol. 34, p. 958; and Amparo of Pablo Salazar, 13 November 1907, SJF, 4th época, vol. 35, p. 237.

52. Amparo of Pablo Salazar, 239.

53. Ibid., 240.

54. Amparo of Mariano Arellanes, 22 February 1907, SJF, 4th época, vol. 30, p. 1081.

55. Amparo of Faustino García, 26 September 1907, SJF, 4th época, vol. 34, p. 480.

56. Amparo of Julio Delgado, 12 February 1908, SJF, 4th época, vol. 36, p. 803.

57. Amparo of Nicolás Mendoza, 26 October, 1907, SJF, 4th época, vol. 34, p. 1125.

58. Ibid.

59. Ibid., 1126–27.

60. Amparo of Demetrio Bustos, 28 January 1908, SJF, 4th época, vol. 36, p. 543.

61. Ibid., 544–45.

62. Amparo of Magdalena Vásquez, 6 March 1908, SJF, 4th época, vol. 37, p. 62.

63. Ibid.

64. Amparo of Estanislao Velueta, 14 October 1908, SJF, 4th época, vol. 40, p. 673.

65. Ibid., 674–75.

66. Ibid., 675–76.

67. Código de Procedimientos Federales, "Exposición de Motivos." Article 758, for example, waives court fees for indigents. Articles 746–49 facilitate the representation of parties in ways that normally would benefit individuals without easy access to a lawyer.

68. "Exposición de Motivos," ibid., 5–9.

69. Baker, *Judicial Review in Mexico*, 44.

70. See Katz, "Labor Conditions"; and Knight, "Mexican Peonage."

71. Wells and Joseph, *Summer of Discontent.* Historian T. M. James has ascertained, by examining the record of unpublished amparo decisions, that the Supreme Court reviewed some amparo petitions arising from Yucatán before 1880 (correspondence with the author, January 2012).

72. Wells and Joseph, *Summer of Discontent*, 155.

73. See, e.g., Turner, *Barbarous Mexico*; Baerlein, *Mexico: The Land of Unrest*; both cited by Knight, "Mexican Peonage," 50.

74. "La Esclavitud—Los Mozos de Tabasco," in *El Socialista*, 10 January 1886, p. 1.

75. "La Esclavitud en México," *El Partido Liberal*, 18 August 1885, quoted in García Cantú, *El socialismo en México*, 389–90. García Cantú collects additional articles by *El Socialista* and other newspapers criticizing scathingly the persistence of forced labor in Chiapas and Tabasco during this period, 381–403.

76. Katz, "Labor Conditions," 2.

77. See Benjamin, *A Rich Land, a Poor People*, 62 and n. 43, quoting Díaz to León, March 1896. This paragraph and the cited correspondence between the governor and Díaz are drawn from Benjamin, 59–66.

78. Benjamin, *A Rich Land*, 63, and n. 50, quoting Díaz to León, May 1896,.

79. Knight, "Mexican Peonage," 51, quoting from Reed, *The Caste War of Yucatán*, 247.

80. Cf. Wells and Joseph, *Summer of Discontent*, 60–63.

81. See González Navarro, "El trabajo forzoso en México," 605–6, citing *El Economista Mexicano*, an influential and prestigious Mexico City business periodical, regarding changing and apologetic statements of hacendados and their supporters on the topic of peonage, 24 April, 1 May, 1909 (Tamaulipas), 4 January 1908 (Chiapas), 2 October 1909 (Valle Nacional), 27 August 1910 (Soconusco coffee growers).

82. Cabrera Acevedo, *La Suprema Corte* [1888–1900], 56.

83. Ibid.

84. See Articles 91 and 96 of the constitution of 1857, as amended 22 May 1900, in Tena Ramírez, *Leyes fundamentales de México*, 712–713.

85. Cabrera Acevedo, *La Suprema Corte* [1888–1900], 41–42, 56–77.

86. Cf. ibid., 46–47.

87. See Wells and Joseph, *Summer of Discontent*, 60–63; Hale, *The Transformation of Liberalism*, chapters 3 and 4.

88. See the Introduction.

89. Amparo of Florencio Roman y Compañeros, 2 December 1874, SJF, pt. 2, vol. 7, p. 192. Cf. Amparo of Dioniso Casas y Socios, 6 May 1882, SJF, 2d época, vol. 4, p. 660, where the Court granted an amparo to a group of textile workers employed in the state of Mexico when a local municipality required them to fulfill night patrol duties that previously employers had paid. Such unpaid municipal duties violated Article 5, as the agent contravening the constitutional guarantee was a public authority.

90. This conclusion is based on my review of the indices of the *Semanario Judicial*.

91. Von Mentz, "Trabajo minero," 593. According to von Mentz, the petition is in the state archive in correspondence to the governor.

92. Many amparo decisions involving criminal matters or the military draft are too brief to indicate the factual nature of the appeal. A review of such opinions did not lead to the identification of any case involving workers in a concerted action, for example, a strike, apart from Florencio Roman. But according to Lozano, *Estudio del derecho constitucional patrio*, 170, the Supreme Court granted thousands of amparos against the arbitrary military draft (the *leva*) through the mid-1870s; Cabrera Acevedo confirms that as of 1890, the Court continued to grant amparos against the leva: see *La Suprema Corte* [1888–1900], 31.

CHAPTER 3: PORFIRIAN INDUSTRIAL RELATIONS AND THE RIGHTS OF LABOR

1. See, e.g., the account of the semi-official Mexico City newspaper *El Imparcial*, 15 October 1902, contending that Mexican workers could not sustain a strike for the duration capable of prejudicing their employer or the public, because of the absence of organization and a strike fund.

2. See González Navarro, "Las huelgas textiles"; and Trujillo Bolio, *Operarios fabriles*, chapter 4. Trujillo cites instances from the 1870s recorded in the files of the municipal archive of Mexico City.

3. See Trujillo Bolio, *Operarios fabriles*, 214, quoting republication of the regulation in *El Socialista*, 6 October 1872, p. 3.

4. Walker, "Porfirian Labor Politics, 258–68. Cf. Hart, *Anarchism and the Mexican Working Class*, chapter 6.

5. Walker, "Porfirian Labor Politics," 278–80. Walker observes disillusionment with governmental policy in the labor press aligned with Díaz as early as 1901, quoting a working-class newspaper normally allied with the government, *La Convención Radical*.

6. See, e.g., *El Imparcial*, 15 and 17 November 1901, describing the large-scale strike of textile workers in Puebla and Tlaxcala where the governor of Tlaxcala called out rural patrols when a strikers' commission arrived from Puebla, while the political prefect tried to persuade workers to return to work.

7. Leal, *Del mutualismo al sindicalismo*.

8. The historiography on the Cananea strike of June 1906 is extensive and encompasses memoirs by some of its leaders. See, e.g., González Ramírez, *La huelga de Cananea*. This account is largely based on Hernández, "Tiempos libertarios," 109–39, in Cardoso, *De la dictadura porfirista*.

9. Hernández, "Tiempos libertarios," 131, 133.

10. Hernández narrates, in passing, how the municipal president acted as an intermediary between the company and the strike committee, while receiving information about the looming strike and conveying it to higher governmental authorities and the Cananea company's management. Hernández argues that the strike was neither unplanned nor a plot formulated by the PLM. "Tiempos libertarios," 124–25.

11. Cockcroft, *Intellectual Precursors*, 136.

12. The PLM program is discussed further in Chapter 4.

13. See, e.g., Hart, *Anarchism and the Mexican Working Class*, 90.

14. Díaz to Dehesa (n.d., but early June 1903), in Dehesa file, Archivo del Estado de Veracruz (hereafter AEV).

15. Carlos Herrera, E. J. P. [political prefect] to the state governor, 15 June 1903, in Dehesa file, AEV.

16. Cf. *El Imparcial*, 26 December 1906: during the major lockout of textile workers, industrialists debated whether to evict their workers. The majority decided against this.

17. See Anderson, *Outcasts in Their Own Land*, whose narrative of the textile workers' struggle in 1906–7 is partly the basis for the subsequent account in this chapter. Furthermore, references to Porfirio Díaz's archive have been guided by citations in Anderson's *Outcasts*. While I analyzed the cited documents with the objective of focusing on legal issues, these documents from the Díaz archive were first identified in Anderson's footnotes and accordingly this account of the 1906–8 labor conflicts (both in the textile and transport sectors) follows (albeit with different readings of the disputes) his pioneering research in the archive and his narrative.

18. See García Díaz, *Un pueblo fabril*, chapter 3, for an analysis of the different factions within the GCOL and local officials' influence on the union throughout 1906.

19. See Anderson, *Outcasts in Their Own Land*, 103–9, for the foundation of the GCOL. Government preoccupation with the PLM's possible instigation of labor conflict was significant: see Letter to Díaz from the governor of Chihuahua, Enrique Creel, 24 July 1906, CPD, 31:8128; Anderson, *Outcasts in Their Own Land*, 120. García Díaz argues that the Porfirian administration by arresting or nearly detaining PLM activists in June 1906 successfully decoupled a developing relationship between the PLM and Orizaba's workers; *Un pueblo fabril*, 98–99.

20. García Díaz, *Un pueblo fabril*, 96–98; according to García, citing two sources, they were consigned to Quintana Roo.

21. "Breves apuntes relativos a los antecedentes de la cuestión obrera en Orizaba y que ofrece al Sr. General Don Rosalino Martínez, Subsecretario de Guerra y Marina, el Licenciado Ramón Rocha, Juez primero de primera instancia de Orizaba," 9 January 1907, CPD, 32:933. Cf. Anderson, *Outcasts in Their Own Land*, 107.

22. Walker, "Porfirian Labor Politics," 281; on this point, Walker disputes Anderson, who asserts 1906 represented a divergence from Porfirian labor policy. See *Outcasts in Their Own Land*, 36, 100.

23. "Breves apuntes," CPD, 32:933. Rocha's brief is dated after the riot or uprising of Río Blanco; García Díaz's narrative emphasizes the closeness of Morales to Rocha and Herrera, and his subordination to them, and cites an earlier memorandum of Rocha to the state governor, dated 13 October 1906; see *Un pueblo fabril*, 99 and n. 20.

24. See José Morales to President Díaz, 16 September 1906, CPD, 31:11375.

25. Ibid.

26. In another letter to Díaz, dated 8 October 1906, Morales again assured Díaz that the GCOL had received the recognition of state authorities, including Díaz's, as he reminded the president and reiterated its objectives as a mutual aid organization to maintain peace and harmony with employers, as well as avoid any political ends; but Morales did not refer to any formal or legal procedure for registration. See Leal, *Del mutualismo al sindicalismo*, 136, n. 420.

27. Quoted in García Díaz, *Un pueblo fabril*, 103–4.

28. Gutiérrez Álvarez, *Experiencias contrastadas*, 178.

29. Morales to Díaz, 8 October 1906, CPD, 31:12749, 49-A; and Anderson, *Outcasts in Their Own Land*, 128–29.

30. Ibid.

31. Morales to Díaz, CPD, 31:12749, 49-A.

32. See García Díaz, regarding deductions for fines being a constant grievance since 1898: *Un pueblo fabril*, 88, 94–95, 109; and Anderson, *Outcasts in Their Own Land*, 105, n. 13, and 130–31. See Chapter 1 for a description of the civil code's allowance of the practice of fining.

33. For Puebla, see Anderson, *Outcasts in Their Own Land*, 130–31; for Orizaba, see also García Díaz, *Un pueblo fabril*, 105–9, 112.

34. See García Díaz, *Un pueblo fabril*, 107–110. Anderson also quotes one manifesto, which invoked patriotic and constitutional ideals, but concludes that workers lost the strike. The strike manifesto is in the federal interior ministry's folder containing much of the material on the Río Blanco uprising, Legajo 817 of the Archivo General de la Nación (hereafter AGN), Ramo de Gobernación.

35. García Díaz, *Un pueblo fabril*, 123–25.

36. Ibid.; Anderson, *Outcasts in Their Own Land*, 133–35.

37. Petition of Gran Liga Nacional Obrera to Francisco Santibañez, 9 September 1906, CPD, 31:11384.

38. Mucio Martínez, governor of Puebla, to General Díaz, 22 September 1906, CPD, 31:11383; Anderson, *Outcasts in Their Own Land*, 128.

39. Díaz to Governor Martínez, 27 September 1906, CPD 31:11385.

40. Gutiérrez Álvarez, *Experiencias contrastadas*, quoting Díaz to Martínez, 1 November 1906, 181.

41. Anderson, *Outcasts in Their Own Land*, 138. On industrialists' concern that neither Díaz nor Martínez were sufficiently repressive, see Gutiérrez Álvarez, *Experiencias contrastadas*, 177.

42. Gutiérrez Álvarez, *Experiencias contrastadas*, 182.

43. The reglamento is reprinted in Gutiérrez Álvarez, *Experiencias contrastadas*, appendix 2.

44. See Gutiérrez Álvarez, *Experiencias contrastadas*, 194, and the copy of it in her third appendix; Anderson, *Outcasts in Their Own Land*, translates most of it in appendix C.

45. Article 21 of the Reglamento, appendix 3 of Gutiérrez Álvarez, *Experiencias contrastadas*, 417.

46. See the discussion of Articles 5 and 13 in Chapter 1.

47. *El Imparcial*, 9 December 1906, p. 1. Historians have described these events in early December as comprising a strike until around December 22, when most of the rest of the country's textile industrialists locked out their employees. One exception is Gutiérrez Álvarez, *Experiencias contrastadas*, 194. Since manufacturers founded the CIM to combat the GCOL, and a periodical reported as early as November 20 that the CIM would respond to a strike in one factory by closing all factories, so that "workers would not have anywhere to go to work," this earlier date for the Pueblan lockout is plausible. Gutiérrez Álvarez, *Experiencias contrastadas*, quoting *El Diario*, 20 November 1906, p. 2, on 182.

48. Walker, "Porfirian Labor Politics," 282, citing *El Imparcial*, 8 December 1906.

49. "El Asunto del Dia," *El Imparcial*, 26 December 1906.

50. *El Imparcial*, 26 December 1906.

51. This is the version of events that the Orizaba prefect Herrera reported subsequently: see his memorandum recounting 7 January 1907, probably dated 16 October 1907, in Dehesa file, AEV.

52. Cf. Hernández, "Tiempos libertarios," 174–75, n. 135; Gutiérrez Álvarez, *Experiencias contrastadas*, 199. The main source for imputing the lockout in Veracruz to Limantour is the critique of his policies by Dehesa, published in *El Diario del Hogar*, 18 June 1911.

53. Walker, "Porfirian Labor Politics," 282–83, citing *El País*, 1 January 1907, and *El Imparcial*, 28, 29, 30 December 1906.

54. Cf. Gutiérrez Álvarez, *Experiencias contrastadas*, 200, 203.

55. Ibid., 203, quoting *El Imparcial*, 3 January 1907; and generally 201–5, regarding the lobbying of Díaz by hard-line industrialists from Puebla.

56. The laudo is reproduced in various texts; see, e.g., "Laudo del Presidente Porfirio Díaz, con motivo de la huelga de los trabajadores de la industria de hilados y tejidos," in Silva Herzog, *Breve historia*, 49–53. Cf. Gutiérrez Álvarez, *Experiencias contrastadas*, 205–8; and Anderson, *Outcasts in Their Own Land*, 151–52.

57. See Anderson, *Outcasts in Their Own Land*,152–54.

58. A. Reynaud letter, from CIM, 6 January 1907, in L. 817, c. 1, AGN, Ramo de Gobernación.

59. Gutiérrez Álvarez, *Experiencias contrastadas*, 208–11; cf. Anderson, *Outcasts in Their Own Land*, 154.

60. "Los Obreros de Río Blanco se Amotinan," *El Imparcial*, 8 January 1907.

61. "Los Sucesos de Río Blanco, Muerte de Dos Agitadores," *El Imparcial*, 10 January 1907, p. 1; Anderson, *Outcasts in Their Own Land*, 163–67.

62. In Puebla, Mendoza prudently changed the name of the union back to what it had been before its affiliation with the GCOL; see Anderson, *Outcasts in Their Own Land*, 169, 174, and 190–92; Gutiérrez Álvarez, *Experiencias contrastadas*, 210.

63. "El Trabajo, el Capital, y el Gobierno," *El Imparcial*, 5 April 1907.

64. Ibid.

65. Cf. Walker, "Porfirian Labor Politics," 284–86, who argues that the CIM had "sharply proscribed Díaz's freedom of action": "Surprised by the lockout, he succumbed to their pressure." Limantour had "extensive ties to French capital and French capital dominated the textile industry." More significantly, "Díaz remained a prisoner of the economic theories which had guided his regime's efforts to develop Mexico . . . that the interests of capital had priority over the needs of labor, that 'profits must be guaranteed to foreign capitalists in order to sustain national progress.' " See also Anderson, *Outcasts in Their Own Land*, 147.

66. "Propaganda Peligrosa, Quienes son los Falsos Amigos de los Obreros," *El Imparcial*, 10 January 1907, p. 1.

67. "Los Obreros de Orizaba Vuelven a sus Labores. Noticias Exageradas Sobre la Huelga," *El Imparcial*, 4 June 1907, p. 8.

68. Maass to Díaz, 29 May 1907, CPD, 66:2010.

69. Maass to Díaz, 30 May 1907, CPD, 32:15823; cf. Anderson, *Outcasts in Their Own Land*, 206 (observing illegal detentions and deportations of workers engaging in strikes in May).

70. "Nuevo y Muy Grave Conflicto Obrero. Mil Quinientos Huelguistas en Orizaba," *El Imparcial*, 28 May 1907, p. 2.

71. *El Imparcial*, 31 May 1907.

72. See Anderson, *Outcasts in Their Own Land*, 207–8, for this and the next paragraph; *El Imparcial*, 28 and 30 May 1907.

73. Dehesa to Díaz, 13 June 1907, CPD, 32:16059.

74. Díaz to Dehesa, 17 June 1907, CPD, 32:16064.

75. Ibid.

76. Dehesa to Díaz, 19 June 1907, CPD, 32:16075.

77. See Attachment to Letter from Dehesa to Díaz, CPD, 32:16076.

78. *El Imparcial*, 4 June 1907, and earlier issues, May 30 and 31.

79. Gómez to Díaz, 30 July 1907, CPD, 32:7558; cf. Anderson, *Outcasts in Their Own Land*, 206.

80. Parlee, "The Impact of United States Railroad Unions." The following account is based partly on Parlee's. See also Leal, *Del mutualismo al sindicalismo*.

81. Parlee, "The Impact of United States Railroad Unions," 458; see generally 452–54.

82. Ibid., 462, quoting *El Imparcial*, 13 August 1906; see also Anderson, *Outcasts in Their Own Land*, 117–19.

83. "Proposiciones Presentadas a la Compañía del Ferrocarril Central Mexicano por la 'Unión de Mecánicos Mexicanos,' " attachment to letter from Cía. Limitada del Ferrocarril Central Mexicano, to Lic. Justino Fernández, 8 August 1906, CPD, 31:9031, cited by Anderson, *Outcasts in Their Own Land*, 118.

84. "Proposiciones," paragraph 1.

85. Shabot, *Los orígenes del sindicalismo ferrocarrilero*, 85–86.

86. Creel to Díaz, 3 August 1906, CPD 31:9889.

87. Díaz to Creel, 8 August 1906, CPD 31:9890.

88. Parlee, "The Impact of United States Railroad Unions," 464; Anderson, *Outcasts in Their Own Land*, 118–19.

89. Parlee, "The Impact of United States Railroad Unions."

90. Cf. *El Imparcial*, 23 July 1901: in its article, "La huelga en el internacional," the semi-official newspaper described the UMM positively, as advancing the interests of Mexican machinists.

91. Parlee, "The Impact of United States Railroad Unions," 463. On Vera's association with the PLM, see Leal, *Del mutualismo al sindicalismo*, 124, n. 370, citing Rodea, *Historia del movimiento obrero ferrocarrilero*, 328–31.

92. Shabot, *Los orígenes del sindicalismo ferrocarrilero*, 67–68, quoting from *El Diario del Hogar*, 10 August 1906.

93. Shabot, *Los orígenes del sindicalismo ferrocarrilero*, 74–75.

94. Ibid., 76.

95. *El Imparcial*, 23 July 1901.

96. Reyes to Díaz, 13 June 1907, Archivo de Bernardo Reyes (hereafter ABR), Carpeta 38, L. 7402, D. 1, F. 1, in Centro de Estudios de Historia de México, Condumex.

97. Ibid., and Díaz to Reyes, 17 June 1907, ABR, C. 38, L. 7413.

98. Díaz to Reyes, decoded telegram, 13 June 1907, ABR, C. 38, L. 7403, D. 1, F. 1.

99. Anderson, *Outcasts in Their Own Land*, 212.

100. Ibid. Cf. Parlee, "The Impact of United States Railroad Unions," 468, who argues that by 1908, the transfer of ownership to the Mexican government of the Ferrocarriles Nacionales contributed to the hardening position of the federal government to the demands of Mexican railway workers. Indisputably, the political situation had changed, and the federal government may well have not wanted to ally itself with workers against a management it was still probably trying to assuage after purchasing majority interests in the principal railway companies.

101. Reyes to Díaz, 28 March 1906, ABR, C. 36, L. 7184, D. 1, F. 2.

102. Ibid.

103. Díaz to Reyes, decoded telegram, 4 April 1906, ABR, C. 36, L. 7186, D. 1, F. 3.

104. Reyes to Díaz, 12 April 1906, ABR, C. 36, L. 7194, D. 1, F. 2.

105. Ibid.

106. Díaz to Reyes, 18 April 1906, ABR, C. 36, L. 7196, D. 1, F. 1. Cf. Anderson, *Outcasts in Their Own Land*, 211, citing the same sources in notes 103–8.

107. Draft Statutes of the Gran Liga Mexicana de Empleados de Ferrocarril, August 1905, partly reproduced in Shabot, *Los orígenes del sindicalismo ferrocarrilero*, 131.

108. Sesion Ordinaria, 24 April 1906, ABR, C. 36, L. 7199, D. 1, F. 2.

109. See Felix Vera's statement, in CPD, 31:5617–20. Vera describes being incarcerated as a result of a trumped-up defamation charge brought by G. Werpell. Cf. Anderson, *Outcasts in Their Own Land*, 214–15, and n. 88.

110. Shabot, *Los orígenes del sindicalismo ferrocarrilero*,144, quoting *El Imparcial*, 21 April 1908.

111. But cf. Shabot, *Los orígenes del sindicalismo ferrocarrilero*, 144–45, who contends it represented an evolutionary moment in the elaboration or articulation of the theory of the strike by the proletariat.

112. See ibid., 156, citing Rodea, *Historia del movimiento obrero ferrocarrilero*, 334–35.

113. Anderson, *Outcasts in Their Own Land*, 215–16; and Parlee, "The Impact of United States Railroad Unions," 468–69.

114. *El Imparcial*, 24 April 1908, p. 1.

115. Reyes to Corral, 18 September 1908, ABR, C. 38, L. 7590, D. 1, F. 1.

116. Corral to Reyes, 22 September 1908, ABR, C. 38, L. 7592, D. 1, F. 1.

117. Leal, *Del mutualismo al sindicalismo*, 118, 131–33.

118. Parlee, "The Impact of United States Railroad Unions," 466, quoting *El Imparcial*, 6 March 1908.

119. Gómez to Governor of Veracruz, 4 March 1910, CPD, 35:3763; cited by Anderson, *Outcasts in Their Own Land*, 266. See also Anderson, "Mexican Workers and the Politics of Revolution," which has informed the discussion of this paragraph and the following ones.

120. Parlee, "The Impact of United States Railroad Unions," 468, quoting Turner, *Barbarous Mexico*.

121. Anderson, *Outcasts in Their Own Land*, 242–47.

122. Ibid., 248, 257–58.

123. "A los Obreros Independientes," dated July 1910, CPD, 35:18474, cited by Anderson, *Outcasts in Their Own Land*, 259.

124. Anderson, *Outcasts in Their Own Land*, 259.

125. Ibid., 261, quoting *El Constitucional*, 2 June 1910.

126. Ibid., 263, quoting *El Constitucional*, 29 April 1910.

127. Leal, *Del mutualismo al sindicalismo*, 117; see also Anderson, "Mexican Workers and the Politics of Revolution."

128. See Chapter 1 for a discussion of Article 925.

CHAPTER 4: TOWARD SOCIAL LEGISLATION

1. See Kennedy, "Three Globalizations of Law and Legal Thought," on which the narrative of this paragraph is largely based. Collier and Collier, *Shaping the Political Arena*, analytically compares labor legislation in Latin America, focusing on the political balances of state and social actors to explain when such legislation was passed in each of the region's major countries; see p. 22 for a figurative overview of the onset of labor reform.

2. Cf. Kennedy, "Three Globalizations," which argues that the social encompassed varying ideological positions, including Catholic social thought, social democracy, and even fascist thought, but not communist, that is, revolutionary challenges to the bourgeois systems then consolidating.

3. Cf. Womack, *Luchas sindicales*.

4. García, "Breves consideraciones."

5. Ibid., Article 22, 416–17.

6. Article 23, in García, "Breves consideraciones," 417.

7. Ibid.

8. "Ley para el Estado de México, por José Vicente Villada," reprinted from the *Gaceta del Gobierno, Periódico Oficial del Estado de México*, 25 May 1904, p. 5, c. 1, in González Ramírez, *La huelga de Cananea*.

9. Gaxiola, "La primera legislación mexicana sobre accidentes del trabajo."

10. "Ley para el Estado de México," in González Ramírez, *La huelga de Cananea*, xlvi.

11. Gaxiola, "La primera legislación mexicana sobre accidentes del trabajo," Articles 3 and 5.

12. Reyes, *De mi vida*, 63.

13. "Ley Sobre Accidentes del Trabajo para el Estado de Nuevo León, por Bernardo Reyes," reprinted from *Compilación de leyes*, Suprema Corte de Justicia, vol. 3, Nuevo León, Decreto 47, 9 November 1906, in González Ramírez, *La huelga de Cananea*, lii.

14. Ley Sobre Accidentes, Art. 3, para. V.

15. "Dictamen del Lic. D. Rafael Rebollar/Opinión emitida por el suscripto a la Academia de Legislación y Jurisprudencia, con motivo de la consulta hecha por la Secretaría de Comunicaciones en el caso de abandono de un tren en marcha por un maquinista," 17 January 1896, reprinted in *Revista de Legislación y Jurisprudencia*, 9 (July–December 1895): 501.

16. Ibid., 502, 503, and 509.

17. Limantour to Corral, 8 April 1907, in Limantour Archive, Fondo CDLIV, Microfilm Roll 42, 1907, Condumex. Regarding the strike, see Chapter 3.

18. Ibid.

19. Corral to Limantour, 30 April 1907, Limantour Archive, Fondo CDLIV, Microfilm Roll 42.

20. Ibid.

21. See Anderson, *Outcasts in Their Own Land*, 217, citing three sources.

22. See Anderson, *Outcasts in Their Own Land*, 219; and "Memorandum relativo a la carta del Señor Daniel Guggenheim dirigida al Señor Presidente de la República," by Olegario Molina, 11 August 1908, CPD, 33:10792, cited by Anderson.

23. Guggenheim to Díaz, 21 July 1908, CPD, 33:10813–18, cited by Anderson, *Outcasts in Their Own Land*, 219.

24. Memorandum, CPD, 33:10792–99.

25. Anderson, *Outcasts in Their Own Land*, 219–20, citing Bernstein, *The Mexican Mining Industry*, 82, 95.

26. Manuel Rivera Collada, letter, 26 January 1907, in Legajo 817, c. 1, AGN, Ramo de Gobernación.

27. Anderson, *Outcasts in Their Own Land*, 234.

28. "Peligros de las Huelgas. El Contrato del Trabajo Debe Reposar en los Intereses de Obreros y Patrones," *El Imparcial*, 2 July 1907. See Chapter 3 for a discussion of the drafting of the reglamento.

29. Ibid.

30. Rodea, *Historia del movimiento obrero ferrocarrilero*, 116–18, cited in Shabot, *Los orígenes del sindicalismo ferrocarrilero*, 106–7.

31. "Programa Definitivo," July 1907, CPD, 32:7143.

32. Anderson, *Outcasts in Their Own Land*, 210. Reyes's support of the Liga's proposal for arbitration, which failed at their convention and to which Corral had objected, is discussed by Anderson, 211.

33. Ibid., 218, citing *El Diario*, 26 April 1908.

34. "Capital y Trabajo," paras. 21–33 of Programa del Partido Liberal y Manifiesto a la Nación, reprinted in Silva Herzog, *Breve historia de la revolución mexicana*, vol. 1.

35. *Diccionario Porrúa de historia, biografía y geografía de México.*

36. Pardo, "La Economía política y la legislación," in *Anuario de Legislación y Jurisprudencia* (1897). Pardo's essay was initially read in a session of the "Concurso Científico de 1895" and sent to the Nacional Colegio de Abogados on August 5, 1895. The *Anuario de Legislación y Jurisprudencia* published it the next year.

37. Ibid.,1–3. But cf. Raat, "Leopoldo Zea and Mexican Positivism."
38. Pardo, "La economía política y la legislación," 4, 6–7, and 12.
39. Ibid., 9–14.
40. Ibid., 17.
41. Ludlow, "El Fondo Histórico," 95, 105.
42. Labastida, "El derecho y la economía política, discurso pronunciado en la inauguración de los estudios del presente año escolar," 7 January 1897, reprinted in *Revista de Legislación y Jurisprudencia.*
43. See Stone, *The Search for Social Peace*, 37.
44. Labastida, "El derecho," 103.
45. Ibid., 98–107.
46. García, "Breves consideraciones," 418.
47. Ibid., 423, 425, 428–29.
48. Fernández Castelló, "La cuestión social," in *Revista de Legislación y Jurisprudencia* (1896).
49. Ibid., 23.
50. Pallares, "Escuela Nacional de Jurisprudencia," 28 August 1889, reprinted in *Revista de Legislación y Jurisprudencia* (1889).
51. Pallares and Reyes Retana, "Reformas al plan de estudios de la Escuela Nacional de Jurisprudencia de México," 2 August 1897, reprinted in *Revista de Legislación y Jurisprudencia*, (1897).
52. Ibid., 469.
53. Ibid., 470–71.
54. Borja Soriano, "Las asociaciones de socorros mutuos a la luz del derecho," *Revista de Legislación y Jurisprudencia* (1899).
55. Ibid., 503.
56. Dorado, "El positivismo en la ciencia jurídica y social italiana," *Anuario de Legislación y Jurisprudencia* (1892). Dorado was born in 1861 and died in 1919. *El positivismo en la ciencia jurídica y social italiana: Economía política, filosofía del derecho, derecho civil, derecho político, derecho romano, otras ramas jurídicas* (Madrid: Imprenta de la Revista de Legislación, 1891) is one of several books he wrote. The World Catalogue List of Records identifies very few locations for this book, one of which is the Universidad Veracruzana Biblioteca Central, in Mexico.
57. Dorado, "El positivismo," 150–51.
58. Ibid., 156–59.
59. Ibid., 172 (emphases in the original).
60. Ibid., 315–17.
61. Ibid., 326–27.
62. Ibid., 327–28.
63. Ibid., 330, n. 1.
64. Ibid., 344 and n. 1.
65. Ibid., 349.
66. Ibid., 350.
67. Dorado, "Hacia un nuevo derecho civil," *Revista de Legislación y Jurisprudencia* (1906). The article had been published earlier in Madrid's journal of the same name.
68. Ibid., 60–61.
69. Ibid., 66, n. 1.

70. Pic, "Legislación industrial," *Boletín de la Secretaría de Fomento* (August 1906).

71. Ibid., 19.

72. This account of Pic is based on Stone, *The Search for Social Peace*, 37–54.

73. Ibid., 25, n.1, 36–38, and 44–45.

74. Stone, *The Search for Social Peace*, 37, citing Pic, *Traité élémentaire de législation industrielle.*

75. This paragraph is based on Goddard, *El pensamiento político y social de los católicos mexicanos*, 144–51.

76. "El Obrero y la Cooperación," *El Imparcial*, 28 January 1907.

77. "Los Viejos Abogados y la Redoma Encantada," *El Imparcial*, 2 February 1907, p. 1.

78. *El Imparcial*, 14 October 1902: "the century of strikes."

79. "El Asunto del Dia," *El Imparcial*, 26 December 1906.

80. See Anderson, *Outcasts in Their Own Land*, 37, describing the interchange between Ramos Pedrueza and Macedo in the Chamber of Deputies, citing the *Diario de los Debates de la Cámara de Diputados, Congreso XX*, 3:667, 675.

CHAPTER 5: LEGISLATING LABOR LAW, 1911–1924

1. See, e.g., Trueba Urbina, *El artículo 123* and *The Mexican Constitution of 1917*.

2. See, e.g., Knight, "The Working Class"; Ruiz, *Labor and the Ambivalent Revolutionaries*; cf. Bortz, *Revolution Within the Revolution*; and Hart, *Anarchism.*

3. See, e.g., the two series, González Casanova, ed., *La clase obrera en la historia de México*, vols. 3 and 5–9; and L. González, ed., *Historia de la revolución mexicana*, vols. 4–16; Carr, *El movimiento obrero*; Middlebrook, *The Paradox of Revolution.* For the 1930s, see, e.g., Hamilton, *The Limits of State Autonomy*; Ashby, *Organized Labor.*

4. *Iniciativa con objeto de crear un Departamento de Trabajo*, 22 September 1911, in Secretaría de Industria, Comercio y Trabajo, *La industria, el comercio y el trabajo en México*, vol. 3, *Del trabajo y la prevision social*, 6–21.

5. Leal and Villaseñor, *En la revolución*, 262.

6. *Iniciativa con objeto de crear un Departamento de Trabajo*, 6, 10–11.

7. Ibid., 18.

8. Carr, *El movimiento obrero*, 1:69; the *Diario Oficial* published the statute on 18 December 1911.

9. For the diplomatic posts held by de la Barra, see Henderson, *In the Absence of Don Porfirio*, 14–15; for his discussion of the progressive consensus, ibid., xi, 11, and 153. Cf. Carr, *El movimiento obrero*, 1:68–69, who contends reticence on the part of Porfirian legislators to bring to a vote the legislation establishing the department, observing that Congress delayed passage.

10. Leal and Villaseñor, *En la revolución*, 249.

11. Ibid., 116–19, 141–49, 154–66; Womack, "The Mexican Revolution," 88–89; Leal, *Del mutualismo al sindicalismo*; Bortz, *Revolution Within the Revolution.*

12. Bortz, "'Without Any More Law," 264.

13. Carr, *El movimiento obrero*, 1:69, as to Ramos Pedrueza's moderate socialism; his service in the Chamber of Deputies (Congress's lower house) is mentioned in Chapter 4.

14. Leal and Villaseñor, *En la revolución*, 270; and Ruiz, *Labor and the Ambivalent Revolutionaries*, 33–34.

15. Rafael Hernández's "Exposición de Motivos," reprinted in Remolina Roqueñi, *El artículo 123*, 23–24.

16. Statement by Lic. Tomás Reyes Retana, in Remolina Roqueñi, *El artículo 123*, 24, 25.

17. Communication No. 24 to the governor of Morelos, from the Minister of Development, 29 January 1912, reprinted in Remolina Roqueñi, *El artículo 123*, 26.

18. Leal and Villaseñor, *En la revolución*, 273–94.

19. Ibid., 295–302. Cf. Bortz, *Revolution Within the Revolution*, chapter 4.

20. "Reglamento para las Fábricas de Hilados y Tejidos en la Republica, Aprobado por la Convención de Industriales reunida en la ciudad de México en el mes de Julio de 1912, aceptado por el Comité Central de Obreros que manda publicar el C. Secretario de Estado y del Despacho de Fomento, Colonización e Industria, por acuerdo del C. Presidente de la República y que comenzará a regir el 1 de Agosto de 1912," signed by Antonio Ramos Pedrueza, 17 July 1912, in AGN, Ramo de Departamento del Trabajo, Caja 106, Exp. 2.

21. Antonio Ramos Pedrueza, "A los obreros de las Fábricas de Hilados y Tejidos de la República," 4 August 1912, in AGN, Ramo de Departamento del Trabajo, Caja 106, Exp. 2.

22. Circular, 24 February 1912, from the director of the Department of Labor, Lic. Antonio Ramos Pedrueza, reprinted in Remolina Roqueñi, *El artículo 123*, 27.

23. Lear, *Workers, Neighbors, and Citizens*, 183–89.

24. Ibid., 310–312; see also Ruiz, *Labor and the Ambivalent Revolutionaries*.

25. Lear, *Workers, Neighbors, and Citizens*, 313–21.

26. See, e.g., "Iniciativa de Ley sobre Uniones Profesionales de la Diputación Colimense," 28 May 1913, Diario de los Debates de la Cámara de Diputados, reprinted in Remolina Roqueñi, *El artículo 123*, 53.

27. Proyecto de Ley de Reformas a las Fracciones VII y XXII del Artículo 73 y al Artículo 309 del Código de Comercio, from Diario de los Debates de la Cámara de Diputados, 17 September 1913, reprinted in Remolina Roqueñi, *El artículo 123*, 55.

28. Ibid. (Articles 11–13.)

29. See the decrees and bills reprinted in Remolina Roqueñi, *El artículo 123*, 212–13.

30. "Manifiesto a la Nación," 26 March 1913, reprinted in Secretaría de Gobernación, *Codificación de los Decretos del C. Venustiano Carranza*, 7.

31. See Leal and Villaseñor, *En la revolución*, 324; cf. Ulloa, *La Constitución de 1917*, 271.

32. Niemeyer, *Revolution at Querétaro*, 19–23; see also Knight, *The Mexican Revolution*, 2:168, 254–56.

33. Knight, *The Mexican Revolution*, 262–63. On the labor component of the social reform program of the Convention, and the conditions under which it was drafted, see Quirk, *The Mexican Revolution*, 242–44.

34. Hall, *Álvaro Obregón*, 100–2.

35. Ibid.

36. Leal and Villaseñor, *En la revolución*, 323, relying on Palavicini's account, suggest that one of Carranza's objections to the Convention was its insistence on completing the terms of the Plan of Guadalupe while reactionaries were still dominant in the economic sector. See also Niemeyer, *Revolution at Querétaro*, 20–21.

37. Palavicini, *Mi vida revolucionaria*, 235.

38. December 12, 1914, Decree, promulgated in Veracruz, reprinted in *Codificación de los Decretos del C. Venustiano Carranza*, 131.

39. See Remolina Roqueñi, *El artículo 123*, and the collection of decrees therein.

40. See, e.g., Decreto, 2 September 1914, issued by Pablo González for Puebla and Tlaxcala and published in *Periódico Oficial del Estado de Puebla*, 15 September 1914, reprinted in Remolina Roqueñi, *El artículo 123*, 67. Remolina reproduces other similar decrees in the same work.

41. Decree of Álvaro Obregón, promulgated 9 April 1915, in Celaya, Guanajuato, and ratified by Venustiano Carranza, published in *El Constitucionalista*, 27 April 1915, and reprinted in Remolina Roqueñi, *El artículo 123*, 94–95.

42. See Knight, "Mexican Peonage"; and González Navarro, "El trabajo forzoso."

43. Decreto, 3 September 1914, published in the *Periódico Oficial del Estado de Puebla*, 18 September 1914, reprinted in Remolina Roqueñi, *El artículo 123*, 68.

44. See Decreto número 4, 11 September 1914, Mérida, Yucatán, published in the *Diario Oficial del Estado de Yucatán*, 12 September 1914, reprinted in Remolina Roqueñi, *El artículo 123*, 66–67.

45. Decreto, San Juan Bautista, Tabasco, 19 September 1914, *Periódico Oficial del Estado de Tabasco*, 19 September 1914, reprinted in Remolina Roqueñi, *El artículo 123*, 68.

46. Ley de Obreros, 30 October 1914, published in *Periódico Oficial del Estado de Chiapas*, 31 October 1914, reprinted in Remolina Roqueñi, *El artículo 123*, 71.

47. Decreto número 11, Cándido Aguilar, Villa de Soledad de Doblado, 19 October 1914, published in *Gaceta Oficial del Estado de Veracruz*, 29 October 1914, reprinted in Remolina Roqueñi, *El artículo 123*, 69–70.

48. Ibid. See also Decreto número 7, given in Xalapa, Ver., 4 October 1914, prescribing Sunday rest, in ibid., 69.

49. Ley de Asociaciones Profesionales de Agustín Millán, 16 October 1915, published in *Gaceta Oficial del Estado de Veracruz*, 14 December 1915, reprinted in Remolina Roqueñi, *El artículo 123*, 99–100.

50. Ley Sobre Asociaciones Profesionales de Cándido Aguilar, 24 January 1916, published in *Gaceta Oficial del Estado de Veracruz*, 8 February 1916, reprinted in Remolina Roqueñi, *El artículo 123*, 119–20.

51. Decreto número 392, Ley del Trabajo, published 15 December 1915 in *Diario Oficial del Gobierno Constitucionalista del Estado de Yucatán*, reprinted in Remolina Roqueñi, *El artículo 123*, 100.

52. Ibid., 101–2.

53. Ibid., 105, 109–10.

54. Palavicini, *Mi vida revolucionaria*, 228–30, 235, 237.

55. See Ley Obrera de Prestación de Servicios and Proyecto de Reformas al Código de Comercio, in Remolina Roqueñi, *El artículo 123*, 72–74.

56. Proyecto de Ley del Salario Minimo y de las Juntas de Aveniencia, Presentadas al C. Jefe de la Revolución por la Sección de Legislación Social, published in *El Pueblo*, 28 January 1915, reprinted in Remolina Roqueñi, *El artículo 123*, 76.

57. Proyecto de Ley de Uniones Profesionales Elaborada por la Sección de Legislación Social Dependiente de la Secretaría de Instrucción Pública, published in *El Pueblo*, 28 January 1915, reprinted in Remolina Roqueñi, *El artículo 123*, 77.

58. See Macías's testimony in the *Diario de los Debates del Congreso Constituyente*, 1:1036, 1044.

59. January 29, 1915, Decree, promulgated in Veracruz, reprinted in *Codificación de los Decretos del C. Venustiano Carranza*, 165.

60. See Proyecto de Ley Sobre Contrato de Trabajo, published on 12 April 1915, in Veracruz, reprinted in Remolina Roqueñi, *El artículo 123*, 83; see also Decreto Número 10, 17 October 1913, reprinted in *Codificación de los Decretos del C. Venustiano Carranza*, 29 (regarding the Ministry of Interior's supervision over the labor department).

61. Palavicini, *Mi vida revolucionaria*, 237–38.

62. Lear, *Workers, Neighbors, and Citizens*, 291. Regarding the COM and its relationship with both workers' organizations and the Constitutionalists, see Hart, *Anarchism*; Ulloa, *La Constitución de 1917*; Carr, "The Casa del Obrero Mundial."

63. Proyecto de Ley Sobre Contrato de Trabajo, in Remolina Roqueñi, *El artículo 123*, 83.

64. Ibid., 88. (See Chapter 4 for a discussion of Dorado and turn-of-the-century social and legal thought.)

65. Remolina Roqueñi, *El artículo 123*, 85.

66. Ulloa, *La Constitución de 1917*, 304–19.

67. Decree, 1 August 1916, published in *Diario Oficial del Gobierno Provisional de la República Mexicana*, 21 August 1916, reprinted in Remolina Roqueñi, *El artículo 123*, 125–26; and see Ulloa, *La Constitución de 1917*.

68. Ulloa, *La Constitución de 1917*.

69. Womack, "The Mexican Revolution," 126–29.

70. Niemeyer, *Revolution at Querétaro*; Hall, *Álvaro Obregón*, 172–79; Knight, *The Mexican Revolution*, 2:473–76. The main account by a key participant in the drafting of Article 123 is Rouaix, *Génesis*, chapters 3 and 4.

71. Niemeyer, *Revolution at Querétaro*, chapters 2, 3, and 4.

72. See, e.g., Knight, *The Mexican Revolution*; P. Smith, "La política dentro de la Revolución"; and Cumberland, *Mexican Revolution*, chapter 9. Quirk, "Liberales y radicales en la revolución mexicana," has contended that there was a strong ideological division between radicals and liberals in Querétaro.

73. See, "Proyecto de Constitución Presentado por el Primer Jefe, Article 73, ¶X," reprinted in Tena Ramírez, *Leyes fundamentales de México*, 764, 783; and *Diario de los Debates*, 1 December 1916, 1:385–99.

74. Niemeyer, *Revolution at Querétaro*, 64–66, and 104–5.

75. "Dictamen sobre el artículo de la Comisión," 26 December 1916 session, *Diario de los Debates*, 1:968–69.

76. Ibid.

77. *Diario de los Debates*, 1:976–78.

78. Ibid., 1:979–80.

79. Ibid., 1: 980–81.

80. Ibid., 1:1011.

81. Ibid., 1:1017–19.

82. *Diario de los Debates*, 28 December 1916 session, 1:1025–28; see Niemeyer, *Revolution at Querétaro*, 54, regarding Macías and Rojas's co-authorship of Carranza's draft constitution.

83. See Cumberland, *Mexican Revolution*, 346, noting the earlier proposal of Froylán Manjarrez.

84. *Diario de los Debates*, 1:1027–28.

85. Ibid., 1:1036

86. Ibid., 1:1037.

87. Ibid., 1:1037–38, 1039.

88. See Oñate, "Administración de justicia," 83–84 (regarding the general animus against lawyers and the judiciary).

89. *Diario de los Debates*, 1:1041.

90. Ibid.

91. Ibid., 1:1042.

92. See Chapters 1 and 2.

93. *Diario de los Debates*, 1:1044.

94. Clark, *Organized Labor*, 49.

95. See Smith, "La política dentro de la Revolución," 379–80 and 377; see also Knight, *The Mexican Revolution*, 2:476.

96. Middlebrook, *The Paradox of Revolution*, 47–48.

97. Ibid.

98. Niemeyer, *Revolution at Querétaro*, 116.

99. *Diario de los Debates*, 1:1051.

100. Niemeyer, *Revolution at Querétaro*, 118.

101. Rouaix, *Génesis*, 103–4.

102. Ibid., 107. Rouaix mentions a few more individuals.

103. Ibid., 117.

104. *Diario de los Debates*, 2:359.

105. Ibid.

106. See Transitory Article 11, Constitución Política de los Estados Unidos Mexicanos, que reforma la del 5 de febrero de 1857, reprinted in Tena Ramírez, *Leyes fundamentals de México*. Interestingly, subsequent litigation to enforce provisions of Article 123, namely, the right to profit sharing, before the date of statutory implementation, failed. See Chapter 6. Macias's and Carranza's framework of deferment evidently prevailed.

107. See Niemeyer, *Revolution at Querétaro*, 122–23, for other changes.

108. See Bensusán Areous, *El modelo mexicano*, 85–92; Bensusán also recognizes Macías's and the renovadores' strategy to structure the new article so as to ensure deferment of its implementation, which was partially foiled by Múgica, as the rights articulated in Article 123 were expanded (see 86–89).

109. *Diario de los Debates*, 2:863; Knight, *The Mexican Revolution*, 2:475.

110. See, e.g., Antonio Díaz Soto y Gama, prologue to *Génesis*, 9; Niemeyer, *Revolution at Querétaro*, 101; Bensusán, "La legislación laboral heredada"; Trueba Urbina, *El artículo* 123; Carr, *El movimiento obrero*, 1:125; and Bortz, "Without Any More Law," 277–78.

111. Article 123 is separate from other chapters in the constitutional text, under its title: "Título Sexto, Del Trabajo y de la Previsión Social" ("Of Labor and Social Welfare"). See Constitución Política de los Estados Unidos Mexicanos, 5 February 1917, reprinted in Tena Ramírez, *Leyes fundamentales de México*.

112. Article 123 is translated and set out completely in Niemeyer, *Revolution at Querétaro*, appendix C; and Branch, *The Mexican Constitution of 1917*, 94–102; here, the focus is on the overall form of the article and its significance. In Spanish, the term *fracción* is used to denote the main parts (paragraphs, clauses, provisions, or sections) of Article 123; this book, consistent with Niemeyer, translates *fracción* as paragraph.

113. Middlebrook, *The Paradox of Revolution*, 47, n. 20.

114. Chapter 6 discusses Paragraphs XX and XXI in detail.

115. See Paragraph XXVII, which nullified abusive stipulations in employment contracts. Transitory Article 13 extinguished until the constitution's effective date all debts owed by workers to employers or their intermediaries. Paragraph XXIV limited the liability of a worker's debt contracted from his or her employer. Paragraph XXV stated that any contracting service would be free to the worker. Tena Ramírez, *Leyes fundamentales de México*, 870–74.

116. See Article 123, Paragraphs XXIII, XXIV, and XXX in Tena Ramírez, *Leyes fundamentales de México*. Paragraph XXX stated that cooperative associations for the construction of low-cost housing were socially beneficial.

117. See Lombardo Toledano, *La libertad sindical*.

118. Cueva, *Derecho mexicano del trabajo* (1938), 117–27.

119. Middlebrook, *The Paradox of Revolution*, 48, citing Remolina Roqueñi, *Evolución*; chapter 4 of Remolina lists state labor laws and their dates of enactment.

120. Clark, *Organized Labor*, 53.

121. Gómez-Galvarriato, "Measuring the Impact," 290–91, and Bortz, *Revolution Within the Revolution*, chapters 6–7, both note that states such as Veracruz and Puebla that passed legislation to enforce Article 123 had strong labor movements.

122. Código del Trabajo del Estado de Yucatán, 2 October 1918, decreed by F. Carrillo, 16 December 1918, reprinted in Secretaría de Industria, Comercio y Trabajo, *Legislación del trabajo*.

123. See Tamayo, *En el interinato*, 35–36.

124. Ley del Trabajo del Estado de Veracruz. Dada en la ciudad de Córdoba, el 14 de enero de 1918, reprinted in Secretaría de Industria, Comercio y Trabajo, *Legislación del trabajo*. For a description of Cándido Aguilar's gubernatorial politics, see Koth, *Waking the Dictator*, 204.

125. Ley del Trabajo del Estado de Veracruz, Arts. 142–52.

126. Ibid., Arts. 153–82.

127. Cueva, *Derecho mexicano del trabajo* (1938), 138–39.

128. See Valenzuela, "1920–1924: . . . y venían de una revolución!," 157.

129. Middlebrook, *The Paradox of Revolution*, 47.

130. See Bensusán Areous, *El modelo mexicano*, 98; Cueva, *Derecho mexicano del trabajo* (1938), 134–35.

131. See Jefe del Departamento to Oficial Mayor of Secretaría de Industria, Comercio y Trabajo, 1 August 1918, Departamento del Trabajo, Caja 132, Expediente 17. See also "Proyecto de Exposición de Motivos para el de la Ley Sobre Conciliación y Arbitraje," n.d. [August 1918], ibid., and "Proyecto de Ley Sobre Conciliación y Arbitraje," Arts. 11, 22, ibid., AGN.

132. "Borador de Exposición de Motivos para el Proyecto de Ley Relativo a Huelgas y Paros," n.d. [August 1918], Departamento del Trabajo, Caja 132, Expediente 16, AGN.

133. "Proyecto de Ley Sobre Huelgas y Paros," n.d. [August 1918], Departamento del Trabajo, Caja 132, Expediente 16, AGN.

134. Clark, *Organized Labor*, 57–59.

135. Carr, *El movimiento obrero*, 1:130–35.

136. "Pacto secreto o convenio privado," 6 August 1919, in Carr, *El movimiento obrero*, appendix C, 2:188–89; see also 2:139–144.

137. Cf. "Convenio" de 13 enero de 1916, in Cámara de Industriales de Orizaba, *La sindicación forzosa* (1922), appendix 1, 15, which stipulates union hiring.

138. Carr, *El movimiento obrero*, 1:145–46, 147, 154–55, 180–81.

139. Ibid., 178, 182–83. The numbers Carr cites, reported by the CROM, are suspect: 50,000 members in 1920; 1,200,000 in 1924. Similarly, the number of strikes reflects official counts. Carr cites the *Estadística Nacional*, May 1928, for the number and outcome of strikes, as reported by Clark, *Organized Labor*, 119, who explains her skepticism about the figures, 119–20.

140. Collado Herrera, *Empresarios y políticos*, 131–32, 134–36. The following narration of events that occurred in Veracruz is largely based on Collado's book.

141. Collado Herrera, *Empresarios y políticos*, 247.

142. Ibid., 250–53. See also the discussion of the federal judiciary's decisions in Chapter 6. The office of the Ministerio Público included public attorneys who could present opinions to the federal judiciary. The office was under the direction of the executive power. See the discussion regarding its establishment during the Porfirian era in Chapter 2.

143. Collado Herrera, *Empresarios y políticos*, 254.

144. Ibid., 255.

145. Ibid., 256, 257–60.

146. Ibid., 290–96, 302, 304.

147. Ibid., 304.

148. Ibid., 314–15; Clark, *Organized Labor*, 102–6.

149. Collado Herrera, *Empresarios y políticos*, 315, 321–25.

150. Address to Secretarios de la H. Cámara de Diputados from A. Obregón, 24 July 1924, in Departamento del Trabajo, Caja 717, Expediente 1, 30–39, AGN; see also Collado Herrera, *Empresarios y políticos*, 325, citing the above, 15–27.

151. "La Ley Reglamentaria del Artículo Ciento Veintitres Constitucional/Proyecto del Ejecutivo que Sera Enviado a las Cámaras/Se Propone la Creación de un Impuesto Hasta de 10 por Ciento Sobre Todos los Pagos que Se Hagan por Concepto de Trabajo/Indemnizaciones por Accidentes, Seguro de Trabajo y Jubilaciones en Bien de la Clase Laborante," n.d. [July 1924], Departamento del Trabajo, Caja 717, Expediente 1, 344–50, AGN.

152. Ibid.

153. Ibid.

154. Ibid.

155. "Solicita el Señor Presidente el Concurso de la Prensa Independiente," n.d. [July 1924], Departamento de Trabajo, Caja 717, Expediente 1, 344–50, AGN. See also Collado Herrera, *Empresarios y políticos*, 325.

156. José Valenzuela, "1920–1924: . . . y venían de una revolución!," 173.

157. Cf. Benjamin, "Laboratories of the New State."

CHAPTER 6: THE SUPREME COURT AND LABOR LAW, 1917–1924

1. See González Casanova, *En el primer gobierno constitucional*, 50–60.

2. *Excélsior*, 21 April 1918, p. 3, reprinted in Cabrera Acevedo, *La Suprema Corte de Justicia* [1917–1920]. This volume identifies a number of the seminal labor cases discussed in this chapter.

3. González Casanova, *En el primer gobierno constitucional*, 54.

4. Ibid., 52–53.

5. Ibid., 53; see also *Excélsior*, 21 April 1918.

6. González Casanova, *En el primer gobierno constitucional*, 53–54.

7. Hijos de Ángel Díaz Rubín, 18 April 1918, SJF, 5th época, vol. 2, p. 1192 (all citations to the *Semanario Judicial* in this chapter and the next are to the 5th época: hence, this series is not cited again specifically).

8. Hijos de Ángel Díaz Rubín at 1195.

9. Ibid., 1194–95.

10. Ibid., 1195; see also Versiones Taquigráficas, 16–18 April 1918, reprinted in Cabrera Acevedo, *La Suprema Corte de Justicia* [1917–1920].

11. Hijos de Ángel Díaz Rubín, 1196.

12. In this case, Article 711 of the Federal Code of Civil Procedure.

13. Hijos de Ángel Díaz Rubín, 1196–97.

14. See Versiones Taquigráficas, 16 April 1918, reprinted in Cabrera Acevedo, *La Suprema Corte de Justicia* [1917–1920], 237.

15. Hijos de Ángel Díaz Rubín, 1198.

16. Versiones Taquigráficas, 17 April 1918, reprinted in Cabrera Acevedo, *La Suprema Corte de Justicia* [1917–1920], 226.

17. *Excélsior*, 4 April 1918, reprinted in Cabrera Acevedo, *La Suprema Corte de Justicia* [1917–1920], 221.

18. "El Conflicto Obrero en Puebla," *Excélsior*, 4 April 1918, p. 8, reprinted in Cabrera Acevedo, *La Suprema Corte de Justicia* [1917–1920], 221.

19. Ibid., 222.

20. See González Casanova, *En el primer gobierno constitucional*, 55–59, on which the paragraph's summary of events is based.

21. Lombardo Toledano, *La libertad sindical*, in *Obras completas*, 3:42–52; and Alvarado, *La reconstrucción de México*, 2:341–42.

22. Cf. Sieder et al., *The Judicialization of Politics in Latin America*, and the essays collected therein, which suggest the process of judicialization occurring more recently in various Latin American countries and on which my argument of the judicialization of labor relations is partly based.

23. Collado Herrera, *Empresarios y políticos*, 252–53.

24. Cervercería Moctezuma, S.A., 14 April 1923, SJF, vol. 12, p. 752; and Cía. Agrícola Francesa y coagraviados, 28 April 1923, SJF, vol. 12, p. 856.

25. Collado Herrera, *Empresarios y políticos*, 250.

26. "Asunto Villa y Alvarez Sucesores," in Versiones Taquigráficas, 10 February 1922.

27. Versiones Taquigráficas, 10 February 1922.

28. Ibid.

29. Ibid.

30. Cervecería Moctezuma, S.A., 14 April 1923, SJF, vol. 12, at 753–55.

31. Ibid., 754–59.

32. Cía. Agrícola Francesa y coagraviados, 28 April 1923, SJF, vol. 12, p. 856.

33. Ibid., 863–64.

34. Versiones Taquigráficas, Sessions of 14 and 28 April 1923.

35. "Asunto: Luz Bringas contra la Junta de Conciliación y Arbitraje y del Presidente Municipal de Orizaba, Ver.," Versiones Taquigráficas, 14 April 1923.

36. Ibid.

37. Ibid., "Asunto Cervecería Moctezuma, S.A.," 14 April 1923 Session.

38. Zorrilla y Miaja, 4 April 1922, SJF, vol. 10, p. 749.

39. Zorrilla y Miaja, 751.

40. Ibid., 752.

41. Cf. Cía. Ferrocarril Sud Pacífico de Mexico, S.A., 10 November 1920, SJF, vol. 7, p. 1405, where the Court had enjoined the Sonoran governor from ordering the railway company not to enter into new contracts with replacement workers during a strike, but let stand a declaration of the board of conciliation and arbitration that the strike was licit.

42. Zorrilla y Miaja, 752–53.

43. Francisco Ortiz Borbolla, sucesion de, 26 December 1922, SJF, vol. 11, p. 1113.

44. Ibid., 1117–19.

45. See Articles 94 and 96, and Transitory Article 5, Constitución Política, reprinted in Tena Ramírez, *Leyes fundamentales de México.*

46. See, e.g., *Diario de los Debates de la Cámara de los Diputados del Congreso de los Estados Unidos Mexicanos, Periodo Extraordinario XXVII Legislatura,* vol. 1, num. 38, 23 May 1917, http://cronica.diputados.gob.mx (accessed 13 August 2008) (indicating the vote for Supreme Court candidates).

47. See "Las Elecciones de Magistrados a la Suprema Corte" and "Elecciones de Magistrados a la Suprema Corte," *Excélsior*, 12 and 13 May 1917, respectively; see also the editions of 18 and 24 May 1917.

48. "Funcionamiento del Poder Judicial," *Excélsior*, 7 May 1917; see also the edition of 13 May 1917.

49. *Excélsior*, 12 May 1917.

50. See Suprema Corte, *Ministros, 1917–2004.*

51. See ibid. and Cabrera, *El poder judicial federal mexicano*, 64–74.

52. "En Congreso General Fue Hecha la Elección de Magistrados a la Suprema Corte," *Excélsior*, 22 May 1919.

53. Marván Laborde, "Ejecutivo fuerte y division de poderes," 153–56.

54. See Carbrera Acevedo, *La Suprema Corte de Justicia* [1920–1924], 23, citing *Excélsior*, 28 October 1919, and Carlos Macías Richard, *Vida y temperamento. Plutarco Elías Calles, 1877–1920* (1995), 292.

55. "La Elección de Magistrados a la Sup. Corte," *Excélsior*, 13 May 1919.

56. *Excélsior*, 22 May 1919.

57. "Pronóstico de *Excélsior* Acerca de los cc. que Integraran la Suprema Corte," *Excélsior*, 11 May 1919.

58. "La Elección de Magistrados a la Suprema Corte de Justicia" and "Quienes Son los C.C. que Forman la Suprema Corte de Justicia," *Excélsior*, 13 and 23 May 1919, respectively.

59. See Suprema Corte, *Ministros 1917–1924*, 1:275.

60. *Excélsior*, 23 May 1919.

61. Valenzuela, "1920–1924: . . . y venían de una revolución!," 158–59.

62. See generally *El Demócrata*, 11, 14, 24, 25, 26, and 27 July 1923.

63. See Emilio Portes Gil's statement in Congress, in *Diario de los Debates, Periodo Extraordinario, XXX Legislatura*, vol. 2, num. 45, Sesion Permanente, 31 May 1923, http://cronica.diputados.gob.mx (accessed 13 August 2008); and "Tampoco Ayer Fue Electa la Suprema Corte," *Excélsior*, 5 June 1923, p. 1.

64. "Por Fin, Van a Ser Hoy Discutidos los Candidatos a Magistrados," *El Universal*, 18 May 1923.

65. "Las Mayorías Parlamentarias Designaron Sus Seis Candidatos a la Magistratura de la Corte," *El Demócrata*, 25 July 1923, p. 1.

66. Article 123, Paragraph XX, states: "Differences or disputes between capital and labor shall be subject to the decisions of a Board of Conciliation and Arbitration, to consist of an equal number of representatives of workers and employers and one from the government." Paragraph XXI states: "If the employer shall refuse to submit his differences to arbitration, the labor contract shall be considered as terminated, and the employer shall be obliged to indemnify the worker by the payment to him of three months' wages and shall incur any liability resulting from the dispute. If the workers reject the award, the contract shall be considered as terminated." See Niemeyer, *Revolution at Querétaro*, 244, from which the translation of the two paragraphs is quoted. See also Chapter 5.

67. "Legal culture" has been defined as "the cluster of attitudes, ideas, expectations, and values that people hold with regard to their legal system, legal institutions and legal rules." See Friedman and Pérez, *Legal Culture in the Age of Globalization*, 2, quoted in Sieder et al., *The Judicialization of Politics*, 12–13.

68. See generally Lombardo Toledano, *La libertad sindical*; Bensusán Areous, *El modelo mexicano*.

69. Remolina Roqueñi, *Evolución*, 43.

70. See Joseph, *Revolution from Without*, 169–72.

71. Ibid., 214.

72. See J. Crasseman Sucesores, S. en C., 2 November 1917, SJF, vol. 1, p. 773; Guillermo Cabrera, 8 March 1918, SJF, vol. 2, p. 772; Francisco Fuentes Vargas, 13 March 1918, SJF, vol. 2, p. 807.

73. Lane Rincón Mines Incorporated, 23 August 1918, SJF, vol. 3, p. 552.

74. Published opinions of amparos in this period frequently mention whether the Ministerio Público recommended conceding or denying the amparo petition.

75. Lane Rincón, 556–57.

76. Remolina Roqueñi, *Evolución*, 44.

77. Clark, *Organized Labor*, 245.

78. See, e.g., Junta de Conciliación y Arbitraje de Veracruz, 23 January 1919, SJF, vol. 4, p. 279, where the board filed the complaint with the Court against a federal judge.

79. Florencio O. Martínez, 3 February 1919, SJF, vol. 4, p. 337.

80. Ibid., 341–42.

81. Ibid., 343.

82. Cía. Minera Victoria y Anexas, S.A., 15 February 1919, SJF, vol. 4, p. 412.

83. Ibid., 417.

84. See excerpt of *Libro de pleno de junio de 1919*, reprinted in Cabrera Acevedo, *La Suprema Corte de Justicia* [1917–1920], p. 77.

85. La Blanca y Anexas, S.A., 11 June 1921, SJF, vol. 8, p. 1015.

86. Ibid. at 1020.

87. Las Dos Estrellas, S.A., 29 June 1922, SJF, vol. 11, p. 794.

88. Versiones Taquigráficas, 29 June 1922.

89. Las Dos Estrellas, 798.

90. Versiones Taquigráficas, 29 June 1922.

91. Las Dos Estrellas, 798.

92. Ibid.

93. Ibid., 799.

94. Ibid., 801–2.

95. The Texas Company of Mexico, 8 February 1923, SJF, vol. 12, p. 286.

96. Ibid., 288–90.

97. See Alfonso Sansores C., 8 February 1923, SJF, vol. 12, p. 291.

98. Ibid., 292–93.

99. Carlos Díaz Ordaz, 24 January 1924, SJF, vol. 14, p. 365.

100. One labor scholar referred to it as the first case in which the Court overturned its earlier case law. Clark, *Organized Labor*, 248, n. 21. Contemporaries also reported the shift in the Court's position. "La Suprema Corte Hizo Justicia a los Obreros," *El Universal*, 29 January 1924.

101. "Las Juntas de Conciliación Son Desde Ayer Autoridades," *El Universal*, 25 January 1924, p. 1.

102. Clark, *Organized Labor*, 193.

103. Carlos Díaz Ordaz, 371–73.

104. "La Corona," Cía. Mexicana Holandesa, S.A., 1 February 1924, SJF, vol. 14, p. 492.

105. Ibid., 498.

106. Ibid. The most significant aspect of the ruling related to the Court's holding that the boards had *imperio*: their determinations would be binding analogously to those of courts. This point is further noted below, in the description of the public conference that accompanied the issuance of the opinion.

107. "Asunto: Compañia Mexicana Holandesa, 'La Corona' S.A.," in Versiones Taquigráficas, 1 February 1924.

108. Ibid.

109. Ibid. Compare "La Corona," at 497, and the opinion's report of the Veracruz junta's argument using the fact of sanctions as evidence of the mandatory nature of board awards.

110. Versiones Taquigráficas, 1 February 1924.

111. Ibid.

112. Ibid.

113. "Los Fallos de la Corte sobre las Juntas de Conciliación," *El Universal*, 4 February 1924, p. 1.

114. See Cueva, *Derecho mexicano del trabajo* (1949), vol. 2, 943–50, on which this and the next paragraph are based.

115. Bassols would become a leading progressive public intellectual in subsequent years.

116. Cueva, *Derecho mexicano del trabajo* (1949), vol. 2, 944–45.

117. "Asunto Compañía de Tranvías Luz y Fuerza de Puebla Contra Actos de la Junta de Conciliación y Arbitraje de Veracruz y Presidente Municipal de Orizaba," in Versiones Taquigráficas, 21 August 1924.

118. Cía. de Tranvías, Luz y Fuerza de Puebla, S.A., 21 August 1924, SJF, vol. 15, p. 508; and *El Universal*, 22 August 1924, p. 1, c. 2.

119. Cía. de Tranvías, 515–16.

120. "Asunto Cía. de Tranvías Luz y Fuerza de Puebla," Versiones Taquigráficas, 21 August 1924.

121. Ibid.

122. Ibid.

123. See generally Middlebrook, *The Paradox of Revolution*, 56–62; Rocha Bandala and Franco, *La competencia.*

124. Cf. Bassols, "Que son, por fin, las Juntas?"

125. See *Excélsior*, 1, 2, and 3 February 1924. But see "La Autoridad de las Juntas de Conciliación," *El Universal*, 26 January 1924, cited in Collado Herrera, *Empresarios y políticos*, 323.

126. See, e.g., "El Pte de la Corte Sostiene que las Juntas de Conciliación y Arbitraje Son Autoridades/Los que Impugnan el Carácter de Autoridad de Dichas Juntas, Dice el Lic. Francisco Modesto Ramírez, Observan una Conducta Contradictoria, a Mi Juicio," *El Universal*, 5 February 1924, p. 4; Carr, *El movimiento obrero*; and Tamayo, *En el interinato*, 34 (citing Carr).

127. See, e.g., Cueva, *El nuevo derecho del trabajo*, 2:530–33; Middlebrook, *The Paradox of Revolution*, 58 and n. 68; and Carr, *El movimiento obrero*, 1:208; the latter two cite Clark, *Organized Labor*, 245–47. Collado Herrera, *Empresarios y políticos*, like Tamayo, *En el interinato*, cites Carr.

128. "Voto de simpatía dado por la H. Cámara de Diputados a la H. Suprema Corte de Justicia de la Nación, por las sentencias pronunciadas por esta en los casos de amparo pedidos por conflictos de trabajo," 7 October 1924, reprinted in SJF, vol. 14, p. 859.

129. Cf. Middlebrook, *The Paradox of Revolution*, 58. One could assert "probable" instead of "possible" in view of the circumstances at the time. But there is evidently no record of such an understanding between Obregón and the justices; the argument is conjectural and circumstantial, however plausible. Interestingly, the Ministerio Público recommended ruling against Veracruz's board in La Corona.

130. María Gambú, Viuda de Maurer, 31 August 1923, SJF, vol. 13, p. 342.

131. Ibid.

132. "Decreto Dando a Conocer los Nombres de las Personas que Integran la Suprema Corte de Justicia de la Nacion," 27 July 1923, SJF, vol. 12, p. 8.

133. See Chapter 5.

134. Bassols, "Que son, por fin, las Juntas?"

CHAPTER 7: LABOR LAW AND SUPREME COURT DECISIONS, 1925–1931

1. See, e.g., Manuel Blanco López, 2 October 1924, SJF, vol. 15, p. 854 (the amparo against the central board of Veracruz is revoked; labor boards have the power to judge, and the matters they can hear are for state law to determine); José García, 6 January 1926, SJF,

vol. 16, p. 37 (the amparo against the central board of Veracruz is revoked; boards are not special tribunals and can resolve conflicts whether they are those of individuals or groups or they arise from executed or existent contracts); and "El Águila," S.A., Cía. Mexicana de Petróleo, 7 February 1925, SJF, vol. 16, p. 238 (the amparo against the San Luis Potosí labor board is revoked; boards are not special tribunals). See also Luis Llerandi, 6 January 1926, SJF, vol. 16, p. 42, where one unsuccessful employer argument was that the matter involved only one worker in a mirror factory. (García and Llerandi probably date to 1925.)

2. See the Introduction, for a summary of the 1928 constitutional reforms.

3. Portes Gil, *Quince años*.

4. "La Planilla de Ministros Para la Suprema Corte Formada por el Presidente Es Muy Bien Recibido," *Excélsior*, 21 December 1928, p. 1.

5. "Protestan Esta Tarde los Señores Magistrados," *Excélsior*, 26 December 1928, p. 1.

6. Bensusán Areous, *El modelo mexicano*.

7. See "Versión taquigráfica del discurso pronunciado por el Lic. Vicente Lombardo Toledano en el mitin celebrado en la Alianza de Ferrocarrileros Mexicanos el día 24 de julio de 1931," published in the magazine *CROM* on 15 November 1931 and reprinted in Lombardo Toledano, *Obras completas*, 7:160, 173, in which the labor leader and lawyer asserts that the Supreme Court has maintained a relatively advanced position in labor and agrarian matters—then adds how a demonstration of 100,000 workers can persuade the Court.

8. See Agustín Vega, 15 April 1925, SJF, vol. 16, p. 874. Cf. Las Sucesiones Acumuladas, Sebastián B. de Mier y Guadalupe Cuevas de Mier, 20 February 1925, SJF, vol. 16, pp. 386, 387–88 (revocation of suspension); and Regino Ramos, 14 January 1926, SJF, vol. 18, p. 97, where the Court held that the board's act of summoning an employer in a dispute in which the complainants' allegations depended on a sharecropping agreement (*contrato de arrendamiento*) did not cause him any prejudice: he could still present his defenses.

9. Vega, 880.

10. Enrique Villar, 30 April 1925, SJF, vol. 16, p. 1023.

11. See also Diario Ortiz Borbolla, 30 April 1925, SJF, vol. 16, p. 1030, where the governor of Puebla and municipal president of Chalchicomula were upheld against the owner of a finca ordered to nominate representatives to a board constituted at his estate. The Court ruled that the order to nominate representatives was in conformance with Article 123 and provisions of the state labor statute. The employer had invoked his rights against coercion under Article 5. The Court did not entertain this argument.

12. Miguel Vélez Gil, 7 August 1925, SJF, vol. 17, p. 362.

13. Cf. Ernesto Vogt, 23 September 1925, SJF, vol. 17, p. 733, where the complainant was an employee whom the central board of Hidalgo found had been discharged justifiably. The Court left the determination undisturbed, rejecting the employee's argument that one of the board members occupied a managerial position in the respondent's business.

14. Tomás Ruiz y Cía., 5 June 1925, SJF, vol. 16, p. 1275.

15. Cía. de Madera, Ltda., 6 August 1925, SJF, vol. 17, p. 342.

16. See María García Trillo, 12 January 1926, SJF, vol. 18, p. 66, where a suspension order was denied for lack of prejudice to the petitioner since the board's declaration that it was competent to hear the matter, which the petitioner alleged did not arise from a labor contract, did not deprive her of any defenses; it was simply the result of a lawful investigatory process.

17. Dominga Cabrera Vda. de Olvera y coag., 20 August 1925, SJF, vol. 17, p. 450.

18. Manuel Parra, 5 March 1929, SJF, vol. 25, p. 1211; Jesús Barrera, 29 July 1931, SJF, vol. 32, p. 1552.

19. See The Utah Construction Co., 13 April 1928, SJF, vol. 22, p. 787; Cía. Petrolera Pierce Oil, S.A., 5 August 1930, SJF, vol. 29, p. 1428; Mario Gómez Daza y coags., 27 November 1930, SJF, vol. 30, p. 1869; and Ferrocarriles Nacionales de México, 12 November 1931, SJF, vol. 33, p. 2161.

20. See Cía. Mexicana de Petróleo "El Águila," S.A., 8 January 1926, SJF, vol. 18, p. 37.

21. The Supreme Court had already reviewed another suspension order arising from a strike in the oil industry. See La Corona, Cía. Mexicana Holandesa, 16 December 1924, SJF, vol. 15, p. 1322. There, eleven justices revoked the suspension of Veracruz's central board's order. The union of workers of La Corona had struck, taking over the refinery of Chijol, including the boilers, cutting telephone lines, and ejecting supervisors from the refinery. The company received notice that the central board was scheduling sessions to investigate and conciliate but refused to recognize the competency of the board, asserting that it was a matter for federal jurisdiction, given the nature of the strike. The federal judge had suspended the board's determination on the basis that the dispute concerned only two private parties. The Court disagreed: a strike affected society and the state. Both were interested in the quick and efficient resolution of large-scale conflicts between labor and capital.

22. "El Amparo en El Águila, en la Suprema Corte/Los Ministros del Más Alto Tribunal del País Comenzaron a Discutir Ayer Este Trascendental Asunto," in *Excélsior*, 8 January 1926, p. 1.

23. "El Paro Que Se Anunciaba Para Hoy, Suspendido," *Excélsior*, 7 January 1926, p. 1.

24. Rivera Castro, *En la presidencia*, 164–67.

25. "Compañia Mexicana de Petróleo El Águila Contra Actos de la Junta de Conciliacion y Arbitraje de Veracruz y del Presidente Municipal de Minatitlan," Versiones Taquigráficas, 7 January 1926. The events outlined in this paragraph are drawn from both the account of Valdivieso Castillo, *Historia del movimiento sindical petrolero*, which is sympathetic to the strikers and critical of the CROM, and the Court secretary's report read in the public conference, which acknowledges that it relies on El Águila's complaint.

26. Valdivieso Castillo, *Historia del movimiento sindical petrolero*, 44–45.

27. Ibid.

28. Clark, *Organized Labor*, 118–19; and Carr, *El movimiento obrero*; cf. Valdivieso Castillo, *Historia del movimiento sindical petrolero*.

29. Cía. Mexicana "El Águila," S.A., SJF, vol. 18, at 39; Valdivieso Castillo, *Historia del movimiento sindical petrolero*, 48–49.

30. "Compañía Mexicana de Petróleos El Águila," Versiones Taquigráficas, 7 January 1926; and "Preparese una Manifestación ante La Corte/La Federación de Sindicatos del D.F. Explica a la Sociedad los Detalles del Grave Conflicto Obrero," in *Excélsior*, 3 January 1926, p. 1. Article 55 of the Ley de Amparo outlines the standard.

31. Versiones Taquigráficas, 7 January 1926.

32. Ibid.

33. Ibid.

34. Ibid.

35. Ibid.

36. Ibid.

37. Versiones Taquigráficas, 8 January 1926.

38. Ibid.

39. Ibid.

40. Ibid.

41. Ibid.

42. Suprema Corte de Justicia, *Ministros, 1917–2004*, 1:193.

43. Versiones Taquigráficas, 8 January 1926.

44. Cía. Mexicana "El Águila," SJF, vol. 18, at 45.

45. "La Corte Ayer Falló el Caso de 'El Águila"/El Amparo Interpuesto por la Cía. Petrolera Fue Negado por el Más Alto Tribunal de la República," *Excélsior*, 9 January 1926, p. 1.

46. Clark, *Organized Labor*, 118–19.

47. Valdivieso Castillo, *Historia del movimiento sindical petrolero*, 51–55.

48. See Haber et al., *The Politics of Property Rights*, 209–11; J. Meyer, *Estado y sociedad con Calles*, 155; L. Meyer, *México y los Estados Unidos*, 173–75 and 271; and Gruening, *Mexico and Its Heritage*.

49. J. Meyer, *Estado y sociedad con Calles*, 155; Valdivieso Castillo, in *Historia del movimiento sindical petrolero*, believes the CROM was both seeking to expand its influence and benefiting from the deal it struck with El Águila, which was also to the company's advantage. The unions sought the assistance and mediation of Jara, but the CROM's involvement appears to have been decisive.

50. Bensusán Areous, *El modelo mexicano*, 119, underscores the recognition of the *cláusula de exclusión* in the Court's ratification of the Veracruz labor board's award as setting a precedent. The judicial opinion certainly lent it greater legitimacy.

51. See, e.g., Cía. Eléctrica de Tampico, S.A., SJF, 11 June 1926, vol. 18, pp. 1178, 1179.

52. See Cía. Carbonífera Consolidada de Sabinas, S.A., 8 December 1927, SJF, vol. 21, p. 1428; Cía. Carbonifera Consolidada de Coahuila, S.A., 17 April 1928, SJF, vol. 22, p. 828 (awards compensating for accident and illness, respectively).

53. See María de Jesús Suc. de García Otamendi, 7 July 1927, and Cía. Electrica de Tampico, S.A., 23 July 1927, SJF, vol. 21, pp. 82 and 246, respectively.

54. See Ferrocarriles Nacionales de México, S.A., 6 September 1930, and Cía. del Ferrocarril Sud Pacífico de México, 14 February 1931, SJF, vol. 30, p. 136, and vol. 31, p. 963, respectively (both involving accidents in which suspensions of the federal board awards were denied). Cf. Compañía Petrolera Rich Mex., S.A., 9 July 1929, SJF, vol. 26, p. 1386 (amparo action dismissed in labor accident complaint made before federal labor board); and Cía. Mexicana Luz y Fuerza Motriz, S.A., 10 May 1929, SJF, vol. 26, p. 297 (amparo petition denied in accident case).

55. See Sociedad Anónima Ferrocarriles Nacionales de México, 11 October 1928, SJF, vol. 24, p. 382; and Cía. Gral. De Inversiones Mineras, 12 April 1930, SJF, vol. 28, p. 2008.

56. See Francisco Rodríguez Toriello, 26 September 1931, SJF, vol. 33, p. 690.

57. See Compañía Constructora "Byrne" S.A., 12 April 1930, SJF, vol. 28, p. 1997; Compañía Maderera de Durango, S.A., 24 January 1931, SJF, vol. 31, p. 430; and "Camionera de Puebla," S.C.L., 31 January 1931, SJF, vol. 31, p. 652.

58. American Smelting and Refining Co., 23 September 1926, SJF, vol. 19, p. 533.

59. See, e.g., Dodson Manufacturing C., S. en C., 13 January 1927, SJF, vol. 20, p. 104, in which substantially similar language was used regarding the denial of a suspension of the award of the central board of Coahuila. The judgment again split 6–5.

60. See, e.g., The Mazapil Copper Co. Ltd., 11 January 1927, SJF, vol. 20, pp. 77, 78, where the application to suspend an award for medical expenses by the Zacatecan central board was denied by the district court. The Court confirmed the denial 11–0.

61. Cf. La Sociedad "Diego y Menéndez," 11 June 1926, SJF, vol. 18, p. 1181, where the Court read the social interest of compliance with Veracruz's labor statute very broadly indeed. There the employer had complained about the requirement of his labor force having to be 80 percent Mexican. The Court largely denied his application to suspend the state authorities' enforcement of the requirement.

62. Eugenio P. Welch, 24 January 1927, SJF, vol. 20, p. 435.

63. Ibid., 438.

64. Ibid., 437–38.

65. See also Mazapil Copper Ltd., 12 November 1929, SJF, vol. 27, p. 1720.

66. See Empresa de Teléfonos Ericsson, S.A., 19 March 1930, SJF, vol. 28, p. 1541.

67. See Ferrocarriles Nacionales de México, S.A., 10 June 1930, SJF, vol. 29, p. 704; see also Unión de Navieros de Cabotaje, 16 May 1931, SJF, vol. 32, p. 230, where the suspension granted also restrained an order to enter into a collective labor contract.

68. The Mazapil Copper Co., Ltd., 19 July 1930, SJF, vol. 29, p. 1035.

69. Cinco Minas Company," 7 August 1930, SJF, vol. 29, p. 1522.

70. La Fabrica de Dulces "La Suiza," S.A., 23 October 1930, SJF, vol. 30, p. 1083.

71. But cf. Silverio Arciniega, 11 July 1924, SJF, vol. 15, p. 161, where the Court affirmed the suspension of an order by the Oaxacan central board to reinstate a railroad machinist or pay him three months' wages, without an explanation. The amparo was eventually denied in November 1927. See Silverio Arciniega, 5 November 1927, SJF, vol. 21, p. 1207.

72. See Ferrocarriles Nacionales de México, 13 November 1929, SJF, vol. 27, p. 1731; Benito Azcano, 16 November 1929, SJF, vol. 27, p. 1868; Dura Mill and Mining Co., 7 January 1930, SJF, vol. 28, p. 51; Alicia Morrison, 8 January 1930, SJF, vol. 28, p. 63; Horacio Uzeta y coags., 15 October 1930, SJF, vol. 30, p. 896; "New England Fuel and Oil Co.," 17 January 1931, SJF, vol. 31, p. 303; Ferrocarriles Nacionales de México, 7 February 1931, SJF, vol. 31, p. 812; and Cinco Minas Co., 24 November 1931, SJF, vol. 33, p. 2521.

73. See Cía. Carbonífera de Sabinas, S.A., 8 December 1927, SJF, vol. 21, p. 1415 (the Court affirmed the order of suspension; the worker would not be harmed irreparably because he had other resources with which to survive); see also Compañía del Ferrocarril Mexicano, 16 November 1929, SJF, vol. 27, p. 1855.

74. See Ferrocarriles Nacionales de México, 15 March 1930, and 6 September 1930, in SJF, vol. 28, p. 1478, and vol. 30, p. 145, respectively.

75. See Ferrocarriles Nacionales de México, S.A., 6 September 1930, SJF, vol. 30, p. 141. Cf. Ferrocarriles Nacionales de México, S.A., 19 July 1930, SJF, vol. 29, p. 1029 (suspension granted against order to pay retirement benefits).

76. See Gremio Unido de Alijadores, Sociedad Cooperativa de Responsabilidad Civil, 17 October 1931, SJF, vol. 33, p. 1380. The Court held that a suspension was inappropriate for wages but allowable for consequential damages; in accord, United Dredging Co., 2 December 1931, SJF, vol. 33, p. 2787.

77. See Paralié C. García, 15 October 1930, SJF, vol. 30, p. 901.

78. See Carlos Valdez y coags., 12 April 1930, SJF, vol. 28, p. 2004; and José Romero y coags., 17 January 1931, SJF, vol. 31, p. 293 (the principle against suspension applies only to workers discharged without justification; here, suspension will keep workers employed).

79. See Cía. Manufacturera del Potrero, S.A., 16 May 1931, SJF, vol. 32, p. 225.

80. See Cía. Trascontinental de Petróleo, S.A., 14 July 1931, SJF, vol. 32, p. 1259.

81. See J. Jesús Vásquez, 8 August 1931, SJF, vol. 32, p. 1787 (the action originated in the federal district).

82. Sindicato Revolucionario de San Bruno y coags., 7 October 1931, SJF, vol. 33, p. 1099.

83. Manuel Oteiza y coags., 17 October 1931, SJF, vol. 33, p. 1397.

84. Cía. Mexicana de Petróleo "El Águila," S.A., 16 March 1929, SJF, vol. 25, p. 1584; Triunfo Bezanilla Testa, 31 January 1931, SJF, vol. 31, p. 662; Benjamín Aguilar Ortiz, 17 April 1931, SJF, vol. 31, p. 2209; Banco Nacional de Crédito Agrícola, 30 May 1931, SJF, vol. 32, p. 572; and Juan Garetto, 8 August 1931, SJF, vol. 32, p. 1783.

85. Unión de Trabajadores de Progreso, "Piedad Luna," 7 November 1931, SJF, vol. 33, p. 1978; Cinco Minas Co., 24 November 1931, SJF, vol. 33, p. 2510.

86. See Cía. Ltda. de Tranvías de San Luis Potosí, 11 October 1927, SJF, vol. 21, p. 1028. Cf. Baudelio Robles y coags., 29 February 1928, SJF, vol. 22, p. 497, applying the same principle of board decision-making power on the basis of conscience so as to deny an amparo against the central board of Jalisco that had absolved the respondent company.

87. Rodolfo Limón, 11 November 1927, SJF, vol. 21, p. 1318.

88. Francisco Real y coags., 7 December 1927, SJF, vol. 21, p. 1397.

89. Emilio Mackeprang, 10 December 1927, SJF, vol. 21, p. 1457. The relevant state law was San Luis Potosí's.

90. Rafael Rivero Rivas, 16 April 1928, SJF, vol. 22, p. 805.

91. United Sugar Companies, S.A., 13 February 1929, SJF, vol. 25, p. 681 (the labor conflict occurred in Sinaloa).

92. See Cía. Minera "Asarco," S.A., 4 March 1929; and The Texas Company, 19 March 1929; in SJF, vol. 25, p. 1170 and p. 1636, respectively.

93. Carlos Gallardo, 12 September 1929, SJF, vol. 27, p. 305.

94. Alicia Morrison, 30 May 1931, SJF, vol. 32, p. 557.

95. Silvestre Faya, 30 May 1931, SJF, vol. 32, p. 565.

96. Cía. Mexicana de Petróleo, "El Águila," S.A., 19 November 1929, SJF, vol. 27, p. 1897. Cf. Ramiro Elorduy, 4 January 1930, SJF, vol. 28, p. 20.

97. Silverio Arciniega, 5 November 1927, SJF, vol. 21, p. 1207 (the denial of the amparo was confirmed; the petitioner could have alleged a violation of his rights only if the Oaxacan central board's act had been outside of the bases of Article 123, in view of the Transitory Article 11); Pedro Villa, 16 March 1928, SJF, vol. 22, p. 645 (amparo revoked; the absence of a statute implementing a provision of Article 123 could not be a reason for delaying board action, which did not violate the petitioner's rights). Cf. Cía. Ltda. de Tranvías de San Luis Potosí, 11 October 1927, SJF, vol. 21, p. 1028 (the denial of the amparo was confirmed, since boards only need to adhere to the law regulating them).

98. Raul Fernández del Valle, 15 April 1929, SJF, vol. 25, p. 1986; see also Sucesión de Cetina Fuentes Basilio, 18 September 1931, SJF, vol. 33, p. 355 (denial of amparo against Yucatán's board: the state civil code was inapplicable).

99. Ricardo Wisbrun, 27 May 1931, SJF, vol. 32, p. 459; see also Ethel Ulfelder May, 1 Oct. 1931, SJF, vol. 33, p. 840; and Modesta Quintanar Vda. de Basurto, 12 June 1931, SJF, vol. 32, p. 899.

100. Compañía Mexicana de Petróleo "El Águila," S.A., 4 November 1925, SJF, vol. vol. 17, p.1195. Cf. Virginia P. de King, 8 September 1926, and Virginia Pernet, 6 October

1926, in SJF, vol. 19, p. 457 and p. 655, respectively. The federal judiciary continued to overturn Veracruz's central board; here the issues were evidentiary as well as procedural and substantive.

101. Sociedad "Miguel E. Padilla e Hijos," 24 April 1925, SJF, vol. 16, p. 965. The Court, compromising, refused to enjoin part of the award to a group of textile workers acting in a concerted manner with the support of the central labor board of the state of Guanajuato but also restrained the board's decision insofar as it ordered a remedy that the workers had not requested (namely, wages accrued while the action was pending). Cf. Sociedad "Vicente Rojí e Hijos," 28 April 1928, SJF, vol. 22, p. 991, where the federal judiciary enjoined the Veracruz central board's order to continue the payment of workers during a shutdown of the factory: boards while resolving disputes according to conscience and equity must still consider only claims expressed in the complaint.

102. Eusebio González, 20 April 1927, SJF, vol. 20, p. 912.

103. Jacinto Collado, 5 November 1927, SJF, vol. 21, p. 1223.

104. E. B. Sloan, 10 January 1928, SJF, vol. 22, p. 90.

105. S. J. Fuller, 11 February 1928, SJF, vol. 22, p. 352.

106. See Cía. Mexicana de Petróleo "El Águila," S.A., 29 January 1929, SJF, vol. 25, p. 381. Sucesión de Chi Ascensión, 16 July 1929, SJF, vol. 26, p. 1526 (since the Yucatán labor code did not stipulate the prescriptive period, it was necessary to refer to the civil and procedural codes; the amparo was confirmed). Cf. Enrique Mañon, 19 July 1929, p. 1551, denying the amparo; and Filogonio Moreno y coagraviados, 9 April 1930, SJF, vol. 28, p. 1900, granting it against the federal labor board for applying local law. See also Eduardo Ruiz y coags., 1 December 1930, SJF, vol. 30, p. 1937, granting an amparo against the federal board over the applicable prescriptive period; cf. Angel Robles y coags., 21 May 1931, SJF, vol. 32, p. 297, denying the amparo when the Tamaulipas central board applied a one-year prescription period based on state law.

107. See, e.g., Urbano Méndez, 30 January 1931, SJF, vol. 31, p. 627.

108. Jesús Villaverde y coags., 25 March 1930, SJF, vol. 28, p. 1624 (granting an amparo against the federal district's central board for absolving the employer of the worker's claim).

109. Amador González, 20 October 1930, SJF, vol. 30, p. 1032 (the amparo was granted against the central board of Durango); "La Providencia," S.A., 21 November 1930, SJF, vol. 30, p. 1734. Cf. Cía. del Ferrocarril Sud-Pacífico, S.A., 24 July 1925, SJF, vol. 17, p. 253(amparo issued where the company had not been cited to the hearing).

110. Bernardo Reynés, 16 May 1930, SJF, vol. 29, p. 224 (the amparo was granted against the Yucatán board; the claimant had the character of a partner, not an employee).

111. Adolfo Ochoa, 18 November 1930, SJF, vol. 30, p. 1699.

112. Huasteca Petroleum Co., 18 April 1931, SJF, vol. 31, p. 2237.

113. Concepción Carvajal Castellanos, 13 June 1931, SJF, vol. 32, p. 936.

114. Competencia en amparo civil entre el juez de distrito de Nuevo León y la Junta Central de Conciliación y Arbitraje del Estado (Gracia Nemesio y colitigante), 7 July 1924, SJF, vol. 15, p. 76. This case was not framed as an amparo action.

115. Ibid., 78–79.

116. "Asunto: Nemesio Gracia and Baldomero Cabral Competencia entre la Junta Central de Conciliación y Arbitraje de Nuevo León y el Juez de Distrito del Mismo Estado," Versiones Taquigráficas, 7 July 1924. The workers complained to the board that the company had wrongfully discharged them because they did not belong to the union.

117. See Cía. del Ferrocarril Sud-Pacífico de México, S.A., 24 July 1925, SJF, vol. 17, p. 253.

118. Ibid., 255.

119. La Cía. Minera y Beneficiadora de Metales "Maravillas y San Francisco," S.A., 18 August 1925, SJF, vol. 17, p. 422. The company had been ordered to indemnify the worker with three months' pay.

120. Ibid., 424, 425.

121. Antonio F. Rodríguez, 11 June 1927, SJF, vol. 20, p. 1124. But cf. The Salinas of Mexico Ltd., 30 August 1927, SJF, vol. 21, p. 604, where the amparo was denied because the extraordinary powers granted to the executive by the legislature did not violate any constitutional rights.

122. Agustín Limón, 30 January 1928, SJF, vol. 22, p. 269. Accord, Otto Tolksdorff, 22 April 1930, SJF, vol. 28, p. 2017.

123. Cía. Pasteurizadora "La Carolina," S.A., 8 February 1930, SJF, vol. 28, p. 674. The litigation occurred in the federal district.

124. See, respectively, Compañía Mexicana de Petróleo "El Águila," S.A., 16 March 1931, SJF, vol. 31, p. 1630; Josefa Sanz Vda. de Solórzano, 28 May 1931, SJF, vol. 32, p. 477; and José Fernández, 6 August 1931, SJF, vol. 32, 1720.

125. See J. Meyer, *Estado y sociedad con Calles*, 159–66.

126. Barrios, *El escuadrón de hierro*, 136; Rodríguez, "The Beginnings of a Movement," 162 (regarding the date of the filing of the amparo petition).

127. Rodríguez, "The Beginnings of a Movement," 163.

128. Donato Muñoz, Dissenting Opinion, 30 December 1927, in Confederación de Transportes y Comunicaciones contra Ferrocarriles Nacionales de México, Expediente 1, Caja 1, of Ramo de la Junta Federal de Conciliación y Arbitraje, AGN.

129. Barrios, *El escuadrón de hierro*, 136–37.

130. Decreto Presidencial que Establece la Junta Federal de Conciliación y Arbitraje, reprinted in Secretaría de Industria, Comercio y Trabajo, *Legislación del trabajo*.

131. Bensusán Areous, *El modelo mexicano*, 141.

132. Confederación de Transportes y Comunicaciones, 4 October 1927, SJF, vol. 21, p. 944.

133. Junta Federal Opinion, 8 December 1927, p. 5, in Confederación de Transportes y Comunicaciones contra Ferrocarriles Nacionales de México, Expediente 1, Caja 1, of Ramo de la Junta Federal de Conciliación y Arbitraje, AGN.

134. Donato Muñoz, Dissenting Opinion.

135. Junta Federal Opinion.

136. Junta Federal Opinion, 7a.

137. See Ley Orgánica del Artículo 4 Constitucional en lo Relativo a La Libertad del Trabajo, published in the *Diario Oficial* 9 January 1926, and reprinted in Cabrera Acevedo, *La Suprema Corte de Justicia* [1924–1928], 271–72; see also Junta Federal Opinion, 9–9a.

138. Junta Federal Opinion, 11a–12.

139. Confederación de Transportes y Comunicaciones, 30 May 1929, SJF, vol. 26, pp. 892, 909.

140. Ibid., 892.

141. See Cabrera Acevedo, *La Suprema Corte de Justicia* [1924–1928], 87–101.

142. See Portes Gil, *Quince años*.

143. Barrios, *El Escuadrón de Hierro*, 161–63.

144. Claro Nevares, 22 April 1931, SJF, vol. 31, p. 2343 (amparo denied; a submission of evidence did not require the federal board to prosecute or act on it). Cf. Compañía Mexicana Holandesa "La Corona," S.A., 22 April 1931, p. 2346, where the amparo was denied, for the Veracruz central board was not obligated to supplement the proof of a party.

145. See Compañía de los Ferrocarriles Nacionales de México, S.A., 26 October 1931, SJF, vol. 33, p. 1630; and Ferrocarriles Nacionales de México, 14 November 1931, SJF, vol. 33, p. 2296.

146. Compañía de los Ferrocarriles Nacionales de México, S.A., 18 February 1930, SJF, vol. 28, p. 945. See also Cía. Minera de Peñoles, S.A., 16 August 1930, vol. 29, p. 1687; the amparo was granted, for boards can decide only what is before them.

147. See Ferrocarriles Nacionales de México, 31 January 1931, SJF, vol. 31, p. 648.

148. Cía. de Ferrocarriles Nacionales de México, 6 February 1931, SJF, vol. 31, p. 761.

149. Cía. de Navegación Interior, S.A., 28 July 1931, SJF, vol. 32, p. 1535; The Mazapil Copper Co., Ltd., 9 October, 1931, SJF, vol. 33, p. 1155.

150. Ferrocarriles Nacionales de México, 26 August 1931, SJF, vol. 32, p. 2090.

151. Ferrocarriles Nacionales de México, 5 November 1931, SJF, vol. 33, p. 1860.

152. See Cía. Industrial de Orizaba, S.A., 19 May 1930, SJF, vol. 29, p. 288.

153. Ibid., 292–93.

154. Ibid., 293.

155. See Chapter 8.

156. See Tomás Urrutia, 24 January 1931, SJF, vol. 31, p. 425; and Sociedad "Alfredo Sordo, Sucres," 14 March 1931, SJF, vol. 31, p. 1575.

157. Cía. Limitada de Luz, Eléctrica, Fuerza y Tracción de Veracruz, 23 September 1924, SJF, vol. 15, p. 723.

158. "Amparo Relativo a la Ley del Trabajo, Promovido por la Cia. Limitada de Luz Eléctrica, Fuerza y Tracción de Veracruz, Contra Actos de la Junta de Conciliación y Arbitraje del Estado de Veracruz," Versiones Taquigráficas, 24 September 1924.

159. Cía. Limitada de Luz Eléctrica, 728–30, citing Bry, book 4, part 1, paras. 801 and 803.

160. "Amparo Relativo a la Ley de Trabajo," Versiones Taquigráficas, 24 September 1924.

161. See The Cubo Mining and Milling Co., 2 October 1924, SJF, vol. 15, p. 849; Luz Bringas y Robles, 4 November 1925, SJF, vol. 17, p. 1187. Cf. Cía. Fundidora de Fierrro y Acero de Monterrey, S.A., 6 October 1926, SJF, vol. 19, p. 663, where the Court denied an amparo, holding that the boards had the power to hear contracts already completed.

162. See Emilio Mackeprang, 10 December 1927, SJF, vol. 21, p. 1457; Cía. Minera "Asarco," S.A., 4 March 1929, SJF, vol. 25, p. 1170; The Texas Company of Mexico, 19 March 1929, SJF, vol. 25, p. 1636; and Juan Sosa Martínez y coags., 13 June 1929, vol. 26, p. 1197.

163. See, e.g., The Cubo Mining and Milling Co., at 852. The case arose in Guanajuato from an award entered 30 October 1922. The Court was already then grappling with the issue of whether a single party could terminate the contract: see Las Dos Estrellas, SJF, vol. 11, p. 794, in Chapter 6.

164. See the cases cited in note 162 above. In The Texas Company of Mexico, SJF vol. 25, p. 1638, for example, the opinion distinguishes between older case law that was superseded by newer case law (jurisprudencia) recognizing the competence of boards to consider both existing and terminated employment contracts.

165. Gustavo Sota, 11 March 1925, SJF, vol. 16, p. 563.

166. Ibid., 566.

167. La Cía. Mexicana de Petróleo "El Águila," S.A., 7 February 1925, SJF, vol. 16, p. 238 (the case originated in San Luis Potosí).

168. See "Asunto: Compañia Mexicana de Petróleo El Águila," 7 February 1925, Versiones Taquigráficas. The vote was 6–4 against granting the amparo.

169. Ángel Orozco, 30 July 1926, SJF, vol. 19, p. 209. The Court refused to grant an amparo involving the hacienda administrator in Jalisco, rejecting the hacienda's argument that the employment contract was a matter for the civil law, holding that the boards could review all labor matters and that the evaluation of proof was for their prudent judgment.

170. Virginia Pernet, 6 October 1926, SJF, vol. 19, p. 655. The decision also turned on the supposed or apparent absence of material evidence of the contract and employment relationship.

171. Ibid., 657.

172. Ibid.; see also Luis Álvarez y Álvarez, 1 December 1927, SJF, vol. 21, p. 1374 (the Court granted an amparo holding that the labor contract had ended with the closure of the business, and the employer could not be deemed to have defaulted on the contract); and Fábrica de Calzado "Atlas," S. en C., 3 January 1928, SJF, vol. 22, p. 28 (termination of a labor contract was done in conformance with Chihuahua's labor statute; no discharge without cause as stated in the twenty-second paragraph of Article 123 had occurred).

173. Enrique Dardón, 2 March 1927, SJF, vol. 20, p. 466.

174. La Sociedad "Diego y Menéndez," 11 June 1926, SJF, vol. 18, p. 1181; Juan Cheing y Alfonso J. Bean, 7 February 1931, SJF, vol. 31, p. 802 (employer appeals from state laws mandating the hiring of Mexicans). Cf. Gabino Terrazas, 24 March 1931, SJF, vol. 31, p. 1884; and Luis Martínez, 17 April 1929, SJF, vol. 25, p. 2034 (regarding overtime pay).

175. See, e.g., Gómez Ochoa y Cía., 7 February 1925, SJF, vol. 16, p. 247 (involving a contract covered by the commercial code); Salvador Milanés, 13 January 1926, SJF, vol. 18, p. 87 (rather than a labor contract, an agreement for an honorarium had existed). Cf. Manuel Hernández P., 21 January 1928, SJF, vol. 22, p. 178. (If the conflict stemming from an employment contract required the application of other laws, a civil law tribunal should adjudicate it; so the amparo was confirmed against the central board of the Federal District.) See also Severiano Sánchez, 4 November 1925, SJF, vol. 17, p. 1191 (involving a matter under the commercial code). Cf. Bernice Rush, 24 December 1926, SJF, vol. 19, p. 1156, where the Court denied an amparo, holding that Article 123 derogated article 328 of the commercial code.

176. La Compañía Mexicana Molinera de Nixtamal, S.A., 23 September 1931, SJF, vol. 33, p. 501.

177. Ibid., 510–11.

178. Ibid., 513 (emphasis added).

179. La Sociedad "Alfredo Sordo, Sucres," 14 March 1931, SJF, vol. 31, p. 1575, 1578.

180. Sociedad Miranda Hermanos y Cía., 21 September 1927, SJF, vol. 21, p. 827; La Sociedad "Zorrilla y Miaja," 6 February 1929, SJF, vol. 25, p. 527; El Sindicato de Obreros Cuauhtémoc y coagraviada, 27 July 1931, SFJ, vol. 32, p. 1500.

181. Camiro, "El Concepto de Paro o 'Lockout.'"

182. See "Cía. del Ferrocarril Urbano de Orizaba," Versiones Taquigráficas, 24 April 1925.

183. But cf. Guillermo Schieman, 13 September 1926, SJF, vol. 19, p. 491, where the Court held it was not justifiable to terminate an employee to lower business costs.

184. See Manuel Rosado, 22 April 1925, SJF, vol. 16, p. 960. See also José Sierra, 20 March 1928, SJF, vol. 22, p. 671 (amparo granted regarding board order to dismiss worker, because of the failure to afford him a hearing); Juan Gil, 13 May 1930, SJF, vol. 29, p. 177 (violating the right to be heard necessitated the amparo against the federal board where it had ordered a worker discharged pursuant to a collective labor contract). Cf. La Cía. Industrial de Orizaba, S.A., 12 June 1925, SJF, vol. 16, p. 1317 (Court declared that the worker had a right for the board to hear his complaint as Article 123 mandated all labor disputes be presented before boards).

185. Efrén Velasco, 5 October 1931, SJF, vol. 33, p. 959.

186. Ibid., 961–62.

187. Ibid., 962.

188. Bruno Méndez, 9 November 1931, SJF, vol. 33, p. 2034.

189. La Orden de Maquinistas y Fogoneros de Locomotores, 15 October 1930, SJF, vol. 30, p. 883.

190. Canto joined the high court in October 1927, replacing a justice who had died. He was thus elected before the constitutional amendment that enabled Portes Gil to nominate justices. But Canto was also elected during Calles's presidency (other justices had joined the bench in July 1923); there was some opposition to his election, too, in the Senate. Portes Gil renominated him; Canto would remain on the bench until 1934, a member of the administrative chamber. Suprema Corte, *Ministros 1917–1924*, 1:141.

191. Bassols, "Que son, por fin, las Juntas de Conciliación y Arbitraje?" Bassols specifically analyzed Court decisions over jurisdictional appeals (*competencias*) between courts and labor boards; the Supreme Court tended to regard them as inappropriate because the boards technically were not law courts under Article 104 of the constitution; but its rulings were inconsistent. Bassols argued that the boards should be deemed courts: they were such in all but name. Cf. Competencia entre la Junta de Conciliación del Distrito Federal y la Junta Federal de Conciliación y Arbitraje, 19 May 1930, SJF, vol. 29, p. 274; and Competencia entre Junta de Conciliación y Arbitraje de Tabasco y Juez de Primera Instancia de lo Civil en Villahermosa, 10 August 1931, SJF, vol. 32, p. 1798.

192. Bassols, "Que son, por fin, las Juntas de Conciliación y Arbitraje?," 191.

193. Bassols, "Que son, por fin, las Juntas de Conciliación y Arbitraje?," 190.

194. Ibid., 190.

195. Ibid., 187, quoting Lombardo Toledano, in *Excélsior*, 27 January 1930.

196. Lombardo Toledano, *La libertad sindical*.

197. See, e.g., Córdova, *En una época de crisis*, 131–32, describing the multiple amparos and failure to enforce them by state authorities in litigation between the United Sugar Company and the sugar workers' union in the state of Sinaloa. Lombardo Toledano, as a lawyer, counseled the union in this litigation.

198. Castorena, for example, compiled decisions of the important labor board of the federal district relating to strikes in *El derecho de huelga en México* (1931). In the introduction, Castorena notes the doctrinal and legal tensions that had arisen in the case-by-case adjudication of the board. Most of the decisions are predicated on the notion of an employment contract between workers and employers.

CHAPTER 8: THE ENACTMENT OF THE FEDERAL LABOR LAW, 1925–1931

1. There is substantial scholarship recounting the process, or aspects of it, that led to the federalization of labor law. See, e.g., Bensusán Areous, *El modelo mexicano*; Middlebrook, *The Paradox of Revolution*; Córdova, *En una época de crisis*; Saragoza, *The Monterrey Elite*. This chapter draws extensively from these works, in addition to other sources cited.

2. Middlebrook, *Paradox*, 48; Clark, *Organized Labor*, 214–15.

3. See Sheffield to Secretary and Undersecretary of State, 22 April 1925, U.S. Department of State (hereinafter cited as "SD"), no. 812.504/621 (*Records of the Department of State Relating to the Internal Affairs of Mexico, 1920–1929* and *1930–1939* [microform]).

4. Ibid.

5. Arthur Schoenfeld, Chargé d'Affaires, a.i., to Secretary of State, 5 June 1925, SD, 812.504/655.

6. Schoenfeld to Secretary of State, 3 June 1925, SD, 812.504/653.

7. Schoenfeld to Secretary of State, 9 June 1925, SD, 812.504/656.

8. Ibid.

9. Peter H. A. Flood, American Vice Consul in Charge to Secretary of State, 17 November 1925, SD, 812.504/736.

10. Flood's letter, *supra*, also described the consternation caused by Veracruz's requirements regarding raising the percentage of Mexicans in labor forces to 80 percent, limiting work schedules to eight hours, and ensuring one day off each week. See also Flood to Secretary of State, 30 October 1925, SD, 812.504/729; and Consul John Wood's correspondence about the commercial houses' struggle with Veracruz's government, and unions, over the 80 percent requirement, Wood to the Secretary of State, 27 October 1925, SD, 812.504/727.

11. Sheffield to Secretary of State, 20 October 1925, SD, 812.504/723.

12. See Congreso de los Estados Unidos Mexicanos, Cámara de Diputados, "Minuta del Proyecto de Ley Reglamentaria del Artículo 123 de la Constitución, Aprobado por la Cámara de Diputados y Enviado Para Su Revisión a la de Senadores," which is dated 9 November 1925, in Archivo Histórico Vicente Lombardo Toledano (AHVLT).

13. Lombardo Toledano to Emilio Barragán, 13 February 1926, in Caja 88, AHVLT.

14. Sheffield to Secretary of State, 12 November 1925, SD, 812.504/735.

15. Sheffield to Secretary of State, 30 November 1925, SD, 812.504/744.

16. See Charles Montague's memorandum enclosed with Sheffield's letter to Secretary of State, 19 November 1925, SD, 812.504/738.

17. Ibid.

18. Sheffield to Secretary of State, 23 November 1925, SD, 812.504/739.

19. See Montague's memorandum in Sheffield to Secretary of State, 19 November 1925, SD, 812.504.738.

20. Sheffield to Secretary of State, 30 November 1925, SD, 812.504/740. This was also the conclusion of the Department of State's solicitor. See Solicitor JRB's letter to Gunther, 9 December 1925, SD, 812.504/742.

21. Sheffield to Secretary of State, 14 December 1926, SD, 812.504/830.

22. Sheffield to Secretary of State, 31 December 1926, SD, 812.504/836.

23. Sheffield to Secretary of State, n.d. (received by 3 June 1927 in Washington), SD, 812.504/860.

24. Ibid.

25. See memorandum enclosed with Sheffield's letter to Secretary of State, 16 May 1927, SD, 812.504/858.

26. Ibid.

27. See Circular Número 2 del Departamento de Trabajo de la Secretaría de Industria, Comercio y Trabajo, sobre la Competencia de Dicha Secretaría para Conocer de los Conflictos entre Trabajadores y Empresas Ferroviarias, 28 April 1926; Acuerdo Presidencial Relativo a la Competencia de la Secretaría de Industria, Comercio y Trabajo, para Conocer de los Conflictos de Trabajo en Materia de Minas y Petróleo, 5 March 1927; Acuerdo Presidencial Relativo a que los Conflictos de Trabajo de la Industria Textil Pasarán a Ser de la Competencia de la Secretaría de Industria, Comercio y Trabajo, 18 March 1927, reprinted in Secretaría de Industria, Comercio y Trabajo, *Legislación del trabajo*. See also Bortz, "The Genesis of the Mexican Labor Relations System."

28. See Decreto Presidencial que Establece la Junta Federal de Conciliación y Arbitraje, in Secretaría de Industria, Comercio y Trabajo, *Legislación del trabajo*, 1078–79.

29. Calles had tried in October 1926 with a legislative initiative to establish such federal labor boards; it was incorporated into the CROM-authored bill and then languished; see Bensusán Areous, *El modelo mexicano*, 141. See also "Labour Legislation Should Be Consistent with the Necessities of Our Living Conditions," translation of article from *CROM* magazine, 1 May 1927, enclosed in correspondence of Sheffield to Secretary of State, 28 May 1927, SD, 812.504/862.

30. See Chapter 7.

31. See "Dictamen Presentado por las Comisiones Unidas Segunda de Puntos Constitucionales y Segunda de Trabajo y Previsión Social Sobre Reformas al Artículo 123 de la Constitución General de la República a Fin de Que Sólo Rija en Toda la Nación un Sólo Código del Trabajo," dated 5 October 1927, published in *Revista CROM*, 15 February 1928, republished in Lombardo Toledano, *Obras completas*, 4:153. The draft law was referenced as the Proyecto de Ley de 24 de Julio de 1924.

32. Schoenfeld to Secretary of State, 14 September 1927, SD, 812.504/887.

33. Schoenfeld to Secretary of State, 17 September 1927, SD, 812.504/888. The letter reported that one of the committees of the employer association drafting another version of the labor bill was comprised of the vice president of El Águila, the National Mining Chamber's president, and Mexico Light & Power Company's general manager—that is, foreign business interests.

34. H. F. Arthur Schoenfeld to Secretary of State, 19 October 1927, SD, 812.504/896.

35. Cf. Bensusán Areous, *El modelo mexicano*, 148, noting the CROM labor bloc's introduction of the bill but also the initiative of the Obregonista legislators, based on Obregón's July 1924 bill, in favor of federalization; they were nonetheless divided around the question of federalization and seemingly stalled.

36. Schoenfeld to Secretary of State, 19 October 1927, SD, 812.504/896.

37. Schoenfeld to Secretary of State, 28 October 1927, SD, 812.504/899.

38. Ibid.

39. Schoenfeld to Secretary of State, 17 May 1928, SD, 812.504/937.

40. Ibid.

41. See Memorandum by Alan F. Winslow, enclosed with letter by Schoenfeld to Secretary of State, 3 July 1928, SD, 812.504/942.

42. Portes Gil, *Quince años*, 127–28. In an unpublished manuscript, Portes Gil dated Obregón's initial commission to prepare the legislation in 1927. See Expediente 37, p. 1 (n.d., possibly 15 January 1930; although it is also apparently a partial draft for *Quince años*), Caja 320, Fondo de Emilio Portes Gil, AGN.

43. Portes Gil, *Quince años*, 129–30. See also Arturo Alvarado, "El Portegilismo." At least two historians are skeptical of the CROM's protestations for labor legislation in view of its power during Calles's presidency. See Saragoza, *The Monterrey Elite*, 156, citing Carr, *El movimiento obrero*.

44. Portes Gil more explicitly repeated his accusations against the CROM in the conclusion of *Quince años*, 545–46, in an excerpt quoted from a riposte to criticism made by Lombardo Toledano in 1940.

45. Ambassador Dwight W. Morrow to Secretary of State, 22 October 1928, SD, 812.504/960.

46. Córdova, *En una época de crisis*, 46.

47. Saragoza, *The Monterrey Elite*, 157.

48. See *CROM*, 1 April 1929, 21–24, reprinted in Lombardo Toledano, *Obras completas*, 5:103.

49. Cf. Middlebrook, *Paradox*, 59.

50. See Lombardo Toledano, *Obras completas*, 5:67–69. No specific date is given for the initial publication in the periodical *CROM*. Excerpts from the convention appeared in *CROM* between 1 December 1928 and 1 July 1929.

51. Lombardo Toledano, *Obras completas*, 5:114.

52. Ibid., 5:114–115 and 117.

53. See Frederick P. Hibbard, Chargé d'Affaires, a.i., to Secretary of State, 28 December 1928, SD, 812.504/994, and the enclosed U.S. embassy translation of "Licenciado Portes Gil's Request of the Senate," published in *Excélsior*, 25 December 1928.

54. "Licenciado Portes Gil's Request of the Senate."

55. Ibid.

56. Morrow to Secretary of State, 6 August 1929, SD, 812.504/1033 (translation by the American embassy).

57. *Excélsior*, 4 August 1929, p. 1.

58. Ley por la cual se Reforman los Artículos 73 y 123 de la Constitución General de la República, 31 August 1929, reprinted in Secretaría de Industria, Comercio y Trabajo, *Legislación del trabajo*, 1207–8.

59. See Garrido, *El partido de la revolución institucionalizada*.

60. See Secretaría de Industria, Comercio y Trabajo (SICT), *Proyecto de Código Federal de Trabajo*, "Exposición de motivos." The statement of purpose or exposition is dated July 1929.

61. SICT, *Proyecto de Código Federal de Trabajo*, xi.

62. Ibid., x.

63. See Bensusán Areous, *El modelo mexicano*, on the code's objective of diminishing labor conflict, 161.

64. SICT, *Proyecto de Código Federal de Trabajo*, xii.

65. The *contrato de equipo* was a labor contractor's arrangement to furnish a group of employees to an employer. The *Proyecto* proposed to apply it to the relationship between

unions and employers; the union would assume some employer responsibilities, such as paying wages. Ibid., xx.

66. SICT, *Proyecto de Código Federal de Trabajo*, xxii–xxiii. Smaller plants employing workers in craft unions also had to sign a collective contract.

67. Ibid., xxv–xxvi.

68. Ibid., xxxii.

69. Ibid., xxxiii.

70. Ibid., xxxiv–xxxv. Córdova lambastes Portes Gil's interpretation; see *En una época de crisis*, 51–52.

71. Córdova, *En una época de crisis*, 54.

72. Ibid., 53–55.

73. "Dictamen Aprobados en la Convención que Convocó la Alianza de Artes Gráficas, para Hacer el Estudio y Objeciones al Proyecto de Código Federal del Trabajo," in *Pro-Paria*, 21 September 1929, 5.

74. Ibid.

75. Lombardo Toledano, "El Contrato de Trabajo y el Proyecto de Código Federal," *Excélsior*, 27 July 1929, reprinted in *Pro-Paria*, 10 August 1929, p. 5.

76. "Grandiosa Manifestación Pro Ley del T." and "Estan Siendo Escuchadas las Objeciones al Proyecto de Código Federal de Trabajo," in *Pro-Paria*, 5 October 1929, p. 1.

77. Saragoza, *The Monterrey Elite*, 159 and n. 32. Most of the articles of *Excélsior* (and the *New York Times* article) examined in the subsequent discussion were first cited by Saragoza.

78. "Observaciones de los Industriales al Proyecto del Código del Trabajo, Sometidas al Sr. Presidente de la República, Lic. Emilio Portes Gil," *Excélsior*, 26 July 1929, pp. 5, 11.

79. "Aspectos de la Cuestión Obrera," *Excélsior*, 15 July 1929, p. 5.

80. "Puntos de Vista Acerca de la Ley de Trabajo," *Excélsior*, 5 August 1929, p. 5.

81. See Chapter 1.

82. Córdova, *En una época de crisis*, 48.

83. "Concienzudos Estudios que hacen a la Ley del Trabajo/Todas las Asociaciones Patronales se Ocupan de Estudiar el Proyecto/El Código y el Crédito de los Industriales," *Excélsior*, 11 September 1929, p. 1.

84. Bensusán Areous, *El modelo mexicano*, 154.

85. "Observaciones de los Industriales del País al Proyecto de Ley Sobre Trabajo," *Excélsior*, 20 September 1929, pp. 1, 3.

86. Ibid.

87. "Seran Públicas las Discusiones de la Ley de Trabajo/Fue Acordado Ayer que los Debates del Proyecto Sean a Puerta Abierta/Un Plazo Prorrogado/Hasta el Día 20 del Presente se Recibirán Observaciones de Patrones y Obreros," *Excélsior*, 10 September 1929, p. 1.

88. "La Industria Reinera Se Resentiría con la Nueva Ley de Trabajo," *Excélsior*, 10 September 1929.

89. "Ford to Mark Time on Mexican Plans. Orders Plant Extension Held up Pending Labor Laws, Mexico City Hears. Studies Planned Measure. President Portes Gil's Project for Federalization Draws Fire on Nation's Employers," *New York Times*, 17 August 1929, p. 21. See also Saragoza, *The Monterrey Elite*, 164.

90. "Objeciones al Nuevo Código sobre Trabajo/El Gerente de la Ford Motor Co. Rebate Tres Puntos del Proyecto que Estudia la Cámara/Contrato Colectivo y Habitaciones

Comodas/También se Refuta lo Relativo a la Indemnización Además de los Tres Meses de Sueldo," *Excélsior*, 26 September 1929, pp. 1, 4.

91. "Ford to Mark Time on Mexican Plans," 21.

92. Herschel V. Johnson, Chargé d'Affaires ad interim to Secretary of State, 27 September 1929, SD, 812.504/1067.

93. Bensusán Areous, *El modelo mexicano*, 154.

94. J. Reuben Clark Jr. to Secretary of State, 13 March 1931, SD, 812.504/1126.

95. Saragoza, *Monterrey Elite*, 166.

96. Bensusán Areous, *El modelo mexicano*, 157–58.

97. Clark to Secretary of State, 13 March 1931, SD, 812.504/1126.

98. Ibid.

99. Ibid.

100. Suárez, *Comentarios*, 21.

101. Suárez, *Comentarios*, 22.

102. Ibid.

103. See SICT, *Proyecto de Código Federal de Trabajo*, vi.

104. Suárez, *Comentarios*, 22–24.

105. Grupo Patronal, *Observaciones y sugestiones*.

106. "Ley del Trabajo al Vapor," in *Pro-Paria*, 14 January 1931. This newspaper has been the organ of the Confederación Sindicalista de Obreros y Campesinos of Orizaba, Veracruz; some scholars consider it the finest labor periodical in Mexico. See Bringas and Mascareño, *Esbozo histórico*, 58–59.

107. "Esta Terminado el Proyecto de Código Federal del Trabajo y Será Conocido Primero en Consejo Colectivo de Ministros," *Pro-Paria*, 17 January 1931, p. 1.

108. *Pro-Paria*, 1 May 1931, p. 1.

109. Clark to Secretary of State, 13 March 1931, SD, 812.504/1126.

110. Ibid.

111. Clark to Secretary of State, 20 March 1931, SD, 812.504/1127.

112. *Proyecto de Ley Federal del Trabajo*, dated and signed by P. Ortiz Rubio on 12 March 1931, in opening session of the 34th Congress, 22 May 1931, *Diario de los Debates de la Cámara de Diputados*, reprinted in *Revista Mexicana del Trabajo*, vol. 4, nos. 1–4 (January–April 1957), 6.

113. *Exposición de motivos del proyecto de ley federal del trabajo*, quoted in *Diario de los Debates de la Cámara de Diputados*, reprinted in *Revista Mexicana del Trabajo*, vol. 4, nos. 1–4 (January–April 1957), 8.

114. Ibid., 11–12.

115. Ibid., 18.

116. Ibid.

117. Clark to Secretary of State, 20 March 1931, SD, 812.504/1127.

118. *Exposición de motivos*, 20.

119. Ibid. The Ley Orgánica is discussed in relation to the federal labor board's decision against the CTC in Chapter 7.

120. *Exposición de motivos*, 20.

121. See "The Attitude of Some Leaders Is Anti-Patriotic," American embassy translation of statement by General Melgar, published in *Excélsior* on 30 April 1931 and enclosed in correspondence of Clark to Secretary of State, 19 May 1931, SD, 812.504/1137; and American embassy translation of Statement of General Melgar, President of the PNR Bloc

in the Congress, as reported in *Excélsior* on 26 April 1931 and enclosed in correspondence by Clark to Secretary of State, 19 May 1931, SD, 812.504/1137.

122. Thus, congressional deputies might have sought labor's support for the amendments they wished to make and indeed made to the project; see Bensusán Areous, *El modelo mexicano*, 190–93; Calles's ultimate support of the changes probably tipped the balance between Sáenz and his detractors, including some deputies and organized labor.

123. U.S. embassy translation of editorial published in *El Universal*, 27 April 1931, enclosed in correspondence of J. Reuben Clark Jr. to Secretary of State, 19 May 1931, SD, 812.504/1137.

124. Ibid.

125. Ibid.

126. Translation of "The Labor Code and Foreign Investments," editorial in *El Universal*, 28 March 1931, enclosed with correspondence of Clark to Secretary of State, 7 April 1931, SD, 812.504/1130.

127. See American embassy translation of "The Labor Law and the People," editorial of *La Prensa*, published on 28 April 1931 and enclosed in correspondence of J. R. Reuben Clark Jr. to Secretary of State, 19 May 1931, SD, 812.504/1137.

128. Córdova in *En una época de crisis*, 109–110, lists the following constituent members of the alliance: the CROM, Comité General de Unificación Obrero Campesina, Confederación de Transportes y Comunicaciones, Confederación Sindicalista de Obreros y Campesinos del Estado de Puebla, Federación Sindical de Trabajadores del Distrito Federal, Confederación General de Trabajadores, Casa del Pueblo, Alianza de Uniones y Sindicatos de Artes Gráficas, Confederación de Electricistas y Similares, Convención Obrera pro Reconstrucción Nacional, and the Liga Nacional Campesina.

129. J. C. Satterthwaite's "Memorandum Covering Proposed Labor Law," in Clark to Secretary of State, 22 May 1931, SD, 812.504/1140.

130. Ibid.

131. Ibid.

132. Ibid.

133. Suárez, *Comentarios*, 24.

134. "Síntesis Taquigráfica, Junta en Chapultepec, Proyecto Ley Trabajo," unpublished transcript, n.d., from Archivo Histórico Aarón Sáenz. It is possible but improbable that this transcript narrates another conference.

135. Joseph C. Satterthwaite's "Memorandum of Proposed Labor Law," in Clark to Secretary of State, 12 June 1931, SD, 812.504/1142.

136. Ibid.

137. Ibid.

138. Ibid.

139. *Diario de los Debates*, 10 July 1931, *Revista Mexicana del Trabajo*, vol. 4, nos. 7–8 (July–August 1957), 129–132.

140. Ibid., 134–135.

141. *Diario de los Debates*, in *Revista Mexicana del Trabajo*, vol. 5, nos. 1–2 (January–February 1958), 317.

142. *Diario de los Debates*, in *Revista Mexicana del Trabajo*, vol. 4, nos. 7–8 (July–August 1957), 136–137.

143. See Article 236 in ibid., 227.

144. Article 243 in ibid.

145. Ibid., 155–156 and 157.

146. See *Diario de los Debates*, in *Revista Mexicana del Trabajo*, vol. 5, nos. 1–2 (January–February 1958), 317; and Bensusán Areous, *El modelo mexicano*, 193–94.

147. "It Is the President's Belief That the Approval of the Labor Law Is a National Necessity," published in *Excélsior* on 28 July 1931 and translated and enclosed with correspondence by J. Reuben Clark Jr. to Secretary of State, 30 July 1931, SD, 812.504/1154. The presidential statement was made on 27 July 1931.

148. See G-2 Report by Robert Cummings, Acting Military Attaché, received at U.S. State Department on 4 September 1931, SD, 812.504/1208.

149. Cueva, *El nuevo derecho mexicano del trabajo* 1:54.

150. *Diario Oficial de la Federación*, 28 August 1931; and Clark, *Organized Labor*, 214.

151. "La CROM ante los Destinos de la Revolución," *Pro-Paria*, 8 August 1931, p. 2.

152. See "Dissatisfaction with the Labor Law. The Alliance of Labor and Peasant Organizations Addresses the President," published in *Excélsior* on 16 August 1931, translated and enclosed in correspondence of J. Reuben Clark Jr. to Secretary of State, 19 August 1931, SD, 812.504/1173.

153. Ibid.

154. "La Ley Federal del Trabajo, Lesiona, No Garantiza, los Intereses Proletarios," speech delivered in Mexico City and published in *Pro-Paria*, 22 August 1931, p. 1.

155. See "The New Labor Law Is Not Satisfactory," published in *Excélsior*, 17 August 1931, translated and enclosed in correspondence of J. Reuben Clark Jr. to the Secretary of State, 19 August 1931, SD, 812.504/1173.

156. "Contra la Ley Federal del Trabajo, El Carácter Fachista del Trabajo," *El Machete*, 15 April 1931, p. 1, reprinted in *El Machete Ilegal*, p. 77.

157. "La Ley del Trabajo, la Cuestión Agraria, y la Lucha de Facciones," in *El Machete*, 1 February 1931, p. 3; and "Contra la Ley Fachista del Trabajo," 15 February 1931, p. 4; both in *El Machete Ilegal*, pp. 59 and 64.

158. "A la Lucha contra la Ley del Trabajo Fachista y Patronal!" *El Machete*, 15 March 1931, p. 1, in *El Machete Ilegal*, p. 69.

159. "El Convenio de la Deuda, la Ley del Trabajo y el 'Plan Preconcebido del Gobierno,'" *El Machete*, 1 April 1931, p. 2, in *El Machete Ilegal*, p. 74.

160. "La Maniobra para Imponer la Ley Fachista," *El Machete*, 10 June 1931, p. 1, in *El Machete Ilegal*, p. 95.

161. "La 'Cruzada Patronal' y el Banquete de los Diputados," *El Machete*, 29 June 1931, p. 3, in *El Machete Ilegal*, p. 101.

162. "La Ley del Trabajo en la Cámara," *El Machete*, 20 July 1931, p. 1, in *El Machete Ilegal*, p. 111.

163. See, e.g., "El Código Federal del Trabajo: Se Presta a Perversas Maniobras de los Capitalistas que Carecen de Escrúpulos para Perjudicar a los Camaradas Trabajadores," *Pro-Paria*, 7 November 1931, p. 3.

164. Clark, *Organized Labor*, 228.

165. See "La Posición de Nuestro Partido ante la Ley del Trabajo," *El Machete*, 30 November and 10 December 1931; and "Organicemos las Violaciones en Masa a la Ley Fachista del Trabajo," *El Machete*, 30 January and 10 February 1932, in *El Machete Ilegal*, pp. 161 and 171, respectively.

166. Bensusán Areous has persuasively argued that the CROM contributed to the shape of labor law substantially in the 1920s. See generally *El modelo mexicano* and "La legislación laboral heredada."

CONCLUSION

1. The cases discussed here were largely selected from Alfonso Lastra y Villar, *Las leyes del trabajo de la República Mexicana.* The publisher and date are not listed in this text, but it must have been completed in 1936 in light of its introduction and the material covered. The book purports to cover all major Court labor opinions issued through 1935 and briefly summarizes their legal points (*tesis*). Over twenty decisions were selected from the work; the complete opinions of these decisions as published in the *Semanario Judicial* were then analyzed.

2. See Cabrera Acevedo, *La Suprema Corte de Justicia* [1929–34], 1:160, reprinting Cárdenas's proposal to the PNR, 11 September 1934.

3. González Casanova contends that the Supreme Court continued to assert a degree of autonomy from the executive power, through 1960; see his *La democracia en México*, 33–36. Since the mid-1990s and further constitutional reform, the Court has manifested greater independence; see Pilar Domingo, "Judicial Independence."

Bibliography

ARCHIVES

Archivo de Colección Porfirio Díaz, Universidad Iberoamericana, Mexico City
Archivo del Estado de Puebla, Puebla
  Federal District Court Collection, Primer Juzgado
Archivo del Estado de Veracruz, Jalapa, Veracruz
  Caja de Dehesa
Archivo General de la Nación, Mexico City
  Fondo de Emilio Portes Gil
  Ramo del Departamento del Trabajo
  Ramo de Gobernación.
  Ramo de la Junta Federal de Conciliación y Arbitraje
Archivo Histórico Aarón Sáenz Garza, Mexico City
Archivo Histórico de la Suprema Corte de Justicia de la Nación, Mexico City
Archivo Histórico Vicente Lombardo Toledano, Mexico City
Archivo Manuel Gómez Morin, Mexico City
Centro de Estudios de Historia de México, Condumex, Mexico City
  Archivo de Bernardo Reyes
  Archivo de José Yves Limantour (Microfilm)
National Archives and Records Service, General Services Administration
  Records of the Department of State Relating to the Internal Affairs of Mexico, 1910–1929
  Records of the Department of State Relating to the Internal Affairs of Mexico, 1930–1939 (Record Group 59) (Microform)

PERIODICALS AND SERIALS

El Demócrata
Diario de los Debates de la Camára de Diputados del Congreso de los Estados Unidos Mexicanos
Diario Oficial de la Federación
El Economista
Excélsior
El Ferrocarrilero
El Foro
El Hijo del Trabajo
El Imparcial
El Machete Ilegal, 1929–1934: edición facsimile. Puebla: Universidad Autónoma de Puebla, Instituto de Ciencias, 1975.

New York Times
Pro-Paria
Revista Mexicana del Trabajo
Semanario Judicial de la Federación (Suprema Corte de Justicia de la Nación)
El Socialista
El Universal

ARTICLES AND BOOKS

Alvarado, Arturo. "El Portegilismo y el movimiento obrero en Tamaulipas 1910–1936." In *75 Años de Sindicalismo Mexicano*. Mexico City: INEHRM, 1986.

Alvarado, Salvador. *La reconstrucción de México, un mensaje a los pueblos de América*. Mexico: J. Ballesca y Cia. Sucs., 1919.

Anderson, Rodney. "Mexican Workers and the Politics of Revolution, 1906–1911." *Hispanic American Historical Review* 54, no. 1 (February 1974): 94–113.

______. *Outcasts in Their Own Land. Mexican Industrial Workers, 1906–1911*. Dekalb: Northern Illinois University Press, 1976.

Armstrong, George. *Law and Market Society in Mexico*. New York: Praeger, 1989.

Arnold, Linda. *Política y justicia: La Suprema Corte mexicana (1824–1855)*. Translated by José Luis Soberanes Fernández and Julián Bunster. Mexico City: Instituto de Investigaciones Jurídicas, UNAM, 1996.

Ashby, Joe C. *Organized Labor and the Mexican Revolution Under Lázaro Cárdenas*. Chapel Hill: University of North Carolina Press, 1963.

Baerlein, Henry. *Mexico: The Land of Unrest*. Philadelphia: Lippincott, 1914.

Baker, Richard D. *Judicial Review in Mexico: A Study of the Amparo Suit*. Austin: University of Texas Press, 1971.

Barrios, Elías. *El escuadrón de hierro*. Mexico City: Ediciones de Cultura Popular, S.A., [1938] 1978.

Bassols, Narciso. "Que son, por fin, las Juntas de Conciliación y Arbitraje?" *Revista General de Derecho y Jurisprudencia* 1 (1930): 185.

Basurto, Jorge. *El proletariado industrial en México (1850–1930)*. Mexico City: UNAM, Instituto de Investigaciones Sociales, 1975.

Bauer, Arnold. "Rural Workers in Spanish America: Problems of Peonage and Oppression." *Hispanic American Historical Review* 59, no. 1 (February 1979): 34–63.

Bazant, Jan. "From Independence to c. 1870." In *The Cambridge History of Latin America*, vol. 3, *From Independence to 1867*, edited by Leslie Bethell. Cambridge: Cambridge University Press, 1985.

Beatty, Edward. *Institutions and Investment: The Political Basis for Industrialization in Mexico Before 1911*. Stanford: Stanford University Press, 2001.

Benjamin, Thomas. "Laboratories of the New State, 1920–1929: Regional Social Reform and Experiments in Mass Politics." In *Provinces of the Revolution: Essays on Regional Mexican History, 1910–1929*, edited by Thomas Benjamin and Mark Wasserman. Albuquerque: University of New Mexico, 1990.

———. *A Rich Land, a Poor People: Politics and Society in Modern Chiapas*, rev. ed. Albuquerque: University of New Mexico, 1996.

Bensusán Areous, Graciela. "La legislación laboral heredada de las luchas revolucionarias: Del constituyente a la ley federal del trabajo de 1931." In *75 Años de Sindicalismo Mexicano*. Mexico City: INEHRM, 1986.

———. *El modelo mexicano de regulación laboral.* Mexico, D.F.: UAM-Xochimilco et al., 2000.

Bernstein, Marvin. *The Mexican Mining Industry, 1890–1950: A Study of the Interaction of Politics, Economics, and Technology.* Albany: State University of New York, 1964.

Bliss, Katherine. "The Science of Redemption: Syphilis, Sexual Promiscuity, and Reformism in Revolutionary Mexico City." *Hispanic American Historical Review* 79, no. 1 (February 1999): 1–40.

Borja Soriano, Manuel. "Las asociaciones de socorros mutuous á la luz del derecho." *Revista de Legislación y Jurisprudencia* 17 (July–December, 1899): 493.

Bortz, Jeffrey. "The Genesis of the Mexican Labor Relations System: Federal Labor Policy and the Textile Industry 1925–1940." *The Americas* 52, no. 1 (July 1995): 43–69.

———. "The Legal and Contractual Limits to Private Property Rights in Mexican Industry During the Revolution." In *The Mexican Economy, 1870–1930: Essays on the Economic History of Institutions, Revolution, and Growth*, edited by Jeffrey Bortz and Stephen Haber. Stanford: Stanford University Press, 2002.

———. *Revolution Within the Revolution: Cotton Textiles Workers and the Mexican Labor Regime, 1910–1923.* Stanford: Stanford University Press, 2008.

———. "'Without Any More Law than Their Own Caprice': Cotton Textile Workers and the Challenge to Factory Authority During the Mexican Revolution." *International Review of Social History* 42, no. 2 (1997): 253–88.

Branch, H. N. "The Mexican Constitution of 1917 Compared with the Constitution of 1857." Supplement to the *Annals of the American Academy of Political and Social Science*, vol. 71. Philadephia: Annals of the American Academy of Political and Social Science, 1917.

Bringas, Guillermina, and David Mascareño. *Esbozo histórico de la prensa obrera en México.* Mexico City: UNAM, 1988.

Buen Lozano, Nestor de. *Derecho del trabajo*, 16th ed. 2 vols. Mexico City: Editorial Porrúa, 2002.

Burgoa, Ignacio. *El juicio de amparo*, 38th ed. Mexico City: Editorial Porrúa, 2001.

Butte, Woodin L. "Stare Decisis, Doctrine, and Jurisprudence in Mexico and Elsewhere." In *The Role of Judicial Decisions and Doctrine in Civil Law and in Mixed Jurisdictions*, edited by Joseph Dainow. Baton Rouge: Louisiana State University Press, 1974.

Cabrera, Lucio. *El poder judicial federal mexicano y el Constituyente de 1917.* Mexico City: UNAM, Coordinación de Humanidades, 1968.

Cabrera, Luis. *Obras completas*, 4 vols. Edited by Eugenia Meyer. Mexico, D.F.: Ediciones Oasis, S.A., 1972–75.

Cabrera Acevedo, Lucio. *La Suprema Corte de Justicia en la república restaurada, 1867–1876.* Mexico, D.F.: Suprema Corte de Justicia de la Nación, 1989.

———. *La Suprema Corte de Justicia a principios del Porfirismo, 1877–1882.* Mexico, D.F.: Suprema Corte de Justicia de la Nación, 1990.

———. *La Suprema Corte de Justicia durante el fortalecimiento del Porfirismo, 1882–1888.* Mexico, D.F.: Suprema Corte de Justicia de la Nación, 1991.

———. *La Suprema Corte de Justicia a fines del siglo XIX, 1888–1900.* Mexico, D.F.: Suprema Corte de Justicia de la Nación, 1992.

———. *La Suprema Corte de Justicia a principios del siglo XX, 1901–1914.* Mexico, D.F.: Suprema Corte de Justicia de la Nación, 1993.

———. *La Suprema Corte de Justicia durante los años constitucionalistas (1917–1920).* Mexico, D.F.: Suprema Corte de la Justicia de la Nación, 1995.

———. *La Suprema Corte de Justicia durante el gobierno del presidente Obregón (1920–1924).* Mexico, D.F.: Suprema Corte de la Justicia de la Nación, 1996.

———. *La Suprema Corte de Justicia durante el gobierno del presidente Plutarco Elías Calles (1924–1928).* Mexico, D.F.: Suprema Corte de la Justicia de la Nación, 1997.

———. *La Suprema Corte de Justicia durante los gobiernos de Portes Gil, Ortiz Rubio y Abelardo L. Rodríguez (1929–1934).* 2 vols. Mexico, D.F.: Suprema Corte de la Justicia de la Nación, 1998.

Cámara de Industriales de Orizaba (Veracruz). *La sindicación forzosa.* Orizaba, Ver., Mexico: n.p., 1922.

Camiro, Maximiliano. "El Concepto de Paro o 'Lockout' y las Fracciones XVII y XIX del Art. 123 de la Constitución Federal." *Revista General de Derecho y Jurisprudencia* 1 (1930): 539.

Camp, Roderic A. *Mexican Political Biographies, 1884–1935.* Austin: University of Texas Press, 1991.

Cardoso, Ciro F. S., Francisco G. Hermosillo, and Salvador Hernández. *De la dictadura porfirista a los tiempos libertarios.* Vol. 3 of *La clase obrera en la historia de México,* edited by Pablo González Casanova. Mexico City: Siglo Veintiuno Editores, 1980.

Carpizo, Jorge. *El presidencialismo mexicano,* 16th ed. Mexico City: Siglo Veintiuno Editores, 2002.

———. "Reformas constitucionales al Poder Judicial Federal y la jurisdicción constitucional, del 31 de diciembre 1994." *Boletín Mexicano de Derecho Comparado* no. 83 (May-August 1995), http://www.juridicas.unam.mx/publica/rev/boletin/cont/83/el/el14.htm (accessed 4 February 2012).

Carpizo, Jorge, and Jorge Madrazo. *Derecho constitucional.* Mexico City: Porrúa, 1991.

Carr, Barry. "The Casa del Obrero Mundial, Constitutionalism, and the Pact of February 1915." In *El trabajo y los trabajadores en la historia de México,* edited by Elsa Cecilia Frost, Michael C. Meyer, and Josefina Zoraida Vásquez. Mexico City: Colegio de México and University of Arizona, 1979.

———. *El movimiento obrero y la política en México, 1910–1929.* 2 vols. Mexico City: SepSetentas, 1976.

Carrera Stampa, Miguel. *Los gremios mexicanos; La organización gremial en Nueva España, 1521–1861.* Mexico City: Edición y Distribucón Iberoamericana de Publicaciones, 1954.

Casar, María Amparo, and Ignacio Marván Laborde, eds. *Gobernar sin mayoría, México 1867–1997.* Mexico City: Editora Aguilar, Altea, Taurus, Alfaguara, S.A., and CIDE, 2002.

Castorena, J. Jesus. *El derecho de huelga en México.* Mexico City: Imprenta Mundial, 1931.

Chassen de López, Francie R. *Lombardo Toledano y el movimiento obrero mexicano, 1917–1940.* Mexico City: Extemporáneos, 1977.

Clagett, Helen Lord, and David M. Valderrama. *A Revised Guide to the Law and Legal Literature of Mexico.* Washington, DC: Library of Congress, 1973.

Clark, Marjorie Ruth. *Organized Labor in Mexico.* Chapel Hill: University of North Carolina Press, 1934; reprint, New York: Russell & Russell, 1973.

Coase, Ronald. *The Firm, the Market, and the Law*. Chicago: University of Chicago Press, 1988.

Coatsworth, John. "Obstacles to Economic Growth in Nineteenth-Century Mexico." *American Historical Review* 83, no. 1 (1978): 80–100.

———. *Orígenes del atraso: Nueve ensayos de historia económica de México en los siglos XVIII y XIX*. Mexico City: Alianza Editorial Mexicana, 1990.

Cockcroft, James. *Intellectual Precursors of the Mexican Revolution, 1900–1913*. Austin: University of Texas Press, 1968.

Código Civil del Distrito Federal y del Territorio de la Baja-California. Mexico City: Imprenta de E. Ancona y M. Peniche, 1871.

Código Penal para el Distrito Federal y Territorio de la Baja-California sobre Delitos del Fuero Común, y para Toda la República Mexicana sobre Delitos contra la Federación. Mexico City: Imprenta del gobierno, a cargo de José María Sandoval, 1871.

Código de Procediminetos Federales, Expedido en Uso de la Autorización que Concedió al Ejecutivo La Ley de 2 de Junio de 1892. Mexico City: Edición Oficial, Tipografía de la Oficina Impresora del Timbre, 1898.

Collado Herrera, María del Carmen. *Empresarios y políticos, entre la restauración y la revolución, 1920–1924*. Mexico City: INEHRM, 1996.

Collier, Ruth B., and David Collier. *Shaping the Political Arena: Critical Junctures, the Labor Movement, and Regime Dynamics in Latin America*. Princeton: Princeton University, 1991.

Córdova, Arnaldo. *En una época de crisis (1928–1934)*. Vol. 9 of *La clase obrera en la historia de México*. Edited by Pablo González Casanova. Mexico City: Siglo Veintiuno Editores, 1981.

———. *La ideología de la revolución mexicana*, 4th ed. Mexico City: Ediciones Era, 1975.

Cormack, Joseph, and F. M. Barker. "The Mexican Labor Law." *Southern California Law Review* 7 (March 1934): 251–94.

Cosío Villegas, Daniel. *La constitución de 1857 y sus críticos*. Mexico City: Secretaría de Educación Pública, 1973.

———. *Historia moderna de México. El Porfiriato: La vida política interior*. Vols. 8 and 9. Mexico City: Editorial Hermes, 1972.

Cueva, Mario de la. *Derecho mexicano del trabajo*, 5th ed. 2 vols. Mexico City: Porrúa hnos. y Cía., 1960.

———. *Derecho mexicano del trabajo*. Vol. 2. Mexico City: Editorial Porrúa, 1949.

———. *Derecho mexicano del trabajo*. Mexico City: Librería de Porrúa Hnos. y Cia., 1938.

———. *El nuevo derecho mexicano del trabajo*. 2 vols. Mexico City: Editorial Porrúa, 1991.

———. "Reflexiones sobre el Primer Congreso Mexicano de Derecho Industrial [1934]." In *El humanismo jurídico de Mario de la Cueva (Antología)*, edited by Ana Luisa Izquierdo y de la Cueva. Mexico, D.F.: UNAM and Fondo de Cultura Económica, 1994.

Cumberland, Charles C., with David C. Bailey. *Mexican Revolution: The Constitutionalist Years*. Austin: University of Texas Press, 1972.

Dawson, John. *The Oracles of the Law*. Ann Arbor: University of Michigan Press, 1968.

Derecho Argentino, *Diccionario Juridico*. http://todoeiure.atspace.com/diccionarios.juridico.v.htm (accessed 13 July 2005).

Diario de los Debates de la Cámara de los Diputados del Congreso de los Estados Unidos Mexicanos. http://cronica.diputados.gob.mx (accessed 13 August 2008).

Diario de los Debates del Congreso Constituyente, 1916–1917, 2nd ed. 2 vols. Mexico City: Gobierno del Estado de Querétaro and INEHRM, 1987.

Díaz, Maria Elena. "The Satiric Penny Press for Workers in Mexico, 1900–1910: A Case Study in the Politicisation of Popular Culture." *Journal of Latin American Studies* 22, no. 3 (October 1990): 497–526.

Diccionario Porrúa de historia, biografía y geografía de México, 6th ed. Mexico City: Editorial Porrúa, 1995.

Disposiciones Complementarios del Código Penal del Edo. de Puebla, colección formada por el Lic. José Mariano Ponton, Defensor de Pobres, 1873–1903. Puebla, 1904.

Domingo, Pilar. "Judicial Independence: The Politics of the Supreme Court in Mexico." *Journal of Latin American Studies* 32 (2002): 705–35.

Dorado, Pedro. "Hacia un nuevo derecho civil." *Revista de Legislación y Jurisprudencia* 31 (July–December, 1906): 41–66.

———. "El positivismo en la ciencia jurídica y social italiana." *Anuario de Legislación y Jurisprudencia,* Año IX (1892): 150 and 306.

Dulles, John W. F. *Yesterday in Mexico; a Chronicle of the Revolution, 1919–1936.* Austin: University of Texas Press, 1961.

Dunham, Arthur Louis. *The Industrial Revolution in France, 1815–1848.* New York: Exposition Press, 1955.

Dunlop, John T. *Industrial Relations Systems,* rev. ed. Boston: Harvard Business School Press, 1993.

Falcón, Romana, and Soledad García. *La semilla en el surco: Adalberto Tejeda y el radicalismo en Veracruz, 1883–1960.* México, D.F.: El Colegio de México, 1986.

Fernández Castelló, Justino. "La cuestión social: Disertación leída por el pasante de derecho Justino Fernández Castelló, en la conferencia de 5 año de la Escuela N. de Jurisprudencia." *Revista de Legislación y Jurisprudencia* 11 (July–December 1896): 7.

Fisher, William. "Texts and Contexts: The Application to American Legal History of Methodologies of Intellectual History." *Stanford Law Review* 49 (1997): 1065–1110.

Fisher, William, Morton Horwitz, and Thomas Reed, eds. *American Legal Realism.* New York: Oxford University Press, 1993.

Fix-Zamudio, Hector. *Ensayos sobre el derecho de amparo,* 2nd ed. Mexico City: Editorial Porrúa and UNAM, 1999.

———. *El poder judicial en el ordenamiento mexicano.* Mexico, D.F.: Fondo de Cultura Económica, 1996

Forbath, William. *Law and the Shaping of the American Labor Movement.* Cambridge, MA: Harvard University Press, 1991.

French, John D. *Drowning in Laws: Labor Law and Brazilian Political Culture.* Chapel Hill: University of North Carolina Press, 2004.

Friedman, Laurence, and Rogelio Pérez-Perdomo. *Legal Culture in the Age of Globalization: Latin America and Latin Europe.* Stanford: Stanford University Press, 2003.

Gallardo y Rionda, J. P. "Las huelgas." *El Socialista,* 27 September 1875, no. 8. Reprinted in *La huelga de los sombrereros, México 1875,* edited by Paco Ignacio Taibo II. Mexico City: Centro de Estudios Históricos del Movimiento Obrero Mexicano, 1980.

Gamboa Ojeda, Leticia. *Los empresarios de ayer. El grupo dominante en la industria textil de Puebla 1906–1929.* Puebla: Universidad Autónoma de Puebla, 1986.

———. *La urdimbe y la trama. Historia social de los obreros textiles de Atlixco, 1899–1924.* Mexico City: Fondo de Cultura Económica & Benemérito Universidad Autónoma de Puebla, 2001.

García, Lic. Francisco Pascual. "Breves consideraciones acerca de la obligación que los dueños tienen de pagar los daños que sufren los trabajadores." *Revista de Legislación y Jurisprudencia* 23 (July–December 1902): 418.

García Cantu, Gaston. *El socialismo en México, siglo XIX.* Mexico City: Ediciones Era, 1969.

García Díaz, Bernardo. *Un pueblo fabril del Porfiriato: Santa Rosa, Veracruz.* Mexico City: Fondo de Cultura Económica, 1981.

———. *Textiles del valle de Orizaba (1880–1925):* Cinco ensayos de historia sindical y social. Xalapa, Ver., Mexico: Universidad Veracruzana, 1990.

Garrido, Luis Javier. *El partido de la revolución institucionalizada: La formación del nuevo estado en México (1928–1945).* Mexico City: Siglo XXI Editores, 1986.

Gaxiola, Jorge F. "La primera legislación mexicana sobre accidentes del trabajo." *Revista de Derecho Industrial* 1, nos. 9–10 (January–February 1932): 541.

Goddard, Jorge Adame. *El pensamiento político y social de los católicos mexicanos, 1867–1914.* Mexico City: UNAM, 1981.

Gómez-Galvarriato, Aurora. "Measuring the Impact of Institutional Change in Capital-Labor Relations in the Mexican Textile Industry, 1900–1930." In *The Mexican Economy, 1870–1930: Essays on the Economic History of Institutions, Revolution, and Growth*, edited by Jeffrey L. Bortz and Stephen Haber. Stanford: Stanford University Press, 2002.

González, María del Refugio. *El derecho civil en México, 1821–1871, apuntes para un estudio.* Mexico City: UNAM, 1988.

———. "El Ilustre y Real Colegio de Abogados de México, una corporación política?" *Secuencia*, no. 27 (1993): 5–26.

———. "Testimonios: Introducción a breve estudio sobre la cuestión de huelgas de obreros." Centro de Estudios Históricos del Movimiento Obrero Mexicano, *Historia Obrera*, Segunda Época, 3, no. 12 (April 1978): 14–19.

González Casanova, Pablo. *La democracia en México*, 4th ed. Mexico City: Ediciones Era, 1971.

———. *En el primer gobierno constitucional (1917–1920).* Vol. 6 of *La clase obrera en la historia de México*, edited by Pablo González Casanova. Mexico City: Siglo Veintiuno Editores, 1980.

González Casanova, Pablo, Samuel León, and Ignacio Marván Laborde, eds. *El obrero mexicano.* 5 vols. Mexico City: Siglo Veintiuno Editores, 1985.

González Navarro, Moisés. "La arcaica libertad: El Artículo 4 contra el Artículo 123." *Historia Mexicana* 39, no. 1 (July–September 1989): 297–312.

———. "Las huelgas textiles en el Porfiriato." *Historia Mexicana* 6, no. 2 (October–December 1956): 201–16.

———. *El Porfiriato, La vida social.* Vol. 4 of *Historia moderna de México*, edited by Daniel Cosío Villegas. Mexico City: Editorial Hermes, 1957.

———. "El trabajo forzoso en México: 1821–1917." *Historia Mexicana* 27, no. 4 (April–June 1978): 588–615.

Gonzalez Prieto, Alejandro. *Proceso formativo de la Ley Federal del Trabajo de 1931.* Mexico City: Instituto Nacional de Estudios del Trabajo, Secretaría del Trabajo y Previsión Social, 1981.

González Ramírez, Manuel, ed. *La huelga de Cananea*. Vol. 3 of *Fuentes para la historia de la revolución mexicana*. Mexico City: Fondo de Cultura Económica, 1956.

Gordon, Robert. "Critical Legal Histories." *Stanford Law Review* 36 (January 1984): 57–125.

Gruening, Ernest. *Mexico and Its Heritage*. New York: Century, 1928.

Grupo Patronal de la República. *Observaciones y sugestiones del Grupo Patronal al Proyecto de Ley Federal del Trabajo*. Mexico City, 1931.

Guerra, Francois Xavier. *México: Del Antiguo Régimen a la Revolución*. Translated by Sergio Fernández Bravo. 2 vols. Mexico, D.F.: Fondo de Cultura Económica, 1988.

Gutiérrez Álvarez, Coralia. *Experiencias contrastadas. Industrialización y conflictos en los textiles del centro-oriente de México, 1884–1917*. Mexico, D.F., and Puebla: El Colegio de México and Instituto de Ciencias Sociales y Humanidades/BUAP, 2000.

Haber, Stephen. *Industry and Underdevelopment: The Industrialization of Mexico, 1890–1940*. Stanford: Stanford University Press, 1989.

Haber, Stephen, Noel Maurer, and Armando Razo. *The Politics of Property Rights: Political Instability, Credible Commitments, and Economic Growth in Mexico, 1876–1929*. Cambridge: Cambridge University Press, 2003.

———. "When the Law Does Not Matter: The Rise and Decline of the Mexican Oil Industry." *Journal of Economic History* 63, no. 1 (March 2003): 1–32.

Hale, Charles. "The Civil Law Tradition and Constitutionalism in Twentieth Century Mexico: The Legacy of Emilio Rabasa." *Law and History Review* 18, no. 2 (Summer 2000): 257–79.

———. *Emilio Rabasa and the Survival of Porfirian Liberalism: The Man, His Career, and His Ideas, 1856–1930*. Stanford: Stanford University Press, 2008.

———. *The Transformation of Liberalism in Late Nineteenth-Century Mexico*. Princeton: Princeton University Press, 1989.

Hall, Linda B. *Álvaro Obregón: Power and Revolution in Mexico, 1911–1920*. College Station: Texas A&M University Press, 1981.

Hamilton, Nora. *The Limits of State Autonomy: Post-Revolutionary Mexico*. Princeton: Princeton University Press, 1982.

Hart, John M. *Anarchism and the Mexican Working Class, 1860–1931*. Austin: University of Texas Press, 1987.

Henderson, Peter V. N. *In the Absence of Don Porfirio: Francisco León de la Barra and the Mexican Revolution*. Wilmington, DE: Scholarly Resources, 2000.

Hepple, Bob, ed. *The Making of Labour Law in Europe: A Comparative Study of Nine Countries up to 1945*. London: Mansell, 1986.

Horwitz, Morton J. *The Transformation of American Law, 1870–1960: The Crisis of Legal Orthodoxy*. New York: Oxford University Press, 1992.

Holden, Robert H. *Mexico and the Survey of Public Lands: The Management of Modernization, 1876–1911*. Dekalb: Northern Illinois University Press, 1994.

Illades, Carlos. *Hacia la república del trabajo: La organización artesanal en la ciudad de México, 1853–1876*. Mexico City: El Colegio de México and Universidad Autónoma Metropolitana Iztapalapa-Consejo Editorial, 1996.

Jaffary, Nora E., Edward W. Osokowski, and Susie S. Porter. *Mexican History, a Primary Source Reader*. Boulder, CO: Westview Press, 2010.

James, T. M. "Liberal Jurisprudence, Labor Tribunals, and Mexico's Supreme Court." *Law and History Review* 27, no. 1 (2009): 87–112.

José Valenzuela, Georgette. "1920–1924: . . . y venían de una revolución! De la oposición civil a la oposición militar." In *Gobernar sin mayoría, México 1867–1997*, edited by María Amparo Casar and Ignacio Marván Laborde. Mexico City: Editora Aguilar, Altea, Taurus, Alfaguara, S.A., and CIDE, 2002.

Joseph, Gilbert M. *Revolution from Without: Yucatán, Mexico, and the United States, 1880–1924*. Durham, NC: Duke University Press, [1982] 1988.

Joseph, Gilbert M., and Daniel Nugent, eds. *Everyday Forms of State Formation*. Durham, NC: Duke University Press, 1994.

Katz, Friedrich. "Labor Conditions on Haciendas in Porfirian Mexico: Some Trends and Tendencies." *Hispanic American Historical Review* 54, no. 1 (February 1974): 1–47.

———. *The Life and Times of Pancho Villa*. Stanford: Stanford University Press, 1998.

———. *La Servidumbre agraria en México en la época porfiriana*. Mexico City: Ediciones Era, 1980 [reissue of SepSetentas, 1976].

Keesing, Donald. "Structural Change Early in Development: Mexico's Changing Industrial and Occupational Structure from 1895 to 1950." *Journal of Economic History* 29, no. 4 (December 1969): 716–38.

Kennedy, Duncan. *A Critique of Adjudication: Fin de Siécle*. Cambridge, MA: Harvard University Press, 1996.

———. "Three Globalizations of Law and Legal Thought: 1850–2000." In *The New Law and Economic Development: A Critical Appraisal*, edited by David M. Trubek and Alvaro Santos. Cambridge: Cambridge University Press, 2006.

Klare Karl. "Judicial Deradicalization of the Wagner Act and the Origins of Modern Legal Consciousness, 1937–1941." *Minnesota Law Review* 62 (1978): 265.

———. "Labor Law as Ideology." *Industrial Relations Law Journal* 4 (1981): 456.

Knight, Alan. "Mexican Peonage: What Was It and Why Was It?" *Journal of Latin American Studies* 18, no. 1 (May 1986): 41–74.

———. *The Mexican Revolution*. 2 vols. Lincoln: University of Nebraska Press, 1990.

———. "The Mexican Revolution: Bourgeois? Nationalist? Or Just a 'Great Rebellion'?" *Bulletin of Latin American Research* 4, no. 2 (1985): 1–37.

———. "The Working Class and the Mexican Revolution, c. 1900–1920." *Journal of Latin American Studies* 16 (May 1984): 51–79.

Knowlton, Robert. "Tribunales federales y terrenos rurales en el México del Siglo XIX: El *Semanario Judicial de la Federación*." *Historia Mexicana* 46, no. 1 (1996): 71–98.

Koth, Karl B. *Waking the Dictator, Veracruz, the Struggle for Federalism, and the Mexican Revolution, 1870–1927*. Calgary: University of Calgary Press, 2002.

Kourí, Emilio. *En busca de Molina Enríquez: Cien años de los grandes problemas nacionales*. Mexico, D.F.: El Colegio de México, 2009.

———. "Interpreting the Expropriation of Indian Pueblo Lands in Porfirian Mexico: The Unexamined Legacies of Andrés Molina Enríquez." *Hispanic American Historical Review* 82, no. 1 (February 2002): 69–117.

———. *A Pueblo Divided: Business, Property, and Community in Papantla, Mexico*. Stanford: Stanford University Press, 2004.

Krauze, Enrique. *Caudillos culturales en la revolución mexicana*. Mexico City: Siglo Veintiuno, 1976.

Labastida, Luis G. "El derecho y la economía política, discurso pronunciado en la inauguración de los estudios del presente año escolar." *Revista de Legislación y Jurisprudencia* 12 (January–June 1897): 93.

Lastra y Villar, Alfonso. *Las leyes del trabajo de la República mexicana interpretadas por la Suprema Corte de Justicia de la Nación.* Mexico: n.p., n.d. [1936].

Leal, Juan Felipe. *Del mutualismo al sindicalismo en México, 1843–1910.* Mexico City: Ediciones El Caballito, 1991.

Leal, Juan Felipe, and José Villaseñor. *En la revolución, 1910–1917.* Vol. 5 of *La clase obrera en la historia de México*, edited by Pablo González Casanova. Mexico City: Siglo Veintiuno Editores, 1988.

Lear, John. "La XXVI Legislatura y los trabajadores de la ciudad de México, 1912–1913." In *El poder legislativo en las décadas revolucionarias, 1908–1934*, edited by Pablo Piccato. Mexico, D.F.: Miguel Ángel Porrúa, 1997.

———. *Workers, Neighbors, and Citizens: The Revolution in Mexico City.* Lincoln: University of Nebraska Press, 2001.

Leroy, Maxime. *Le Code Civil et le Droit Nouveau.* Paris: G. Bellais, 1904.

———. *El derecho consuetudinario obrero: Sindicatos, bolsas de trabajo, federaciones profesionales, cooperativas, doctrinas e instituciones.* Mexico City: Secretaría de Industria, Comercio y Trabajo, 1922–1926.

Lombardo Toledano, Vicente. "Las fuentes del derecho industrial." *Revista General de Derecho y Jurisprudencia* 1 (1930): 5–17.

———. *La libertad sindical en México.* Mexico City: Universidad Obrera Mexicana, [1926] 1974.

———. *Obras completas.* Puebla: Gobierno del Estado de Puebla, 1990.

Lomnitz, Claudio. *Vicios públicos, virtudes privadas: La corrupción en México.* Mexico City: CIESAS and Miguel Ángel Porrúa, 2000.

López, C. D. *Sociedades y sindicatos, contribución a la legislación obrera.* Mexico City: Secretaría de Hacienda y Credito, 1918.

Lozano, José María. *Estudio del derecho constitucional patrio en lo relativo a los derechos del hombre*, 2nd ed. facsimile. Mexico City: Editorial Porrúa, S.A., [1876] 1972.

Ludlow, Leonor. "El Fondo Histórico de Hacienda en la Biblioteca Miguel Lerdo de Tejada." *América Latina en la Historia Económica*, no. 11 (January–June, 1999): 95.

Madero, Francisco. "Plan de San Luis Potosí." In Arnaldo Córdova, *La ideología de la revolución mexicana.* Mexico, D.F.: Ediciones Era, 1982.

Margadant, Guillermo. *Introducción a la historia del derecho mexicano*, 18th ed. Naucalpan, Edo. de Mexico: Editorial Esfinge, S. de R.L. de C.V., 2001, 2007.

Martínez, Rafael de la Torre. "Las huelgas. Disertación leída en el Colegio de Abogados." Mexico City: Imprenta del "Federalista," 1875.

Marván Laborde, Ignacio. "Ejecutivo fuerte y división de poderes: El primer ensayo de esa utopia de la Revolución Mexicana." In *Gobernar sin mayoría, México, 1867–1997*, edited by María Amparo Casar and Ignacio Marván Laborde. Mexico City: Editora Aguilar, Altea, Taurus, Alfaguara, S.A., and CIDE, 2002.

Mayagoitia y Hagelstein, Alejandro. "De real a nacional: El Ilustre Colegio de Abogados de México." www.bibliojuridica.org/libros/1/133/19.pdf (accessed 15 May 2011).

Means, Robert C. "Mexican Commercial Law, 1854–1884." *Boston College International and Comparative Law Review* 2, no. 2 (1979): 299–335.

Méndez, Juan E., Guillermo O'Donnell, and Paulo Sérgio Pinheiro, eds. *The (Un)rule of Law and the Underprivileged in Latin America.* Notre Dame, IN: University of Notre Dame Press, 1999.

Mendieta y Nuñez, Lucio. *Historia de la facultad de derecho.* Mexico City: UNAM, 1975.

Merryman, John Henry, and Rogelio Pérez-Perdomo. *The Civil Law Tradition: An Introduction to the Legal Systems of Europe and Latin* America, 3rd ed. Stanford: Stanford University Press, 2007.

Mexico. Departamento del Trabajo. *Memoria del Primer Congreso Mexicano de Derecho Industrial.* Mexico City: Talleres Gráficos de la Nación, 1934.

Mexico. Secretaría de Gobernación. *Codificación de los Decretos del C. Venustiano Carranza, Primer Jefe del Ejército Constitucionalista, Encargado del Poder Ejecutivo de la Unión.* Mexico City: Imprenta de la Secretaría de Gobernación, 1915.

———. *Constitución Política de los Estados Unidos Mexicanos, Edición Oficial.* Mexico City: Imprenta de la Secretaría de Gobernación, 1917.

Mexico. Secretaría de Industria, Comercio y Trabajo. *Ley Federal del Trabajo.* Mexico City: Talleres Gráficos de la Nación, 1931.

———. *La industria, el comercio y el trabajo en México durante la gestión administrativa del Señor Gral. Plutarco Elías Calles*, vol. 3, *Del trabajo y la previsión social.* Mexico City: Tip. Galas, Mex., 1928.

———. *Proyecto de Código Federal de Trabajo para los Estados Unidos Mexicanos que Somete el C. Lic. Emilio Portes Gil, Presidente de la República, al H. Congreso de la Unión.* Mexico City: Talleres Gráficos de la Nación,1929.

———. Departamento del Trabajo. *Legislación del trabajo de los Estados Unidos Mexicanos.* Mexico City: Talleres Gráficos de la Nación, [1928] 1930.

Meyer, Jean, with Enrique Krauze and Cayetano Reyes. *Periodo 1924–1928, estado y sociedad con Calles.* Vol. 11 of *Historia de la revolución mexicana*, edited by Luis González. Mexico D.F.: Colegio de México, 1977.

Meyer, Lorenzo. *México y los Estados Unidos en el conflicto petrolero (1917–1942)*, 2nd ed. Mexico, D.F.: Colegio de México, 1972.

Meyers, Frederic. *Mexican Industrial Relations from the Perspective of the Labor Court.* Los Angeles: Institute of Industrial Relations, University of California, 1979.

Middlebrook, Kevin J. *The Paradox of Revolution: Labor, the State, and Authoritarianism in Mexico.* Baltimore: Johns Hopkins University Press, 1995.

Mijangos y González, Pablo. *El nuevo pasado jurídico mexicano.* Madrid: Universidad Carlos III de Madrid and Editorial Dykinson, 2011.

Miller, Richard. "Labor Legislation and Mexican Industrial Relations." *Industrial Relations* 7, no. 2 (February 1968): 171–82.

Mirow, M. C. *Latin American Law: A History of Private Law and Institutions in Spanish America.* Austin: University of Texas Press, 2004.

———. "Marbury in Mexico: Judicial Review's Precocious Southern Migration." *Hastings Constitutional Law Quarterly* 35 (Fall 2007): 41–97.

Molina Enríquez, Andrés. *Los grandes problemas nacionales.* Mexico City: Imprenta de A. Carranza e hijos, 1909.

Moreno Cora, Silvestre. *Tratado del juicio de amparo conforme a las sentencias de los tribunales federales.* Mexico City: Tip. Y Lit. "La Europea" de J. Aguilar Vera y Compañía (S. en C.), 1902.

Moreno-Brid, Juan Carlos, and Jaime Ros. *Development and Growth in the Mexican Economy: A Historical Perspective.* Oxford: Oxford University Press, 2009.

Morris, James O. *Elites, Intellectuals, and Consensus: A Study of the Social Question and the Industrial Relations System in Chile.* New York: Cornell University and W. F. Humphrey Press, 1966.

Morris, Stephen D. *Corruption and Politics in Contemporary Mexico*. Tuscaloosa: University of Alabama, 1991.

Nickel, Herbert J. "Zur Immobilität und Schuldknechtschaft Mexikanischer Landarbeiter vor 1915." *Saeculum* 27, no. 3 (1976): 289–328.

Niemeyer, E. V., Jr. *Revolution at Querétaro: The Mexican Constitutional Convention of 1916–1917*. Austin: University of Texas Press and Institute of Latin American Studies, 1974.

North, Douglas. *Institutions, Institutional Change, and Economic Performance*. Cambridge: Cambridge University Press, 1990.

Oñate, Santiago. "Administración de justicia y composición de conflictos laborales." In *El derecho laboral*, edited by Graciela Bensusán Areous. Vol. 4 of *El obrero mexicano*, edited by Pablo González Casanova, Samuel León, and Ignacio Marván Laborde. Mexico City: Siglo Veintiuno Editores, 1985.

Palavicini, Felix F. *Mi vida revolucionaria*. Mexico City: Ediciones Botas, 1937.

Pallares, Eduardo. *La jurisprudencia de la Suprema Corte de Justicia. Colección debidamente clasificada y extractada de las sentencias de más importancia, pronunciadas por la Suprema Corte de Justicia de la Nación; a partir del mes de junio de 1917 hasta junio de 1919*. Mexico City: Herrero Hermanos Sucesores, 1921.

Pallares, Jacinto. "Escuela Nacional de Jurisprudencia, exposición de motivos de la reforma al plan de estudios de esta escuela." *Revista de Legislación y Jurisprudencia* 1 (January–July 1889): 63.

Pallares, Jacinto, and T. Reyes Retana. "Reformas al plan de estudios de la Escuela Nacional de Jurisprudencia de México." *Revista de Legislación y Jurisprudencia* 13 (July–December 1897): 467.

Pardo, Emilio, Jr. "La economía política y la legislación." *Anuario de Legislación y Jurisprudencia, Sección de Estudios de Derecho* 13 (1896–97): 1–19.

Parlee, Lorena. "The Impact of United States Railroad Unions on Organized Labor and Government Policy in Mexico (1880–1911)." *Hispanic American Historical Review* 64, no. 3 (August 1984): 443–75.

Pasquel, Leonardo. *La revolución en el Estado de Veracruz*. Mexico City: INEHRM, 1971–72.

Pérez-Perdomo, Rogelio. *Latin American Lawyers: A Historical Introduction*. Stanford: Stanford University Press, 2006.

Pic, Paul. "Legislación industrial: Evolución histórica de la reglamentación legal del trabajo industrial, desde la antigüedad hasta el Siglo XX." *Boletín de la Secretaría de Fomento*, 2nd epoca, III, no. 1, *Industrias nuevas y aplicaciones industriales en general* (August 1906): 14.

———. *Traité élémentaire de législation industrielle. Les lois ouvriéres*, 2nd ed. Paris: Arthur Rosseau, 1903.

Piccato, Pablo. *City of Suspects: Crime in Mexico City, 1900–1931*. Durham, NC: Duke University Press, 2001.

Pizarro Suárez, Nicolas. *La huelga en el derecho mexicano*. Mexico City: Ediciones Insignia, 1938.

Portes Gil, Emilio. *Quince años de política mexicana*. Mexico City: Ediciones Botas, 1941.

Prieto, Guillermo. *Obras completas*, vol. 25, edited by Boris Rosen Jélomer. Mexico City: Consejo Nacional para la Cultura y las Artes, 1992.

Quirk, Robert. "Liberales y radicales en la revolución mexicana." *Historia Mexicana* 2, no. 4 (April–June 1953): 503–28.

———. *The Mexican Revolution, 1914–1915: The Convention of Aguascalientes*. Bloomington: Indiana University Press, 1960.

Raat, William D. "The Anti-Positivist Movement in Prerevolutionary Mexico, 1892–1911." *Journal of Inter-American Studies and World Affairs* 19 (February 1977): 83–98.

———. "Ideas and Society in Don Porfirio's Mexico." *The Americas* 30 (July 1973): 32–53.

———. "Leopoldo Zea and Mexican Positivism: A Reappraisal." *Hispanic American Historical Review* 48, no. 1 (February 1968): 1–18.

Rabasa, Emilio. *La Constitución y la dictadura: Estudio sobre la organización política en México*. Mexico: Tip. de "Revista de revistas," 1912.

Rebollar, Lic. Rafael. "Dictamen del Lic. D. Rafael Rebollar/Opinión emitida por el subscripto á la Academia de Legislación y Jurisprudencia, con motivo de la consulta hecha por la Secretaría de Comunicaciones en el caso de abandono de un tren en marcha por un maquinista." *Revista de Legislación y Jurisprudencia* 9 (July–December, 1895): 501.

Reed, Nelson. *The Caste War of Yucatán*. Stanford: Stanford University Press, 1964.

Reich, Peter L. "Recent Research on the Legal History of Modern Mexico." *Mexican Studies/Estudios Mexicanos* 23 (Winter 2007): 181–93.

Reglamento de la Sociedad Paz y Unión en las Artes para Auxilios Mutuos. Mexico City: Imprenta Francisco Díaz de Leon, 1875.

Remolina Roqueñi, Felipe. *El artículo 123*. Mexico City: Ediciones del V Congreso Iberoamericano de Derecho del Trabajo y de Seguridad Social, 1974.

———. *Evolución de las instituciones y del derecho del trabajo en México*. Mexico City: Junta Federal de Conciliación y Arbitraje, 1976.

Reyes, Rodolfo. *De mi vida, memorias políticas*. Vol. 1. Madrid: Biblioteca Nueva 1929.

Reyes Heroles, Jesús. *El liberalismo mexicano*. 3 vols. Mexico, D.F.: UNAM, 1957–61.

Reyna Muñoz, Manuel. *La Crom y la Csum en la industria textil (1928–1932)*. Mexico City: Universidad Autónoma Metropolitana, Azcapotzalco, 1988.

Reynolds, Clark. *The Mexican Economy: Twentieth-Century Structure and Growth*. New Haven: Yale University Press, 1973.

Rivera Castro, José. *En la presidencia de Plutarco Elías Calles (1924–1928)*. Vol. 8 of *La clase obrera en la historia de México*, edited by Pablo González Casanova. Mexico City: Siglo Veintiuno Editores, 1983, 1987.

Rocha Bandala, Juan Francisco, and José Fernando Franco. *La competencia en materia laboral: Evolución*. Mexico City: Editorial Cárdenas, 1975.

Rodea, Marcelo. *Historia del movimiento obrero ferrocarrilero, 1890–1943*. Mexico: n.p., 1944.

———. "La Huelga de 1926–1927." In *Cuatro sindicatos nacionales de industria*, edited by Centro de Estudios del Movimiento Obrero y Socialista. Mazatlán: Universidad Autónoma de Sinaloa, 1988.

Rodríguez, Miles Vincent. "The Beginnings of a Movement: Leagues of Agrarian Communities, Unions of Industrial Workers, and Their Struggles in Mexico, 1920–1929." PhD diss., Harvard University, 2010.

Rosemblatt, Karin Alejandra. "Charity, Rights, and Entitlement: Gender, Labor, and Welfare in Early Twentieth Century Chile." *Hispanic American Historical Review* 81, no. 3–4 (August-November 2001): 555–585.

Rosenzweig, Fernando. "La industria." In vol. 7, part 1, of *Historia moderna de México, El Porfiriato: La vida económica*, edited by Daniel Cosío Villegas. Mexico City: Editorial Hermes, 1965.

Rouaix, Pastor. *Génesis de los artículos 27 y 123 de la Constitución Política de 1917*, 2nd ed. Mexico City: INEHRM, 1959.

Ruiz, Ramón Eduardo. *Labor and the Ambivalent Revolutionaries: Mexico, 1911–1923*. Baltimore: Johns Hopkins University Press, 1976.

Salvatore, Ricardo D., Carlos Aguirre, and Gilbert Joseph, eds. *Crime and Punishment in Latin America: Law and Society Since Late Colonial Times*. Durham, NC: Duke University Press, 2001.

Saragoza, Alexander M. *The Monterrey Elite and the Mexican State, 1880–1940*. Austin: University of Texas Press, 1988.

Schjolden, Line. "Sentencing the Social Question: Court-Made Labour Law in Cases of Occupational Accidents in Argentina, 1900–1915." *Journal of Latin American Studies* 41, no. 1 (February 2009): 91–120.

Serna de la Garza, José María. "The Concept of *Jurisprudencia* in Mexican Law." *Mexican Law Review*, new series, 1, no. 2 (January–June 2009): 131–45.

Shabot, Esther. *Los orígenes del sindicalismo ferrocarrilero*. Mexico: Ediciones El Caballito 1982.

Sieder, Rachel, Line Schjolden, and Alan Angell, eds. *The Judicialization of Politics in Latin America*. New York: Palgrave Macmillan, 2005.

Sikkink, Kathryn. *Ideas and Institutions: Developmentalism in Brazil and Argentina*. Ithaca: Cornell University Press, 1991.

Silva Herzog, Jesús. *Breve historia de la revolución Mexicana*, vol. 1, *Los antecedentes y la etapa maderista*. Mexico City: Fondo de Cultura Económica, 1960.

Smith, Peter H. "La política dentro de la Revolución: El Congreso Constituyente de 1916–1917." *Historia Mexicana* 22, no. 3 (January–March 1917): 363–95.

Smith, Robert Freeman. *The U.S. and Revolutionary Nationalism in Mexico, 1916–32*. Chicago: University of Chicago Press, 1972.

Snodgrass, Michael. *Deference and Defense in Monterrey: Workers, Paternalism, and Revolution in Mexico, 1890–1950*. Cambridge: Cambridge University Press, 2003.

Sonenscher, Michael. *Work and Wages: Natural Law, Politics, and the Eighteenth-Century French Trades*. Cambridge: Cambridge University Press, 1989.

Speckman Guerra, Elisa. "Justice Reform and Legal Opinion: The Mexican Criminal Codes of 1871, 1929, and 1931." In *Reforming the Administration of Justice in Mexico*, edited by Wayne A. Cornelius and David Shirk. Notre Dame and San Diego: University of Notre Dame Press and Center for U.S.–Mexican Studies, University of California, San Diego, 2007.

Steinfeld, Robert J. *Coercion, Contract, and Free Labor in the Nineteenth Century*. Cambridge: Cambridge University Press, 2001.

Stone, Judith F. *The Search for Social Peace: Reform Legislation in France, 1890–1914*. Albany: State University of New York, 1985.

Suárez, Eduardo. *Comentarios y recuerdos (1926–1946)*. Mexico City: Editorial Porrúa, 1977.

Suarez-Potts, William. "The Mexican Supreme Court and the *Juntas de Conciliación y Arbitraje*, 1917–1924: The Judicialisation of Labour Relations After the Revolution." *Journal of Latin American Studies* 41, no. 4 (2009): 723–55.

———. "The Railroad Strike of 1927: Labor and Law After the Mexican Revolution." *Labor History* 52, no. 4 (November 2011): 399–416.

Suprema Corte de Justicia de la Nación. *Historia del amparo en México*, vol. 5, 2nd ed. Mexico City: Suprema Corte de Justicia de la Nación, 2000.

———. *Ministros, 1917–2004: Semblanzas*. 2 vols. Mexico City: Suprema Corte de Justicia de la Nación, 2005.

Taibo II, Paco Ignacio, ed. *La huelga de los sombrereros, México 1875*. Mexico City: CEHSMO, 1980.

Tamayo, Jaime. *En el interinato de Adolfo de la Huerta y el gobierno de Álvaro Obregón (1920–1924)*. Vol. 7 of *La clase obrera en la historia de México*, edited by Pablo González Casanova. Mexico City: Siglo Veintiuno Editores, 1987.

Taylor, Matthew M. *Judging Policy: Courts and Policy Reform in Democratic Brazil*. Stanford: Stanford University Press, 2008.

Taylor, Michael C. "Why No Rule of Law in Mexico? Explaining the Weakness of Mexico's Judicial Branch." *New Mexico Law Review* 27 (W. 1997): 141–66.

Tena Ramírez, Felipe, ed. *Leyes fundamentales de México, 1808–2005*, 24th ed. Mexico City: Editorial Porrúa, 2005.

Tomlins, Christopher L. *Law, Labor, and Ideology in the Early American Republic*. Cambridge: Cambridge University Press, 1993.

———. *The State and the Unions: Labor Relations, Law and the Organized Labor Movement in America, 1880–1960*. Cambridge: Cambridge University Press, 1985.

Trueba Urbina, Alberto. *El artículo 123*. Mexico City: Talleres Gráficos Laguna, de A.B. Arzate, 1943.

———. *Evolución de la huelga*. Mexico, D.F.: Ediciones Botas, 1950.

———. *The Mexican Constitution of 1917 Is Reflected in the Peace Treaty Versailles of 1919*. New York: n.p., 1974

Trujillo Bolio, Mario. *Operarios fabriles en el Valle de México, 1864–1884*. Mexico, D.F.: Colegio de México and Centro de Investigaciones y Estudios Superiores en Antropología Social, 1997.

Turner, John Kenneth. *Barbarous Mexico*. Austin: University of Texas, [1910] 1969.

Ulloa, Berta. *La Constitución de 1917*. Vol. 6 of *Historia de la revolución mexicana, 1914–1917*, edited by Luis González. Mexico City: El Colegio de Mexico, 1983.

Unger, Roberto Mangabeira. *Knowledge and Politics*. New York: Free Press, [1975] 1984.

———. *Law in Modern Society: Toward a Criticism of Social Theory*. New York: Free Press, 1976; 1st paperback ed., 1977.

Valdivieso Castillo, Julio. *Historia del movimiento sindical petrolero en Minatitlán, Veracruz*. Mexico, D.F.: n.p., 1963.

Vigil, J. M. "La cuestión de huelgas." *El Siglo Diez y Nueve*, séptima época, T. 54 (12 September 1872), p. 1. Reprinted in Centro de Estudios Historicos del Movimiento Obrero Mexicano, *Historia Obrera*, Segunda Época 1, no. 2 (September 1974): 30.

Von Mentz, Brígida. "Trabajo minero y control social durante el Porfiriato: Los operarios de dos poblaciones contrastantes." *Historia Mexicana* 50, no. 3 (2001): 555–607.

Walker, David. "Porfirian Labor Politics: Working Class Organizations in Mexico City and Porfirio Díaz, 1876–1902." *The Americas* 37, no. 3 (January 1981): 257–89.

Weldon, Jeffrey. "The Political Sources of Presidencialismo in Mexico." In *Presidentialism and Democracy in Latin America*, edited by Scott Mainwaring and Matthew Sober. Cambridge: Cambridge University Press, 1997.

Wells, Allen, and Gilbert M. Joseph. *Summer of Discontent, Seasons of Upheaval: Elite Politics and Rural Insurgency in Yucatan, 1876–1915*. Stanford: Stanford University Press, 1996.

Wilkie, James, and Edna Monza. *México visto en el siglo* XX. Mexico City: Instituto Mexicano de Investigaciones Económicas, 1969.

Womack, John, Jr. "The Mexican Revolution, 1910–1920." In *The Cambridge History of Latin America*, vol. 5, edited by Leslie Bethell. Cambridge: Cambridge University Press, 1986.

———. "Luchas sindicales y liberalismos sociales, 1867–1993." *Para una historia de América,* vol. 2, *Los nudos* 1, edited by Marcello Carmagnani, Alicia Hernández Chávez, and Ruggiero Romano. Mexico City: El Colegio de México and the Fondo de Cultura Económica, 1999.

Zamora, Stephen. *Mexican Law*. Oxford: Oxford University Press, 2007.

Zarco, Francisco. *Crónica del Congreso Extraordinario Constituyente, 1856–1857*. Mexico City: Colegio de Mexico, 1979.

Zimmerman, Eduardo. "Intellectuals, Universities and the Social Question: Argentina, 1898–1916." In *Essays in Argentine Labor History, 1870–1930*, edited by Jeremy Adelman. London: Macmillan Press, 1992.

Index

The authorized representative in the EU for product safety and compliance is:
Mare Nostrum Group
B.V Doelen 72
4831 GR Breda
The Netherlands

www.ingramcontent.com/pod-product-compliance
Lightning Source LLC
LaVergne TN
LVHW091524200926
848483LV00002B/298
* 9 7 8 0 8 0 4 7 7 5 5 1 9 *